DK Guide to Public Speaking

Lisa A. Ford-Brown

3rd Edition

Pearson

Text design, page layout,
and cover design:
Stuart Jackman

Portfolio Manager: Karon Bowers
Content Producer: Nicole Conforti
Content Developer: Brenda Hadenfeldt
Portfolio Manager Assistant: Dea Barbieri
Product Marketer: Christopher Brown
Field Marketer: Kelly Ross
Content Producer Manager: Melissa Feimer
Content Development Manager: Sharon Geary
Content Developer, Learning Tools: Amy Wetzel
Art/Designer: Blair Brown
Digital Producer: Amanda Smith
Full-Service Project Manager: Alverne Ball
Compositor: Integra Software Services, Inc.
Printer/Binder: LSC Communications/Crawfordsville
Cover Printer: Phoenix Color/Hagerstown
Cover Credits: Hero Images/Getty Images; Rawpixel.com/Fotolia; Steve Debenport/Getty Images; Hill Street Studios/Getty Images

Acknowledgments of third party content appear on page 484, which constitutes an extension of this copyright page.

Library of Congress Cataloging-in-Publication Data

Names: Ford-Brown, Lisa A. author.
Title: DK guide to public speaking / Lisa A. Ford-Brown, Columbia College.
Description: 3rd edition. | Boston : Pearson, 2017. | Includes
   bibliographical references and index.
Identifiers: LCCN 2016020580 | ISBN 9780134380896
Subjects: LCSH: Public speaking—Handbooks, manuals, etc.
Classification: LCC PN4129.15 .F67 2017 | DDC 808.5/1—dc23
LC record available at https://lccn.loc.gov/2016020580

1   16

Student Edition

ISBN-10:   0-13-438089-4
ISBN-13: 978-0-13-438089-6

Contents

TAB 2: RESEARCHING

CONTENTS   v

PLEASE
KEEP OFF THE GRASS.

How to Use This Book

This book contains nine tabs. **Tabs 1–5** explain the creative process for public speaking, and **Tabs 6–9** discuss the basic types of speaking. The chart to the right gives a quick overview.

Within the chapters, headings are in question-and-answer format—to ask common questions that beginning speakers have and to provide clear answers. Each chapter-opening contents section also serves as a list of **learning objectives** for that chapter. Every chapter ends with a **Chapter Review** section that reinforces these learning objectives by reviewing them one more time.

See pages 20–21 for more tips on using this book to study and to create a speech.

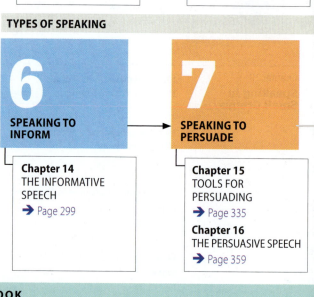

THE CREATIVE PROCESS FOR PUBLIC SPEAKING

1 STARTING

Chapter 1
OVERVIEW OF PUBLIC SPEAKING
➔ Page 1

Chapter 2
GETTING TO KNOW YOUR AUDIENCE AND SITUATION
➔ Page 25

Chapter 3
SELECTING YOUR TOPIC AND PURPOSE
➔ Page 47

2 RESEARCHING

Chapter 4
LOCATING SUPPORT MATERIALS
➔ Page 67

Chapter 5
SELECTING AND TESTING SUPPORT MATERIALS
➔ Page 103

TYPES OF SPEAKING

6 SPEAKING TO INFORM

Chapter 14
THE INFORMATIVE SPEECH
➔ Page 299

7 SPEAKING TO PERSUADE

Chapter 15
TOOLS FOR PERSUADING
➔ Page 335

Chapter 16
THE PERSUASIVE SPEECH
➔ Page 359

What's New in This Edition

1

Revel™ Educational technology designed for the way today's students read, think, and learn

When students are engaged deeply, they learn more effectively and perform better in their courses. This simple fact inspired the creation of Revel: an immersive learning experience designed for the way today's students read, think, and learn. Built in collaboration with educators and students nationwide, Revel is the newest, fully digital way to deliver respected Pearson content. Revel enlivens course content with media interactives and assessments—integrated directly within the author's narrative—that provide opportunities for students to read about and practice course material in tandem. This immersive educational technology boosts student engagement, which leads to better understanding of concepts and improved performance throughout the course.

Learn more about Revel

http://www.pearsonhighered.com/revel/

In every chapter, interactive features promote comprehension and mastery of core concepts in ways that will engage students. These features include:

- **Audio Excerpts** – In-line audio allows students to hear short speech excerpts as they read, giving them a better appreciation of these examples than can be gained from a printed text. These excerpts are identified in color both in print and in Revel and are identified by red audio buttons in Revel.

> Sample Oral Citation for Interview Material
>
> In a personal interview I conducted last month, local dentist Dr. Marvin Jones said that his office will donate supplies and a day of free checkups to support the city's health literacy campaign in schools. ◀))

▪ **Full-Length Speech Outlines with Audio Annotations** – Three complete preparation outlines (two informative, one persuasive) and one complete transcript (speech of inspiration) of student speeches are accompanied by audio annotations that highlight good outlining form and explain some of the choices the speakers made while preparing their outlines and speeches.

▪ **Videos with Accompanying Video Self-Checks** – Videos bring to life additional examples, speeches, and explanations of communication principles across a variety of public speaking situations. Sample speeches allow students to see speeches being delivered and provide extra help for students in developing and delivering their own speeches. Many videos are accompanied by video self-checks that allow students to test their knowledge of the content and information in the videos.

▪ **Self-Assessments** – Self-assessment instruments and other self-reflexive activities allow students to analyze their own communication styles, enabling them to learn and grow as a speaker over the duration of the course.

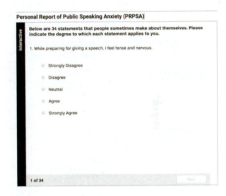

▪ **Interactive Figures** – Figures and illustrations in the text (such as the transactional process of communication and Maslow's hierarchy of needs) have been animated to make complex concepts easier to understand through interactivity.

▪ **Integrated Writing Opportunities** – Questions for review and reflection are integrated into the text, giving students an opportunity to stop and think about the content presented and to respond in a written format. These writing opportunities take the form of Journal prompts for individual student response and Shared Writing prompts that allow students to respond to and discuss the same questions as their classmates.

For more information about all the tools and resources in Revel and access to your own Revel account for *DK Guide to Public Speaking*, go to www.pearsonhighered.com/revel

2

Additional incorporation of learning objectives: Learning objectives are emphasized throughout. As in previous editions, each chapter module starts with an objective-reinforcing question that students should be able to answer completely after reading the chapter. Additionally, each chapter's table of contents and review section pair the headings and objectives, and objectives are repeated at the bottoms of pages. Each Revel interactive is designed to further support the objectives, providing opportunities for application, self-checks, and reflection.

3

Expanded coverage of mediated presentations: More information on analyzing the mediated audience, using technology, finding tutorials, preparing and practicing, recording, and delivering video will help students give effective mediated presentations. Videos in Revel show recorded speeches, virtual meetings, and more.

4

Updated MLA citation style: MLA citation guidelines and examples have been fully updated to reflect the *MLA Handbook*, 8th edition. Writing exercises in Revel help students practice citing sources.

5

New speech outlines and examples: Two new, complete, annotated preparation outlines of informative student speeches are featured in Chapters 6 and 14, along with new related examples (working and delivery outlines, introductions and conclusions, and more). Many other new and updated examples appear throughout, including a new speech of introduction and a new after-dinner speech excerpt. Revel includes audio for annotations and many excerpts.

6

New sample presentation aids and illustrations: Chapter 11 includes new sample slides and updated templates from PowerPoint and Prezi. Many other illustrations and photos have been updated throughout the text, including library portal and database examples.

Additional Features

A powerfully visual DK design and comprehensive coverage combine for an easy-to-navigate resource that equips students with the tools to be effective public speakers. Based on extensive research and usability studies, this guidebook gives students the practical information they seek, supported by the concepts and theories instructors want.

1

Designed for easy navigation and use: Tabs, color-coded chapters, process charts, and question-and-answer heading formats help students quickly find answers to questions on any part of the speech process. Blue cross-references guide students to related

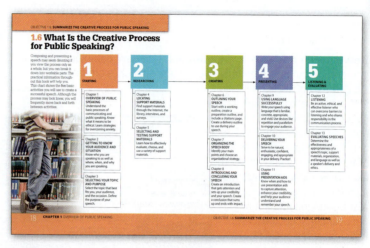

sections. Revel includes links between the table of contents, chapter contents, and modules to help students navigate the text.

2

Presents concepts visually, supported by text: The pairing of visuals and detailed explanations allows students to get an overview at a glance and read on for specifics. In Revel, many visuals are animated to further help students understand concepts.

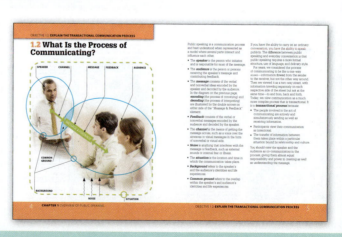

3

Driven by examples: This text teaches by example with its intricate weaving of scenarios, annotated speeches, and diverse examples in an easy-to-find blue font, including comparisons of ineffective and effective techniques. In Revel, many examples include audio clips so students can hear as well as see speech excerpts, oral citations, and more.

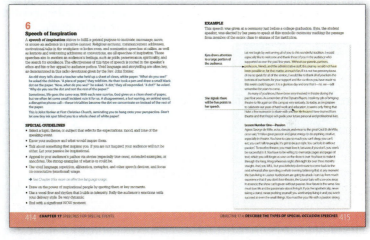

4

Emphasizes confidence-building: Starting with a section in Chapter 1 on overcoming apprehension, the text then features blue "Confidence Booster" sections throughout to help students deal with fears and be well prepared. Revel includes videos and self-assessments that students can use to further understand and control their anxiety.

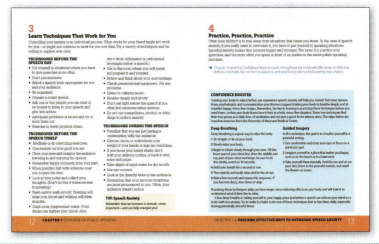

5

Emphasizes ethics at every stage:
Building on ethics and avoiding plagiarism, "Practicing Ethics" sections are integrated into each chapter. Many of these sections in Revel are paired with a Journal prompt or other writing exercise.

PRACTICING ETHICS: Cite Sources

Whether blatant or no-citation, intentional or accidental, plagiarism is highly unethical and can be damaging. Be diligent in citing your sources during your speech and on your outline. Citing sources will build your credibility.

6

Correlates with NCA learning outcomes:
Learning objectives correlate with the National Communication Association's Learning Outcomes in Communication. A guide in the back of the book points to where each outcome is addressed in the text. Revel includes links to the relevant chapters and learning objectives.

7

Based on how students do research: The research chapters in Tab 2 are designed around the astounding array of resources available to students today. Coverage emphasizes how to evaluate sources and how to cite them orally and in written form. Revel includes audio and video examples of using and citing sources in speeches as well as interactive writing exercises to practice creating citations.

8

Includes checklists and tip boxes for practical application: Extensive use of checklists gives students practical tools to help them create and evaluate their speeches at each stage of the process. Tip boxes provide useful information and advice along the way. Revel features interactive versions of the checklists.

CHECKLIST for Evaluating Working Main Points

☐ Does each main point cover only one key idea?

☐ Are my main points similarly constructed (are they parallel)?

☐ Am I roughly balancing the time spent on each point?

☐ Do my main points relate back to the central idea?

TIP: Length

• Your introduction should be less than 15 percent of your total speech time.

• Your conclusion should be less than 5 percent of your total speech time.

9

Covers presentation aids in a truly visual way: Chapter 11, "Using Presentation Aids," takes full advantage of the cutting-edge and visual nature of the text to explain and showcase the variety of aids available to students today—and the best ways to maximize their use. Videos in Revel show additional examples as they are incorporated into speeches.

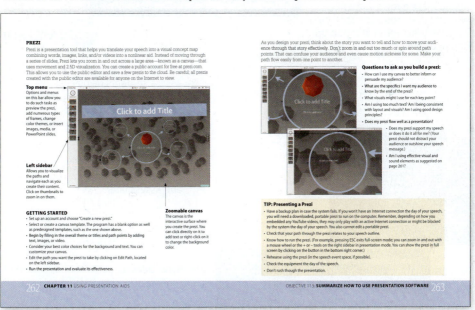

Instructor and Student Resources

MediaShare   A one-stop media-sharing tool that facilitates interactive learning

MediaShare is a learning application for sharing, discussing, and assessing multimedia. Instructors easily can assign instructional videos to students, create quiz questions, and ask students to comment and reflect on the videos to facilitate collaborative discussion. MediaShare also allows students to record or upload their own videos and other multimedia projects, which they can submit to an instructor and peers for both evaluation via rubrics and review via comments at time-stamped intervals. Additionally, MediaShare allows students working in a group to submit a single artifact for evaluation on behalf of the group.

MediaShare offers a robust library of pre-created assignments, all of which can be customized, to give instructors flexibility.

Pearson

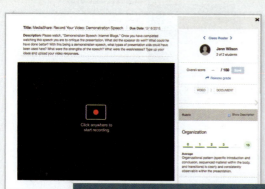

Record video directly from a tablet, phone, or other webcam (including a batch upload option for instructors) and tag submissions to a specific student or assignment.

- Assess students using customizable, Pearson-provided rubrics or create your own around classroom goals, learning outcomes, or department initiatives.

- Grade in real time during in-class presentations or review recordings and assess later.

- Set up learning objectives tied to specific assignments, rubrics, or quiz questions to track student progress.

- Sync slides to media submissions for more robust presentation options.

- Set up assignments for students with options for full-class viewing and commenting, private comments between you and the student, peer groups for reviewing, or as collaborative group assignments.

- Use MediaShare to assign or view speeches, outlines, presentation aids, video-based assignments, role plays, group projects, and more in a variety of formats including video, Word, PowerPoint, and Excel.

Time-stamped comments provide contextualized feedback that is easy to consume and learn from.

- Embed video from YouTube via assignments to incorporate current events into the classroom experience.

- Ensure a secure learning environment for instructors and students through robust privacy settings.

- Upload videos, comment on submissions, and grade directly from our MediaShare app, available free from the iTunes store and GooglePlay. To download, search for "Pearson MediaShare."

Create quiz questions for video assignments to ensure students master concepts and interact and engage with the media.

Additional Resources

Key instructor resources include an Instructor's Manual (ISBN 0-13-440310-X), Test Bank (ISBN 0-13-440313-4), and PowerPoint Presentation Package (ISBN 0-13-440225-1). These supplements are available at www.pearsonhighered.com /irc (instructor login required). MyTest online test-generating software

(ISBN 0-13-440315-0) is available at www.pearsonmytest.com (instructor login required).

For a complete listing of the instructor and student resources available with this text, please visit the Pearson Communication catalog at www.pearsonhighered.com /communication.

Acknowledgments

This book was a labor of love for many people, and I was blessed to work with a great team and to have folks from my professional as well as personal lives offering support. Thanks go to everyone whose work, input, and contributions are reflected in this book, including: at Pearson and Dorling Kindersley, Karon Bowers (Publisher, Communication), Brenda Hadenfeldt (Development Editor), Stuart Jackman (Design Director for DK Education), Laura Coaty (Director of Learner Insight), Sophie Mitchell (Publishing Director for DK Education), Becky Brown (Product Marketer), and Kelly Ross (Senior Field Marketing Manager); Tharon Howard, Director of the Clemson University Usability Testing Facility, and his team, including Wendy Howard; undergraduate students at both Clemson University and Tri-County Technical College who participated in usability studies; undergraduate students at the University of Cincinnati who participated in focus groups; Faculty Advisory Board members, additional focus group participants, and reviewers (listed on pages xxiii-xxvi); student and research assistants Gabrielle Mistretta, Steven Dotson, Crystaldawn Arnold, Jared Reichel, and Karissa King; Columbia College students Caitlin Jenkins Campbell, Andria Caruthers, Desiree Chong, Rachel Coleman, Kelly Feisel, Tori Gehlert, Ashley Hardy, Brianna Hickman, Charity J. Hunter, Candace Johnson, Megan Kelly, Katherine Mancuso, Milos Milosavljevic, Logan Park, Shakeera Schneller, Kylie E. Stephenson, Jessica Ucci, Christopher Vietti, and Rachel K. Wester; and speech contributors Dorinda K. Stayton, Kimberly Albrecht-Taylor, and the Rev. John Yonker (Columbia, MO).

Throughout this project, I have been fortunate to enjoy the support and assistance of many colleagues on the Columbia College campus. I wish to thank: President Scott Dalrymple, David Starrett, David Roebuck, Peter Monacell, and the Humanities Department; the entire Columbia College Technology Services group (specifically Gary Stanowski, Stefanie McCollum, B. J. Donaldson, Matt Meininger, Jennifer Tice, and Michael Van Duser); and Danny Campbell, Janet Caruthers, Tonia Compton, Lucia D'Agostino, Johanna Denzin, Gretchen Hendrickson, Brandi Herrman, Barry Langford, Michael Lyman, Peter Neely, Kaci Smart, and Laura Smith.

I would like to thank several exceptional educators who have influenced me both professionally and personally: Sheron J. Dailey, C. Sue Davis, Mary Carol Harris, Harriet McNeal, Dan P. Millar, Ron Pelias, Elyse Pineau, and David Worley.

I am extremely grateful to the Ford, Camp, and Brown families for all the support and understanding—especially Bruce Brown.

What an adventure this was, and I thank ALL of you.

Lisa A. Ford-Brown

Faculty Advisory Board

Shae Adkins, Lone Star College–North Harris; **Allison Ainsworth**, Gainesville State College; **Mary Alexander**, Wharton County Junior College; **Julie Allee**, Indiana University South Bend; **Barbara Baron**, Brookdale Community College; **Kate Behr**, Concordia College; **Constance Berman**, Berkshire Community College; **Kimberly Berry**, Ozarks Technical College; **Kirk Brewer**, Tulsa Community College, West Campus; **Ferald Bryan**, Northern Illinois University; **Rebecca Carlton**, Indiana University Southeast; **Gary Carson**, Coastal Carolina University; **Wendy R. Coleman**, Alabama State University; **Diana Cooley**, Lone Star College–North Harris; **Karin Dahmann**, Blinn College; **Natalie Dorfeld**, Thiel College; **Kelly Driskell**, Trinity Valley Community College; **Robert D. Dunkerly**, College of Southern Nevada; **Steve Earnest**, Coastal Carolina University; **Katrina Eicher**, Elizabethtown Community and Technical College; **Kristina Galyen**, University of Cincinnati; **Jo Anna Grant**, California State University, San Bernardino; **Christa Tess Kalk**, Minneapolis Community and Technical College; **Tressa Kelly**, University of West Florida; **Sherry Lewis**, University of Texas at El Paso; **Daniel Leyes**, Brookdale Community College; **Terri Main**, Reedley College; **Anne McIntosh**, Central Piedmont Community College; **James McNamara**, Alverno College; **Donna Munde**, Mercer County Community College; **John Nash**, Moraine Valley Community College; **William Neff**, College of Southern Nevada; **Karen Otto**, Florida State College at Jacksonville; **Maria Parnell**, Brevard Community College, Melbourne; **Katherine Rigsby**, University of South Alabama; **Kristi Schaller**, University of Georgia; **Michael Shannon**, Moraine Valley Community College; **Pam Speights**, Wharton County Junior College; **Janice Stuckey**, Jefferson State Community College; **Jane Varmecky**, Tulsa Community College, Southeast Campus; **Jenny Warren**, Collin County Community College, Spring Creek; **Rebecca Weldon**, Savannah College of Art and Design; **Susan Wieczorek**, University of Pittsburgh at Johnstown; **Susan Winters**, University of Cincinnati; **Brandon Wood**, Central Texas College; and **Quentin Wright**, Mountain View College.

Focus Group Participants

Carolyn Babcock, Savannah College of Art and Design; **Cameron Basquiat**, College of Southern Nevada; **Shirene Bell**, Salt Lake Community College; **Linda Brown**, El Paso Community College, Transmountain Campus; **Dawn Carusi**, Marietta College; **Helen Chester**, Milwaukee Area Technical College; **Russ Church**, Middle Tennessee State University; **Kathleen D. Clark**, University of Akron; **Janis Crawford**, Butler University; **Dale Davis**, University of Texas at San Antonio; **Ella Davis**, Wayne County Community College; **Shannon Doyle**, San Jose State University; **Jeanne Dunphy**, Los Angeles City College; **Jennifer Fairchild**, Eastern Kentucky University; **Jeff Farrar**, University of Connecticut; **Katie Frame**, Schoolcraft College; **Kathy Golden**, Edinboro University of Pennsylvania; **Don Govang**, Lincoln University; **Joy Hart**, University of Louisville; **James Heflin**, Cameron University; **Terry Helmick**, Johnson County Community College; **Wade Hescht**, Lone Star College–North Harris; **Heather Hundley**, California State University, San Bernardino; **Lynae Jacob**, Amarillo College; **Jim Kuypers**, Virginia Tech; **Libby McGlone**, Columbus State Community College; **Terri Moore**, Brevard Community College, Melbourne; **Tim Pierce**, Northern Illinois University; **Sherry Rhodes**, Collin County Community College, Courtyard Center; **Rebecca Robideaux**, Boise State University; **David Schneider**, Saginaw Valley University; **April DuPree Taylor**, University of South Alabama; **Paaige Turner**, Saint Louis University; **Julie Weishar**, Parkland College; and **Charla Windley**, University of Idaho.

Reviewers

Donald Abel, Amarillo College; Helen Acosta, Bakersfield College; Brent Adrian, Central Community College, Grand Island; Bob Alexander, Bossier Parish Community College; Jeffrey Anderson, Tidewater Community College; Krista Appelquist, Moraine Valley Community College; Brenda Armentrout, Central Piedmont Community College; Ann Atkinson, Keene State College; Jackie Augustine, Victor Valley College; Kevin Backstrom, University of Wisconsin Oshkosh; Cynthia L. Bahti, Saddleback College and Orange Coast Colleges; Erin Baird, University of Oklahoma; Elise Banfield, Genesee Community College; Bryan Barrows, Lone Star College-North Harris; Kristin Barton, Dalton State College; Jennifer Huss Basquiat, College of Southern Nevada; Sharon Beal, Long Beach City College and California State University, Fullerton; Polly Begley, Fresno City College; Tim Behme, University of Minnesota, Twin Cities; Christopher Bell, University of Colorado, Colorado Springs; Belinda Bernum, Mansfield University; Denise Besson-Silvia, Gavilan College; Melanie Lea Birck, Bossier Parish Community College; Mardia Bishop, University of Illinois; Carol Bliss, California State Polytechnic University; Tonya Blivens, Tarrant County College, Southeast Campus; Robert Boller, University of Hawaii at Manoa; Beverly McClay Borawski, Pasco-Hernando Community College; Jeffrey Brand, Millikin University; LeAnn Brazeal, Kansas State University; Heather Brecht, Ithaca College; Michele Bresso, Bakersfield College; Stefne Lenzmeier Broz, Wittenberg University; Jackie Bruscella, University of Oklahoma; Barbara Ruth Burke, University of Minnesota, Morris; Donna Burnside, University of Texas at Brownsville; Nicholas Butler, Arizona State University; Dennis Cali, University of Texas at Tyler; Mary Carver, University of Central Oklahoma; Connie Caskey, Jefferson State Community College; Jennifer Chakroff, Kent State University; Angela Cherry, Laney College; Robert Christie, DeVry College; Carolyn Clark, Salt Lake Community College; Benjamin J. Cline, Western New Mexico University; Cindy Cochran, Kirkwood Community College; Jodi Cohen, Ithaca College; Teresa Collard, University of Tennessee at Martin; Leslie Collins, Modesto Junior College; Ron Compton, McHenry County College; Linda Carvalho Cooley, Reedley College; Lisa Coulter, Murray State College; Andrea Davis, University of South Carolina Upstate; Quinton D. Davis, University of Texas at San Antonio; Tasha Davis, Austin Community College, Round Rock; Isabel del Pino-Allen, Miami Dade College; Laura Deshaies, Cleveland Community College; Susan Dobie, Humboldt State University; Natalie Dudchock, Jefferson State Community College; Ann Duncan, McLennan Community College; Janine W. Dunlap, Freed-Hardeman University; Rachel Dwiggins-Beeler, Contra Costa College; Evangeline East, Solano Community College; Kristen Eichhorn, SUNY Oswego; Marty Ennes, West Hills College Lemoore; Heather Erickson, Emerson College; Diane Ferrero-Paluzzi, Iona College; James M. Floss, Humboldt State University; Vanessa Forcari, California State University, East Bay; Jeffrey Fox, Northern Kentucky University; Rebecca Franko, California State Polytechnic University; Barbara Franzen, Central Community College; Mark Frederick, Tidewater Community College; Stacy Freed, University of Tennessee at Martin; Todd S. Frobish, Fayetteville State University; Mark S. Gallup, Lansing Community College; Joseph M. Ganakos, Lee College; Laura Garcia, Washington State Community College; Donna Goodwin, Tulsa Community College; Donna Gotch, California State University, San Bernardino; Sandra E. Grayson, Mississippi College; Robert Greenstreet, East Central University; Howard Grower, University of Tennessee; Angela Grupas, St. Louis Community College, Meramec; Karen Hamburg, Camden County College; William Harpine, University of South Carolina Aiken; Carla Harrell, Old Dominion University; Richard Harrison, Kilgore College; Megan Hart, Cumberland County College; Vickie Harvey, California State University, Stanislaus; April Hebert, College of Southern Nevada; Linda Heil, Harford Community College; Anne Helms, Alamance Community College; Linda Hensley, Southwestern College; Lisa Katrina Hill, Harrisburg Area Community College, Gettysburg; Tim Horne, University of North Carolina at Charlotte; Allison Horrell, Spartanburg Community College; Marcia W. Hotchkiss,

Tennessee State University; **Christopher Howerton**, Woodland Community College; **Teresa Humphrey**, University of South Carolina Aiken; **Mary Hurley**, St. Louis Community College at Forest Park; **Nancy Jennings**, Cuyamaca College; **Katie Johnson**, Black Hawk College; **Karyn Jones**, Clemson University; **Robert Kagan**, Manchester Community College; **Pamela Kaylor**, Ohio University Lancaster; **Rebecca M. Kennerly**, Georgia Southern University; **Peter Kerr**, Asbury University; **Susan Kilgard**, Anne Arundel Community College; **Ray Killebrew**, Missouri Baptist University; **Sandra King**, Anne Arundel Community College; **Loretta Kissell**, Mesa Community College; **Brian Kline**, Gainesville State College; **Krista Kozel**, Doña Ana Community College; **Staci Kuntzman**, University of North Carolina at Charlotte; **Kristina Langseth**, Minneapolis Community and Technical College; **Cindy Larson-Casselton**, Concordia College; **Bohn Lattin**, University of Portland; **Jeffrey Lawrence**, Ivy Tech Community College, Columbus/Franklin; **Michael Lee**, College of Charleston; **Robert Leonard**, Sinclair Community College; **Charles E. Lester**, Palm Beach Atlantic University; **John Levine**, University of California, Berkeley; **Derrick Lindstrom**, Minneapolis Community and Technical College; **Darren Linvill**, Clemson University; **Karen Lollar**, Metropolitan State University of Denver; **Steve Madden**, Coastal Carolina University; **Kristen Majocha**, University of Pittsburgh at Johnstown; **Jodie D. Mandel**, College of Southern Nevada; **Reed Markham**, Daytona State College, DeLand; **Ginger K. Martin**, Guilford Technical Community College; **Tami Martinez**, Indiana University South Bend; **Sujanet Mason**, Luzerne County Community College; **Sarah Mathews**, Southwestern Michigan College; **Leola McClure**, MiraCosta College; **James R. McCoy**, College of Southern Nevada; **Dee Ann McFarlin**, North Central Texas College; **Deborah Socha McGee**, College of Charleston; **Miriam McMullen-Pastrick**, Penn State Erie, The Behrend College; **James McNamara**, Alverno College; **Delois Medhin**, Milwaukee Area Technical College; **Shellie Michael**, Volunteer State Community College; **Josh Miller**, Los Angeles Valley College; **Mike Monsour**, Metropolitan State University of Denver; **Barbara Montgomery**, Colorado State University, Pueblo; **Eric Moreau**, College of Southern Nevada; **Lynnette Mullins**, University of Minnesota, Crookston; **Heidi Murphy**, Central New Mexico Community College; **Thomas Murray**, Fitchburg State University; **W. Benjamin Myers**, University of South Carolina Upstate; **Alexa Naramore**, University of Cincinnati; **Kay E. Neal**, University of Wisconsin Oshkosh; **Mary T. Newman**, Wharton County Junior College; **Deborah Nolan**, Ivy Tech Community College; **Rebecca Nordyke**, Wichita State University; **Christine North**, Ohio Northern University; **Erin Obermueller**, Concordia College–New York; **Elizabeth Reeves O'Connor**, Rochester Institute of Technology; **Tami Olds**, Northern Virginia Community College; **Mary Oulvey**, Southwestern Illinois College; **Zachary Owens**, University of Cincinnati; **Mariusz Ozminkowski**, California Polytechnic State University, Pomona; **Kate Pantinas**, Ivy Tech Community College; **Deborah Panzer**, Nassau Community College; **Daniel Paulnock**, Saint Paul College; **Jean Perry**, Glendale Community College; **Charlotte Petty**, University of Missouri at St. Louis; **Tonia East Phanor**, Edison State College; **Shirlee Pledger**, Fullerton College; **Mihaela Popescu**, California State University, San Bernardino; **Mike Posey**, Franklin University; **Renee Post**, Cumberland County College; **Shelly Presnell**, Shasta College; **Ann Preston**, St. Ambrose University; **C. Thomas Preston**, Gainesville State College; **Marlene M. Preston**, Virginia Tech; **Shannon Proctor**, Highline Community College; **Brandi Quesenberry**, Virginia Tech; **Rita Rahoi-Gilchrest**, Winona State University; **Michele Ramsey**, Penn State Berks; **Rasha Ramzy**, Georgia State University; **Paul R. Raptis**, Gainesville State College; **Jessica Reeher**, SUNY Oswego; **Catherine Reilly**, Dominican College; **Elizabeth Richard**, Saint Louis University; **Maryanna Richardson**, Forsyth Technical Community College; **William Richter**, Lenoir-Rhyne University; **Heather Ricker-Gilbert**, Manchester Community College; **Greg Rickert**, Bluegrass Community and Technical College; **B. Hannah Rockwell**, Loyola University Chicago; **Terry Rogers**, Casper College; **Estrella Romero**, Riverside City College/Riverside Campus; **Alisa Roost**, Hostos Community College; **Douglas Rosentrater**, Bucks County Community College; **Kimberly Ross-Brown**, Bluegrass Community and Technical College;

TAB 1
Starting

1
OVERVIEW OF PUBLIC SPEAKING

1.1 When Will You Use the Skills Offered in This Book?

1 In Your Public Life
2 In Your Professional Life
3 In Your Personal Life

1

In Your Public Life

Taking the time now to understand the public speaking process will help you:

- Improve your ability to speak out about issues in your community and larger society.
- Become more culturally sensitive.
- Become a better consumer of public communication from others through the development of your critical thinking skills.

Engaging in public speaking is empowerment at its purest. We live in a country that honors its people with the freedom of speech; as citizens, we can use that freedom to improve our lives and those of future generations. Someday, you may find yourself the president of a local community project to keep children drug-free. You may find yourself appointed the neighborhood spokesperson when a large corporation wants to purchase land in your neighborhood for a new construction project. When family members struggle to pay their medical bills, you may find yourself speaking out for medical reform. You will encounter numerous times throughout your life when you will need to have the courage to speak out publicly on issues that concern you and those you care about.

> **PRACTICING ETHICS: Understanding**
>
> When evaluating and responding to the communication of a speaker, strive to understand his or her point of view, needs, and behavior. Create a caring and mutual learning environment when responding to a message. For example, when you disagree with someone's message, listen carefully to the entire message as an option before you judge it.

2
In Your Professional Life

Individuals who develop effective communication skills get better grades, more promotions, and higher pay, and they have more overall success in their educational and professional careers. No matter what major you select or what profession you end up working in, you will need to be an effective speaker.

Learning how to outline or cite sources is as important in a science research class as it is in a speech class, and learning how to listen will help you in all your classes as well as in your professional relationships. Today, most two- and four-year college courses in any field have an oral presentation requirement.

When looking for a job, you will find that most employers place a high emphasis on good written and oral communication skills when hiring and evaluating their employees. The basic job interview is quite possibly the most difficult persuasive communication most of you will undertake.

3
In Your Personal Life

Personal benefits relate to your self-development and self-esteem. When you engage in public speaking, you learn more about yourself and others as well as how to be a better listener and overall person.

For example, think about the beliefs you hold related to topics like abortion or gay marriage. Can you articulate why you hold these beliefs and support them? What can you learn about yourself when you publicly articulate your feelings related to these topics? How can you learn from listening to others who agree or disagree with your feelings?

The self-esteem benefit may be the most important at this point in your public speaking mission. Most beginning speakers have some fear or stage fright related to giving a speech. Ironically, the single best way to beat the stage-fright monster is to give many speeches. Once you realize that you can give a speech and that most audiences are more forgiving than you think, you will find confidence in yourself that you didn't know existed.

TIP: Unleash Your Potential

Research consistently demonstrates the importance of communication skills to your ability to get and keep a job. Sources such as the National Association of Colleges and Employers, the American Association of Retired Persons, and business professor Marcel M. Robles show that key to your success are the abilities to communicate well in writing and verbally; to listen; to be organized; to be creative; to be analytical; to make decisions and solve problems; to be cooperative; to be persuasive; to be a life-long learner; to be proficient in computers, reading, and math; and to have a good work attitude, manners, ethics, and confidence. Each of these skills is either directly or indirectly related to your public speaking skills. Developing and honing your communication competence will benefit you in every aspect of your life.

1.2 What Is the Process of Communicating?

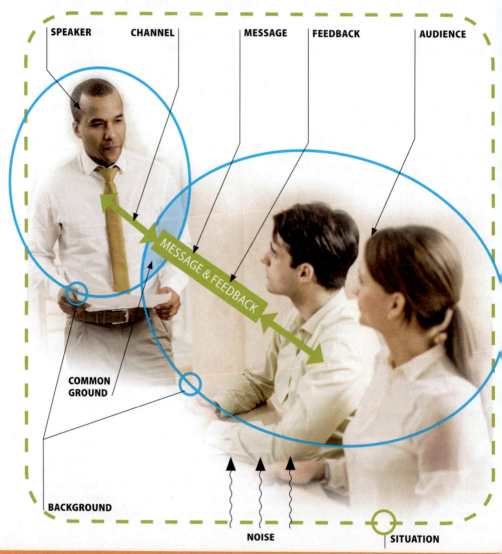

SPEAKER   CHANNEL   MESSAGE   FEEDBACK   AUDIENCE

MESSAGE & FEEDBACK

COMMON GROUND

BACKGROUND

NOISE   SITUATION

Public speaking is a communication process and best understood when represented as a model where several parts interact and influence each other.

- The **speaker** is the person who initiates and is responsible for most of the message.

- The **audience** is the person or persons receiving the speaker's message and contributing feedback.

- The **message** consists of the verbal and nonverbal ideas encoded by the speaker and decoded by the audience. In the diagram on the previous page, **encoding** (the process of conveying) and **decoding** (the process of interpreting) are illustrated by the double arrows on either side of the "Message & Feedback" element.

- **Feedback** consists of the verbal or nonverbal messages encoded by the audience and decoded by the speaker.

- The **channel** is the means of getting the message across, such as a voice over the airwaves or visual messages in the form of nonverbal or visual aids.

- **Noise** is anything that interferes with the message or feedback, such as external sounds or internal fear or illness.

- The **situation** is the location and time in which the communication takes place.

- **Background** refers to the speaker's and the audience's identities and life experiences.

- **Common ground** refers to the overlap within the speaker's and audience's identities and life experiences.

If you have the ability to carry on an ordinary conversation, you have the ability to speak publicly. The difference between public speaking and everyday conversation is that public speaking requires a more formal structure, use of language, and delivery style.

For years, we considered the process of communicating to be like a one-way street—information flowed from the sender to the receiver, but not the other way around. Then we viewed it as a two-way street, with information traveling separately on each respective side of the street but not at the same time—to and from, back and forth. Today, we view communication as a much more complex process that is transactional. It is a **transactional process** because:

- The people involved in the act of communicating are actively and simultaneously sending as well as receiving information.

- Participants view their communication as intentional.

- The transfer of information between them takes place within a particular situation bound by relationship and culture.

You should view the speaker and the audience as co-communicators in the process, giving them almost equal responsibility and power in creating as well as understanding the message.

1.3 How Can You Be a Successful Public Speaker?

1 **Be Audience Centered**

2 **Be Knowledgeable, Creative, and Organized**

3 **Use Appropriate Appeals**

4 **Use Appropriate Presentation Techniques**

5 **Practice Again and Again**

We often know when we hear or see successful public speakers, even if we can't always put our finger on why we like them. Good public speaking habits seem to slide right on by, unnoticed, while the speakers can move us and change our lives.

So what makes a good speaker? Scholars have wrestled with this question for centuries, but deep down, you already know the answer. Think about President John F. Kennedy or Martin Luther King, Jr. Search the Internet for recent famous commencement speeches by First Lady Michelle Obama, celebrities such as Stephen Colbert or Maya Rudolph, or Apple CEO Tim Cook; think about what you like. Even if you disagree with their viewpoints, it is hard to deny that they all had or have good communication skills. Like you, they initially had certain skills that needed more work. For example, former Prime Minister of England Margaret Thatcher reportedly took voice-training courses to change her high voice to a lower one—a pitch that was culturally perceived to be authoritative.

Beginning speakers often see perfection as the key to success, only to be disappointed. No one is perfect, but successful public speaking grows out of the following qualities.

1

Be Audience Centered

Have you ever heard someone say, "You can't understand me until you have walked in my shoes"? This phrase reflects theorist and philosopher Kenneth Burke's notion of identification, as discussed in his book *A Rhetoric of Motives*. **Identification** (also called *empathy*) is the human need and willingness to understand as much as possible the feelings, thoughts, motives, interests, attitudes, and lives of others. As human beings, we are born separate but spend much of our lives looking for what we share with others. Identification is at the core of being **audience centered**. Audience-centered speakers create and deliver their speeches while identifying and considering the unique characteristics and viewpoints of their audience. Being audience centered will guide you in selecting appropriate topics and help you in creating ways for your audience to connect with your topic.

→ Chapters 2 and 3 show you how to analyze your audience and select a topic.

2

Be Knowledgeable, Creative, and Organized

When the great artist Michelangelo was 88 years old, he allegedly wrote, "I am still learning." To be a successful speaker, you must be diligent and know as much as possible about your topic, audience, occasion, language, and methods of delivery right up to the moment the speech ends.

Bring your knowledge to life by being creative. Individuality, uniqueness, imagination, resourcefulness, and vision are all qualities of creativity. Imagine if Martin Luther King, Jr., had said "hope" rather than "dream." Imagine if Michael Jackson hadn't envisioned the video for "Thriller." We might not have one of the greatest speeches of all time, or music videos as we now know them might never have existed. Think outside the box and take chances that will set you apart from others.

Be organized. Successful speakers effectively organize their speeches to focus and engage their audiences.

→ Tabs 1–3 help you develop your knowledge, use your creativity, and organize your speech.

> If I had to go back to college again — knowing what I know today — I'd concentrate on two areas: learning to write and to speak before an audience. Nothing in life is more important than the ability to communicate effectively.[1]

PRESIDENT GERALD R. FORD

3
Use Appropriate Appeals

The great philosopher Aristotle wrote in the *Rhetoric* about the influence certain appeals (also called *proofs*) have on the credibility of a speaker and his or her speech. Aristotle argued that your credibility and that of your speech stem from *logos*, *ethos*, and *pathos*.

Logos appeals to your audience's ability to reason or work through your ideas logically. You use this sort of appeal when you organize a speech and support your speech with material your audience will accept through reasoning.

For example, if you want to persuade your audience that the 2015 Panama drought, which forced the Panama Canal Authority to limit ship draft, was a product of natural climate variables and global warming created by humans, you must support this claim with current facts presented reasonably.

Ethos is the appeal of reliability. Your audience must view you and your support materials as reliable. You use this appeal when you demonstrate to the audience that you have their best interest in mind and are confident in the quality of your support materials as well as of the sources you quote. Your audience must view you as trustworthy, competent, objective, and enthusiastic for you to have high ethos.

One of the best methods for creating ethos is to use and cite sources from a variety of appropriate and current support material. If you are trying to inform your audience about the healthiest fruits, for example, you should cite the work of nutritionists and not just fruit growers.

Pathos appeals to the audience's emotions to maintain their interest or to convince them of your intent. You create pathos through effective use of support materials and language. For example, imagine you are giving a speech to convince others to volunteer or offer donations to rebuild areas affected by severe storms and flash flooding that hit the Midwest in December 2015. You could use pictures or stories depicting the devastation to appeal to a sense of compassion. Speakers engaging an audience's emotions must be careful to balance this appeal with ethos and logos.

You must use a combination of these appeals to get your audience to listen, to understand your message, and, ultimately, to react the way you intend. Skillful and ethical speakers learn when and how to use appeals appropriately.

→ Chapter 15 shows you how to use appeals in your speech.

4

Use Appropriate Presentation Techniques

Think about how you talk to your best friend compared with how you speak to someone like your mother or grandfather. Most likely, you do not use the same language and speaking style with your friend that you do with an older relative.

The same is true for speaking effectively in public. Speakers must think about the topic, audience, situation, and intent of their speeches when they select their verbal and nonverbal behavior and their delivery style. For example, reading from a manuscript about your trip to the state fair will seem strange and too formal.

Most of the speeches you will give in a class or your everyday life will use an *extemporaneous* style. Speaking extemporaneously requires you to logically organize the speech, practice sufficiently, and use minimal notes while giving the speech.

Choosing your words carefully for each speaking situation, employing the best vocal and physical delivery techniques possible, and using presentation aids when necessary must be considered with each new speaking event.

→ Tab 4 offers guidance on appropriate behavior, delivery styles, and presentation aid usage.

5

Practice Again and Again

In the first century BCE, Roman author Publilius Syrus wrote, "Practice is the best of all instructors." Most often, beginning students do not practice enough or exactly as they plan to give their speeches. Bad habits (such as putting off writing a speech until the last minute, just reading over the speech instead of practicing it, or practicing it only once) can cause many problems. Practicing helps you hone all your skills, locate issues that are not working within the speech, and develop confidence. Let your mind and body become familiar with your speech.

Practicing will boost your confidence and make you a better speaker. You will begin to actually enjoy giving a speech (yes, you will!) if you work on how you feel about your abilities. Like creating a speech, boosting your confidence is a process that takes work and time. Most people have some level of anxiety about public speaking, and the next few pages will help you start to control that anxiety.

→ See Chapter 10 for rehearsal guidelines.

TIP: Practicing

Using the exact delivery outline and rehearsing in the actual space with the specific equipment you will use during the speech will help you prevent major problems.

1.4 How Can You Overcome a Fear of Public Speaking?

1 Understand What Is Happening

2 Face Your Fear Head On

3 Learn Techniques That Work for You

4 Practice, Practice, Practice

1

Understand What Is Happening

When Jenna needs to prepare for a speech, she dreads it so much that she puts it off until the last minute. Then, when she gives the speech, her voice cracks. Sergei feels like his mouth is full of cotton and his legs shake as he gives his speeches. Jenna and Sergei are mentally and physically reacting to their fears of public speaking.

Communication apprehension is a term scholars give to the fears you may have when engaging in a communicative interaction with one or more persons. The uneasiness and fearfulness you might feel when preparing or giving a speech is *speech anxiety*.

The feelings you might have about giving a speech can be very similar to the nervousness you feel the first time you talk to someone you are attracted to. Either of these fears can be so intense that you avoid the situation, and they can manifest into physical distress such as sweaty hands or shaky knees.

When you fear something, no matter what it is, your body enters into the fight-or-flight response, which releases hormones to help you either fight or flee the thing causing you anxiety. Your body reacts to the hormones, and your heart and breathing rates go up; your blood vessels constrict, forcing the blood from your limbs to your vital organs; and your muscles tense. In prehistoric times, you would be ready to fight or run from a predator. In current times, this is how your body reacts to any situation causing alarm, such as giving a speech. Common symptoms of anxiety are listed on the next page.

COMMON ANXIETY SYMPTOMS

- Tight throat, producing a high pitch
- Dry mouth
- Shaky hands or legs
- Nausea
- Perspiration
- Skin changes (paleness, red patches)
- Cold, clammy, or sweaty hands
- Cold nose or ears
- Fast pulse and breathing rate
- Trembling lips
- Avoiding eye contact
- Adding vocal pauses and fillers ("ah," "um," "like," "you know")
- Multiple trips to the restroom
- Memory issues or inability to concentrate
- Overwhelming feeling of anxiousness
- Any inward or outward physical response that isn't normal for you

You might experience one or more of these symptoms when you begin to prepare the speech, just before the speech event, during the speech, and even after a speech. You can turn any of these symptoms into a positive reaction if you realize what your body and mind are trying to tell you. Preparing a solid speech, being familiar with the speaking environment, and practicing more will often help reduce your anxiety. Learn to control the situation rather than letting your anxiety control you.

2
Face Your Fear Head On

One of the first steps to controlling your anxiety is identifying the underlying reason why you are anxious. The most common causes of speech anxiety for many beginning speakers are:

- Lack of public speaking experience
- Negative public speaking experience in the past
- Fear of looking "stupid" or failing in front of peers
- Fear that the audience will laugh
- Fear of being the center of attention
- Fear of forgetting everything
- A belief that no one else feels like this
- Fear of speaking and using presentational equipment at the same time
- Fear of not being like the rest of the audience (especially true for returning students and nonnative students)
- Fear of failing the class based on speech performance

Often, just naming what we are afraid of will help us see how unfounded our fears might be. However, there are techniques you can use to minimize the influence of your anxiety. Throughout this book, "Confidence Booster" boxes (such as the one on page 13) offer insights that may help you respond to your physical and psychological reactions. Note that they are labeled "Confidence Booster," not "Anxiety Eliminator." A certain amount of intense reaction energizes you and prepares you for the event.

3
Learn Techniques That Work for You

Controlling your anxiety is an individual process. What works for your friend might not work for you—or might not continue to work for you over time. Try a variety of techniques and be willing to explore new ones.

TECHNIQUES BEFORE THE SPEECH DAY

- Put yourself in situations where you have to give speeches more often.
- Don't procrastinate.
- Select a speech topic appropriate for you and your audience.
- Be organized.
- Prepare a sound speech.
- Ask one or two people you can trust to be honest to listen to your speech and give you advice.
- Anticipate problems or issues and try to work them out.
- Exercise to lower physical stress.

TECHNIQUES BEFORE THE SPEECH ITSELF

- Meditate or do stretching exercises.
- Concentrate on how good you are.
- Close your eyes and imagine the audience listening to and enjoying the speech.
- Remember happy moments from your past.
- When possible, talk with someone near you to pass the time.
- Look at your notes and collect your thoughts. (Don't do this if someone else is speaking.)
- Yawn and/or walk around. Yawning will relax your throat and walking will relax muscles.
- Drink room-temperature water. (Cold drinks can tighten your throat. Also,

don't drink caffeinated or carbonated beverages before a speech.)
- Get to the room where you will speak and prepare it and yourself.
- Notice and think about your surroundings.
- Check presentational equipment. Fix any problems.
- Listen to calming music.
- Breathe deeply and slowly.
- Don't eat right before the speech if you often feel nauseous when anxious.
- Do not use tranquilizers, alcohol, or other drugs to reduce anxiety.

TECHNIQUES DURING THE SPEECH

- Visualize that you are just having a conversation with the audience.
- Gesture, move, or redistribute your weight if your hands or legs are trembling.
- If you know your hands shake, don't hold your delivery outline, or back it with some stiff paper.
- Take drinks of tepid water for dry mouth.
- Use eye contact.
- Look at the friendly faces in the audience.
- Remember that your nervous symptoms are more pronounced to you. Often, your audience doesn't notice.

TIP: Speech Anxiety

Remember that nervousness is normal—even important—and can help energize you!

4

Practice, Practice, Practice

Often your instinct is to stay away from situations that cause you stress. In the case of speech anxiety, if you really want to overcome it, you have to put yourself in speaking situations. Ignoring anxiety makes that monster bigger and stronger. The more you practice your speeches, and the more often you speak in front of an audience, the easier public speaking becomes.

→ Chapter 10 and the Confidence Booster boxes throughout the book offer more on effective delivery methods, tips on how to practice, and practical guidance for lowering your anxiety.

CONFIDENCE BOOSTER

Training your body to adjust before you experience speech anxiety will help control that inner demon. Many psychologists and communication practitioners suggest training your body to breathe deeply and to visualize happy, stress-free images. Remember, the key to training is practicing these techniques before you need them, so that your body learns how it feels in a truly stress-free situation. These two techniques find their true power as a daily form of meditation and not just a quick fix for intense stress. The steps below are based on exercises from the University of Maryland Medical Center.

Deep Breathing

Deep breathing is a great way to relax the body.

1 Sit straight or lie on your back.

2 Slowly relax your body.

3 Begin to inhale slowly through your nose. Fill the lower part of your chest first, then the middle and top part of your chest and lungs. Be sure to do this slowly, over 8 to 10 seconds.

4 Hold your breath for a second or two.

5 Then quietly and easily relax and let the air out.

6 Wait a few seconds and repeat this sequence. If you become dizzy, slow down or stop.

Guided Imagery

In this technique, the goal is to visualize yourself in a peaceful setting.

1 Get comfortable and close your eyes or focus on a particular spot.

2 Imagine yourself in a place that makes you happy, such as on the beach or in a hammock.

3 Take yourself there mentally. Feel the sun and air on your skin, listen to the peaceful sounds, and smell the flowers or ocean.

Practicing these techniques daily can have major stress-relieving effects on your body and will train it to understand what it feels like to relax.

A few deep breaths or taking yourself to your happy place just before a speech can refocus your mind on a body with less anxiety. Try to make it a habit to do one of these techniques four to five times daily, especially during potentially stressful times.

1.5 How Can You Be an Ethical Public Speaker?

1 Understand Ethics

2 Support and Endorse Freedom of Expression

3 Value Diversity

4 Be Sensitive to the Power of Language

5 Use Reliable Evidence, Logic, and Reasoning

6 Cite Sources to Avoid Plagiarism

7 Accept Responsibility for Your Communication

1

Understand Ethics

Being ethical means much more than just following the rules. Rules are part of the equation, but ethics grows out of our need to develop social relationships with others and our responsibilities within those relationships. For you to construct and maintain good relationships, others must view you as trustworthy, competent, objective, and passionate about what you do and support.

Your *ethics*, or a set of standards that guide you to good and honorable behavior, helps others see you in a positive manner. A standard of ethics is absolutely necessary for maintaining your relationships in your personal and professional lives. Therefore, ethics should become a part of every decision you make as you create your speeches and judge the speeches of others. For example, as Milo researches a persuasive speech, he finds credible information that indicates part of his position may be wrong. To be ethical, Milo shouldn't ignore or skew this information. He should adapt or change his position.

"Practicing Ethics" boxes, such as the one below, appear throughout the book to help you be aware of ethical issues in your speech and maintain high standards.

PRACTICING ETHICS: Be Truthful

Being ethical as a public speaker begins with telling the truth.
- Seek out correct information.
- Don't leave out or skew information for your own benefit.
- Allow your audience to see options.
- Create a strong, detailed message.

2
Support and Endorse Freedom of Expression

The *First Amendment* of the U.S. Constitution (adopted in 1791) states, "Congress shall make no law … abridging the freedom of speech, or the press…." As a public speaker, you are morally and legally obligated to comply with laws that protect others. Practicing all of the guidelines on pages 14–17 will help you protect the rights of others. Also keep the following in mind:

- Be careful to debate ideas rather than attack people.
- Keep your feelings in check, especially if you feel angry.
- Do not use your words to incite violence, defame, or slander, or use hate speech. This type of unethical behavior is not protected or a right granted by the First Amendment.
- Above all, remember that the First Amendment is a form of protection and empowerment, not censorship and disenfranchisement.

3
Value Diversity

As an ethical speaker, you must work at recognizing every member of your audience and respect his or her needs and motives. Avoid **ethnocentrism**, or the assumption that your own group or culture is better than all others. Create a sense of inclusion, not exclusion. Be respectful and helpful.

→ Chapter 2 helps you get to know your audience.

4
Be Sensitive to the Power of Language

Words have the power to heal and to destroy. As an ethical speaker, you must be aware of your language choices and their power. Overly emotional language can cloud your audience's ability to reason. Offensive language directed at someone's race, ethnicity, religion, gender, or culture is inappropriate at the very least and can be the fuel for hate groups at its worst. Use language for the good of others.

→ Chapter 9 discusses how to use language effectively and ethically.

5
Use Reliable Evidence, Logic, and Reasoning

To be ethical, you must dedicate yourself to using reliable evidence, tight organization, and careful reasoning (avoiding fallacies). When speaking publicly, you have the opportunity to alter people's lives. Be careful with that responsibility. As Aristotle wrote in "De Caleo" ("On the Heavens"), "The least initial deviation from the truth is multiplied later a thousandfold."

As with language, use evidence, logic, and reasoning for the good of others. Research the whole story, don't twist facts for your own benefit, and never intimidate or oppress with your speech.

→ Tabs 2 and 3 show how to select evidence and organize a speech.

→ Chapters 15 and 16 help you create sensible reasoning and avoid fallacies.

6
Cite Sources to Avoid Plagiarism

Avoiding plagiarism is all about protecting the words, ideas, and illustrations created by someone else, no matter if the creation is published or unpublished. When you intentionally or accidentally use all or a portion of someone else's words, ideas, or illustrations without giving proper credit, you commit the unethical and potentially harmful act of **plagiarism.** Plagiarism is not acceptable and may prevent you from passing a class, get you placed on academic probation, or force you to resign from a position.

TYPES OF PLAGIARISM

Recognizing the different types of plagiarism and adhering to preventive techniques will help you avoid plagiarizing in your speech.

- **Blatant plagiarism** can occur either when speakers take an entire speech or document and present it as their own or when a speaker takes pieces of information from other sources and links the parts together, creating an entire speech out of someone else's words, ideas, or illustrations. Both of these forms are clearly intentional and highly unethical acts. In both forms, the speaker claims the works of others as his or her own and makes no attempt to recognize the original author.

PRACTICING ETHICS: Cite Sources

Whether blatant or no-citation, intentional or accidental, plagiarism is highly unethical and can be damaging. Be diligent in citing your sources during your speech and on your outline. Citing sources will build your credibility.

- **No-citation plagiarism** occurs when speakers fail to give source credit to a specific part of their speech that has been taken from another source. This form of plagiarism can occur once or several times throughout a speech, even when the speech is created mainly by the speaker or when other sources are cited correctly. This form of plagiarism may be accidental but is still unethical. Be sure you have carefully cited all your sources.

AVOIDING PLAGIARISM

When you are not the researcher, writer, or creator of the material you are using, you are borrowing the material and must properly acknowledge the source on your outline and during the speech. Potential examples of material you must cite are:

- Quotations
- Paraphrased material
- Facts
- Definitions
- Statistics
- Illustrations
- Pictures or photos
- Icons or drawings
- Graphics or maps
- Videos
- Music

In essence, if you did not create everything related to the material you are using, you must cite the sources. This includes anything downloaded from the Internet, in electronic format, printed, or copied.

Here are some guidelines to help you avoid plagiarizing.

- Read and make sure you understand your institution's and instructor's plagiarism policies.

- Different institutions and instructors can have different plagiarism guidelines. For example, some instructors will allow you to use the topic and research from a paper you submit in another class as the groundwork for a speech. However, other instructors would view this as plagiarism. If in doubt, ask for clarification before it becomes an issue.

- Do your research early so you have enough time to properly prepare. Students are more tempted to cut corners and commit plagiarism when they are rushed and stressed about finishing the speech. Plus, you will have time to prepare effective oral citations.

- Utilize a variety of sources.

- Keep detailed notes on any sources you use and the material you find there. That way, you won't be tempted to not give an effective citation because you don't have the necessary information.

- Use your own words, sentence structure, and organizational structure.

- Follow the class assignment rules for citing sources on your outline, on your source page, and during your speech.

- Consult plagiarism.org for further help with preventing plagiarism.

→ Tab 2 offers oral citation examples, and pages 120–123 and 146–151 provide further guidelines for creating oral and written citations.

7
Accept Responsibility for Your Communication

In this age of very open disclosure and easy access to recording devices, we cannot always predict the long-term effects related to what we say or do. In just a short period of time, your words and actions can go viral. You don't need to look far for numerous accounts of individuals saying things and doing things that come back to cause them problems in the future or cause harm to others. Most newspapers have at least one story about a bullying incident, a politician who says something inappropriate, or a person losing his or her job for an unfortunate remark.

Almost everything you say or do has the potential to have positive and negative effects on your life and the lives of others. If you need to take a stance that may be risky, make sure you are willing to stand by your words and actions, not only in the immediate short-term speaking situation, but in the long term as well. Be willing to admit an error and make it right.

CHECKLIST for Avoiding Plagiarism

❏ Have I read and understood my institution's and instructor's plagiarism policies?

❏ Have I started my research early?

❏ Am I using a variety of sources and keeping detailed notes on them?

❏ Am I creating an oral citation for any borrowed material in my speech?

❏ Am I including proper written citations on my outline and source page?

❏ Am I following the class assignment rules for oral and written citations?

1.6 What Is the Creative Process for Public Speaking?

Composing and presenting a speech may seem daunting if you view the process only as a whole, but you can break it down into workable parts. The practical information throughout this book will help you. This chart shows the five basic activities you will use to create a successful speech. Although the process may look linear, you will frequently move back and forth between activities.

1 STARTING

2 RESEARCHING

Chapter 1
OVERVIEW OF PUBLIC SPEAKING
Understand the basic processes of communicating and public speaking. Know what it means to be ethical. Learn strategies for overcoming anxiety.

Chapter 2
GETTING TO KNOW YOUR AUDIENCE AND SITUATION
Know who you are speaking to as well as where, when, and why you are speaking.

Chapter 3
SELECTING YOUR TOPIC AND PURPOSE
Select the topic that best fits you, your audience, and the occasion. Define the purpose of your speech.

Chapter 4
LOCATING SUPPORT MATERIALS
Find support materials through the Internet, the library, interviews, and surveys.

Chapter 5
SELECTING AND TESTING SUPPORT MATERIALS
Learn how to effectively evaluate, choose, and use a variety of support materials.

3 CREATING

Chapter 6
OUTLINING YOUR SPEECH
Start with a working outline, create a preparation outline, and include a citations page. Create a delivery outline to use during your speech.

Chapter 7
ORGANIZING THE SPEECH BODY
Identify your main points and choose an organizational strategy.

Chapter 8
INTRODUCING AND CONCLUDING YOUR SPEECH
Create an introduction that gets attention and sets up your credibility and your speech. Create a conclusion that sums up and ends with impact.

4 PRESENTING

Chapter 9
USING LANGUAGE SUCCESSFULLY
Write your speech using language that is familiar, concrete, appropriate, and vivid. Use devices like repetition and parallelism to engage your audience.

Chapter 10
DELIVERING YOUR SPEECH
Strive to be natural, enthusiastic, confident, engaging, and appropriate in your delivery. Practice!

Chapter 11
USING PRESENTATION AIDS
Know when and how to use presentation aids to capture attention, enhance your credibility, and help your audience understand and remember your speech.

5 LISTENING & EVALUATING

Chapter 12
LISTENING
Be an active, ethical, and effective listener who can overcome barriers to listening and who shares responsibility in the communication process.

Chapter 13
EVALUATING SPEECHES
Determine the effectiveness and appropriateness of a speech's topic, support materials, organization, and language as well as a speaker's delivery and ethics.

Learning with This Book

Using This Book to Study

The overall goal of this course is to make you a better public speaker. To achieve this goal, the author of your text and your instructor have certain learning objectives supporting this main goal. You should think of these learning objectives as the tools you need to become a better speaker.

Table of Contents and Headings: Each chapter in this book is divided into sections related to specific learning objectives. To make these objectives useful to you as a student, each section starts with a question you should be able to answer completely. The

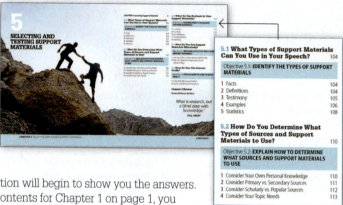

headings under each question will begin to show you the answers. If you turn to the table of contents for Chapter 1 on page 1, you can see the important questions for this chapter. Use the table of contents at the beginning of each chapter for studying as you read that chapter.

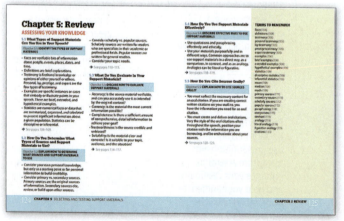

Chapter Review: At the end of each chapter, you will find two pages dedicated to reviewing once again the learning objective questions and terms you need to remember. Each question and review term has a cross-reference back to the related pages in the chapter. Use these references to help you review the details for tests and for understanding the speech creation process.

Using This Book to Create a Speech

Creating a speech is a lot like running a race, solving a puzzle, or playing a video game. You evaluate the other players and the situation, you research your options, you organize your strategy, and you plan an effective attack or move. You select a path to take, and you follow it—one step at a time—to the finish line.

Step-by-Step Tab Structure: In the first five tabs of this book, you will encounter the tools and activities to help you along the path of creating the best communicative events you can. In the last four tabs, you will see those tools and activities put into practice when creating an informative, persuasive, or special occasion speech as well as when communicating in a professional setting or a small group.

1 STARTING → **2** RESEARCHING → **3** CREATING → **4** PRESENTING → **5** LISTENING & EVALUATING

Practical Pointers: At the end of each tab section, you will find a page dedicated to frequently asked questions and further support on creating a speech. Review these pages as you begin the creation process, and return to them when you find yourself stuck for new ideas or resources.

Use the steps in this book to conceive a great speech and to believe in your heart of hearts that you can deliver it. Take a deep breath, stand tall, walk to the lectern, and believe in yourself. You can achieve success and confidence in speaking!

As American civil rights activist Jesse Jackson once said,

> If my mind can conceive it, and my heart can believe it, I know I can achieve it.[2]

Chapter 1: Review

ASSESSING YOUR KNOWLEDGE

1.1 When Will You Use the Skills Offered in This Book?

Objective 1.1: **IDENTIFY WHEN YOU WILL USE EFFECTIVE COMMUNICATION SKILLS**

You will use effective communication skills in your public, professional, and personal life.

→ See pages 2–3.

1.2 What Is the Process of Communicating?

Objective 1.2: **EXPLAIN THE TRANSACTIONAL COMMUNICATION PROCESS**

The communication process is transactional, or a fluid process that gives the speaker and the listener equal status in creating meaning when communication occurs. The speaker and the listener are actively involved and simultaneously sending and receiving information. They view their communication in this interaction as intentional. The transfer of information between the speaker and listener takes place within a particular situation.

The components of the transactional model of communication are the:
- Speaker
- Audience/listener
- Message that is encoded or decoded
- Feedback
- Channel
- Noise
- Situation
- Background of the speaker and audience
- Common ground between the speaker and the audience

→ See pages 4–5.

1.3 How Can You Be a Successful Public Speaker?

Objective 1.3: **STATE HOW TO BE A SUCCESSFUL PUBLIC SPEAKER**

- You strive to be audience centered.
- You are knowledgeable, creative, and organized.
- You use appropriate appeals (logos, ethos, and pathos).
- You use appropriate presentation techniques.
- You practice repeatedly.

→ See pages 6–9.

1.4 How Can You Overcome a Fear of Public Speaking?

Objective 1.4: **DESCRIBE EFFECTIVE WAYS TO OVERCOME SPEECH ANXIETY**

Speech anxiety is the uneasiness and fearfulness you may feel when preparing or giving a speech. The best method for overcoming your fears is to understand what is happening; face your fear head on; learn techniques that help you reduce your fears; and practice, practice, practice.

→ See pages 10–13.

1.5 How Can You Be an Ethical Speaker?

Objective 1.5: **EXPLAIN HOW TO BE AN ETHICAL SPEAKER**

To be an ethical public speaker, you must:
- Understand that ethics is a set of standards guiding you to good and honorable behavior that helps you develop social relationships with others.
- Support and endorse freedom of speech (the First Amendment).
- Value diversity.

- Respect the power of language.
- Use reliable evidence, logic, and reasoning.
- Cite sources to avoid plagiarism.
- Accept responsibility for your communication.

→ See pages 14–17.

1.6 What Is the Creative Process for Public Speaking?

Objective 1.6: **SUMMARIZE THE CREATIVE PROCESS FOR PUBLIC SPEAKING**

Creating a speech is a process, which means it is most manageable if you take it one step at a time. Don't expect to create a quality speech by skipping steps or forgetting what you learned in previous activities. The five basic activities you will use to create a successful speech are:

- **Start** the process by getting to know your audience and situation before you move on to selecting a topic and purpose.
- **Research** your speech by locating material from the Internet, library, interviews, and surveys. You must effectively evaluate, choose, and use a variety of support materials.
- **Create** the speech text by working through several types of outlines, selecting an appropriate organizational strategy, and citing your sources on the outline and during the speech. Create an effective introduction and conclusion.
- **Present** your speech using effective language, delivery, and presentation aids.
- **Listen and evaluate** the speeches of others in an active and ethical manner. Give productive criticism, and seek out criticism of your own speeches to be a better speaker.

The process of creating a speech is imaginative, original, artistic, inventive, resourceful, and inspirational.

→ See pages 18–19.

TERMS TO REMEMBER

speaker (5)
audience (5)
message (5)
encoding (5)
decoding (5)
feedback (5)
channel (5)
noise (5)
situation (5)
background (5)
common ground (5)
transactional process (5)
identification (7)
audience centered (7)
logos (8)
ethos (8)
pathos (8)
communication apprehension (10)
speech anxiety (10)
ethics (14)
First Amendment (15)
ethnocentrism (15)
plagiarism (16)
blatant plagiarism (16)
no-citation plagiarism (16)

2

GETTING TO KNOW YOUR AUDIENCE AND SITUATION

2.1 Why Do You Need to Know Your Audience and Situation?

1 You Will Make Better Speech Decisions

2 You Can Foster Audience Attention and Goodwill

3 You Will Feel More Confident

Think about how you feel when someone cannot remember your name. Or does not repeat a message when there is a loud noise interfering with your understanding. These behaviors can make you feel like you do not exist or are not important or that what you believe does not matter.

Speaking to an audience that you have not taken the time to learn about creates similar feelings in others. It is a necessity and your ethical responsibility as a speaker to appreciate your audience and understand the situation if you want to succeed. This type of audience centeredness, as discussed in Chapter 1, is not easy or something that just happens. You have to work at it.

Speaking from an audience-centered standpoint begins with **audience and situation analysis**—a systematic investigation of characteristics that make your audience and speaking situation unique.

This chapter will help you understand the importance of audience and situation analysis, offer several methods for conducting an analysis, and help you identify what to look for when you conduct the analysis.

Your audience gives you everything you need.... There is no director who can direct you like an audience.[1]

FANNY BRICE

1

You Will Make Better Speech Decisions

Adapting to your audience and the situation should begin immediately after you receive a public speaking assignment or engagement. That way, every decision you make about the speech is grounded in who you are speaking to and under what conditions. If you don't know your audience or the speaking event, you could choose an inappropriate topic, select the wrong source materials, or use a delivery style that doesn't work in your speaking situation.

2

You Can Foster Audience Attention and Goodwill

To be an effective speaker, you must have your audience's attention and willingness to participate in your speech. Audiences want you to recognize that they are a unique group of individuals, not one mass without personality—that they have a set of norms, values, preferences, or ideas that influence the ways they interact with other people and ideas. The more you know about an audience's frame of reference and the situation that brings them to your speech, the better you can foster their attention and goodwill while you are speaking.

3

You Will Feel More Confident

Speaking competence relates to how well you communicate with others. No matter if you are communicating with an audience of similar members or one with multiple diverse social, personal, or cultural identities, your communication will be considerably better if you demonstrate effective speaking competence. Stephen Littlejohn and Karen Foss in *Theories of Human Communication* call this intercultural competence and identify three components:

Identity knowledge means knowing what is distinctive about an audience.

Mindfulness means being conscientiously aware of and paying attention to those distinctions.

Negotiation skill is the ability to respond to audience differences through sensitivity, politeness, willing adjustment, and collaboration. Littlejohn and Foss suggest that you have achieved effective negotiation when your audience understands you and feels respected.

> **TIP: Audience and Situation Analysis**
>
> Potential questions to ask:
> - What are the specific interests of this audience?
> - What details should be covered for this audience?
> - What language and support materials will work best for them?
> - What could be potential audience expectations and reactions?
> - What situational obstacles could affect the speech?
>
> The deeper you analyze, the better you can answer these questions and formulate new ones.

2.2 What Do You Need to Know About Your Audience?

1 Attitudes
2 Beliefs
3 Values

1

Attitudes

Attitudes are persistent psychological responses, predispositions, or inclinations to act one way or feel a particular way—usually positive or negative—toward something. For instance, you might like New York City better than Chicago, you may not trust anything found on the Internet, or you may like to date men that are tall and have dark hair. The longer someone holds an attitude, the more information he or she usually has to support it—and the harder it is to change.

Your audience's attitudes can influence how they respond to you, your topic, the situation, and even smaller details such as your support material, delivery style, or presentation aids.

For example, if you are planning to give a persuasive speech on the positive attributes of tweeting and most in your audience hold a somewhat negative feeling about the over-popularity of electronic devices, the audience will be less likely to accept your position. You will need to work hard to establish your credibility early in the speech. Don't ignore their attitude or criticize it. Let the audience understand that you know their point of view, and try to move them in a positive direction from that vantage point. You will also need to select valid examples that clearly support online social networking services.

CONFIDENCE BOOSTER

Fear of the unknown is a major creator of speech anxiety. Analyzing your audience and the situation has the added benefit of helping you feel more comfortable in front of them. You can prepare for what can happen and prevent some stressors.

2
Beliefs

Beliefs are those things a person accepts as plausible based on interpretation and judgment, such as believing in a religion or philosophy.

For example, you may believe it is the responsibility of humans to take care of the planet, Internet bullying is harmful, or the United States has a responsibility to help other countries in times of disaster. Some beliefs may be easily accepted with only a little knowledge, whereas others take time to accept or may be very controversial.

As with attitudes, beliefs affect how an audience perceives and responds to a speaker, a topic, support material, or other elements of a speech. If you believe the death penalty is wrong, that belief will influence your response to any speech about the death penalty.

As another example, imagine you are listening to a speech arguing that the world will end soon. Like most people, you wake everyday believing the world will continue and find it hard to believe that the end is near. Without verifiable data to support the prediction of a catastrophic event, the speaker has little hope of convincing you.

3
Values

Values relate to worth or what a person sees as right or wrong, important or unimportant, desirable or undesirable, and they shape our attitudes and beliefs. Values are our principles, such as cherishing family over professional success. Other examples of values held by many in the United States are independence, progress, freedom of speech, life, good health, honesty, wealth, and education. When you are from or belong to a country, culture, or religion, you may be expected to hold and share common values with the other members.

For example, many countries, the United States included, have struggled with their values when considering how to help refugees fleeing the war in Syria. Supporters arguing that we should allow Syrian refugees into this country value helping those in need of a safe haven. Opponents of allowing the refugees into this country are stressing the value of national safety over offering assistance. Not all reactions will be this extreme, but when giving a speech with the potential to challenge values, be extra careful with what you say. Remember that your message has consequences.

Beliefs, values, and attitudes make up the audience's **identity.** Of course, you will never fully know your audience's specific beliefs, values, and attitudes about every issue in your speech, but knowing as much as possible about them will help you make your speech more meaningful and you more confident.

2.3 What Specific Traits Do You Need to Investigate?

1 Personal Traits
2 Psychological Traits
3 Social Traits

1

Personal Traits

Personal traits (sometimes referred to as *demographics*) include age, gender, sexual orientation, household type, education, occupation, income, and disabilities. Each characteristic may help provide insight into what's important to your audience, how they will feel about given issues, and what they accept as true.

The key to using personal traits effectively is to make yourself aware of possible traits present in your audience but not to compartmentalize or stereotype the audience. *Stereotyping* is false or oversimplified generalizing applied to individuals based on group characteristics.

Allow the traits to guide but not dictate your interactions. Although the personal traits you might need to consider are almost endless, a few are listed in the checklist below and on the next page.

CHECKLIST for Personal Traits

❏ What's the age range of my audience? What's the average age?

❏ Who are the audience members specifically? What do I know about their gender? Sexual orientation? Occupations? Education? Households? Disabilities?

❏ What's the average income or socioeconomic level?

❏ What might the audience already know about my potential topics?

NOTE: Not all of these questions will apply to every speaking event, but you should do your best to know as much as possible about the audience.

Remember to:

- Be respectful of gender and sexual orientation. No matter whether your audience is predominantly male or female, gay or straight, being insensitive will hurt your reputation and perpetuates negative stereotypes.
- Recognize that you may have few "traditional" household members in your audience. According to the U.S. Census Bureau, only 2 percent of all U.S. households in 2010 were "traditional."
- Remember that high levels of education do not always equate with intelligence. College graduates are not smart about everything, and some very intelligent people are self-taught. However, the more education your audience has, the more they are exposed to different topics and language.
- Be cautious about connecting income levels and occupations—not all lawyers are highly paid, for instance.
- Consider that you may have audience members with disabilities. They often have unique insights and may have certain communicative challenges.

GENERATIONAL TRENDS

This table, based on *We Are Generation Z* by Vivek Pandit and *When Generations Collide* by Lynne Lancaster and David Stillman, describes some generational trends you can consider to help you understand how age might influence your audience.

Born before 1945 *(Traditionalists)*	*Defining word:* **loyal** Marry once, "save for a rainy day," little formal education, conservative, respect authority and America, not easily persuaded
Born 1946–1964 *(Baby Boomers)*	*Defining word:* **optimistic** More educated, committed to belonging, political, very competitive, spend rather than save, divorce and remarry, cynical of and challenge authority
Born 1965–1980 *(Generation X)*	*Defining word:* **skepticism** Product of divorce, single parents, or blended homes; resourceful and independent; count on peers more than on family; influenced by media; struggle with money
Born 1981–1999 *(Millennials or Generation Y)*	*Defining word:* **realistic** Smart, confident, practical, tech savvy, concerned about personal safety, influenced by friends and media, appreciate diversity, can be very biased
Born 2000– *(Generation Z)*	*Defining word:* **connected** Truly mobile generation; identities extend into the digital world; techno-entrepreneurs; concerned with world uncertainty, the economy, and digital surveillance; switch jobs often; accustomed to extended family living together; sense of entitlement; can be very tolerant

2
Psychological Traits

The ***psychological traits*** of your audience pertain to their needs and motivations. In *Motivation and Personality*, psychologist Abraham Maslow outlined a classic theory demonstrating how people's needs motivate them to respond in certain ways. For example, if buying or doing something will help people satisfy a need, they are more likely to make that purchase or do that activity. Maslow fine-tuned his theory by identifying five levels of needs, which are *hierarchical*. In other words, you must fulfill some of the basic needs before the other needs become crucial. **Maslow's hierarchy of needs** is best represented as a pyramid, with basic needs at the bottom, giving support to the higher levels.

SELF-ACTUALIZATION NEEDS

SELF-ESTEEM NEEDS

SOCIAL NEEDS

SAFETY NEEDS

PHYSIOLOGICAL NEEDS

Physiological needs are related to continued existence and include food, water, general comfort, and sex. These are the most basic and necessary for a person to live. A speech on "How to Eat Healthy on a Budget" highlights this level of need.

Safety needs relate to what we need to feel secure, such as a roof over our heads and security in our own homes. A speech demonstrating how to be ready in times of disaster evokes this type of need.

Social needs are those feelings we have about belonging. Most of us want to give and receive love, be close to others, and be supported. We have a strong need to feel a part of groups such as family, friends, or religion. Pep rallies and speeches given during new student orientations on college campuses strive to fulfill this need.

Self-esteem needs relate to our strong need for respect from others we view as important, much as you may have felt when you were a teenager and wanted your parents to trust you and be proud of you. Pride, prestige, self-respect, accomplishment, recognition, and the need for success are aspects of

this need. Speeches given at graduations usually focus heavily on self-esteem needs.

Self-actualization needs relate to the need to feel achievement connected to personal identity, independence, happiness, and potential. An example of a self-actualization speech would be Grammy- and Academy Award–winning music icon, cancer survivor, and activist Melissa Etheridge giving a motivational speech to a group of breast cancer survivors. Her 2005 song "I Run for Life" characterizes this need.

CHECKLIST for Psychological Traits

- ❏ What needs might my audience have?
- ❏ Is there a level of needs where my audience has significant concerns?
- ❏ Because of their needs, will my audience be positive, apathetic, or negative toward my potential speech topics?
- ❏ How might I use their needs to show relevance to my topic or to persuade them?

3
Social Traits

Your audience's **social traits** relate to how they are affected by or identify with other groups of people. Two types of groups can influence your audience—those by choice and those by birth.

SOCIAL TRAITS BY CHOICE

The "by choice" group are people your audience members choose to connect with, such as political parties; hobby communities; athletic teams; and religious, professional, social, or civic organizations. Studying these group connections can give you obvious but significant insights into how your audience will relate to you and your topic. For example, avid hunters may react negatively to a speech arguing for new hunting regulations unless they see a benefit to hunters or the animal population.

SOCIAL TRAITS BY BIRTH

The second group includes those relationships your audience members have with others by birth and by growing up within certain societies—specifically race, ethnicity, and culture.

Race is the biological differences of humankind, often noticeable in physical markers such as color and texture of hair, color of skin and eyes, shape of facial features, and bodily build and proportions.

Ethnicity stems from our national and religious affiliations.

Culture is the system that teaches a set of objectives and rules that help us survive and gain societal acceptance within our community. Individuals learn, share, and convey culture from generation to generation.

Race, ethnicity, and culture mold a person's identity and, therefore, will directly influence how he or she responds to issues.

Given how diverse our towns, offices, schools, and digital lives have become, understanding the social traits of the audience is a speaker's ethical imperative and a key to success. However, simply knowing you have a diverse audience is not that helpful. The following pages look at some ways audience members' race, ethnicity, and culture can impact your speech.

CHECKLIST for Social Traits

❏ What organizations will sponsor the speaking event?

❏ What organizations might be represented at the event?

❏ What other social affiliations might influence my speech (such as hobbies or athletic teams)?

❏ What professions might be represented?

❏ What religions might be represented?

❏ What cultures, ethnicities, and races might be represented?

PRACTICING ETHICS: Traits

• Avoid negative stereotypes.

• Understand that some traits can change due to significant events, trends, and opportunities during a particular time in history.

• Respect diversity, all the time!

U.S. POPULATION DIVERSITY

According to the U.S. Census Bureau in 2010, the nation is getting more racially and ethnically diverse as well as much older.

The chart below shows some projections for U.S. population diversity by 2060. Given their different cultural heritages, their personal struggles, and the struggles represented in previous generations of their families, "minorities" have unique perspectives, needs, and motivations that you must keep in mind. For example, they tend to consider issues such as equal opportunity, immigration laws, English as the official U.S. language, and minority representation in high-level government and private offices more carefully than people in the "majority."

We are a country built and empowered by our diversity. Appreciate diversity and, at every stage of your speech process, consider it an opportunity rather than an obstacle.

CULTURAL TENDENCIES

In *Culture's Consequences*, Geert Hofstede's Value Dimension model offers a helpful way to look at cultural tendencies and might help you adapt appropriately to a culture (or cultures). See the table on the following page. Keep in mind that these are tendencies, not individual responses. You will rarely, if ever, find someone who fits them exactly. Let the dimensions guide, not define, your interactions.

As a speaker, you must be aware of and sensitive to cultural tendencies when you select a topic and source materials, create an argument, craft your language, and adjust your delivery style.

Be mindful of what is distinctive about your audience and respond to those differences through sensitivity, politeness, concern, willing adjustment, and collaboration.

PROJECTED U.S. POPULATION DIVERSITY (each figure = 1%)

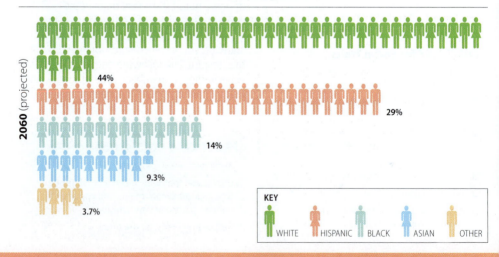

KEY — WHITE · HISPANIC · BLACK · ASIAN · OTHER

2060 (projected): 44%, 29%, 14%, 9.3%, 3.7%

HOFSTEDE'S FIVE DIMENSIONS OF CULTURE

DIMENSION	EXPLANATION	EXAMPLE COUNTRIES	AUDIENCE RESPONSE
High Power vs. Low Power	**High-power cultures** have clear, defined lines of authority and responsibility.	**High-power countries** Guatemala, Mexico, Venezuela, Arab countries	**High-power audiences** will respond well to material from credible sources.
	Low-power cultures blur these lines.	**Low-power countries** Germany, Costa Rica, Great Britain, Denmark, U.S.	**Low-power audiences** like equality and options.
Individualist vs. Collectivist	**Individualist cultures** stand for self.	**Individualist countries** U.S., Australia, Great Britain, Canada, Netherlands, Italy, France, Denmark, Germany	**Individualist audiences** will respond better to an emphasis on personal reward.
	Collectivist cultures stand for the group.	**Collectivist countries** Venezuela, Pakistan, Costa Rica, Peru, Taiwan, Chile, South Korea	**Collectivist audiences** will respond best to emphasis on community and sense of duty.
Competitive vs. Nurturing	**Competitive cultures** stress competitiveness, assertiveness, ambition, wealth, and material possessions.	**Competitive countries** Japan, Austria, Venezuela, Italy, Ireland, Greece, Switzerland, Mexico, Great Britain, U.S., Germany	**Competitive audiences** will respond to emphasizing strength, winning, gaining an edge, and material success.
	Nurturing cultures stress relationships, quality of life, sexual equality, and care of the environment.	**Nurturing countries** Sweden, Norway, Chile, Costa Rica, Netherlands, South Korea, Denmark, Finland, Portugal, Thailand	**Nurturing audiences** will respond well to nurturing language, caring behavior, and equality.
High-uncertainty Avoidance vs. Low-uncertainty Avoidance	**High-uncertainty cultures** strive to avoid uncertainty and ambiguity through stability.	**High-uncertainty countries** Greece, Portugal, Japan, Peru, Spain, France, Costa Rica, Mexico, Israel, Belgium	**High-uncertainty audiences** need clear logic, detailed information, and small steps to initiate change.
	Low-uncertainty cultures are tolerant of the unusual, new ideas, and other people.	**Low-uncertainty countries** Singapore, Jamaica, Denmark, Ireland, U.S., India	**Low-uncertainty audiences** don't need as much detail, are willing to be more adventurous, and embrace change.
Long-term Orientation vs. Short-term Orientation	**Long-term cultures** value persistence, thriftiness, future, a strong work ethic, structure, and status.	**Long-term countries** China, Taiwan, Japan, South Korea, Brazil	**Long-term audiences** respond to detail, persistence, seeing what benefit there is for the future.
	Short-term cultures emphasize time and are concerned with short-term results, try to "cheat" old age, seek quick gratification, and deemphasize status.	**Short-term countries** Great Britain, Canada, the Philippines, U.S.	**Short-term audiences** want quick results with almost instant gratification. How will this get the job done?

2.4 What Do You Need to Know About the Speaking Situation?

1 Place and Audience Size
2 Time
3 Occasion

CHECKLIST for Place and Audience Size

❏ Will I be giving the speech inside or outside? If outside, what are the plans if there is bad weather?

❏ Is there a lectern or table if I need one?

❏ How large will the audience be? In what arrangement?

❏ Will I be visible to the whole audience?

❏ Are there issues to consider for audience members with disabilities?

❏ Will I have the equipment I need? Can I practice with it? What are my backup plans?

❏ Can I control the heating, lighting, and sound?

❏ Whom do I contact for help with any logistics?

❏ Does this place have significance for the audience?

1

Place and Audience Size

Imagine this scene: You are a shorter-than-average person about to give a commencement address from behind a solid wooden lectern, on a stage that is three feet above the floor where the first few rows of your audience are sitting. These audience members will see only the top of your head, if they can see you at all.

Or imagine giving a speech outdoors on a windy day—from loose manuscript pages.

Both of these examples highlight how important it is to consider the environment where you will be speaking and to plan ahead. A simple, short platform for the first speaker prevents embarrassment. A manuscript printed on heavy paper and attached in a binder prevents the second speaker's need to run after flying pages.

You may know that your public speaking classroom is where you will give the speech. But such familiarity is a luxury you rarely have, and even in the classroom, you need to prepare. What if someone has taken the lectern to another room? You should always try to visit the space prior to your speech so that you can make changes if necessary and possible.

Know what equipment you will need and make sure it will be there. Make a backup plan if the equipment does not show up or is not working. Also, find out how large the audience will be. Audience size could influence how formal (for larger audiences) or informal (for smaller ones) your style can be. For a large audience, you may need more equipment, such as a microphone. Use the checklist at left to help you prepare.

2
Time

Time has two factors. The first are general elements related to the time of day, day of the week, rotation of speakers, events before the speaking event, and length of speaking time. Each element could influence your speech positively or negatively. For instance, holding audience attention during an after-dinner speech can be challenging because the audience has just eaten and may be tired.

The second factor is time's influence on your relationship with the audience. For example, if this is the first time the group hears you speak, you will likely be careful to build your credibility (ethos). If they have heard you speak many times and have responded favorably, you might be a bit less formal. For example, recall how your professor or your boss related to you when you first met. How does she or he relate to you now? Is there a difference? Has your relationship evolved over time?

Use the checklist below to see how time will affect your speech.

CHECKLIST for Time

❑ How much time will I have to speak?

❑ How early should I arrive?

❑ What day of the week and time of day will I speak? How might these influence my speech?

❑ Where do I fall in the rotation of speakers? How might other speeches influence mine?

❑ Is there late-breaking news I should consider?

❑ Is this the first time this audience will hear me speak? What is our relationship?

3
Occasion

Think about *why* your audience is gathered to hear your speech. How might the occasion influence their feelings about you and your topic? Are they a captive audience, required to be there, who do not feel like they can leave? Or are they a voluntary audience who made the choice to hear your speech?

Audiences required to attend an event, such as students at a graduation or employees at a job-required meeting, can be apathetic, negative, or impatient. You might even experience some of these reactions in your classroom, as your audience has to be there regularly and must listen to many speeches. Captive audiences are not impossible to reach, but you must be extra dynamic and interesting to gain their attention.

Mood is another consideration. Is the situation celebratory? Somber? Businesslike? Your speech should reflect and respect the appropriate mood.

Use the checklist below to assess your occasion.

CHECKLIST for Occasion

❑ Is this a special occasion?

❑ What does the audience expect out of this event? Why are they here?

❑ What will be the mood of the day?

❑ How will the audience respond to the topic?

❑ Does this audience have any social norms or expectations I should know about?

❑ Who's in charge of the event, and what is their relationship with the audience?

2.5 How Do You Analyze the Audience and Situation?

1 **Stop, Think, and Brainstorm**

2 **Interview**

3 **Survey**

4 **Research**

1

Stop, Think, and Brainstorm

As a speaker, you should start your audience and situation analysis by thinking about what you already know, followed by brainstorming with others about the audience and situation. Simply taking the time to be mindful of what you (or someone close to you) might know could save valuable time. Turn to friends, relatives, teachers, or peers and ask them what feelings or knowledge they have about the audience and your speech ideas. Sometimes fresh eyes can see connections and issues that we cannot when we are so involved in the process.

For example, Trang is the president of the student body at a small liberal arts college. The college plans to build a new residence hall but needs to raise student fees to help fund the project. In her role as student president, Trang must conduct several informational sessions about the project and the fee increase. Several of her friends are excited about the new hall but concerned about the fee increase. Trang knows she needs to get a better idea of how the fee increase will influence her audience. She brainstorms about who might give her the best information and decides it might be beneficial to talk with the admissions and financial aid directors, the dean of students, and the building committee as well as to survey students.

2
Interview

Interviewing someone connected with the speaking event, a person familiar with the audience membership, or members of the audience are excellent ways to learn about your audience and situation. The interview can be in person, over the phone, by e-mail, or by regular mail.

→ See pages 88–91 in Chapter 4 for more on how to conduct an interview.

BASIC INTERVIEW GUIDELINES
- Consider what you need to know about your topic, audience, and situation.
- Plan your questions to get the best responses.

  Open-ended questions allow the interviewee to give a detailed response and often will give you valuable information you had not anticipated.

  Closed-ended questions are used when you want general, quantifiable information.
- Be willing to add questions that come to mind as you conduct the interview, but make sure you are conscious of how long the interview is running.
- Always end the interview by asking if you have missed anything important that would help you understand your audience better.

Trang, for example, made an appointment to meet with the Dean of Student Life and constructed a few interview questions.

Meeting with Dean Ortiz
Sept. 10th @ 1:00
Reece Hall 203

1. What prompted the College to decide to build the new hall?

2. Were students a part of that decision? Were students a part of the process?

3. What will the hall look like, and how will it be different from the ones we have now?

4. How much will the fees increase?

5. How will that affect our current students? Will there be students who can't continue in their education because of the increase? Are there plans for the College to help those students in some way?

6. Can you think of anything else I need to know to help me inform my peers about this decision?

An open-ended question encourages a detailed answer.

More closed-ended questions prompt the interviewee to respond with one word or a very short answer.

3
Survey

Written surveys or questionnaires are helpful for gathering information from a large pool of people—and often from your audience. Surveys may contain open- and closed-ended questions but should tend toward the closed-ended.

Because a good cross section of the student body can be found at the Student Union, Trang created a survey and asked students at the union to complete it. See her survey below.

Use familiar language.

Ask necessary demographic questions.

Make no assumptions about your respondents.

Use neutral responses—don't be biased or leading.

Ask only one thing in each question.

Use a clean, consistent structure for the overall questionnaire.

Proposed Residence Hall and Fee Increase Questionnaire

1. What is your class rank? _____

2. What is your sex? _____ Male _____ Female

3. Do you live on campus or off? _____On campus _____Off campus

4. What are your feelings about the building of a new hall?

_____ Support it even with the fee increase   _____ Oppose it because of the fee increase

_____ Would support it without the fee increase   _____ Oppose it no matter what

Other (please specify): _____

5. If you support the building of the new hall, what is your number one reason for doing so?

_____ Need more rooms on campus   _____ Other halls are old

_____ Closer to my classes   _____ Like the new building design options

Other (please specify): _____

6. If you oppose the building of the new hall, what is your number one reason for doing so?

_____ I don't care because I will graduate before it is finished

_____ I like the other halls

_____ I don't see why we need it

_____ I don't like the new building design options

_____ I don't support the fee increase

Other (please specify): _____

Trang greeted each student and explained her survey. She made a conscious effort to survey equally across class rank and between males and females. After collecting a good number of surveys, Trang studied the information so that she could use it to understand the students' concerns and needs. Everyone was excited about the hall, especially those who might get to live there. Most students saw a need for a new hall but were concerned about the fee increase. Of the students who opposed the hall, 95 percent did so because of the increase.

Trang decided that she would focus her speeches on how the college planned to help students deal with the fee increase rather than why they needed a new hall.

→ See pages 92–95 in Chapter 4 for a detailed discussion on question construction for surveys.

4
Research

Simple detective work can be a great way to analyze your audience, especially if they are part of a larger group or organization. Often groups and organizations publish information about their membership, goals, mission, facilities, activities, and accomplishments. The information might be on the Internet (does the group have a website?) or in brochures, press releases, newspaper and magazine articles (can you locate a city magazine promoting local groups?), or annual reports.

Opinion polls, census data, almanacs, local and city government archives, and historical societies are good sources as well. You may find some of them online or through your local library. These sources are useful for general data about a population. For example, how many African Americans hold college degrees?

Trang searched online for information about types of residence halls being built nationwide and the impact the new construction projects had on fees at those institutions.

www.usa.gov

www.census.gov

2.6 How Can You Adapt to Your Audience and Situation During the Speech?

1 Adapt to External Noise
2 Adapt to Internal Noise

No matter how much you know about your audience and the situation, you cannot think of everything ahead of time, and unpredictable things can happen. The communication process has too many variables that can change the outcome.

Even with the unpredictable nature of the process, you can learn to control and minimize the effect on your ability to communicate. One aspect to pay special attention to is the "noise" that pushes its way into the communication process. This noise may interrupt the audience's ability to listen and your ability to communicate.

Chapter 12 will talk more about the importance of listening—for both the speaker and the audience—as well as how noise becomes a barrier to active listening. For now, you should realize that effective listening can only happen when the speaker and audience members are willing to work at it, by identifying and eliminating the noise.

→ See Chapter 12 for more on how speakers and audience members can effectively listen to one another.

1
Adapt to External Noise

External noise occurs or originates outside of the mind or body and can be classified into two categories.

Environmental barriers:
sounds, movement, light, darkness, heat, cold, hard seats

Linguistic barriers:
misread verbal and nonverbal messages such as slang, jargon, technical words, and body language that differs across cultures

Anything from a loud lawn mower outside the window, to a computer that will not connect to the Internet, to a campus emergency the morning before your speech can change the best-laid plan, making it difficult for you to listen to your audience and for them to listen to you. Just remember:

- Stay calm.
- Pay attention to the noises affecting you and your audience.
- Be willing to adjust. Adjustments you might need to make could be:
  - Pausing for that noisy lawn mower or turning off a loud projector
  - Offering another definition or example when your audience seems confused
  - Removing slang or other language choices not effective for a given audience
  - Eliminating distracting nonverbal behavior (such as tapping a pencil on the lectern)

2
Adapt to Internal Noise

Internal noise occurs or originates inside of the mind or body and can be classified into two categories.

Physiological barriers:
hunger, sickness, disabilities, pain

Psychological barriers:
negative thoughts about the topic, distraction outside of the situation (such as a fight with a partner), fear, egocentrism, racism, sexism, homophobia

Adapting to internal noise may require more work than adjusting to external noise. Points to keep in mind:

- If your audience's attention is wandering, call on members, move around the room, or vary your delivery.
  → Chapter 10 offers more on delivery.
- Be a creative, dynamic speaker and your audience will want to listen.
- Pay attention to the nonverbal behavior of your audience. The way people are sitting or their facial expressions are great feedback on how to adapt to the moment. For instance, if listeners seem confused, slow down and offer more examples to help them understand.
- Anticipate a potentially negative response and lessen the effect.
- Ultimately, realize that your audience is ethically responsible for listening to you.

In most cases, the audience will view you as a better speaker for being in enough control to handle problems—and to pull them back into the speech.

Chapter 2: Review

ASSESSING YOUR KNOWLEDGE

2.1 Why Do You Need to Know Your Audience and Situation?

Objective 2.1: **EXPLAIN THE IMPORTANCE OF AUDIENCE AND SITUATION ANALYSIS**

Audience and situation analysis is a systemic investigation of characteristics that make your audience and speaking situation unique. Knowing as much as you can about your audience and speaking situation will:
- Help you make better speech decisions
- Help you foster audience attention and goodwill
- Help you feel more confident

➔ See pages 26–27.

2.2 What Do You Need to Know About Your Audience?

Objective 2.2: **ARTICULATE WHAT YOU NEED TO KNOW ABOUT THE AUDIENCE**

Attitudes, beliefs, and values make up your audience's identity. Attitudes are persistent psychological responses, predispositions, or inclinations to act one way or feel a particular way. Beliefs are those things a person accepts as plausible based on interpretation and judgment. Values relate to worth or what a person sees as right or wrong, important or unimportant, desirable or undesirable.

➔ See pages 28–29.

2.3 What Specific Traits Do You Need to Investigate?

Objective 2.3: **DESCRIBE THE SPECIFIC AUDIENCE TRAITS TO ANALYZE**

- Personal traits such as age, gender, sexual orientation, household type, education, occupation, income, and disabilities
- Psychological traits related to audience needs and motivation
- Social traits by choice and by birth

Be aware that focusing too much on trends and traits can lead to stereotyping.

➔ See pages 30–35.

2.4 What Do You Need to Know About the Speaking Situation?

Objective 2.4: **ARTICULATE WHAT YOU NEED TO KNOW ABOUT THE SITUATION**

- Place and audience size
- Time
- Occasion

➔ See pages 36–37.

2.5 How Do You Analyze the Audience and Situation?

Objective 2.5: **EXPLAIN THE PROCESS FOR ANALYZING THE AUDIENCE AND SITUATION**

- Stop, think, and brainstorm
- Interview
- Survey
- Research

➔ See pages 38–41.

2.6 How Can You Adapt to Your Audience and Situation During the Speech?

Objective 2.6: **IDENTIFY WAYS TO ADAPT TO THE AUDIENCE AND SITUATION DURING THE SPEECH**

Noises are anything that can interfere with the communication process. They can be external (outside of the mind or body) or internal (inside the mind or body).

External noises can be environmental or linguistic. Environmental barriers can be things like a fire engine siren during a speech. Linguistic barriers can be language issues such as slang.

Internal noises can be physiological or psychological. If an audience member is sick, that can be a physiological barrier. If an audience member is sexist, that can be a psychological barrier.

When giving a speech, stay calm, pay attention to your audience's needs, and be willing to adjust.

→ See pages 42–43.

TERMS TO REMEMBER

audience and situation analysis (26)
speaking competence (27)
identity knowledge (27)
mindfulness (27)
negotiation skill (27)
attitudes (28)
beliefs (29)
values (29)
identity (29)
personal traits (30)
stereotyping (30)
psychological traits (32)
Maslow's hierarchy of needs (32)
social traits (33)
race (33)
ethnicity (33)
culture (33)
external noise (43)
environmental barriers (43)
linguistic barriers (43)
internal noise (43)
physiological barriers (43)
psychological barriers (43)

3

SELECTING YOUR TOPIC AND PURPOSE

TIP: Civic and Professional Speaking

In or outside of the classroom, your situation and the audience will frequently dictate your topic selection. To narrow your topic in these cases, you should:
• Start early.
• Determine the expected overall topic.
• Focus your specific purpose for the given audience and situation.

3.1 How Do You Select a Topic?

1 Identify the General Purpose of Your Speech

2 Create an Idea Bank

3 Select Your Topic

TIP: General Purpose

You can have only one general purpose—to inform, to persuade, or to accentuate (entertain, celebrate, etc.). Using an entertaining delivery style does not necessarily make your purpose to entertain. Your general purpose is your overriding goal for the whole speech.

1

Identify the General Purpose of Your Speech

Identifying the general purpose of your speech will help you narrow your topic options. The *general purpose* is the unrestricted aim of your speech, which can fall into three different categories.

To inform. The giving of information is the aim of this general purpose. Speeches focusing on topics such as "How to Make a Kite," "The History of Hershey's Chocolate," and "The Life and Career of Drake" are examples of speeches to inform.

To persuade. When your goal is *to reinforce*, *to change*, or *to influence* the attitudes, values, beliefs, or actions of your audience, you aim to persuade. Speeches arguing for health care reform or rallying members of the Republican party to support a candidate are examples of speeches to persuade.

To accentuate a special occasion. *To entertain*, *to celebrate*, or *to commemorate* is the aim of a special occasion speech. A wedding toast, a graduation speech, or a speech given by a breast cancer survivor to women recently diagnosed with breast cancer each has the aim to accentuate a special occasion.

If you are giving a speech for class, the assignment likely tells you the general purpose. When you are invited to speak, the audience or the occasion may dictate your general purpose. You may in some cases have the flexibility to choose. For a commencement speech, for example, unless the invitation indicates your purpose, you can choose to inform, persuade, inspire, or entertain.

2
Create an Idea Bank

An *idea bank* is a list of general words and phrases that could be speech topics for you. Here's how to create an idea bank.

- Evaluate your speech assignment, the audience, and the speaking situation. Often this will help you limit your topic ideas.

  → See Chapter 2 for how to evaluate your audience and situation.

- Write down your idea bank by hand. Using paper rather than a computer allows your mind to see connections and jump more quickly from idea to idea.

- Make a list of potential topics. The next few pages will show you three methods for filling your idea bank: searching for topic ideas, brainstorming, and exploring your general purpose. Often, a combination of all three methods will produce the best topics. Later you will narrow your list, but for now, include as many ideas as you can that you find interesting and appropriate for the audience and situation.

TIP: Judging Topics

Be careful not to judge a topic too quickly. Some topics may appear to be a waste of time but can be used creatively. For example, making bubble tools and soap solutions may seem unworthy for a college class. However, if your audience consists of parents or elementary education majors, or if it is close to finals week, you might be giving your audience information they can use to involve their children or students in the creative process or a great activity to alleviate the stress of studying.

SEARCHING FOR TOPIC IDEAS

One way to create an idea bank is by *searching*—browsing print publications, reference works, websites, or other media and materials for subject ideas. For example, you can look through acceptable newspapers or magazines you already have access to at home, online, or in a library, such as the Sunday paper in your area, *Time*, *National Geographic*, *The Week*, or *Smithsonian*.

You can also watch a news broadcast, search an academic database at the library, or browse the Internet. A few places you might look include About.com, Ask.com, ratespeeches.com, or Yahoo! Directory. The idea bank shown below is one example created by searching ratespeeches.com and thinking about what is currently popular.

IDEA BANK
Sharks
Goats
Drones
Childcare - evolution of
Turntables
Things you need at college
Prisoner rehabilitation
African food
Hoverboards
Barefoot running

BRAINSTORMING

Brainstorming is a process that will stimulate your creative thinking through "free association" or "clustering." To brainstorm topics, follow these guidelines.

Free Association

- On a sheet of paper, write down everything you can think of that could be a topic. To get started, take a personal inventory. Think about your hobbies, interests, experiences, abilities, talents, values, attitudes, or beliefs. If that is difficult for you, work with someone who knows you well and have him or her brainstorm with you about your interests, experiences, abilities, and so on. Conducting a quick search for topics as previously outlined might help prime your brainstorming session as well.

- Don't eliminate anything at this stage. Consider everything a potential speech topic and write it down. When you select a topic, you will eliminate the ideas that don't work as well.

- Setting a time limit of 4 or 5 minutes might spur you to think quickly and prevent you from judging an idea.

Below is an example of an idea bank created through free association.

Idea Bank (Free Association)

Building a camera	Cameras	Netflix
Exotic pets	Stonehenge	Road trips
Online classes	Women photographers	Marvel
Space travel	Candy making	Maroon 5
Sinkholes	Soap making	KPOP
Sloths	Embroidery	The Royals
Wilderness survival	Molecular gastronomy	
Sailing	Protein shakes	

At this point, you may have enough ideas to move on to the narrowing process. However, you might try a clustering technique with a few of the ideas in the bank to discover even more ideas. Clustering can help you see the possible main points of your speech as well.

Clustering

- Look at the ideas you have in your current idea bank, and select one that seems interesting or could be something to build on. For example, "cameras" is a very broad topic that might lead to other topics.
- Using another sheet of paper, write that idea in the center of the paper and circle it. This idea is now a focal term from which you will cluster new ideas.
- Look at your focal term and let your mind wander to all the topics linked to it. Write those linked ideas around the focal term and draw lines to connect them to it. Some will have a direct relationship and some will not.
- Next, consider each linked idea as a potential focal term, and circle those that seem like good ones.
- Now, link ideas from each new focal term. Continue this until you can't make new links or you fill the page. See the "cameras" clustering example below.

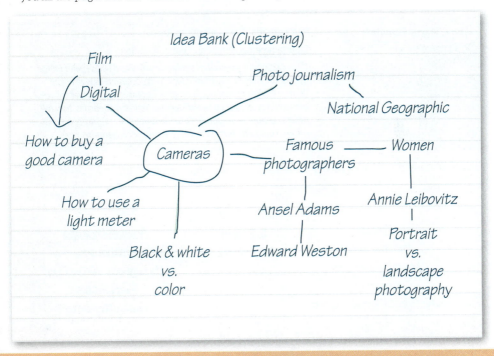

EXPLORING YOUR GENERAL PURPOSE

Exploring your general purpose can also lead to speech topics. In situations where you are told what your general purpose must be, this method is a good place to start your topic selection process. You can create columns for the different types of speeches and topic categories that fit your purpose. The following table offers some categories you can use to generate ideas.

If Your General Purpose Is ...	Your Potential Topic Categories Are ...

To inform: To describe
            To explain
            To demonstrate
	Object, person, animal, place, or event
	Concept or issue
	Process

If Your General Purpose Is ...	Your Potential Topic Categories Are ...
To persuade:	Attitudes, beliefs, values, behaviors/actions, or policies *(For topics under any of these categories, think about reinforcing, changing, or creating new attitudes, beliefs, etc.)*

If Your General Purpose Is ...	Your Potential Topic Categories Are ...
To accentuate a special occasion:	Entertainment, celebration, commemoration *(These categories are not as straightforward and will depend on the goal of the speech. You must adapt to the occasion as well as the audience. Most special occasion speeches take place at events such as weddings, graduations, christenings, retirement parties, funerals, award ceremonies, inaugurals, dinners, holiday celebrations, fund-raisers, campaign banquets, conferences, or conventions.)*

Below is one example of an idea bank created by exploring a general purpose.

IDEA BANK

Places	*To inform*	*Animals/Insects*
Panama Canal	*To describe*	*Seahorses*
Mount Rushmore		*Portuguese Water Dog*
Key West		*Red pandas*
The Great Dismal Swamp		*Leafcutter ants*

3
Select Your Topic

Ask yourself a series of focus questions to help identify topics that will work well and eliminate topics that will not.

- Which topics in my idea bank will work for my general purpose?
- Which topics fit the speech assignment or request?
- Which topics are most familiar to me?
- Which topics am I most comfortable or credible speaking about?
- Which topics have positive aspects for the audience, occasion, speaking event, or timing of the event? Which topics might cause a negative reaction from the audience or are not appropriate?
- Which topics are new or unique to this audience?
- Which topics are worth the audience's time and attention?

For example, suppose you are a member of a miniature aircraft group that has asked you to give an informative talk. You brainstorm topics that are your strengths and create an idea bank (see above right). You ask yourself the focus questions and cross out topics, such as "die-cast military models," that other members are already very familiar with or were discussed in recent months. Thinking about current popular interest in drones, you reason that members might like to hear a talk related to those crafts. Plus, you own several drones and did thorough research before spending a lot of money on them. The drones topic passes the test created by the focus questions.

Idea Bank for Model Aircraft Group

~~Repairing landing gears~~

(Drones)

~~Model helicopters~~

~~Starter kits for younger operators~~

~~Miniature air strips around the Las Vegas area~~

~~Die-cast military models~~

Do some preliminary research to see if you can locate current, quality materials on the topic. As you research, ask these questions:

- Are there enough materials to create a speech that fits into my allotted speech time?
- Is there a variety of quality materials for the topic?
- Will I be able to locate and review the materials in time to prepare effectively for my speech?

If you are having trouble finding support materials, you may want to return to your idea bank for a new topic.

→ Tab 2 explains how to do research and evaluate support materials.

PRACTICING ETHICS: Topics

Your topic should not be harmful to you or your audience, and it should not break any laws or rules.

3.2 How Do You Narrow Your Topic?

Narrowing your topic may not seem all that difficult or important, but the scope of your topic can make or break your speech.

A well-defined topic will help you:

- Achieve the general purpose of your speech. A topic that is too broad will not be thorough enough to be informative, persuasive, or celebratory.

- Reduce the time you spend researching and writing the speech.

- Increase your confidence for giving the speech. If you feel you are trying to cover too much material in a few minutes or you cannot remember all of the speech, your nervousness will increase. A narrow topic allows you to focus on an appropriate amount of material and to feel confident that your speech is not overloaded.

- Effectively deliver your speech at a comfortable rate. A speech that tries to cover too much will run long or seem rushed because you will talk too fast. A narrow topic helps keep the length down and allows you to speak at an understandable rate.

- Keep your audience focused on your topic. A well-defined topic will help audience members follow your speech and can prevent their minds from wandering.

The measure of choosing well is whether a [person] likes and finds good in what he [or she] has chosen.[1]

CHARLES LAMB

Although you can narrow your topic in different ways, the main result of any method you use should be a focused, effectively written *central idea* (thesis statement). Your instructor may prefer a certain method, or the following steps can help you create a focused speech topic.

IDENTIFY THE SPECIFIC PURPOSE OF YOUR SPEECH	The *specific purpose* of your speech is a single statement that combines your general purpose, your audience, and your objective. The *objective* is the outcome or behavior you want your audience to experience or adopt after hearing your speech. → See pages 56–57.
IDENTIFY THE CENTRAL IDEA OF YOUR SPEECH	The *central idea* (also called a *thesis statement, theme,* or *subject sentence*) is a concise, single sentence summarizing and/or previewing what you will say in your speech. → See pages 58–59.
EVALUATE YOUR CENTRAL IDEA	Once you have created an initial central idea, you need to evaluate it. An effective central idea is vital to a successful speech because everything you say in your speech should relate back to this one complete statement. → See pages 60–61.
CONSTRUCT A WORKING OUTLINE	A *working outline* is a brief sketch of the body of your speech. The working outline will contain what you have composed so far—your topic, general purpose, specific purpose, and central idea—plus working main points to guide your research. → See pages 62–63.

CONFIDENCE BOOSTER

If giving a speech seems daunting to you, try to select a topic that is familiar and will be interesting to research. You can then keep your research focused, spend more time practicing, and use your nervous energy to feed your excitement.

3.3 How Do You Create a Central Idea?

1 **Identify the Specific Purpose of Your Speech**

2 **Identify the Central Idea of Your Speech**

3 **Evaluate Your Central Idea**

1

Identify the Specific Purpose of Your Speech

Identifying your specific purpose is the first step in creating a focused central idea. The ***specific purpose*** of your speech is a single statement that combines your general purpose, your audience, and your objective. The ***objective*** of the specific purpose describes the outcome or behavior you want your audience to experience or adopt. Notice how the specific purpose examples at the top of the next page identify what the speakers want their audiences to take away from the speeches.

CHECKLIST for Evaluating a Specific Purpose

❏ Does my specific purpose contain my general purpose, my audience reference, and my objective for the speech?

❏ Is my specific purpose an infinitive statement (to inform, to convince, to motivate, to inspire)?

❏ Am I using clear, concise language?

❏ Does my specific purpose identify exactly what I want to discuss?

❏ Does my specific purpose focus on only one speech topic?

❏ Does my specific purpose relate to the audience? Does it work with the occasion and time? Is it appropriate for me?

❏ Will the scope of my specific purpose fit the time allowed for the speech?

EXAMPLES OF SPECIFIC PURPOSES

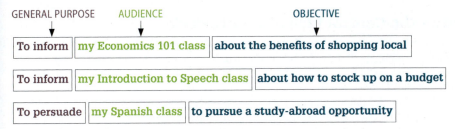

GENERAL PURPOSE | AUDIENCE | OBJECTIVE

To inform | my Economics 101 class | about the benefits of shopping local

To inform | my Introduction to Speech class | about how to stock up on a budget

To persuade | my Spanish class | to pursue a study-abroad opportunity

The above examples follow these guidelines for composing a specific purpose:

- Begin with an infinitive form ("To …") that reflects the general purpose, such as "To inform," "To persuade," or "To commemorate."
- Specify the audience. In the first example, the audience is "my Economics 101 class."
- State the objective. In the first example, the objective is to give the audience information "about the benefits of shopping local."
- Use clear, concise language. Avoid filler words or technical or long descriptions. For instance, the first example does not say, "the awesome economic benefits of buying food, tools, paper goods, and clothes from small grocers, non-chain stores, and online."
- Focus on only one speech topic. "The benefits of buying locally and online" would be two distinctly different speech topics.

Returning to your drone speech, you could construct a specific purpose this way:

GENERAL PURPOSE | AUDIENCE | OBJECTIVE

To inform | the Southern Las Vegas Model Aircraft Group members | about how to buy their first drone

Your specific purpose should contain the key information and be concise, as the drone example shows. Once you have constructed a specific purpose, always evaluate it using the checklist to the left.

If you have a sound specific purpose, you are ready to identify and compose your central idea.

2

Identify the Central Idea of Your Speech

The ***central idea*** (also called a *thesis statement, theme,* or *subject sentence*) is a concise, single sentence summarizing and/or previewing what you will say in your speech. Any decision you make about your main points or support materials should connect back to the theme of this central idea.

How the central idea differs from the specific purpose can seem confusing, but the difference lies in how each functions. First, the specific purpose identifies the objective of your speech. Then, the central idea summarizes and/or previews the ideas your speech will cover in order to achieve its objective. Here are a few examples demonstrating how the specific purpose relates to the central idea. The objective of each specific purpose is shown in blue.

If Your Specific Purpose Is ...	Your Central Idea Could Be ...
To inform my Economics 101 class **about the benefits of shopping local**	Supporting local businesses keeps your money local and benefits the community.
To inform my Introduction to Speech class **about how to stock up on a budget**	College students can save a lot of money if they plan ahead by avoiding name brands, using coupon apps, and buying in bulk with friends.
To persuade my Spanish class **to pursue a study-abroad opportunity**	In addition to being a great way to challenge your language-learning ability, studying abroad grants you a unique experience and makes you stand out when applying for jobs.

Notice how the second central idea example—stocking up on a budget—previews the speech's main points (avoiding name brands, using coupon apps, and bulk buying). Some instructors may require you to preview your main points in this way as a standard part of your central idea.

WHAT DOES AN EFFECTIVE CENTRAL IDEA INCLUDE?

Let's compose a central idea for the speech on drones. Start by looking at your specific purpose and identifying your objective.

SPECIFIC PURPOSE

To inform the Southern Las Vegas Model Aircraft Group members about how to buy their first drone

OBJECTIVE

Your central idea will then summarize and/or preview what you will cover in your speech to achieve your objective. Here is one possible central idea:

CENTRAL IDEA

Model aircraft enthusiasts interested in owning a drone should consider the type of drone, the cost, and drone regulations.

Notice how this example:

- Considers what your audience—the model aircraft group members identified in your specific purpose—will need or want to know.
- Previews what your speech will include: in this case, the "type of drone, the cost, and drone regulations." This information comes from your preliminary knowledge and research.
- Focuses on only one speech topic: how to buy your first drone.
- Uses simple, clear language that is not figurative or ambiguous. In the drone example, you would want to avoid using technical language that isn't common to aircraft enthusiasts just entering the drone market. If need be, define terms or procedures, or simplify them for a listener with little-to-basic skill or construction knowledge.
- Is a complete sentence, with a noun phrase and a verb phrase.
- Is a declarative statement, not a question.

These are all qualities your central idea should have in order to be effective.

→ The next two pages show you how to evaluate a central idea for these qualities.

3
Evaluate Your Central Idea

To evaluate your central idea for effectiveness, study it from two perspectives. First, check the mechanics; that is, make sure your central idea is written correctly, with the proper parts, construction, and focus. Secondly, assess your central idea as it relates to your speech event and audience. Use the following guidelines and the checklist on the next page to help you evaluate it.

MECHANICALLY SOUND

To be mechanically sound, your central idea should meet all four of the following criteria.

- **Your central idea should be a complete sentence.** A complete sentence contains a noun phrase and a verb phrase and can stand alone.

INCORRECT:

Good uses for Pinterest, an online virtual bulletin board.

CORRECT: | The noun phrase

Pinterest, an online virtual bulletin board, | is useful for collecting creative ideas and images.

| The verb phrase

Although the incorrect example ends with a period, it is only a noun phrase; without a verb phrase, it is not a complete sentence. The correct version contains both noun and verb phrases and can stand alone.

- **Your central idea should be written as a statement, not a question.**

INCORRECT:

How safe are energy drinks?

CORRECT:

Many energy drinks contain high amounts of sugar, caffeine, and other additives that in large quantities can cause serious health issues.

Asking a question—as in the incorrect example—can help you think about your speech, but your central idea needs to be a declarative sentence, as in the correct example.

> **TIP: Refining Your Central Idea**
>
> Keep in mind that your central idea might change slightly as you do research and organize the speech. Be open to refining it as you move through the creative process.

- **Your central idea should use clear, simple, and direct language.** To be clear, use language familiar to the audience and words that are concrete. Avoid vague or filler language and qualifying phrases that can lessen the impact of your central idea.

INCORRECT:	CORRECT:
Some believe basically that the radiation silently emitted from cell phones can cause cancer.	Cell phones emit tiny amounts of radiation, which scientists believe may be linked to certain types of brain cancer.

In the incorrect example, "some believe" is vague (who are the "some"?). "Basically" is a filler word that serves no purpose, and "silently" is unnecessary because all radiation is silent. The correct example drops the filler words and directly specifies "scientists believe" as well as what types of cancer may be caused by the radiation.

- **Your central idea should focus on only one speech topic.**

INCORRECT:	CORRECT:
Kickbikes and elliptical trainers are low-impact, high-intensity pieces of exercise equipment.	The kickbike, a European bicycle-scooter hybrid, is a low-tech, low-impact, and high-intensity piece of exercise equipment.
Two nouns connected with a conjunction ("and") may indicate that you have more than one speech topic.	CORRECT: An elliptical trainer is a low-impact and high-intensity piece of exercise equipment.

In the incorrect example, "kickbikes" and "elliptical trainers" are two equal topics that could each get a speech-length treatment. Notice how each of the correct examples previews possible points ("low-tech," "low-impact," etc.) while focusing on a single speech topic.

APPROPRIATE FOR THE EVENT AND AUDIENCE

Because your central idea is a combination of your broad topic, general purpose, and specific purpose, your central idea should, at this stage, be appropriate and focused enough for the event. However, you need to continue to assess whether the topic is still narrow enough for the time allotted, interesting enough to grab your audience's attention, unique enough to not waste their time with something they already know, and accessible enough to not be too technical or confusing for them.

CHECKLIST for Evaluating a Central Idea

- ❏ Is the central idea written as one complete sentence?
- ❏ Is the central idea written as a statement (not a question)?
- ❏ Does the statement use clear, simple, and direct language?
- ❏ Does the central idea focus on only one speech topic?
- ❏ Can I cover this central idea in the time allotted for my speech?
- ❏ Is the central idea worth my audience's time and attention?

3.4 How Do You Construct a Working Outline?

The construction of a speech is a creative process, with many ways you can approach it. Some beginning speakers find that creating a working outline at this point helps them focus and transition into the research phase of creating a speech.

A ***working outline*** is a brief (usually handwritten) sketch of the body of your speech. This outline will help you stay on track while researching your speech and give you direction on what to look for. The working outline will contain what you have composed so far—your topic, general purpose, specific purpose, and central idea—plus working main points to guide your research. The working main points may or may not be the main points you use in your final outline, but they serve the same purpose. Main points, which you will learn more about in Chapter 6, form the skeletal structure, or backbone, that makes up the body of your speech; they are the two to five most important ideas to know about your topic. ***Working main points*** are early drafts of your main points. They may be awkward in format and can change significantly as you research your topic.

→ Chapter 7 explains how to finalize your main points as you compose your speech.

CHECKLIST for Evaluating Working Main Points

❏ Does each main point cover only one key idea?

❏ Are my main points similarly constructed (are they parallel)?

❏ Am I roughly balancing the time spent on each point?

❏ Do my main points relate back to the central idea?

To construct your working main points:

1. Turn to your central idea for categories. Write down your central idea and highlight its important issues. Evaluate the highlighted issues to see if you can discover two to five main categories with one distinct key idea per category.

CENTRAL IDEA:

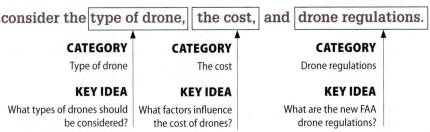

Model aircraft enthusiasts interested in owning a drone should consider the type of drone, the cost, and drone regulations.

CATEGORY	CATEGORY	CATEGORY
Type of drone	The cost	Drone regulations
KEY IDEA	**KEY IDEA**	**KEY IDEA**
What types of drones should be considered?	What factors influence the cost of drones?	What are the new FAA drone regulations?

2. Sum up each of your categories with a statement or question, as shown in each key idea above. These are your working main points. Your final main points must be statements, but for now, questions may seem easier to formulate and may help focus your research. Write in complete sentences, make your points parallel in structure, and balance them so that you will spend roughly equal time on each.

TOPIC: Drones

GENERAL PURPOSE: To inform

SPECIFIC PURPOSE: To inform the Southern Las Vegas Model Aircraft Group members about how to buy their first drone

CENTRAL IDEA: Model aircraft enthusiasts interested in owning a drone should consider the type of drone, the cost, and drone regulations.

MAIN POINT #1: What types of drone should be considered?

MAIN POINT #2: What factors influence the cost of drones?

MAIN POINT #3: What are the new FAA drone regulations?

The preliminary research you did when selecting your topic can help you compose working main points, which will continue to evolve as you prepare your speech. Use the checklist on the left to evaluate your working main points.

Chapter 3: Review

ASSESSING YOUR KNOWLEDGE

3.1 How Do You Select a Topic?

Objective 3.1: **SUMMARIZE HOW TO SELECT A TOPIC**

- Identify the general purpose of your speech, which will be one of the following:
  - To inform
  - To persuade
  - To accentuate a special occasion
- Create an idea bank through techniques like searching through publications, websites, or other media; brainstorming through free association or clustering; or exploring your general purpose.
- Select a topic that works best for you, your audience, and the situation by asking and answering a series of focus questions. Do some preliminary research to see if quality materials are available on the topic.

→ See pages 48–53.

3.2 How Do You Narrow Your Topic?

Objective 3.2: **EXPLAIN HOW TO NARROW A TOPIC**

Having a well-defined topic will help you create an effective speech. There are several methods for narrowing your topic. However, the following steps will help you create a focused central idea.
- Identify the specific purpose of your speech.
- Identify the central idea of the speech.
- Evaluate your central idea.
- Construct a working outline.

→ See pages 54–55.

3.3 How Do You Create a Central Idea?

Objective 3.3: **DESCRIBE HOW TO CREATE A CENTRAL IDEA**

- You should identify your specific purpose. The specific purpose is a single statement that combines your general purpose, your audience reference, and your objective. The objective describes the outcome or behavior you want your audience to experience or adopt.
- You should identify one complete sentence that summarizes and/or previews what you will say in your speech. This is the actual central idea.
- You should evaluate your central idea. Is it a complete sentence with a noun and verb phrase? Is it a declarative statement, not a question? Are you using clear, simple, and direct language? Does the central idea focus on only one speech topic? Can you cover the material suggested in the central idea in your allotted speech time? Is the central idea worthy of your audience's time and attention?

→ See pages 56–61.

3.4 How Do You Construct a Working Outline?

Objective 3.4: **DEMONSTRATE HOW TO CONSTRUCT A WORKING OUTLINE**

A working outline is a brief sketch of the body of your speech. It should contain your topic, general purpose, specific purpose, central idea, and working main points. This outline will help you stay on track while researching your speech and gives you direction on what to look for. To create a working outline, you should:
- Turn to your central idea for categories that might be working main points. Preliminary research can also help you identify categories.
- Sum up each of your categories with a statement or question. Try to write in complete thoughts. Note that the final main points in your preparation outline must be statements, not questions.

→ See pages 62–63.

TERMS TO REMEMBER

general purpose (48)
idea bank (49)
brainstorming (50)
specific purpose (56)
objective (56)
central idea (58)
working outline (62)
working main points (62)

Practical Pointers for Tab 1

FAQs

What if I'm still nervous about giving a speech?

Being somewhat concerned or anxious is normal. However, you can work on minimizing your anxiety right up to the end of the speech.

For example, dry mouth, tight throat, and shakiness seem to be the most common anxiety symptoms for the beginning speaker. Here are some additional suggestions for lessening their effects:

- **Dry mouth:** Using lip balm and taking small sips of water right before the speech may help. If the dry mouth is severe, take a few small sips of water during the speech. Be careful that they don't become distracting, and never chew gum during a speech.

- **Tight throat:** While calmly practicing your speech, pay attention to how your throat feels when it is relaxed and talking. Work to recognize how to keep your throat and vocal cords relaxed. Before the speech, hum softly, do vocal exercises, and breathe deeply. Breathing from your diaphragm rather than your upper chest will help relax your throat.

- **Shakiness:** Exercise and movement can help. A couple of hours before the speech, mild exercise might help relieve built-up tension that will worsen as you give the speech. Try to gesture or move around during the speech, when appropriate, to relax those shaky muscles.

Do I have to analyze my audience and situation if I'm just giving a speech in class?

Yes. Analyzing your audience and situation is central to almost every decision you make regarding any speech you give. In class, it may be more important than in other situations because your audience can be very apathetic or distracted.

What if I have trouble coming up with working main points?

Ask yourself questions such as: What do I know about this topic? What are the three most important things to know about this topic? What should my audience know about this topic?

If that doesn't help, brainstorm with a friend or family member with similar questions, or do some preliminary research on the Internet to help you focus on three to five working points.

ADDITIONAL SUPPORT

If you are still struggling with researching your audience and situation or creating an idea bank, these resources might help you locate further information or topic ideas:

gallup.com
pewresearch.org
pewglobal.org
ropercenter.cornell.edu
infoplease.com
norc.org
buzzfeed.com
news.google.com

4

LOCATING
SUPPORT
MATERIALS

4.1 Where Do You Locate Support Materials?

Research is the act of investigating, evaluating, and summarizing information. Good research skills help you find effective **support materials** (or *evidence*)—information that explains, elaborates, or validates your speech topic. Support materials come from different **sources** such as books, magazines, journals, and websites. You can locate many support materials and sources by using the Internet, libraries, interviews, and surveys.

For example, Logan is preparing a speech on basketball and wants to use some startling statistics about one of the best professional basketball players of all time. However, he also wants to choose a player not everyone in his class knows. Logan asks a librarian for help. She recommends first searching the Internet for a list of great players and then looking for a specific player from that list. Within minutes, Logan has the opening to his speech:

> According to the NBA Encyclopedia Playoff Edition at NBA.com, as of December 2015, which NBA star is the only player to score 4,000 points in a season? Who set the NBA single-game record for most points (100) and the most rebounds (55)? Who was nicknamed the "Big Dipper"? If you answered Wilt Chamberlain, you are correct.

TIP: Personal Sources

Don't forget to consider your own available personal sources. If your topic is something you are interested in, you may own books, objects, memorabilia, records of an event, video, pictures, or other related items. This is often a great place to start your research.

Where can you start? One tool that covers many bases is a library's online portal (see one example below). Searching a portal is an effective way to do preliminary research on the library's holdings and resources as well as to access online databases or reference material. Online access is also helpful when you need more information or you forget a citation and cannot get back to the physical library quickly. Most library portals allow you to:

- Search their catalogs and databases just as you would if you were sitting in the library (see the librarian for any special log-on requirements for databases).
- Utilize other services such as getting help with citing sources.

So explore your library portal and learn what it has to offer.

However, don't be afraid to go to the library. The reference librarian can save you time, as his or her job is to help you find information and resources. If researching is a relatively new process for you, begin with a face-to-face discussion with your librarian. He or she can help you learn how to use the resources designed to make your search faster and more effective. Whenever you ask a librarian for help, take the following items with you:

- Your speech assignment and any notes you have about it
- Your working outline
- Any research you have already completed

→ See pages 76–87 for more about the resources inside a library.

Because of the Internet and the quality of U.S. libraries, and the widening ability to interview experts or conduct surveys, you have a vast amount of information at your fingertips. The next sections offer guidance on when and how to use these resources.

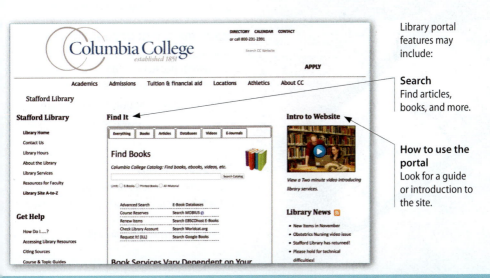

Library portal features may include:

Search
Find articles, books, and more.

How to use the portal
Look for a guide or introduction to the site.

4.2 What Does the Internet Have to Offer You?

1 Search Engines
2 Commercial Websites
3 Nonprofit Organization Websites
4 Blogs
5 Personal Websites

1

Search Engines

Search engines are the specific tools you use to search for information on the web. You can access them through web browsers (such as Chrome, Safari, Internet Explorer, or Mozilla Firefox). When you type search terms into an engine, it will then send back *hits*, or a list of web pages, files, images, and other items.

SOME GENERAL SEARCH ENGINES

Google	www.google.com
Yahoo!	www.yahoo.com
Bing	www.bing.com

SOME METASEARCH ENGINES

Metasearch engines search other engines and specialized sites.

Dogpile	www.dogpile.com
Excite	www.excite.com
ixquick	www.ixquick.com

SEARCHING THE INVISIBLE WEB

To search the invisible web or deep net—information not accessible via general search engines—use sites such as these:

Google Scholar	scholar.google.com
Alexa	www.alexa.com

TIP: Search Terms

- Connect multiple search terms with *and, or,* or *not.*
- The first word in your search term gets the most emphasis.
- Use quotation marks around a phrase.

The following pages will show you how to locate and use types of websites and blogs in your research. **Websites** usually consist of multiple, unified pages beginning with a home page. A website may be created and maintained by an individual, group, business, or organization. The contents of a website might include images, video, articles, facts, statistics, digital documents, and links to related websites. The table below provides tips on how to evaluate online sources. Use common sense—don't believe everything you read on the Internet.

➜ See Chapter 5 for a detailed discussion on evaluating all sources.

Specific types of sources, such as newspapers or magazines, also can be found using search engines.

➜ See pages 80–87 for more information on these types of sources.

WHAT SHOULD YOU EVALUATE?	HOW CAN YOU EVALUATE THIS INFORMATION?	TIPS
Accuracy: Does the information seem plausible?	• Check for citations. • Investigate the authors. • Verify content with other sources.	• Citations are usually located at the bottom of the page. • Look for an "About Us" link to find information or Google the authors. • Locate the same information in other sources.
Responsibility: Who is responsible for this website? What are their qualifications related to your topic?	• Look at the page header. • Study the site address (URL) for clues. • Scroll to the bottom of the home page for copyright information.	• Look for author information and research their qualifications. • Look for who owns the site and research their connection to the information.
Impartiality: Could this site be biased? How are the site creators affiliated?	• Check for advertisements that may indicate a bias. • Check for a mission statement. • Consider who the site is targeting as an audience.	• Some websites pay to be the top results in a search engine. They may be called sponsored links. • Look for a link such as "Our Mission," "FAQ," or "About Us."
Currency: When was this site created? Is it important to your topic to have the most current information possible?	• Check for a copyright date or date of last update at bottom of home page. • Verify content with other sources.	• If a site has no copyright date, look for a date when material (such as an article or blog entry) was posted. • Check citation dates for recency.

2

Commercial Websites

Commercial websites are sites created and maintained by for-profit businesses or organizations. These websites are typically promotional but can include newspapers, television networks, and video and image services (e.g., YouTube or Google Maps).

For a speech on the Water Efficient Maize Project (WEMA) led by the African Agricultural Technology Foundation (AATF) in Kenya, Tobi discovered that the U.S.-based company Monsanto is a partner in the project. So Tobi searched the company's website for details. On the Monsanto site (shown below), she found this quotation to use in her speech.

> Three-quarters of the world's most severe droughts over the past 10 years have occurred in Africa, making farming risky for millions of smallholder farmers, most of whom are women and rely on rainfall to water their crops. Maize is the most widely grown staple crop in Africa—more than 300 million Africans depend on it as their main food source. Maize production is severely affected by drought, which can lead to unpredictable and low yields, and at worst, complete crop failure.

Leading into this quotation, Tobi used the oral citation shown at the end of this page.

WHEN TO USE
- To locate information about a company
- To gather support materials from sites of respected news organizations
- To find current or popular-culture materials
- To find presentation aids (cite the sources)

ADVANTAGES
- Can offer information unavailable in print
- May be current (be sure to check dates)
- May be seen by your audience as reliable

DISADVANTAGES
- Are often biased toward the interests of the site owner or paid advertisers, if any
- May require verifying information with other sources or may not be verifiable
- May not credit all sources of information

TIPS ON LOCATING
- Use a search engine to find a specific site if you have one in mind, or search on your topic to locate related sites.

SAMPLE ORAL CITATION
According to the story "Water Efficient Maize for Africa," found on Monsanto.com on December 1, 2015, three-quarters of the most severe droughts in the last 10 years have occurred in Africa.

3

Nonprofit Organization Websites

Nonprofit organization websites are sites for local, national, and international not-for-profit groups dedicated to issues or causes such as UNICEF, MADD, the Special Olympics, or the Magic Johnson Foundation. Their URLs often end with ".org."

Suppose you are researching a speech for a service learning assignment. You and your classmates are required to participate in civic responsibility activities as part of your degrees, and you want to inform your audience about an opportunity to honor veterans. On the Central Missouri Honor Flight website, you discover information about the program, which flies veterans to Washington, D.C., to see the war memorials honoring their service. You find this statistic a good use of pathos (emotional appeal):

> Now, with more than 640 WWII veterans dying each day, time to express our thanks to these brave men and women is running out.

The site (shown below) also contains photos, stories, and information on how individuals can help. You can use the site to collect some support materials. See the end of this page for a sample oral citation.

WHEN TO USE

- To locate detailed information about a particular issue or organization
- To locate emotional appeal examples

ADVANTAGES

- Can provide background and current information about a service or issue
- Are usually considered reliable sources
- Tend to use accessible language

DISADVANTAGES

- Have set goals or agendas, which may bias how information is presented
- May not include author credentials
  - May accept paid advertisements, which may signal the site's information is biased

TIPS ON LOCATING

- Search online using the name of the organization or the issue it supports.

SAMPLE ORAL CITATION

According to centralmissouri honorflight.com on November 1, 2015, the Central Missouri program has "transported over 1,900 veterans on 31 flights to Washington" since 2009.

4

Blogs

A ***blog*** is a website or page that contains regular postings by its author(s)—often in the form of a journal—and may allow visitors to comment. Blogs exist for almost any topic. When created by authorities, they can offer unique, credible information; but keep in mind that most blogs will represent specific opinions or points of view.

Types of blogs include:

- Personal blogs (including Twitter)
- Corporate blogs (often for marketing)
- Subject blogs (politics, travel, fashion, etc.)
- Media blogs (comprised of videos, links, etc.)

Bruce is giving a speech on the U.S. employment situation because it has been in the news lately. On the White House blog (shown below), Bruce found information he could use in his speech, such as:

> Today we learned that private-sector employment rose by 197,000 jobs in November. Private employment growth in September and October was revised up by a combined 52,000 jobs, bringing October's growth to 304,000—the best month of the year so far.

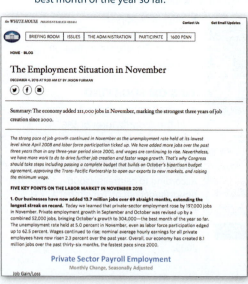

WHEN TO USE

- To find examples of public opinion
- To find new developments about your topic (to verify with other sources)
- To gauge if a topic is controversial or of current general interest

ADVANTAGES

- Can provide current information
- Can be helpful in gauging public opinion
- Can offer unique material

DISADVANTAGES

- Are often biased toward the opinions of the blogger(s)
- May require verifying information with other sources
- May not credit all sources of information
- May not be acceptable support material in some college classes. Ask your instructor.

TIPS ON LOCATING

- Use blog search engines (Google Blog Search, Blogarama, Technorati).

SAMPLE ORAL CITATION

According to the White House blog on December 4, 2015, the economy added 211,000 jobs in November.

5

Personal Websites

Personal websites are created by groups or individuals and focused on topics of personal interest. These sites, if created by a credible source, can offer personal or expert testimony. Much like blogs, personal websites can be created by anyone with skills and equipment, and they may represent specific opinions.

Karissa is an art major who likes to work in nontraditional forms. Recently she has been working with fiber, and she came across a print of a quilt by fiber artist Annette Kennedy. Inspired by her work, Karissa decided to select Kennedy as one of the nontraditional artists she would speak about to a class. Karissa accessed the artist's personal website (shown below), where she found digital images of Kennedy's works and information about the artist. During the speech, Karissa used this direct quotation from the artist's biography:

> I love and am inspired by the beauty in nature. I have always been an avid amateur photographer. These things coupled with my love of fabric and color have lead me to my journey of creating landscape and pictorial art quilts from personally taken photographs.

Karissa also found several images to display during the speech. See a citation at the end of this page.

Longs Peak Rhapsody

WHEN TO USE
- To find material that humanizes your topic
- To find personal information about the site author(s)

ADVANTAGES
- Can be reliable support if author is a recognized expert on your topic
- Can offer unique material

DISADVANTAGES
- Can be written by anyone, regardless of his or her credentials (research the author's credibility)
- May require verifying information with other sources
- Are often promotional or biased toward the opinions of the author
- May not credit all sources of information
- May not be acceptable support material in some college classes. Ask your instructor.

TIPS ON LOCATING
- Use the search engines discussed on page 70.

SAMPLE ORAL CITATION
According to the official website of fiber artist Annette Kennedy on December 10, 2015, *Longs Peak Rhapsody* is an award-winning work from 2011.

4.3 What Does the Library Have to Offer You?

1 The Catalog

2 Databases

3 Books

4 Newspapers

5 Magazines

6 Newsletters

7 Journals

8 Reference Librarians

You should always include the library in your research adventures. In most college towns, you have a library on or affiliated with your campus and a public library. In some larger cities, you may find additional libraries dedicated to specialized topics. All of these libraries may have something to offer your speech topic.

The college library will have more academically oriented information such as historical analysis and scientific research.

The public library will offer you access to local history and statewide statistics as well as popular books, newspapers, and magazines.

Special libraries are usually connected or related to a famous person (such as a presidential library), company, organization, government agency, or museum. You may need special permission to access the stacks in these libraries.

Many libraries also provide an interlibrary loan (ILL) service. ILL allows you to request items located at other libraries that will be delivered to your library. This service can give you access to much more material, but it can be time consuming (often more than a month for delivery) and can have associated fees.

TIP: Know Your Requirements

Most college speech assignments require that you use a certain amount of material from the library, rather than relying only on the Internet. Check your assignment and ask your instructor.

1
The Catalog

All libraries have a catalog system, typically an electronic search engine, designed to help you locate materials physically owned by the library and other libraries in the area. See an example below. Items in the library's database are cataloged according to subjects and related subjects as assigned by the Library of Congress. Usually you can search for publications by title, author, or subject. The librarian can help you determine what search terms to use to target your research. You should always pay attention to the related subjects listed, for other possible routes to take in your search. The tips given earlier for search engines are helpful here as well.

Contact a librarian: You can ask a librarian a question.

TIP: Visiting Other Libraries

If you want to use a library you are not affiliated with, check the library's website or call for its visiting patron policies. In many cases, a letter of introduction from the director of a library where you are already a patron will help you gain access.

Multifaceted search
This library lets you search all its collections and locations. You can also search items by format (print, audio, etc.) and other criteria.

Finding materials
You can locate books, articles, and other materials by searching catalogs and databases.

2

Databases

Although search engines such as Google can help you find general information, they do not access everything.

Most libraries subscribe to **databases**, or extensive collections of published works (such as magazine, newspaper, and journal articles) in electronic form, making material easy to search and locate. Databases contain descriptions and citation information about articles (title of article and publication, author, publication date, etc.), and they often include the full text of the articles. A database itself is not a source you will orally cite in your speech; it is a portal for finding a large amount of support materials from many different sources, all in one place.

Different databases may focus on different subject areas. For instance, ERIC (Education Resources Information Center) covers education research. Others specialize in arts, sciences, law, or business. Your reference librarian can tell you what databases are available at your library and what disciplines they cover. Your library's website will likely include a link to these databases.

MULTIPLE-SUBJECT DATABASES

Multiple-subject databases contain sources across a vast spectrum of disciplines and periodicals. Use these to research broadly and then to narrow your topic. Some common ones include:

- Academic Search Elite/EBSCOhost
- LexisNexis
- JSTOR (shown on page 79)
- Project MUSE

SPECIALIZED DATABASES

Specialized databases contain sources related to specific disciplines or topics. Use these to focus your research once you have your topic narrowed. Some common ones include:

- Bloom's Literary Reference Online (literary criticism and resources)
- CQ Weekly (coverage of acts of Congress)
- ERIC (education)
- OVID (science and health care)
- Standard & Poor's NetAdvantage (business)

TIP: Using Databases

You search in databases much like you search in the library's catalog or with a search engine. A search screen from one common database (JSTOR) is shown on the next page. As with a search engine, you have options for basic and advanced searching.

- Put limits on your search by defining attributes. You may be able to limit your search by discipline or subject, to full-text articles only, or to recent articles only. Always start with a full-text search. You may find all you need this way.

- Use broad key words rather than specific phrases or language for your initial search.

- If a database has more than one "search" box, use them. For example, you can search for "2015 drought," "California," and "Nevada."

- Check to see if the database has an online thesaurus to browse for subjects that match your speech topic. Once you have some results, look at the subject or descriptor field for related terms you can search on, and redo your search.

- Search more than one database.

- Ask your librarian for help if you have questions or find using a database intimidating.

Basic search
On this site, you can
use the home screen
for a basic search.
Enter key terms
related to your topic.

Advanced search
Investigate how you can
limit your search , such as
by item type or date, or do
a detailed search.

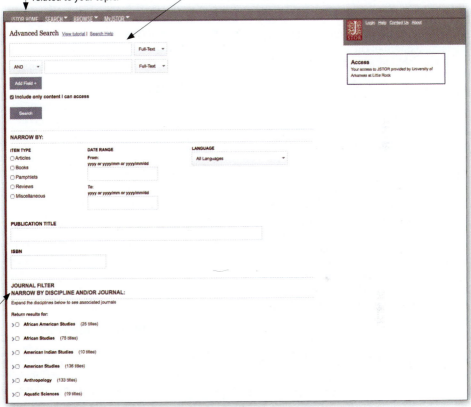

Discipline search
Some sites have
additional searching
and browsing options,
such as by academic
discipline or journal.

3
Books

You might use any of several types of books for support materials. A book may be written by a single author, multiple authors, corporate authors, or government authors.

Types of books include:

- Nonfiction books (when credible, offer factual information about people, places, events, things, animals, etc., and are written by reliable authors)
- Fiction books (authors invent creative stories)
- Edited collections (compilations of essays or articles, written by multiple authors but related topically)
- Anthologies (compilations of short stories, poetry, or plays)

Lacey has been asked to give a presentation on cooking gluten-free at a local food show. In the book *The Spunky Coconut Cookbook: Gluten-Free, Casein-Free, Sugar-Free*, she found lists of equipment needs and numerous recipes. Before giving the audience a couple of the recipe examples, Lacey included an oral citation (see sample at the end of the next column). Also, Lacey included the source on printed copies of a recipe she distributed to the audience at the end of her speech.

WHEN TO USE

- To find important detail and contextual information about your topic
- To locate facts, statistics, and examples

ADVANTAGES

- Often considered extremely reliable
- Usually contain a large amount of detailed information
- Often have bibliographies or source notes leading you to additional material
- Often contain quotable passages for emotional appeals

DISADVANTAGES

- May not have current information (check the copyright date and verify information with current sources)
- Require more time to read and glean information, due to length

TIPS ON LOCATING

- Search for your topic on sites such as Amazon or Library of Congress (www.loc.gov) to identify books to seek at the library.
- Search the library catalog.

SAMPLE ORAL CITATION

In her 2011 book, *The Spunky Coconut Cookbook*, Kelly Brozyna offers several easy gluten-free recipes.

4
Newspapers

Newspapers are published daily, weekly, or biweekly and can be local, national, or international. They contain news, information, opinions, and advertisements. Articles tend to focus on politics, crime, business, health, art/entertainment, society, and sports.

After the November 2015 terrorist attacks in Paris, Brigitte wanted to inform her class about how the terrorists used modern tools to carry out the attacks. Brigitte found this information in the November 20, 2015, online edition of the *Miami Herald*:

> The Paris attackers used an online gaming chat function to discuss their plans. To stay in touch, they used a social media app designed to protect Russian citizens from the prying eyes of their secret police. And, later, after they'd killed 130 and wounded another 351, the remaining members of a terror cell that was on the verge of launching yet another attack in Paris [were] found and arrested or killed early Wednesday when the GPS functions on their phones and rental cars gave away the group's locations and travel histories.

See one of Brigitte's oral citations at the end of this page.

WHEN TO USE

- To find current facts and statistics
- To locate extended examples
- To support current events or topics

ADVANTAGES

- Often viewed as current and reliable
- Feature condensed information
- Use accessible language

DISADVANTAGES

- Rarely cite references
- May require finding other in-depth sources
- May be outdated quickly

TIPS ON LOCATING

- Search the library databases.
- Public libraries often carry local and some national newspapers.
- Academic libraries often carry local, national, and international newspapers.
- Some newspapers are also online (note that online editions can be different from print editions).

SAMPLE ORAL CITATION

A November 20, 2015, *Miami Herald* online article, "Paris Attacks Show the Good and Bad of High-Tech Revolution" by Matthew Schofield, reports that one attacker sent this text message from a phone discovered near the theater. "Off we go, we begin."

5
Magazines

Magazines are published on a regular schedule (weekly, monthly, or quarterly) and contain a range of articles, often related to a theme or focus. Magazines are generally financed by advertisements as well as a purchase or subscription price.

Magazines can be local, regional, national, or international. Some focus on popular culture (e.g., *Vogue* or *GQ*), whereas others tend toward educational topics (e.g., *Scientific American* or *National Geographic*). Magazines, especially for general readers, often use accessible and vivid language.

For example, Nico is studying to be a marine biologist and knows several of his classmates are interested in marine life. He finds an article on the phenomenon of seamounts and the ecosystem they create for marine life and decides to give an informative speech on seamounts. He uses this definition in his speech:

> According to Gregory Stone, in his September 2012 *National Geographic* article "Mountains in the Sea," "Seamounts generally form when volcanic mountains rise up from the seafloor but fail to reach the surface."

See the end of this page for another sample from Nico's speech. Nico cites the same article as the source of an image he uses in a presentation aid.

WHEN TO USE
- To find facts, statistics, and examples
- To support current events or topics

ADVANTAGES
- Often viewed as current and reliable
- Feature condensed information
- Use accessible language

DISADVANTAGES
- May not give background information
- May require finding other in-depth sources
- May be outdated quickly

TIPS ON LOCATING
- Search the library databases.
- Libraries often have many magazines and may archive old issues.
- Some magazines have websites, but they may differ from print versions or contain only old issues.

SAMPLE ORAL CITATION
> This image, from Gregory Stone's September 2012 *National Geographic* article titled "Mountains of the Sea," is an expanse of cabbage coral attached to the slope of a seamount.

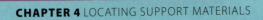

6
Newsletters

Newsletters are regularly distributed mini-publications produced by clubs, churches, societies, associations, businesses, and government agencies. Their purpose is to provide concise information about a group or one main topic of interest. Newsletters can be delivered in printed or electronic form.

Because many college students don't eat a healthy diet, Sean wants to inform his classmates about how to make healthier food choices. In a National Institutes of Health newsletter, Sean found several tips; he created a visual aid for listing them and used them in his speech:

Tips for Eating Out

· Choose foods that are steamed, broiled, baked, roasted, poached, or lightly sautéed or stir-fried.

· Ask for fat-free or low-fat milk instead of cream for coffee or tea.

· Pick food without butter, gravy, or sauces— or ask to have the food without it.

· Choose a low-calorie salad dressing and ask for it on the side.

· Pick drinks without added sugar, such as water, fat-free or low-fat milk, unsweetened tea, or diet iced tea, lemonade, or soda.

WHEN TO USE

- To locate information on specific groups or topics
- To find a group's stance on an issue
- To discover or follow current events

ADVANTAGES

- Contain information specific to an organization or topic
- Offer material not found elsewhere
- Give information in condensed form

DISADVANTAGES

- May give incomplete information
- May use specialized language
- May not cite sources or authors
- May be biased or promotional

TIPS ON LOCATING

- Search for a website maintained by the group or author of the newsletter.
- May be in a library's periodical or reference section; ask your librarian.
- Contact the organization.

SAMPLE ORAL CITATION

According to the September 2015 issue of "News in Health," published by the National Institutes of Health, here are some tips for eating out.

7
Journals

Journals are academic and professional publications issued at regular intervals, such as quarterly. Journals typically use *peer review*, in which experts in the appropriate field evaluate the articles before they are accepted for publication.

Journals are topic specific and tailored for a certain audience. For example, the *Journal of the American Medical Association* is written for medical professionals. Journals exist in most major fields.

Mitali is majoring in film. In her film history class, she must give a presentation on the films of Martin Scorsese. The assignment requires including critical reviews as well as Scorsese's film history. So Mitali turns to some of the journals of her field. In the *Journal of Film and Video*, she finds this article:

"Geographies of Desire: Postsocial Urban Space and Historical Revision in the Films of Martin Scorsese"

Mitali found some descriptive quotations in the article, and the endnotes offered other articles she could research for support materials. See the end of this page for how she began one of her oral citations.

WHEN TO USE
- To find detailed facts and statistics
- To locate expert testimony
- When highly credible sources are needed
- With a highly educated audience

ADVANTAGES
- Have extremely high credibility
- Are written and peer reviewed by experts or specialists in the field
- Include extensive bibliographies where you may find further sources

DISADVANTAGES
- Are written in a formal style that may need to be adapted for your audience
- Use language specific to the field that may be difficult to understand

TIPS ON LOCATING
- Search the library databases.
- Academic libraries often carry selected scholarly/professional journals in print.

SAMPLE ORAL CITATION

In her article "Geographies of Desire: Postsocial Urban Space and Historical Revision in the Films of Martin Scorsese"—published in the Spring/Summer 2010 issue of the *Journal of Film and Video*—Professor Sabine Haenni argues that...

8
Reference Librarians

Some of the most helpful library resources are people: Reference librarians are specially trained to respond to your library needs and assist you in your research. They often are up to date on current issues, trends, and topics. They know what types of sources and services are available to you, and they can show you how to effectively use services—such as databases—to get what you need and to save time. They may also interact directly with your instructors and know what is important for your assignments. For all of these reasons, it is a good idea to physically visit the library early in your research and talk to a reference librarian.

PRESENTATION AID EQUIPMENT ASSISTANCE

At some institutions, you may find a library conference room with all the same presentation equipment as your classroom. Most institutions allow students to reserve these rooms for practice. Also, reference librarians may hold workshops on using the equipment or can give you one-on-one assistance. See what your school has available.

ACCESS TO SPECIAL COLLECTIONS OR RARE BOOKS

Many libraries house special collections or rare books that are unique to that library. Items in special collections may include rare works, historical records (archives), manuscripts, personal correspondence, photographs, or physical items and artifacts. Because these items are rare, fragile, and often valuable, they are usually stored in a controlled environment known as *closed stacks*. You cannot check out these items and may need to present identification or a letter of reference to gain access, if access is available. Reference librarians are usually the ones who will give you access to these special collections and are very knowledgeable about what the collections contain.

> When the going gets tough, the tough get a librarian.[1]
>
> JOAN BAUER

4.4 What Can You Find Both on the Internet and in Libraries?

1 Government Resources
2 Reference Works

1

Government Resources

Government resources are information sources created by local, state, and federal governmental agencies. They can include books, reports, bills, pamphlets, maps, websites, or other documents.

WHEN TO USE
- To locate statistics and facts
- To locate policy information
- To locate practical information

ADVANTAGES
- Are often viewed as highly credible
- Are often very current
- Often contain unique information
- Often have extensive bibliographies

DISADVANTAGES
- May not include citation information
- May be difficult to locate the specific publication you are looking for

TIPS ON LOCATING
- Search the Internet using the city or state name, or ask your librarian how to locate government holdings.
- Public libraries are often good sources.
- Go to www.usa.gov/federal-agencies/a for a list of sites.
- The U.S. Government Publishing Office website (www.gpo.gov) offers information about federal government publications.

SAMPLE ORAL CITATION
In 2015, the city's official website noted that more than 9,000 accidents occur yearly nationwide due to drivers' running lights.

2
Reference Works

A reference work is a compilation of information such as facts, data, and definitions arranged for easy access. Many printed reference works have a corresponding website.

Some examples are:

- Dictionaries (general and subject specific)
- Encyclopedias (general and subject specific)
- Thesauruses
- Yearbooks or annuals (e.g., *Statistical Abstracts*, *Facts on File Yearbook*)
- Atlases
- Grammar handbooks and style manuals
- Books of quotations
- Biographical reference books (e.g., *International Who's Who*)

WHEN TO USE

- To locate brief definitions or segments of information
- To locate statistics and facts
- To assist you in using language effectively
- To start your research and get a broad base of information to build upon

ADVANTAGES

- Are great places to begin your research
- Are useful places to get brief statistics, facts, and quotations
- Are helpful in constructing your outline

DISADVANTAGES

- May offer information that is too brief
- Can focus on obscure facts or definitions that are not popularly acceptable or used
- May be user-created sites, such as Wikipedia, which may not always be accurate and so are not viewed as credible. The source lists within these references may help you locate reliable primary sources, but always check with your instructor to see if using such user-created references is acceptable for your assignment.

TIPS ON LOCATING

- Check the reference section of your library or ask a reference librarian.
- Typing in a key word or phrase or asking a search engine a question will pull up many online references. Some commonly used Internet references are:

> Merriam-webster.com
> Infoplease.com
> Biography.com
> Refdesk.com
> The World Factbook

SAMPLE ORAL CITATION

As defined in the *Longman Dictionary of American English*, 4th edition, xenophobia is "an extreme fear or dislike of people from other countries."

CONFIDENCE BOOSTER

Allowing yourself to take the necessary time to effectively research your topic will not only help you compose a great speech, but also increase your confidence. When you spend time building your knowledge about a topic, you become more comfortable talking about it.

4.5 How Can You Gather Support Materials in an Interview?

1 Prepare for the Interview

2 Conduct the Interview

3 Use Media-Assisted Interviews If Necessary

Interviews are information-gathering sessions where you (the *interviewer*) ask either one person or a group (the *interviewee/interviewees*) a series of prepared questions. As a student at an institution of higher education, you have access to many experts across numerous fields as well as a large number of people who could offer lay testimony. Conducting personal interviews could offer you:

- Excellent expert information not available by other means
- Firsthand experience or feelings about the topic
- Leads on where and how to locate other support materials
- The ability to increase the credibility of your speech as well as to make your speech more personable
- Insight into your audience's perspective, if you interview them directly

> ### TIP: Finding People to Interview
>
> When conducting your research, look for organizations related to your topic. Think about groups, societies, businesses, clubs, institutions, associations, or museums that might have helpful information or publications. Interview someone if you can. For example:
>
> - If you are doing a speech on inexpensive spring break travel packages or how to prepare for a flight with all the new regulations, interview a travel agent.
> - If you need local or state history, interview someone at a historical society or museum.
> - If you need information on composting, interview someone at the local extension agency, agricultural school, or farmers' market association.

1
Prepare for the Interview

SET UP A TIME AND A LOCATION

- Set the time around your interviewee's schedule. Set start and end times and stick to them. Most interviews should last no longer than 30 to 60 minutes.
- Select a location that is comfortable for the interviewee and that is quiet, with few interruptions (away from phones if possible).
- Reconfirm the time and place with your interviewee.

WRITE YOUR QUESTIONS

- Research the interviewee's background, and be sure your questions are appropriate to his or her expertise.
- Ask questions that help you gather the types of support materials (examples, facts, etc.) you need.
- Use more open-ended questions than closed-ended questions. **Open-ended questions** encourage discussion or longer responses. This type of question may start with *who, what, where, when, why,* or *how.* For example:

  How do you feel about the proposed emergency notification system?

  Closed-ended questions prompt one-word or short answers (often "yes" or "no"). For example:

  Do you support the proposed emergency notification system?

- Collect information that will establish your interviewee's credibility with your audience:

  What's your exact title?

  How long have you worked for your company?

DECIDE HOW TO RECORD THE INTERVIEW

- Note taking alone may work if you plan to summarize and the interview is brief.
- Use audio or video recording for direct quotations, detailed facts or statistics, or complex material. Take notes as a backup. As an ethical interviewer, you must have permission to audio or video record an interview. Some schools might require written permission, or you might just document the permission at the beginning of the recorded interview. After you have turned on the recording device, you might say to the interviewee:

  Are you aware I am recording this interview? Do I have your permission to do so? Thank you, and if at any time you would like me to stop the recording, just say so.

PRACTICING ETHICS: Conducting Interviews

When you conduct interviews for a speech, remember:

- Always be respectful of your interviewee's time.
- Always get permission from your interviewee if you want to make an audio or video recording of the interview.

2
Conduct the Interview

To conduct a successful interview, you should:

- Pay attention to your appearance. Be well groomed and dress appropriately.
- If you are using any equipment, make sure it works.
- Arrive on time and begin the interview on time.
- Thank the interviewee for his or her time.
- Explain your topic and speech goal.
- Give the interviewee time to respond to each question.
- Allow yourself to think of **follow-up questions**, or new questions that occur to you based on the interviewee's answers so far. However, be careful not to do this too often or you may run out of time.
- Ask the interviewee to clarify anything if you do not understand.
- Be an active listener.

  → See Chapter 12 for listening tips.

- Near the end of the interview, check your notes to see if you have the information you need.
- End your interview with a question such as:
  Is there anything else I should know?
  Is there anyone else you recommend I speak with?
- End the interview on time.
- Thank the interviewee again, and ask if you can follow up if questions arise later.

- Take a few minutes immediately after the interview to make additional notes while the conversation is still fresh in your mind.
- Send the interviewee a thank-you note. If appropriate, you might offer to share your outline or invite him or her to your speech.

Use the checklist on this page to help prepare for and conduct your interview.

SAMPLE ORAL CITATION FOR INTERVIEW MATERIAL

In a personal interview I conducted last month, local dentist Dr. Marvin Jones said that his office will donate supplies and a day of free checkups to support the city's health literacy campaign in schools.

CHECKLIST for Interviewing

❏ Did I set up an appropriate time and place for the interview?

❏ Do my questions collect background information as well as necessary support materials?

❏ Are most of my questions open-ended?

❏ Do I have a means for recording the interview?

❏ On the day of the interview, am I well groomed and dressed appropriately?

❏ Do I have everything I need to conduct the interview (questions, notebook, recorder, address, etc.)?

❏ After the interview, did I send a thank-you note?

3

Use Media-Assisted Interviews If Necessary

Sometimes meeting face-to-face for an interview is impossible. When necessary, you can use the telephone, video calling, e-mail, or instant messaging to conduct the interview. However, realize that these forms of information collection are not as effective as sitting face-to-face with the interviewee. You cannot use as many questions with e-mail, and instant messaging will force an interviewee to take longer to respond. Also, people tend to craft their written words differently and more carefully. You might lose the dramatic effect of an oral narrative and will certainly lose the nonverbal responses from your interviewee.

For example, when responding to you in a carefully written message, the interviewee may eliminate emotional or connotative language or description. You would then lose the vocal rate, intonation, and stress or physical behaviors (paralanguage) often associated with varying emotions, which might otherwise have helped you assess the significance of the material gathered and know how to present it during the speech.

Still, when you need testimony from a particular person or group, media-assisted interviews are better than no interview at all.

Most of the guidelines on preparing for and conducting in-person interviews will still apply for media-assisted interviews. In general, always follow good etiquette and be respectful of your interviewee and his or her time.

A few reminders and tips:

- Set up a specific time for a phone interview.
- For an interview via e-mail or a similar method, contact the interviewee in advance to formally request the interview.
- If you are sending written questions, limit how many you ask. A good guideline is to ask no more than five open-ended questions and five closed-ended questions (or questions requiring very short answers). Proofread them for any errors in spelling or grammar.

PRACTICING ETHICS: Using Interview Evidence

When using information collected from an interview, you have an ethical responsibility to:

- Report the information as accurately as possible. Quote and paraphrase correctly and in context. You might even ask the interviewee to listen to your speech or read over the outline prior to the speech event.
- Protect the interviewee from painful effects that might occur when you reveal something intimate or distressing about him or her to a larger audience. If an interviewee has requested anonymity or if you think you should protect his or her identity for any reason, use a pseudonym in your speech instead of an interviewee's real name. During the speech, inform the audience that you have changed the name to protect the privacy of the individual. If you feel that the person's identity is crucial to your speech, consult with your instructor.

4.6 How Can You Gather Support Materials with a Survey?

1 Create the Survey
2 Conduct the Survey

Surveys are similar to interviews in that their purpose is to collect information. However, they help you collect quantifiable information from a large group of individuals known as the **population**. The responses given to survey questions are not as wide open as in an interview, and the survey is usually self-administered—requiring careful construction of the questions.

Depending on your survey's focus, you can collect opinions and/or factual information from the individuals in your population. The polls we hear about prior to major elections are examples; they are statistics collected by administering surveys. When collecting support materials for a speech, you use surveys in the same way.

For example, if you are giving a persuasive speech on your school's intentions to install an emergency notification system for students, staff, and faculty, knowing how the student body and staff feel about this system would help you focus your speech as well as give you statistics related to community opinion.

Surveys can be beneficial because they:

- Are a valuable way to collect information from a large number of people
- Allow you to collect a wide variety of information
- Are relatively easy and economical to administer
- Can be simple to interpret, if your survey is simple and brief

You can find many survey tools available online for free. Search using phrases such as "free survey tools" or "free survey maker."

1
Create the Survey

Most surveys are short and self-administered, so crafting your questions is very important. Unlike interviews, surveys benefit from using more closed-ended questions. Before you begin writing questions, take a few moments to focus on what specific information you want to collect, including demographic information important to your data and topic.

→ See Chapter 2 for more information about demographics.

As you create your questions, use clear and appropriate language, ask about only one issue in each question, and try to accommodate all possible answers.

INEFFECTIVE:

1. Tell me why you shop at the farmers' market and what you buy.

This is really two open-ended questions in one, which may take too long to answer. The respondents may give incomplete responses or answer only one of the questions.

EFFECTIVE:

1. Out of the following reasons, why do you shop the farmers' market? Please check all that apply.

.... Value

.... Quality of products

.... Variety of organic products

.... Location of the market

.... Supporting local farmers

.... Other

          Please explain ....

          ....

This question asks about only one issue and offers specific responses plus an option to add one not supplied. You could quickly gather information with this question.

CHECKLIST for Surveys

❏ Am I asking only one thing in each question?

❏ Am I using language that is clear and appropriate to my respondents?

❏ Did I use mostly closed-ended questions?

❏ Did I keep the questionnaire short and simple?

Continuing with the farmers' market topic, a more developed survey would look like this.

→ See page 40 for another sample survey.

FARMERS' MARKET SURVEY

Make questions easy to read, in a consistent format.

1. Are you from Jackson City?
   .... Yes
   .... No

2. If you are not from Jackson City, do you live in Lawrence County?
   .... Yes
   .... No

3. What is your sex?
   .... Female
   .... Male

4. What is your age?
   .... Younger than 20
   20–39
   40–59
   .... 60 or older

5. How often do you visit the farmers' market?
   .... First time
   .... Weekly
   .... Every two weeks
   .... Monthly
   .... Periodically during the season

6. Why do you shop the farmers' market? (Check all that apply.)
   .... Value
   .... Quality of products
   .... Variety of organic products
   .... Location of the market
   .... Supporting local farmers
   .... Other
   Please explain ....
   ....

7. Which products do you purchase weekly? (Check all that apply.)
   .... Organic vegetables
   .... Vegetables
   .... Plants
   .... Cut flowers
   .... Cheese
   .... Meat
   .... Eggs
   .... Honey
   .... Homemade baked goods
   .... Handmade products
   .... Other
   Please explain ....
   ....

Use specific language.

2
Conduct the Survey

Once you have your survey written and reproduced (if necessary), you are ready to administer it. Most likely, you will only survey a **sample**, or portion, of the population you are researching.

Determining your sample size can be complicated if you need a low margin of error (high reliability) that what you say about the population is correct. The primary guidelines for selecting and determining the size of your survey sample are the following:

Select individuals who represent subgroups across the entire population.

Your sample should represent different genders, ages, races, religions, social statuses, and so on, if these are important to your survey. Achieving a representative sample can be difficult. To help achieve the appropriate variety:

- Be sure you ask demographic questions in the survey so that you can see if you are getting a representative sample. For example, the survey on the previous page asks demographic questions that might be helpful in analyzing the data related to farmers' markets (see questions 1–4). However, in certain situations, you may need to reword or ask different questions that are more sensitive to individuality, such as asking about sexual orientation or political and religious affiliations. Be considerate when asking personal demographic questions.

- Select individuals randomly (e.g., every tenth student) from a general and complete list, such as your campus phone directory or e-mail directory.

Survey a large-enough sample. "Large enough" means you are reasonably confident your sample represents the population and your audience will find your results credible.

Factor in the location. Be aware of how the location where you are going to conduct the survey can influence the results. Surveying students in the science building may mean most of your respondents will be science majors—which may or may not be appropriate, depending on your survey's goals.

SAMPLE ORAL CITATION FOR SURVEY MATERIAL

In my February survey of 85 out of the 120 new employees here at the plant, more than two-thirds indicated a high level of satisfaction with their jobs.

TIP: Review Your Questions

Once you have drafted a survey, you might be wise to let someone who knows how to create an effective survey (such as an instructor) take a look at it.

4.7 How Do You Research Effectively?

1 Prepare to Research
2 Be an Ethical Researcher
3 Take Thorough Notes
4 Gather Citation Information

1

Prepare to Research

Taking time to map out a research strategy before you start the research process will save you valuable time and will help you focus in on quality support material. Here are some helpful hints for creating a research strategy.

- Before you begin your research, read Chapter 5 to guide you on the types of support materials you may find and how you might use each type.

- Create a list of types of support materials you may want to locate. For example, do you need an extended example for an attention-getter? Do you need statistics to prove a point? Do you need definitions? Do you need visuals to help explain complex ideas or concepts?

- Think about which local library or libraries might offer the best information for your speech and where you will go within the library to locate materials. If your topic is professional or academic, your institution's library might be better than a city or county library.

- Consider what material you might locate online. Taking a few minutes to search online at this point might help you focus on what you need to look for in the library as well.

- Create a list of local experts that you might interview about your speech topic.

→ Chapter 5 helps you prepare to research.

2
Be an Ethical Researcher
AVOIDING PLAGIARISM

In Chapter 1, you read about plagiarism, and it is important to revisit this information as you start your research. Plagiarism is the intentional or accidental use of someone else's work or ideas, including those of other students, without giving proper credit. It does not matter if this work is unpublished or published; copyrighted or not, you still need to cite the source within the oral speech, on your outline, and on any applicable presentation aids. Page 16 lists materials you must cite when using them in a speech. Remember, there are two types of plagiarism:

- Blatant plagiarism—occurs either when speakers take an entire speech or document and present it as their own or when speakers take pieces of information from other sources and link them together, creating an entire speech of someone else's words or ideas.

- No-citation plagiarism—occurs when speakers fail to give source credit to a specific part of their speech that is borrowed from another source.

The best practice is to cite the creator of anything you use if you didn't create it or it isn't common knowledge. An example of common knowledge is that Rome is the capital of Italy.

Be sure your research notes are clearly matched to their sources. Keep track of when you are directly quoting versus paraphrasing source material. Use ellipsis dots (...) to indicate deletions from direct quotations.

→ See page 99 for more on source citations.

GETTING THE WHOLE STORY

Preventing plagiarism is an important step toward being an ethical speaker but is only a portion of your ethical responsibility when collecting and using support material. As you conduct an ethical search for material, think about the following suggestions.

- Cover as many aspects and views of your topic as possible. Make sure you research the whole story and other perspectives. For example, don't rely on one book or article for your entire speech. Also, consider sources that might present a different view to your topic.

- Record information correctly and double-check or verify with another source when necessary. For example, if a statistic seems unbelievable, verify it from another reliable source.

- Always try to use primary sources.

  → See page 111 for help on identifying primary sources.

- Be true to the author's intention.

- Use the checklist below as you research, to keep in mind five important characteristics of effective support materials.

CHECKLIST for Evaluating Support Materials

- ❏ Is the information accurate?
- ❏ Is the information current and timely?
- ❏ Is the information complete? Am I missing anything?
- ❏ Will my audience view the information and the source as trustworthy?
- ❏ Is the information suitable for my audience?

3
Take Thorough Notes

Taking detailed notes is the key to good research, so establish a note-taking system. Most students use one of three basic methods:

- Take notes on note cards; on sheets of paper; or electronically on a tablet, computer, or phone.

- Photocopy from sources, print pages, or save PDFs containing support materials. Software such as OneNote, Zotero, or Mendeley can be helpful.

- Use a combination of written note taking and copying/printing/saving.

Any of these methods can be effective, but handwritten or typed notes (either alone or in combination with the other methods) can work especially well when creating a speech. Here are some helpful hints for tackling the task of thoroughly researching your topic.

- As you read, be ready to type or write. You don't want to waste time re-locating sources and materials.

- Use a separate card, piece of paper, or electronic file for each major research category in your speech, and create a logical naming system for them. For example, you might name an electronic file "intro and conclusion material" or "Main point 1 information." Or, you might have a series of note cards categorized as "introduction material" or "Main point 1." Your working outline will help you with these broad naming systems.

- You should always record written citation information before you begin to record information from each source (including

any sources for borrowed presentation aids). If using cards or paper, make sure you have a method for connecting all cards or pages to a specific citation. Creating correct and effective written and oral citations begins when you start your research.

→ See page 99 for how to gather citation information.

- Leave extra space between entries so you can add comments as you go. If you are working with note cards, use one for each segment of information.

- Make your notes as detailed as possible. You don't want to struggle to decipher your own notes.

- Collect more support material than you might think you need. It is always better to have too much than not enough.

- Considering and recording how you might orally cite each segment of information while you have the source in front of you might be helpful later. This is particularly important when using secondary sources, as you will need to note the primary sources they are quoting.

- Keep your notes in a safe place, and back up often if using an electronic method.

> **TIP: Keeping Track**
>
> If you use a combination of note taking and photocopying, make sure you have a method to match your notes with the right photocopy so that you can create accurate source citations.

4
Gather Citation Information

Most beginning speech classes require students to use the style manual of either the *Modern Language Association (MLA)* or the *American Psychological Association (APA)* to cite sources properly in the written outline.

Creating your speech outline and oral citations will be much easier if you adhere to your assigned style as you take your research notes. Keep your style manual handy so that you can refer to it for citation specifics. The majority of libraries have the most recent version of the commonly used manuals in their reference collections.

Most major style formats will require some or all of the following information.

- Author and/or editor names
- Title of the main source (book, magazine, newspaper, website, etc.)
- Title of a specific article, essay, or other item being used from within a larger main source
- Publisher or, for a website, the sponsoring organization
- Date of publication
- Date of retrieval for electronic sources
- Web address (URL) for a website
- The issue, volume, and/or number of a periodical (especially a journal), if given
- The name of the database you used to access a source, if applicable
- The digital object identifier (DOI), if one is given
- Page numbers

Collect as much of this information as you can while you are researching, even if you are not sure how much of it you will need, to avoid having to search for it again later. Photocopies of title pages and copyright pages, or printouts of web pages that show URL information in the headers and footers, can help serve as backups to your notes. The URL is the most commonly forgotten piece of information; if there is no DOI, APA style requires including the URL in the citation, and MLA style recommends it.

Citing your sources correctly on your outline and during your oral presentation is the only way to prevent plagiarism.

→ See pages 120–123 and 146–151 for how to create oral and written citations.

TIP: Copyright Laws and Fair Use

Copyright helps the creators of written and artistic works to control the use of their works. In the classroom, fair use rules allow you to use most copyrighted works if cited correctly.

Outside of the classroom, you are more restricted and need to get permission to post, copy, or distribute the works of others. This includes posting on websites and other social media forums.

See www.copyright.gov or www.umuc.edu /library/libhow/copyright.cfm for more details about fair use.

Chapter 4: Review

ASSESSING YOUR KNOWLEDGE

4.1 Where Do You Locate Support Materials?

Objective 4.1: **IDENTIFY WHERE TO LOCATE SUPPORT MATERIALS**

Good research skills help you find effective *support materials* (or *evidence*)—information that explains, elaborates, or validates your speech topic. Support materials come from different sources such as books, magazines, journals, and websites. You can locate many support materials and sources by using the Internet, libraries, interviews, and surveys.

→ See pages 68–69.

4.2 What Does the Internet Have to Offer You?

Objective 4.2: **DESCRIBE THE DIFFERENT INTERNET TOOLS AND SOURCES**

Search engines, commercial websites, nonprofit organization websites, blogs, and personal websites are all online resources for locating support material. When using these resources for a specific class, make sure they are acceptable and appropriate.

→ See pages 70–75.

4.3 What Does the Library Have to Offer You?

Objective 4.3: **DESCRIBE THE DIFFERENT LIBRARY TOOLS AND SOURCES**

Library resources include the catalog, databases containing collections of published works, books, newspapers, magazines, newsletters, journals, and reference librarians.

→ See pages 76–85.

4.4 What Can You Find Both on the Internet and in Libraries?

Objective 4.4: **DESCRIBE SOURCES FOUND BOTH ON THE INTERNET AND IN LIBRARIES**

Although you can often find many of the previously discussed sources online and in libraries, the most common sources that consistently reside in both places are government resources and reference works. Government resources can include books, reports, bills, pamphlets, maps, websites, and other documents. Reference works are such tools as dictionaries, thesauruses, yearbooks or annuals, or atlases.

→ See pages 86–87.

4.5 How Can You Gather Support Materials in an Interview?

Objective 4.5: **DISCUSS PREPARING AND CONDUCTING AN INTERVIEW**

Interviews are information-gathering sessions where you ask either one person or a group a series of prepared questions about a topic. You need to prepare for the interview by setting up a time and location for the interview and writing your questions ahead of time. Conduct your interview in person or through media-assisted devices such as the telephone, video calling, or e-mail. When conducting the interview, dress appropriately, listen carefully, ask follow-up questions, and thank the interviewee.

→ See pages 88–91.

4.6 How Can You Gather Support Materials with a Survey?

Objective 4.6: **DISCUSS PREPARING AND CONDUCTING A SURVEY**

Surveys help you collect quantifiable information from a large population. As with an interview, you want to create your survey questions with care and typically in a closed-ended format. Keep the survey simple and short. When conducting the survey, select individuals that represent the population you need to research, make sure it is a large-enough sample, and think about the best place to conduct the survey.

→ See pages 92–95.

4.7 How Do You Research Effectively?

Objective 4.7: **DESCRIBE SOME EFFECTIVE RESEARCH TECHNIQUES**

- Prepare to conduct the research. Map out a research strategy by thinking about the types of sources and support materials you may want to locate.

- Be an ethical researcher. Respect others' works by avoiding plagiarism, and research well to "get the whole story" on your topic.

- Take thorough notes. Use a system that allows you to collect detailed support material and match it to the correct sources.

- Gather citation information. Check your style manual for the types of information you will need to collect in order to create proper citations.

→ See pages 96–99.

TERMS TO REMEMBER

support materials (68)
sources (68)
search engines (70)
hits (70)
websites (71)
blog (74)
databases (78)
interviews (88)
open-ended questions (89)
closed-ended questions (89)
follow-up questions (90)
surveys (92)
population (92)
sample (95)

5

SELECTING AND TESTING SUPPORT MATERIALS

What is research,
but a blind date with
knowledge.[1]

WILL HENRY

5.1 What Types of Support Materials Can You Use in Your Speech?

1 Facts
2 Definitions
3 Testimony
4 Examples
5 Statistics

1
Facts

Facts are verifiable bits of information about people, events, places, dates, and times. Most audiences will accept a fact with minor support or a simple oral citation and will not require an extended logical argument to prove the fact. The fact must be typical and from a recent reliable source. For example:

> The Washington Monument was reopened to the public on May 12, 2014, after being damaged in a 2011 earthquake.

2
Definitions

For a classroom speech on digital piracy, Jonah used a definition to gain his audience's attention:

> When you hear the word *piracy*, do you think of *Pirates of the Caribbean*? Or do you think about bootlegged copies of DVDs or music? If you answered yes to the latter question, you know that such copying can constitute digital piracy. According to Judy Strauss and Raymond Frost, in their 2013 book *E-Marketing*, this form of "piracy" is "installing computer software or other copyrighted intellectual property (such as music or movies) that the individual did not purchase."

In general, ***definitions*** are brief explanations designed to inform your audience about something unfamiliar. As you can see in Jonah's speech, a definition can also be used as a language or persuasive device. How you define a word or phrase can persuade your audience to focus their attitudes or beliefs about that word or phrase in a certain way.

3
Testimony

Testimony is firsthand knowledge or opinions, either your own or from others. It tends to be interpretive or judgmental.

Personal testimony is from your own personal experience or point of view. For example, Monica, a student, included her own story in an informative speech on adoption:

> Imagine you are six years old and your little sister is three, and the state takes you away from your birth parents. Imagine not knowing where you will live, where you will go to school, or if your little sister will go with you. That was my life when I was six. But my story has a happy ending: My sister and I were adopted by great people we now call Mom and Dad.

Monica's audience will probably view her expertise on this subject as high because she lived the experience. However, relying entirely on your own personal testimony is never a good idea. You can use it in your introduction to build your credibility or as brief examples periodically in a speech. But you must support your knowledge with other sources; never use it as the main type of source in a speech.

Lay testimony (or *peer testimony*) occurs when an ordinary person other than the speaker bears witness to his or her own experiences and beliefs. When Senator John McCain included "Joe the Plumber's" comments in the October 15, 2008, presidential debate, he was using the testimony of an ordinary person to demonstrate problems with then-senator Barack Obama's plan to solve the economic crisis.

Prestige testimony draws its effectiveness from the status of the person testifying, which often stems from his or her popularity, fame, attractiveness, high-profile activities, or age, if older. For example, advertisements and political statements that feature famous movie stars or sports figures are using prestige testimony. This testimony tends to be less credible logically but may appeal emotionally.

Expert testimony is testimony from a person the audience recognizes as an expert. The expert must be in a field related to your topic—a doctor for a medical topic, a teacher for an education topic, a scientist for a scientific topic, and so on. An expert's specialty can also be a factor; an eye doctor, for instance, is not an expert on heart surgery. Identifying your source's expertise to your audience is crucial:

> In a November 24, 2015, online press release of the Centers for Disease Control and Prevention, the director of the CDC, Dr. Tom Frieden, stated, "With about 40,000 HIV infections newly diagnosed each year in the U.S., we need to use all available prevention strategies."

CHECKLIST for Testimony

- ❏ If I am using personal testimony, do I support it with other sources?
- ❏ If I am using lay testimony, will my audience identify with the people giving the testimony and view them as credible?
- ❏ If I am using prestige testimony, will the audience view the person's reputation positively?
- ❏ If I am using expert testimony, do I tell my audience why the person is an expert?
- ❏ Are all the testimonies I use relevant to my topic?
- ❏ Is the person testifying free of bias?

4
Examples

Examples are specific instances or cases that embody or illustrate points in your speech. The content of the examples may embody or illustrate items, people, events, places, methods, actions, experiences, conditions, or other information. They act as samples, patterns, models, or standards that help your audience understand and accept your points. Effective examples bring life to your speech, making your topic vivid and concrete for your audience.

Examples fall into three categories: brief, extended, and hypothetical.

TIP: Using Examples

You can use examples to:
- Start your introduction. Often the extended example works best to grab audience attention.
- Clarify difficult ideas.
- Strengthen a point.
- Build emotional intensity. Several brief examples in a row work well.
- Give a personal touch to your speech.

CHECKLIST for Examples

❑ Will the audience view my example as typical, relevant, and believable?

❑ Is the example representative of the larger group or category that it stands for?

❑ Do I have enough examples to support my point?

❑ Am I sure that no counterexamples can disprove my point?

BRIEF EXAMPLES

Specific instances illustrating a single general notion are *brief examples*. You use this type of example to quickly illustrate something, and you can use several back-to-back to demonstrate frequency.

EXTENDED EXAMPLES

(also known as *stories, narratives, illustrations,* or *anecdotes*)

Extended examples are more detailed examples, allowing the audience to linger a bit longer on the vivid, concrete images the examples create. You can use a narrative or story in your introduction as an attention-getting device; in speeches with a general purpose to inspire; or as support material where you need to help your audience understand or make connections to your point or access their emotional responses. A good story must use language and imagery effectively to create—or transport the audience to—the world being described. The story has to fit together and be plausible in the eyes of the audience.

→ See Chapter 9 for more on effective language usage.

HYPOTHETICAL EXAMPLES

Examples based on the potential outcomes of imagined scenarios are *hypothetical examples*; they gain their power from future possibilities. An effective hypothetical example requires the speaker and the audience to have faith that the projected outcome *could* occur. In other words, the example is not real in the present but could happen in the future.

A brief example in a speech about album sales might look like this:

> In an age when single song purchases and streaming seem to be the norm, there is still hope for album sales. For example, Adele's blockbuster album *25* broke the all-time one-week sales record in just four days.

Suppose you are preparing a persuasive speech on controlling the spread of HIV in South Africa. You find the article "Women, Inequality, and the Burden of HIV" in the February 17, 2005, issue of the *New England Journal of Medicine*. Editing a small portion of the article, you create an extended example:

> Thandi Dlamini grew up in a crowded four-room house with 13 family members. As the youngest girl, she was charged with cooking, cleaning, and caring for her elders. At age 19, she met her first boyfriend. From the perspective of Thandi and the other women in her community, he was quite a catch—he was older, unmarried, and financially stable. She dreamed that one day he would offer to pay her *lobola* (bride price) and she would have her own home. Several months after meeting, he and Thandi had sexual intercourse, and she says this was her first encounter.
>
> Nine months later, she gave birth to a daughter, Zama. The baby was sick from the beginning and by six months of age was seriously failing to thrive. After being tested for HIV, Thandi was given three tragic pieces of information: She had given her daughter HIV, no treatment was available, and Zama would not live long.
>
> *Ichilo*. Disgrace. *Amahloni*. Shame. This is how Thandi describes her feelings after leaving the hospital. Thandi's boyfriend left after he heard about the baby, and Zama died shortly after that.

For instance, a speech on emergency preparedness could use a hypothetical example about local risks:

> Cities such as ours along the Mississippi River would experience great destruction if an earthquake erupted on the New Madrid Fault. One hundred years ago, when the fault last erupted, the force was so intense it changed the path of the Mississippi. That was before we settled the area and built many of our homes and businesses in big cities near the fault. If a similar quake occurred today, we could have major destruction and fatalities. Recovery would take months. Would you have enough food and water for your entire family for a week? Do you have an emergency plan to react to a quake or to contact family members? Do you have necessary medical supplies? Are you prepared?

5

Statistics

Statistics are numerical facts or data that are summarized, organized, and tabulated to present significant information about a given population (people, items, ideas, etc.). When you use statistics correctly, your audience will view them as factual and objective. Statistics should not scare or confuse you or your audience.

Descriptive statistics aim to describe or summarize characteristics of a population or a large quantity of data. For example:

> WNBA Los Angeles Sparks player Candace Parker was the the 2008 and 2013 MVP, and she has a career average of 17.8 points, 1.4 steals, 9.1 rebounds, and 32.1 minutes of playing time per game as of December 17, 2015, according to wnba.com.

The average (or *mean*) of this player's statistics over her career gives the audience an idea of her talent in a brief snapshot. As another example, if you survey your entire speech class and calculate the percentage results of the survey, you are generating descriptive statistics.

Inferential statistics aim to draw conclusions about a larger population by making estimates based on a smaller sample of that population. For example:

> Gallup.com reports that eleven percent of Americans approve of the job Congress is doing as of December 17, 2015.

This example says that only 11% of all Americans approve of the job Congress is doing. Yet the Gallup data, like most poll statistics in the news, are inferential. They come from only a portion of the population;

if the poll is trustworthy, the portion is assumed to be representative of the whole.

As another example, if you poll only *one-third* of the students taking speech classes at your school and then make predictions about *all* students taking speech classes there, you are calculating inferential statistics.

COMMON STATISTICAL MEASUREMENTS

Different statistical data can make different measurements as well. A **mean**, a **median**, and a **mode** are some of the most common measurements used in speeches.

WHAT IS IT?	EXAMPLES
A **mean** is an average of a set of numbers.	The ages of five students in a survey are 18, 19, 21, 27, and 34. Add them together, divide by 5, and your mean is 23.8.
A **median** is the "middle value" in your set of numbers after you have placed them in increasing order.	The median of the above ages is 21. If you have an even number of ages (18, 19, 21, 27), locate the two middle numbers, add them, and divide by 2 (20).
A **mode** is the number that occurs the most in your set.	19 is the mode in this set: 21, 18, 19, 27, 19. You may have more than one mode if multiple numbers occur with the same frequency, and you may not have a mode at all if each number in your set occurs only once.

WHEN TO USE STATISTICS

As you will learn in Chapter 9, words are very powerful, and most have emotional meaning that makes straightforward understanding difficult. That is the reason most people respond favorably to statistics. However, using statistics effectively depends on when you use them, their reliability, and the way you present them.

- Use statistics if they directly connect to what you are speaking about.
- Use them to make abstract ideas real or to validate an argument.
- Use them if your credibility is low.

HOW TO EVALUATE THE RELIABILITY OF STATISTICS

- Make sure the source of your statistics is a reliable source and, preferably, unbiased. Inform your audience of any biases the source of the statistics may have if you must use that source.
- Make sure your statistics are accurate. Check any calculations to confirm that they are correct.
- Verify important statistics with multiple sources for better validity.
- Do research to confirm that the collection, interpretation, and reporting methods for the statistics were ethical and valid, and that the sample is representative.
- If the statistics are based on a poll, any differences shown by the poll should be less than the poll's margin of error.
- Assess how you report the statistics to make sure you do not twist their meaning for the benefit of your speech.

HOW TO PRESENT STATISTICS

- Explain clearly to your audience what the numbers mean. Brief examples and visual aids often help make statistics understandable.
- Comparing statistics can help explain them. Be sure to compare like things.
- Use them with stories, illustrations, or ancedotes to make the statistics more memorable.
- Compare a statistic over time.

  In 2014 there were 12 car-related deaths during the holiday weekend, in 2015 there were 10, and in 2016 there were 6.

- Avoid or simplify complicated statistics.
- Use statistics in moderation. Too many can make your audience stop listening.
- Use the most appropriate statistical measurement. For example, look at the mean and the mode examples on the previous page. When considering the students' ages, the mean is 23.8; the median is 21 and determines those in the lower half of the age range. You could then say,

  Students under 21 are youngest in this group.

- Use language that hints at how important your statistics are. For example:

  If you remember one thing from this speech, designated driver programs save lives!

- When giving the statistics, use facial expressions that relate to the data (surprise, shock, or sadness), speak slower than your usual speech, and articulate distinctly.

  → See Tab 4 for help with language, delivery, and presentation aids.

5.2 How Do You Determine What Types of Sources and Support Materials to Use?

1 **Consider Your Own Personal Knowledge**

2 **Consider Primary vs. Secondary Sources**

3 **Consider Scholarly vs. Popular Sources**

4 **Consider Your Topic Needs**

1

Consider Your Own Personal Knowledge

Use your personal experience as an added value to your speech but not for your *entire* speech. Even when you know a considerable amount about your topic, you need to demonstrate to your audience that your knowledge is credible. The best way to do that is to cite other material supporting your ideas or position.

WHEN CAN YOU USE YOUR OWN PERSONAL KNOWLEDGE?

Use your personal experience to build your own ethos (credibility) and to give a personal face to your topic. Your personal experience can be an excellent source of examples, definitions, facts, and emotional appeal. Again, use other sources for the bulk of your speech, to support your ideas and establish your credibility and reliability. Without support, your personal knowledge may be dismissed by your audience.

An *ineffective* use of personal experience would be giving a speech about your summer vacation to Africa with only a step-by-step account of your trip and your opinion of it. An *effective* use of personal experience would be to use information from historical documents about places you visited, published travel guides, articles, and books on Africa for the bulk of the speech. Then you could add your personal experience throughout, giving life to the facts.

CONFIDENCE BOOSTER

If you know you have interesting, current, and reliable materials, you can be proud of your speech and confident about giving it.

2

Consider Primary vs. Secondary Sources

One of the first source and support material decisions you need to make is whether to use primary or secondary sources or both. Each of these types of sources plays an important role in formal speech composing.

WHAT IS IT?	EXAMPLES
Primary sources are the original sources of the information. Primary source material is the closest to what is being reported on or studied; it is not being quoted by a second party.	Original research reports, photographs, graphics, videos, or documentaries; historical brochures or pamphlets; autobiographies; novels; poems; some speeches; letters or e-mails; diaries or blogs; some websites; eyewitness accounts
	Interviews, surveys, or field research you conduct about your topic
Secondary sources cite, review, or build upon other sources. Secondary sources quote or paraphrase primary sources.	Most newspaper and magazine articles; some journal articles; reviews; biographies; reprinted photographs or graphics; some websites quoting other sources
	Most speeches you give are themselves secondary sources. Rarely, if ever, should you give a speech where you do not use information from other primary and secondary sources to support your speech.

WHEN DO YOU USE PRIMARY OR SECONDARY SOURCES?

Both primary research and secondary sources will offer strong support materials for certain topics. Sometimes, one is better than the other, but you will usually use both.

For example, if you are giving a speech about parking needs on your campus or the potential need for an on-site day care at your corporate headquarters, you will need to do primary research to get a feel for the local needs. Using secondary research from other institutions or corporations that have positively implemented the program that you are arguing for will strengthen your argument even further.

In another speech, you might focus mostly on cancer statistics collected by physicians at major medical clinics, to motivate your audience to stop smoking or to incorporate healthier eating habits. When you quote these statistics, you are using information from a secondary source. However, sprinkling personal narratives from real people you personally interview throughout those statistics humanizes the numbers and allows you to use primary source materials as well.

3

Consider Scholarly vs. Popular Sources

The basic differences between scholarly and popular sources are as follows.

WHAT IS IT?	CHARACTERISTICS	EXAMPLES
Scholarly sources are written for readers who are specialists in their academic or professional fields.	• Are written by authors with academic credentials related to your topic • Discuss and research topics at length • Use very technical language • Aim to educate specialists • Cite all sources supporting the research	Articles in journals, books, or research databases, or on professional web pages
Popular sources are written for general readers.	• Are often written by journalists • Tend to be short discussions • Use common language • Aim to educate and/or entertain the general public • Often cite no sources or give sources that are brief and incomplete	Articles in newspapers, magazines, newswires, or popular-culture databases; news-related web pages

WHEN DO YOU USE SCHOLARLY OR POPULAR SOURCES?

Choosing to use scholarly or popular sources depends heavily on your topic and your audience, but you will always use at least one type and may use both. The main reason you would rely on one more than the other resides in the *credibility of the author* and the *reliability of the information.*

Most audience members will view scholarly research as more trustworthy and accurate than information from popular sources. However, some topics will not need that level of integrity or will relate more to popular culture than to academia. Even within these two categories, you will discover varying degrees of credibility and reliability. A well-regarded popular source that focuses on a subject is credible and reliable for a speech on that topic (such as *Fortune* magazine for finance issues), whereas you will be hard pressed to find an audience that values information from the many tabloids on the market today.

4

Consider Your Topic Needs

Some topics demand special consideration when you are selecting your sources or support materials. The guidelines in this table are only suggestions, not steadfast requirements or limitations. Remember, always keep your relationship with the topic as well as your audience in mind as you make your decisions about support materials and sources.

TOPICS WITH SPECIAL DEMANDS	TYPES OF SUPPORT MATERIALS	TYPES OF SOURCES
Controversial or highly emotional topics	Statistics, examples, expert testimony, definitions, facts	Rely more on scholarly or highly respected or focused popular sources. Primary sources are a necessity.
Topics with a purpose to incite emotions or inspire	Examples (especially narratives), lay and expert testimonies	Popular sources tend to contain more emotionally evocative examples and lay testimony. Expert testimony will more often be found in scholarly sources or your own primary research (interviews and surveys).
Technical topics	Definitions, facts, brief examples, statistics	Rely more on scholarly or highly respected or focused popular sources. Primary sources are a necessity. If the audience is unfamiliar with the topic, include definitions of technical terms.
Abstract topics	Definitions, facts, brief examples (precise narratives)	Use scholarly or focused popular sources.
Topics relating to current events	Statistics, examples, testimony, facts, definitions	Current events will require you to rely more on popular sources because the topics are too new to appear in scholarly sources. Scholarly sources may offer historical comparisons to the current topic.
Topics your audience knows well	Depends on the topic, but unique examples, statistics, facts, and testimony will help you inspire the audience to listen.	Depends on the topic, but the key here is finding unique information to keep your knowledgeable audience interested and learning.

5.3 What Do You Evaluate in Your Support Materials?

1 **Accuracy**
2 **Currency**
3 **Completeness**
4 **Trustworthiness**
5 **Suitability**

1
Accuracy

Several years ago, a student majoring in biology wanted to persuade her class to be open to the potential of cloning for medical reasons. She began her speech with an extended example from published research, unaware that the research had recently been declared invalid. The student had used only one source and failed to verify the information with any other sources; as a result, she used an inaccurate example that hurt her credibility.

Accuracy is an ethical consideration for the original creators of the information and for you. Accurate support materials must meet two standards.

- First, the information should be verifiable from the original source as well as supported by multiple sources. You should use only materials you can verify as accurate or from an extremely reliable source.

- Second, you must use your support materials within their original context. Do not twist the information to fit an agenda that does not match the author's intent.

The accuracy of the information's creator or source is out of your control. However, you can attempt to verify information with other sources, evaluate your sources for accuracy, and always use sources that are extremely reliable. Even trusted sources can occasionally report false information. Your ethical responsibility is to present the most accurate, verifiable support materials possible.

2

Currency

If your audience knows more recent information about your topic than your speech reflects, your credibility and the potential for your speech to achieve its general purpose will drop considerably.

- First, you must make sure you have the most current information possible about your topic, which is not as easy as it sounds.

  For instance, if you are researching online, you can easily pull up outdated web pages that seem to have current information. Always check the copyright date of the page or the last time it was updated. Usually, you can find that information at the bottom of the first page (the home page). If you cannot locate a date, verify the information with another source.

- Second, if your topic is not one that is changing rapidly, a good general research rule to follow is to use information published or collected in the past five years. Some exceptions might be if your topic is historical, the older material is very important, or no recent information is available.

- Third, you need to be as current as possible with your information right up to the moment you give your speech. Changes can happen quickly, especially if your topic is unpredictable or related to current events. You are responsible for knowing about new developments that affect your topic.

  For example, suppose you had been scheduled to give a speech on February 5, 2015, and your topic was an informative speech on Pluto. You would have needed to make last-minute adjustments to your speech and visuals, because NASA's New Horizons Spacecraft returned new images of Pluto and its largest moon, Charon, on February 4, 2015.

Some of the best speech topics are unpredictable (which is what makes them interesting), so do not be afraid of these topics. Just be diligent and stay on top of the latest information.

TIP: Staying Current

Listening to a national news show while you are dressing, driving, cleaning, or cooking is an easy way for you to stay current. You can also subscribe to a respected national paper or news magazine or read one online. *The Week* magazine is an excellent condensed version of a week of information.

3
Completeness

If you intend to inform or persuade your audience, you need a sufficient amount of comprehensive, detailed information to achieve your goal. Two or three examples are not enough to demonstrate or prove your central idea or even show a trend. Persuasive speeches, especially, need complete information behind them to be ethical and influential.

For example, in recent years, many U.S. cities have supported the use of tasers by law enforcement personnel. As new data and more examples are available about the potential harm these devices can render, more citizens are changing their views about tasers. Two or three examples might illustrate a minor point about the hazards of tasers but are not complete enough to sway opinion or effectively inform an audience of how harmful tasers are overall. To give complete information, you may need to summarize several types of examples or incorporate wide-ranging national statistics about injuries or deaths caused by tasers.

TIP: Sufficient Support

There is no formula for how much support is enough, but you can get an indication by thinking about what you are asking your audience to understand or agree to. The more you want your audience to accept or change—or the less your audience already knows about the topic—the more support materials you need.

4
Trustworthiness

Your support materials' trustworthiness is similar to your ethos: It is measured by your audience's opinion, not yours. If your *audience* does not have the necessary information or respect to view your support materials as credible, they are not.

- Select materials from credible sources and help your audience view them as such. The audience should see the author or creator of the information as an expert on the topic. Provide the audience with the author's or creator's credentials (education, training, position, and/or other experience that relates to your topic).

- Select materials from unbiased sources. The author or creator of the materials should not have a hidden agenda—or if there is one, you need to inform your audience of that bias or not use the materials.

- Be diligent in holding electronic sources to high standards of credibility. As noted earlier, the Internet provides a lot of information, but anyone can easily create or change a website. Always ask:

  – What is the purpose of the site?

  – What type of site is it?

  – Who sponsors the site? Who contributes?

  – Are there advertisements on the site, and, if so, how might they bias the information?

  – When was the site created? Has it been updated recently?

  → See page 71 for more tips on evaluating online sources.

5
Suitability

Your support materials are suitable when your audience is able to view the materials as relevant to them, to the topic, and to the occasion.

For example, suppose you are from a country where water shortages are a concern, and you want to give a persuasive speech about water conservation to students in an area of the United States where water is abundant. Using data, examples, personal narrative, and other information related only to other countries currently experiencing water shortages—such as several along the equator—will not resonate with your U.S. audience. You must use at least some support materials demonstrating the effects of water shortages within the United States.

You never want to have a moment when your audience questions why you said something or views your materials as awkward or inappropriate.

To demonstrate suitability:

- Use support materials with a purpose that is clear and concrete.

  → See the section "Use Your Materials Purposefully and in Different Ways" on page 119.

- Use materials that relate back to your central idea.

- Include information that shows your audience why the materials are relevant to them, to the topic, and to the occasion.

- Use support materials acceptable to the situation. For example, if you are giving a speech at a professional organization, you need material from professional or academic sources. Remember that in the academic setting, blogs, tweets, or personal websites are not always viewed as trustworthy or suitable. If you wish to use these types of Internet sources, make sure that your instructor allows them, and then verify trustworthiness and content.

PRACTICING ETHICS: Support Materials

Manipulating your support materials to prevent your audience from being rational—or to make them overly emotional—is extremely unethical behavior. Remember these ethical guidelines when using support materials.

- Present hypothetical examples as such—not as factual.
- Present prestige testimony honestly and not as expert testimony.
- Interpret and represent statistics fairly and accurately.
- Use a variety of support materials and sources.
- Include and note primary sources orally during your speech.
- Research thoroughly for alternate points of view.
- Use and quote materials in their correct context. Do not omit information.
- Use reliable, trustworthy sources.
- Give proper oral citations (include some variation of the date of publication, type of publication, title, author, and highlights of author's credentials). See pages 120–123 for guidelines.
- Disclose any agendas or biases a source might have.

5.4 How Do You Use Support Materials Effectively?

1 **Use Quotation and Paraphrasing Effectively**

2 **Use Your Materials Purposefully and in Different Ways**

1

Use Quotation and Paraphrasing Effectively

The bulk of your speech should be your words and organization, but quoting your sources at key points can provide compelling additional support. Directly quoting from a source is generally more effective than paraphrasing. Quote precisely if the material is short and says something better than you can or is memorable. In your speech, signal a direct quotation orally by using a technique such as:

> Craig Welch writes in his November 2015 *National Geographic* article, "A Blueprint for a Carbon-Free America," "Today only 13 percent of U.S. electricity comes from renewables."

Paraphrase when the section you wish to use is long, wordy, unclear, or awkward for you to say. **Paraphrasing** restates the content of the material in a simpler format and in your own words, using language appropriate for your audience. For example, here is a section of text from Aristotle's *Rhetoric*:

> The modes of persuasion are the only true constituents of the art: everything else is merely accessory. These writers, however, say nothing about enthymemes, which are the substance of rhetorical persuasion, but deal mainly with nonessentials.

Here is how a speaker might paraphrase this:

> According to the *Rhetoric*, Aristotle believed that logic was the only true method of persuasion and that everything else was merely ornamentation. Other classical scholars focused on less-vital aspects of rhetoric and ignored the enthymeme, the classical logical argument.

Remember, when you summarize, quote, or paraphrase the work of others, you must cite the source orally and in your outline.

2
Use Your Materials Purposefully and in Different Ways

You will use most support materials for one of four purposes.

- To clarify unfamiliar or abstract information
- To hold your audience's attention
- To help your audience remember important aspects of your speech
- To prove a claim your speech makes

To achieve the purpose of each of your support materials, you can employ different approaches. Here are four common ones to try.

DIRECT

The easiest and most common way to use support materials is to be simple and straightforward. Here, you identify and use materials for what they are: examples, facts, definitions, testimony, or statistics.

For example, for a class speech on Argentine football (soccer) player Diego Maradona, Felipe creates this sentence:

> In the 1986 World Cup quarter-final round, Diego Maradona scored two goals now known as the "Hand of God" and the "Goal of the Century."

This statement is a direct use of support materials—in this case, Felipe simply presents facts as facts.

COMPARISON

When you use support materials to point out similarities between two or more ideas, things, factors, or issues, you are using them as a **comparison**. For example, Felipe wants to assert that Maradona was as great a player as the famous Brazilian Pelé:

> Diego Maradona and Pelé each made it to four FIFA World Cup finals.

CONTRAST

When you use support materials to point out differences between two or more ideas, things, factors, or issues, you are using them in **contrast**. Felipe tries this:

> Pelé won three FIFA World Cups in his career, whereas Diego Maradona won only one.

Felipe's contrast of the players' World Cup successes is correct, but highlighting this contrast might suggest that Pelé was a better player than Maradona, not that they were equal.

ANALOGY

An **analogy** helps explain the unfamiliar by comparing and contrasting it to what is familiar. The key to using analogy is for your audience to be familiar with one of the two things being compared and contrasted. There are two types of analogies:

- **Literal analogy** compares and contrasts two like things.

  > Although Maradona and Pelé came from different playing backgrounds, their similar, exceptional career successes make them the greatest footballers of all time.

  Felipe can discuss Pelé and Maradona as two like things—successful players. You might use literal analogy if you are advocating once choice over another.

- **Figurative analogy** compares and contrasts two essentially different things.

  > Diego Maradona is like a god to many Argentines.

  Felipe can use this analogy to highlight Maradona's popularity.

5.5 How Do You Cite Sources Orally?

1 **Collect the Necessary Content**
2 **Create and Deliver Oral Citations**

1 Collect the Necessary Content

You know that when you write a paper you need to cite your sources. When you write and give a speech, you also need to use citations. *Citations* are the oral and written credits for the original sources of the support materials you are using.

As a speechwriter in a class, you will need to use both oral and written citations—oral during the speech and written ones on the outline. Chapter 6 will help you with written citations, and writing style manuals offer specific guidelines on how to format written in-text citations and source pages for your outlines.

Here we are concerned with the oral citations. During a speech, the oral citations you use must always be incorporated so that the audience clearly hears them, because listeners do not have the outline or source page. Compared to a written paper, however, your oral citation is not as detailed. Your first citation of a source will be the most detailed, and any later reference to the same source needs just enough information to connect it back to the original.

For example, Nina is doing a presentation on how to attract hummingbirds to your backyard. She created a list of flowers known for their appeal to "hummers," from an article in an issue of *Birds and Blooms*. Her oral citation is:

> As Danielle Calkins notes in her June/July 2011 *Birds and Blooms* article, "Hummingbird Award Winners," these are 10 great plants to attract these tiny birds.

This could be Nina's first oral citation for this source during her speech.

The table below suggests the potential content of your first oral citations for different sources. Use it to help you collect the necessary information for your oral citations.

Your oral citation should include enough information so that proper credit is given and so that an audience member could locate the item being cited if he or she desired to do so.

If you need to create a written text of your speech (such as an outline), or a works cited or reference page, you will need more-specific information.

→ See pages 99 and 146–151 for more information on written citations and style manuals.

CONTENTS OF ORAL CITATIONS

TYPE OF SOURCE	WHAT TO INCLUDE IN YOUR ORAL CITATION
Website	Identify it as a website; give title of web page, site sponsor, and either the date of publication, last update, or when you accessed it; may include article title.
Magazine or journal	Identify it as an article; give name of magazine or journal, author and qualifications, and date of publication; may include article title.
Newspaper	Identify it as an article; give name of paper, author and qualifications, and date of issue; may include article title.
Book	Identify that it is a book; give title, author and qualifications, and date of publication.
Government document	Provide title, name of agency or branch of government publishing it, and date of publication.
Brochure or pamphlet	Identify it as a brochure or pamphlet; give title, who published it, and date of publication.
Reference works	Provide title and date of publication.
Videotape, DVD, or CD	Provide title of tape or disk and date.
Television or radio	Provide title of the show, channel or network, and date of broadcast.
Interview conducted by you	Identify yourself as the interviewer; give name and identity of the person interviewed and date of interview.

The next section offers examples and advice on how to construct and deliver your oral citations.

2

Create and Deliver Oral Citations

The main rule of oral citation is to make sure you cite everything you borrow from another source. This includes words, phrases, sentences, paragraphs, photos, diagrams, video and audio clips, graphs, and so on. If the item is not original to you, you must cite the source.

Your citations should not be too repetitive, misplaced, or boring. You want your audience to listen to them. Follow these suggestions:

Use variety when possible. Once you have given a detailed oral citation, subsequent citations for the same source can be shorter. For example, recall that Nina's first citation was very detailed:

> As Danielle Calkins notes in her June/July 2011 *Birds and Blooms* article, "Hummingbird Award Winners," these are 10 great plants to attract these tiny birds.

Her second citation of this source might use the author's last name and the article title.

> Again, Calkins, in her article, "Hummingbird Award Winners,"…

If Nina cites the same article again, she might include only a very brief reference:

> AAS stands for All-America Selections, according to Calkins.

After you have cited a source three or four times, if the citations are close together, you can use a simple citation like Nina's last one.

Do not put every citation at the beginning or end of a quotation, summary, or paraphrase. Write them in different ways. Variety is the key to avoiding ineffective repetition and keeping your audience's attention.

Place your citations with the information being borrowed. A common error is to group all citations together at the beginning of a point or to add them on to the end of the speech.

INEFFECTIVE:
The material from this section of my speech came from a special issue of *Time* magazine, April 19, 2010; Rachel Carson's book *Silent Spring;* and the spring 2016 *Nature Conservancy* magazine.

The proper way to orally cite your sources is to cite each at the time you use it in the speech. If you have a lot of summarized information from one source, you might use this type of oral citation to begin the section:

MORE EFFECTIVE:
The information summarized in my next point comes from the 2002 edition of *Silent Spring* by Rachel Carson.

If using visuals from another source, it is best to cite the source on your presentation aid and to orally note the citation during the speech.

CITATION ON A PRESENTATION AID:
Zigrosser, Carl. *Prints and Drawings of Käthe Kollwitz.* Dover Publications, 1969.

ORAL CITATION:
This 1927 self-portrait of Käthe, from the book *Prints and Drawings of Käthe Kollwitz,* depicts a solemn Käthe.

To draw your audience's attention to the written citation, you might gesture at its location on the aid. Placing the written citation in the same location on every aid will help guide your audience's eyes to it each time.

Be enthusiastic about your sources. Be proud of the research you did to support your speech. Speak clearly and maintain good volume as you cite sources. Use a variety of inflection that demonstrates your enthusiasm.

Practice saying your citations when you rehearse your speech. If you practice, you will remember better to include your citations; they will become more familiar; and you can further craft them to be effective. The table below shows the five types of support materials and gives sample beginnings for orally citing each type.

SAMPLE ORAL CITATIONS

TYPE OF SUPPORT MATERIALS	BEGINNING OF AN ORAL CITATION
Examples	"As Desdemona says in Shakespeare's *Othello*..." "Let me give you two examples of identity theft. The first comes from the May 10th issue of *Newsweek*..."
Facts	"As published in the July 2015 issue of the *Conservationist*, the diet of a largemouth bass consists of..."
Definitions	"*Time* magazine—in its March 10, 2014, issue—defines..."
Testimony	"In an interview I conducted last October with Dr. James Wing in our history department, Dr. Wing said..." "As Chantal Smith, an eyewitness to the plane crash, said in January..."
Statistics	"'Eight out of 10 child safety seats are not properly installed,' according to the National Transportation Safety Board's website on October 1, 2012." "In the December 12, 2015, issue of Lancet, available online at..."

→ Chapter 6 on outlining and Chapter 10 on delivery offer more citation examples and advice.

PRACTICING ETHICS: Oral Plagiarism

Not citing—or ineffectively citing—your sources during your oral presentation is plagiarism and unethical. Remember to cite all sources when you use someone else's ideas, thoughts, terms, data, audio, and visuals.

CHECKLIST for Oral Citations

❑ Does my citation include the necessary information?

❑ Am I citing everything borrowed from another source?

❑ Am I presenting my oral citations in a variety of formats?

❑ Are my citations properly placed?

❑ Have I practiced saying my citations within my speech, and do they seem to be a natural part of the speech?

Chapter 5: Review

ASSESSING YOUR KNOWLEDGE

5.1 What Types of Support Materials Can You Use in Your Speech?

Objective 5.1: **IDENTIFY THE TYPES OF SUPPORT MATERIALS**

- Facts are verifiable bits of information about people, events, places, dates, and time.
- Definitions are brief explanations.
- Testimony is firsthand knowledge or opinions of either yourself or others. Personal, lay, prestige, and expert are the four types of testimony.
- Examples are specific instances or cases that embody or illustrate points in your speech. There are brief, extended, and hypothetical examples.
- Statistics are numerical facts or data that are summarized, organized, and tabulated to present significant information about a given population. Statistics can be descriptive or inferential.

→ See pages 104–109.

5.2 How Do You Determine What Types of Sources and Support Materials to Use?

Objective 5.2: **EXPLAIN HOW TO DETERMINE WHAT SOURCES AND SUPPORT MATERIALS TO USE**

- Consider your own personal knowledge, but only as a starting point or for personal information to build credibility.
- Consider primary vs. secondary sources. Primary sources are the original sources of information. Secondary sources cite, review, or build upon other sources.

- Consider scholarly vs. popular sources. Scholarly sources are written for readers who are specialists in their academic or professional fields. Popular sources are written for general readers.
- Consider your topic needs.

→ See pages 110–113.

5.3 What Do You Evaluate In Your Support Materials?

Objective 5.3: **DISCUSS HOW TO EVALUATE SUPPORT MATERIALS**

- Accuracy: Is the source material verifiable, and can you accurately use it as intended by the original context?
- Currency: Is the material the most current information possible?
- Completeness: Is there a sufficient amount of comprehensive, detailed information to achieve your goal?
- Trustworthiness: Is the source credible and unbiased?
- Suitability: Is the material clear and concrete? Is it suitable to your topic, audience, and the situation?

→ See pages 114–117.

5.4 How Do You Use Support Materials Effectively?

Objective 5.4: **DESCRIBE EFFECTIVE WAYS TO USE SUPPORT MATERIALS**

- Use quotations and paraphrasing effectively and ethically.
- Use your materials purposefully and in different ways. Common approaches are to use support materials in a direct way, as a comparison, in contrast, and as an analogy. Analogies can be literal or figurative.

→ See pages 118–119.

5.5 How Do You Cite Sources Orally?

Objective 5.5: **EXPLAIN HOW TO CITE SOURCES ORALLY**

- You must collect the necessary content for an oral citation. If you are creating correct written citations on your outline, you have the information you need for an oral citation.
- You must create and deliver oral citations. Vary the style of the oral citations often throughout the speech, position your citation with the information you are borrowing, and be enthusiastic about your sources.

→ See pages 120–123.

TERMS TO REMEMBER

facts (104)
definitions (104)
testimony (105)
personal testimony (105)
lay testimony (105)
prestige testimony (105)
expert testimony (105)
examples (106)
brief examples (106)
extended examples (106)
hypothetical examples (106)
statistics (108)
descriptive statistics (108)
inferential statistics (108)
mean (108)
median (108)
mode (108)
primary sources (111)
secondary sources (111)
scholarly sources (112)
popular sources (112)
paraphrasing (118)
comparison (119)
contrast (119)
analogy (119)
literal analogy (119)
figurative analogy (119)
citations (120)

Practical Pointers for Tab 2

FAQs

Are there other tips for locating information on the Internet? I can't find anything related to my narrowed topic.

- Use specific search terms or phrases. Try to break down your topic into individual concepts. Try different words or phrases that mean the same thing or are similar.
- Look for options on the search page (scrolling down the page, if needed) to further limit the search by factors such as date or only full text.
- Ask a librarian to help you get started with an effective search. Be sure to bring along your assignment, your research notes so far, and your working outline.

Can I use a website or software to create citations?

It is always best to ask your instructor about his or her policy for creating your citations. Most instructors want you to learn what it takes to write correct source citations, and the best way to do that is by actually doing it.

If it is acceptable to use a website or software, you still need to check the final format. The electronic versions are not always correct or current, and formatting can be lost or changed depending on what printer or computer you are using. So always check each entry for correct content and proper format.

Are there types of support material that don't need citations?

The general rule is that if your material is common knowledge or fact, you don't need documentation. For example, it is common knowledge that there are seven days in a week, that George Washington was the first U.S. president, and that Africa is a continent. However, determining what is common knowledge or fact can be difficult. It may be best to cite sources even in some cases of common knowledge and fact. It really can't hurt and will help build your ethos.

ADDITIONAL SUPPORT

If you are struggling to locate material, try these resources or ask a librarian for assistance.

To locate only websites, try these:

The Open Directory Project	dmoz.org
Best of the Web	botw.org

To locate relevant blog material, try these:

IceRocket	icerocket.com
Technorati	Technorati.com
Regator	regator.com

Beyond YouTube or Bing, Google, and Yahoo! Videos, try these to locate multimedia material:

Blinkx	blinkx.com
FindSounds	FindSounds.com
Library of Congress	loc.gov

If you need more help with citing sources and understanding plagiarism, explore plagiarism.org.

TAB 3
Creating

6 OUTLINING YOUR SPEECH

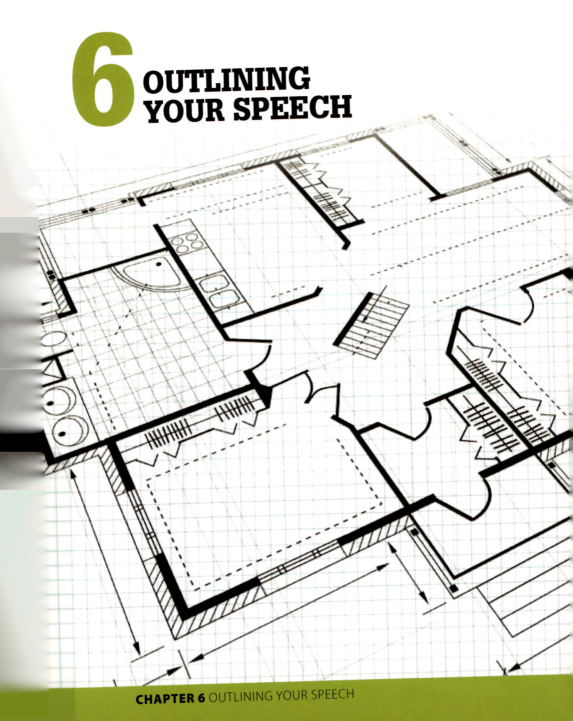

6.1 What Are the Parts of an Outline?

1 Introduction
2 Body of the Speech
3 Conclusion
4 Source Page

Why do I need an outline? is possibly the question most frequently asked by beginning speakers.

Much like a building designed by an architect, successful speeches contain distinctive features and components that are carefully structured for a particular function and pleasing effect. Your outline is the blueprint you use to make sure everything is properly supported, in the right place, and easy to maneuver. An outline helps you:

- Ensure that your main points relate to your central idea.
- Select the appropriate organizational strategy and keep it consistent.
- Make sure your subpoints are related and subordinate.
- Evenly distribute your support materials and investigate the quality of the material.
- Formulate links between parts of the speech.
- Design a speech your audience can follow and recall.

So, let's look at the specific parts of an outline.

Order and simplification are the first steps toward the mastery of a subject — the actual enemy is the unknown.[1]

THOMAS MANN

1
Introduction

The *introduction* opens the speech, grabs the audience's attention, and previews the speech.

→ See Chapter 8 for how to create an introduction.

2
Body of the Speech

The *body* contains the central portion of the speech, including the main points, the multiple layers of subordinate points, and the links. It is fundamentally what you want to tell your audience about the topic.

Main points are the essential ideas you must cover or the main claims you wish to make, and they directly relate to your central idea. Most speeches will have two or three main points, but some speeches (usually process or persuasive) will have more— around five.

Subpoints (also called *subordinate points* or *supporting points*) offer information to support and relate back to the main point. You can have multiple layers of subpoints (e.g., your subpoints can have their own subpoints).

Links (also called *transitions*) act much like hyperlinks on your computer, which serve to make a logical jump between two places on your computer. Links in your speech will make logical connections between parts of your speech.

→ See "What Can You Use to Link Your Speech Parts Together?" on pages 144–145.

3
Conclusion

The *conclusion* ends your speech and takes one last moment to summarize and reinforce your main ideas and "wow" your audience.

→ See Chapter 8 for how to create a conclusion.

4
Source Page

Many instructors will require a page at the end of your preparation outline that indicates the sources you used in your speech. You will create this page just as you do for a formal research paper, often using the style manual for the Modern Language Association (MLA) or the American Psychological Association (APA). Style manuals are guides for writing and documenting research. Your instructor may require you to purchase a style manual, you may be able to use one located in your library's reference section, or you can consult relevant websites (see page 190 for a suggestion). Make sure you have the correct style manual and that it is the most current. Certain software packages (including Word) can help you adhere to a style, although you should always check the citations and page format for accuracy.

→ See "How Do You Create a Source Page?" on pages 148–151.

CONFIDENCE BOOSTER

Knowing your material is the best way to lower your anxiety, and the best way to learn it is to be exceedingly meticulous, comprehensive, and systematic when creating your outline.

6.2 How Can You Create an Effective Outline?

1 **Record the Topic, Specific Purpose, and Central Idea**

2 **Use Full Sentences**

3 **Cover Only One Issue at a Time**

4 **Develop the Introduction and Conclusion**

5 **Use Correct Outline Format**

6 **Use Balanced Main Points**

7 **Employ Subordination**

8 **Plan Out Formal Links**

9 **Use Proper Citations**

1
Record the Topic, Specific Purpose, and Central Idea

You should include the topic, specific purpose, and central idea at the top of the outline as a title framing the speech. Doing so will help you keep these elements of your speech in the forefront of your mind as you create the rest of the outline.

2
Use Full Sentences

Write each outline component in full sentences (but see Tip box below). This forces you to think in complete thoughts and will help you learn the speech as well as gauge its length. If you use only words or phrases in the preparation outline, you may struggle for the right words when giving the speech.

INCORRECT

> I. The beginning of soccer

CORRECT

> I. The game of soccer, or association football, has changed significantly since its beginnings.

TIP: Different Types of Outlines

Not every quality on pages 130–135 is necessary for different types of outlines. For example, you will include very few full sentences in your delivery outline. If you are not sure what your assignment requires, ask your instructor.

→ See pages 136–143 for outline examples.

3

Cover Only One Issue at a Time

Covering only one issue at a time in each outline component will help you keep your speech simple enough for delivery and will keep you from writing the speech as a manuscript. The best method is to write only one sentence per component in the body of the speech.

INCORRECT

I. The city of Anna Point needs to institute a plan to decrease the waste going to its landfill ==because== the landfill will be full in two years ==and== the waste contaminates waterways ==and== causes health risks ==or== death to humans, pets, ==and== wildlife.

Avoid using words such as **and**, **or**, **because**, or **but** to connect two independent issues in one sentence.

CORRECT

I. The city of Anna Point needs to institute a plan to decrease waste going to its landfill.
    A. Each year, tons of recyclable waste end up in Anna Point's local landfill.
        1. The city estimates that each of the 56,202 residents threw out approximately 4.29 pounds a day last year.
        2. At that rate, the waste will use up the remaining landfill space in two years.
    B. Much of the waste is . . .

4

Develop the Introduction and Conclusion

Most instructors suggest creating your introduction and conclusion after you create the body of the speech. The introduction will include an attention-getter, a statement about your credibility, material demonstrating relevance to the audience, and a preview of the speech. The conclusion will contain a summary, audience response statement, and "WOW" statement. For now, recognize that they are an integral part of the preparation outline. Beginning speakers tend to cut corners in the development of a speech by deciding to improvise the introduction and conclusion as they speak. This practice sets you up for serious problems at critical moments.

→ See Chapter 8 for how to create effective introductions and conclusions.

5
Use Correct Outline Format

The format of an outline should be very systematic, helping you to logically structure your speech and aiding you in your delivery. You should always use correct outline formatting in the body of the speech. The following guidelines will help you.

DISTINGUISHING MAIN POINTS

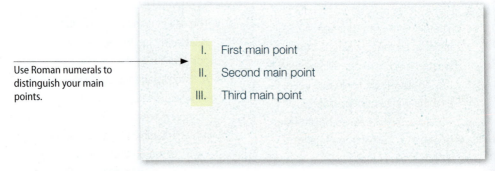

Use Roman numerals to distinguish your main points.

I. First main point

II. Second main point

III. Third main point

PATTERN OF SYMBOLS

Use a consistent pattern of symbols (e.g., uppercase letters, numbers, and lowercase letters).

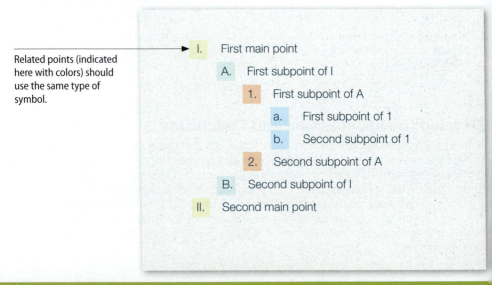

Related points (indicated here with colors) should use the same type of symbol.

I. First main point

  A. First subpoint of I

    1. First subpoint of A

      a. First subpoint of 1

      b. Second subpoint of 1

    2. Second subpoint of A

  B. Second subpoint of I

II. Second main point

SUBPOINTS

Each subpoint must have at least two subdivisions if it has any. Think of it like cutting up an apple. If you cut up an apple, you have at least two pieces. You may end up with more pieces, but you cannot divide something without a result of at least two.

For example, subpoint A has two subdivisions, 1 and 2 (indicated here with colors).

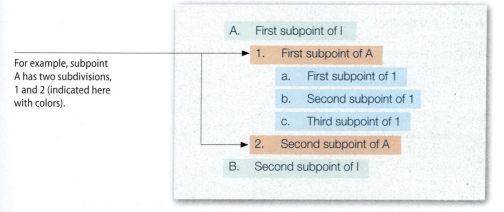

ALIGNMENT OF POINTS IN YOUR OUTLINE

Your main points should line up closest to the left margin of the page, and each subsequent subdivision should be indented further to the right.

Each main point should align left (align the periods), and each level of subpoints should be indented further to the right.

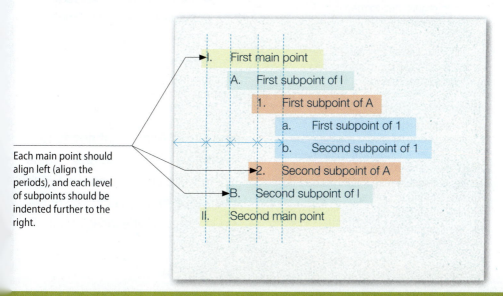

6
Use Balanced Main Points

Your main points should be equal in importance to each other. This is called a *standard of balance*. The main points will directly relate to the overall topic but should not overtly relate to each other. Each main point should coordinate with the others. For example, below are three relatively balanced main points:

> ▶ **Specific purpose:** To inform my coaching class about the development of soccer
>
> I. A brief look at early soccer explains its historical significance.
>
> II. As the game gained popularity, regulations formed out of necessity.
>
> III. Today, as an internationally popular sport, soccer has a distinct setup.

Notice that each point is unique and relates back to the specific purpose.

Each of the above points is manageable in scope and should take roughly the same amount of time to present; the "brief look" in point 1 might be a bit shorter in duration.

→ See Chapter 7 for details on how to logically organize your main points.

7
Employ Subordination

The components of your outline following each main point should be properly subordinate to the point above them. In other words, any statement that comes under a point must not be equal to or of greater importance than the point directly above it.

An easy test for this is to read the main point, mentally insert "because," and then read the subpoint. If doing so makes a logical connection between the main point and the subpoint, the subpoint is subordinate. For example, here is a main point followed by its first subpoint:

> I. The city of Anna Point needs to institute a plan to decrease waste going to its landfill.
> A. Each year, tons of recyclable waste end up in Anna Point's local landfill.

You can test the connection by mentally inserting "because":

Main point I

The city of Anna Point needs to institute a plan to decrease waste going to its landfill **because** each year, tons of recyclable waste end up in Anna Point's local landfill.

Subpoint A

8
Plan Out Formal Links

You should include links between major components of the speech. An effective speaker will lead the audience almost effortlessly from one point to another, and formal links will make this seem smooth, not jolting. For example:

> Now that we understand soccer's history and development of regulations, let's look at the international sport it is today.

→ See pages 144–145 for how to write effective links.

9
Use Proper Citations

Include in-text citations within the outline itself and a page with sources listed according to an acceptable style manual. In the outline, you can do your in-text citations one of two ways. Your first option is to follow your style manual. This example follows the MLA style of using *parenthetical citations*, or placing the citation information in parentheses at the end of a sentence:

> I. A brief look at early soccer explains its historical significance.
>   A. Soccer can trace its roots back to China's Han dynasty and game of Cuju (Goldblatt).

Alternatively, you could incorporate the citation into the outline text. This method is especially useful for beginning speakers. For example:

> I. A brief look at early soccer explains its historical significance.
>   A. According to David Goldblatt in his 2008 book *The Ball Is Round: A Global History of Soccer*, soccer can trace its roots back to China's Han dynasty and game of Cuju.

Before you decide how to cite your sources within the outline text, make sure you first check your instructor's requirements.

→ See pages 146–151 for more help with citations.

6.3 What Are the Different Types of Outlines?

1 The Working Outline
2 The Preparation Outline
3 The Delivery Outline

1

The Working Outline

Working outlines are usually handwritten attempts to organize your thoughts as you progress through the early stages of creating a speech—especially as you do research. These outlines will change often and will be a combination of complete thoughts, words, and phrases. Think of them as a way to record your thoughts, narrow in on your main points, and play around with organizational strategies.

For example, Garrett owns a greyhound. Several of his friends thought it was a difficult dog to own and expressed some misconceptions about the breed. Garrett decided to do his informative speech about greyhounds, and he created the working outline below. Later, he will change his main points into declarative sentences.

TOPIC: Greyhounds

GENERAL PURPOSE: To inform

SPECIFIC PURPOSE: To inform my COMM 110 class about the evolution of the greyhound breed

CENTRAL IDEA: Since humans first started cooperating with greyhounds, these speedy dogs have evolved as a complex breed to keep up with human advancements.

MAIN POINT #1: What is the early history of greyhounds?

MAIN POINT #2: What is the relationship they have with humans?

MAIN POINT #3: What are the misconceptions about the breed?

2

The Preparation Outline

Preparation outlines (also known as *formal* or *full-sentence outlines*) will be much longer and more detailed than working outlines. Designing a preparation outline allows you the opportunity to give the necessary time, effort, and thought to creating a successful speech.

The entire outline will adhere to correct outline form. The introduction, body, and conclusion will be clearly marked and connected with detailed links. Each outline component will be written as a complete sentence, and main points in particular should be declarative sentences. The outline will end with a complete and correct source page listing all the sources cited in the speech. You should follow your instructor's requirements for how to present the outline, but in most cases, it will be:

- Typed
- Double-spaced
- Formatted in a specific and consistent way
- Handed in prior to or on the day you give your speech

The basic format of a preparation outline should look similar to the template at right. This template is the standard pattern you can use to create most speech outlines.

You can see Garrett's complete preparation outline on the next few pages.

Student name   Class
Date   Instructor name

Topic
Specific purpose
Central idea

INTRODUCTION
    Attention-getter
    Credibility material
    Relevance to audience
    Preview of speech

(Link from introduction to first main point)

BODY
    I. First main point
        A. Subpoint
        B. Subpoint
            1. Subpoint of B
            2. Subpoint of B
            3. Subpoint of B

(Link between first and second main points)

    II. Second main point
        A. Subpoint
        B. Subpoint
            1. Subpoint of B
            2. Subpoint of B
        C. Subpoint

(Link between second and third main points)

    III. Third main point
        A. Subpoint
            1. Subpoint of A
               a. Subpoint of 1
              b. Subpoint of 1
            2. Subpoint of A
        B. Subpoint
        C. Subpoint

(Link to conclusion)

CONCLUSION
    Summary statement
    Audience response statement
    WOW statement

        Works Cited (or References)

Garrett McCloud
10 February 2015

COMM 110
Dr. Daniels

Topic: Greyhounds

Specific purpose: To inform my COMM 110 class about the evolution of the greyhound breed

Central idea: Since humans first started cooperating with greyhounds, these speedy dogs have evolved as a complex breed to keep up with human advancements.

INTRODUCTION

> By labeling the parts of the introduction, Garrett is sure he has included all he needs to grab his audience's attention. When necessary, he includes proper in-text source citations. He follows APA guidelines for his outline.

Attention-getter: A big bag of rat poison, a dog, and a family busy preparing Thanksgiving dinner. If you think these three things sound like a list of ingredients for disaster, you're right. Nancy Moen's article "Dogs on Call" tells us that, in November of 2012, Gunner the chocolate lab ate about half that bag of rat poison. Luckily for his family, the Harrisons, Elmo was there. Elmo isn't the family's other dog. He didn't pull Gunner out of danger or alert the family like in some Lassie movie. In fact, Elmo wasn't even at the site of the incident. Even so, Elmo the retired racing greyhound, along with a team of veterinarians, is responsible for Gunner surviving that night—but we'll get to that in a minute. Once treasured coursing hounds owned only by the wealthy, greyhounds have become something of an invisible breed, working behind the scenes like Elmo.

Relevance to audience: Although you might think greyhounds aren't a popular Midwest dog, it is important to note that our state has three active greyhound rescue agencies and 120 have been adopted in our state since January 2015.

Credibility material: I routinely work with a local rescue group to socialize greyhounds and promote awareness of the breed, and I'm always surprised to learn how many people have never seen a greyhound other than on the side of a bus or in *The Simpsons*.

> Garrett's main points mirror the order and construction of his preview.

Preview of speech: Since we first started cooperating with greyhounds, the world has changed a lot, but these speedy dogs have kept up with our advancements. Let's look at the history of these dogs, how they are medical marvels, and why they can make good companion animals.

(**Link:** Let's begin historically.)

BODY

I. We can see them clearly in the history of civilization and, more recently, on racetracks.
   A. According to the American Kennel Club (2015), there are fossil records and paintings depicting sighthound-shaped dogs dating as far back as 8,000 B.C.
      1. Sighthounds are a family of dog breeds that share similar characteristics.
      2. Breeds such as the saluki, basenji, whippet, borzoi, and of course the greyhound are in the sighthound family.
   B. The earliest evidence of sighthounds was found in Egypt, but sighthounds eventually made their way into Western Europe.

All of Garrett's main points and subpoints are properly indented and aligned.

1. An informational pamphlet published by Rescued Racers states that sighthounds were brought into England by the Celts and Romans in the 9th century.
   a. By the end of the 18th century, competitive coursing events, in which greyhounds or teams of greyhounds were set loose to chase live hares, had developed in England (The Greyhound Database, 2004).
   b. The English also began keeping pedigrees of their hounds around this time (Rescued Racers).
      i. It's pretty awesome that they did that, and even more awesome that The Greyhound Database has uploaded all of those records.
      ii. Using that site, I was able to trace my dog's bloodline back to the year 1780.
      iii. This is actually a drawing of one of his ancestors from 1790s (The Greyhound Database, 2014).
2. In the early 1900s, coursing events gave way to modern greyhound racing, which is easier to control and monitor and removes the need for live rabbits (The Greyhound Database, 2004).
   a. The premise is that a white, fluffy object on a mechanical arm, placed too far ahead for the dogs to reach, is moved rapidly around an oval track, exciting the dogs' natural instinct to chase prey.
   b. Greyhound racing enjoyed a fair bit of popularity and is still quite a big deal in Europe, but a decline in interest and concerns about animal welfare have led many tracks to close (The Greyhound Database, 2004).
   c. Greyhounds in the U.S. generally race until they are between two and four years of age, with some kept longer for breeding (Rescued Racers).
C. Although racing is mostly concentrated in Florida, the greyhound's first big job in America was here in the Midwest.
   1. They were imported from Europe in the 1800s.
   2. Their job was to help farmers defend their crops against jackrabbits (The Greyhound Database, 2004).

(**Link**: Now that you have a historical background, let's look at how they are medical marvels.)

He distinguishes his main points with Roman numerals.

II. Due in part to some characteristics unique to sighthounds, we often humanely study rescued greyhounds for medical purposes rather than euthanizing them when they stop performing on the track.
   A. Multiple studies conducted at Ohio State University culminated in a 2011 report documenting several physiological differences between sighthounds and other dogs. Some of these features make them very useful in a medical sense.
      1. For one, sighthounds have a higher percentage of red blood cells than non-sighthounds (Zaldívar-López et al., 2011).
         a. The typical concentration of red blood cells in sighthounds, between 50% and 63%, would signify a diseased state in any other type of dog. (Zaldívar-López et al., 2011).

    b. This also means that they can provide more plasma per unit of blood, as the percentage of platelets in the blood is lowered (Zaldívar-López et al., 2011).

   2. Additionally, between 50% and 70% of all greyhounds, compared to less than 20% of all other dogs, have a blood type that can be universally donated to all other dogs (Zaldívar-López et al., 2011).

   3. Their lean, muscular shapes, thin skin, and thick veins make it easy to draw blood, and their large size makes donation safe for them (Zaldívar-López et al., 2011).

   4. Given these features, it's easy to understand why dogs like Elmo (mentioned in my introduction) are indispensable to veterinary hospitals.

   5. When Gunner needed a blood transfusion, Elmo was able to provide enough blood in a compatible type to effectively save his life.

  B. There are also medical drawbacks to having such a unique physiology.

   1. Veterinarians must be aware of these genetic quirks in order to effectively treat sighthounds.

    a. A vet who expects a greyhound's body to behave like any other dog's can grossly misdiagnose a greyhound or prescribe wildly inaccurate treatment.

    b. One example of a potential misdiagnosis is the greyhound's blood pressure.

    c. It is significantly higher than that of other breeds, and in the past led to many misdiagnoses of hypertension, or abnormally high blood pressure (Zaldívar-López et al., 2011).

   2. M. H. Court's article "Anesthesia of the Greyhound" (1999) adds that sighthounds also metabolize drugs differently.

  (**Link**: Finally, let's look at how greyhounds fare as a pet.)

 III. More and more, greyhounds are being considered pets and not just racers or medical marvels.

  A. Happily, the same group that conducted the medical analyses determined that roughly 180,000 greyhounds were placed in homes between 1990 and 2011—a big improvement from just having them all put down. (Zaldívar-López et al., 2011).

  B. However, there are a few incorrect assumptions about the breed that prevent even more people from considering adoption.

   1. Myth number one: Greyhounds are high-energy dogs who need lots of space to run all the time.

    a. Despite their speed, these dogs are notoriously lazy.

    b. Though they are the fastest dog in the world, greyhounds are often referred to as the 45 mph couch potato.

    c. They are sprinters, not endurance runners.

    d. This actually makes them fantastic apartment dogs despite their large size, which ranges from about 55 to 65 lbs. for females and 70 to 80 lbs. for males.

He uses an appropriate pattern of symbols for related subpoints, such as the lowercase letters under this subpoint 1.

Garrett includes all links in his outline.

2. Myth number two: Greyhounds are aggressive.
   a. This myth springs from the basket muzzles often worn by greyhounds.
   b. While every individual dog is different, greyhounds do not tend to be aggressive.
   c. Worn on the track to help keep dogs from getting too excited, the muzzles are also handy for keeping greyhounds from sticking their long, skinny faces into things that might be dangerous.
3. Myth number three: Greyhounds are not small-dog or cat safe.
   a. This can vary by the individual dog and situation, as with any breed.
   b. However, most greyhounds can easily learn to get along with cats, small dogs, and children.

As in the introduction, Garrett labels the parts of his conclusion, highlighting their functions.

CONCLUSION

Summary statement: Whether they're whirlwind coursing hounds, blood donors, or pets, greyhounds are all around us.

Audience response statement: Next time you see a bus with the Greyhound logo or watch Santa's Little Helper curl up on the Simpsons' rug, remember that you now know the place these grand dogs have in our lives.

WOW statement: Just don't blink, or you might miss them!

References

American Kennel Club. (2015). Greyhound detail. Retrieved from http://www.akc.org /dog-breeds/greyhound/detail/

Court, M. H. (1999, February). Anesthesia of the sighthound. *Clinical Techniques in Small Animal Practice*, 14(1), 38–43. doi: 10.1016/S1096-2867(99)80025-5

The Greyhound Database. (2004). Greyhound track overview: USA. Retrieved from http://www.greyhound-data.com/stadia.htm?land=us

The Greyhound Database. (2014). Pedigree of Swale McBones. Retrieved from http:// www.greyhound-data.com/d?d=swale+mcbones&x=18&y=11

Moen, N. (2012, May 29). Dogs on call. *Mizzou Wire*. Retrieved from http://mizzouwire .missouri.edu/stories/2012/donor-dogs/index.php

Rescued Racers. (n.d.). Informational pamphlet.

Zaldívar-López, S., Marín, L. M., Iazbik, M.C., Westendorf-Stingle, N., Hensley, S., & Couto, C. G. (2011, December). Clinical pathology of Greyhounds and other sighthounds. *Veterinary Clinical Pathology* 40(4): 414–425. doi: 10.1111/j.1939-165X.2011.00360.x

For each source used in the speech, he includes a proper citation on his source page. Again, he follows APA guidelines.

He double-spaces his source page and uses a hanging indent for each entry.

3
The Delivery Outline

Delivery outlines will maintain the tight structure of the preparation outline but will eliminate much of the detail because you will know it by memory after writing the speech and doing some preliminary practicing. Create and use this outline as early as possible in the rehearsal stage of your speech. It is important that your "mind's eye" becomes familiar with the layout of this outline. You know you have become familiar enough with it when you can anticipate moving on to the next note card or page without looking down. This outline should assist you but not be a crutch. If you find that you want to read directly from it most of the time, it has too much detail. A delivery outline will also have delivery and presentation hints highlighted at key points during your speech. You should set up your delivery outline format with what you find the most useful and comfortable. The following is only one example, showing the note cards Garrett used during his speech.

CARD # 1

- A big bag of rat poison, a dog, and a family busy preparing Thanksgiving dinner (slide)
- Nancy Moen's article "Dogs on Call" November of 2012
- Three active greyhound rescue agencies
- 120 adopted in our state since January 2015
- I work with a local rescue group
- The history of these dogs, how they are medical marvels, and why they can make good companion animals

(**Link**: Historically)

CARD # 2

I. History of civilization and racetracks
   A. Fossil records and paintings as far back as 8,000 B.C. (AKC)
      1. Sighthounds—a family of dog breeds
      2. Saluki, basenji, whippet, borzoi, and greyhound
   B. The earliest evidence of sighthounds found in Egypt
   C. Greyhound's first big job in America
      1. Imported 1800s (slide x3)
      2. Defend their crops (Greyhound Database, 2004)
        (slide)

SLOW DOWN

(**Link**: Medical marvels)

II. Medical purposes rather than euthanizing
   A. Multiple studies conducted at Ohio State University culminated in a 2011 report
      1. Higher % of red blood cells than non-sighthounds
      2. Between 50% and 70% have a universal blood type
      3. Easier and safer donation
      4. Help veterinary hospitals
      5. Elmo's connection to Gunner
   B. Medical drawbacks

(**Link:** Greyhounds as pets)

III. Greyhounds as pets
   A. Roughly 180,000 greyhounds were placed in homes (slide x2)
   B. Myths
      1. High-energy dogs (slide)
      2. Aggressive (slide)
      3. Not small-dog or cat safe (slide)

Conclusion
• Whirlwind coursing hounds, blood donors, or pets
• Remember the place they have in our lives
• Just don't blink, or you might miss them!

(slide of me and my greyhound)

→ See Chapters 10 and 11 for more on delivery and presentation aid hints.

6.4 What Can You Use to Link Your Speech Parts Together?

1 Transitions
2 Signposts
3 Internal Previews
4 Internal Reviews

1 Transitions

Transitions are words or phrases signaling movement from one point to another as well as how the points relate to each other. Transitions fall into the following categories.

TYPE OF TRANSITION	EXAMPLES
Time transitions are words and phrases that demonstrate a passing of time.	Let's move on to … Now that we have … We are now ready … In the future … Meanwhile … Later … Next …
Viewpoint transitions demonstrate a change in your view of a situation.	On the other hand … However … Conversely … Although … But …
Connective transitions simply unite related thoughts.	Also … Another … In addition … Moreover … Not only …, but also …
Concluding transitions signal the end of a section within the speech or the ending of the entire speech.	Therefore … Thus … As a result … Finally … In conclusion … To summarize …

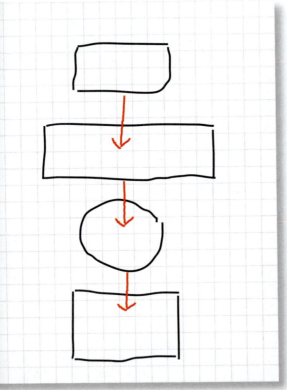

2
Signposts

Signposts are words or phrases that signal to the audience where they are with regard to related thoughts and/or what is important to remember. Some of the most common signposts are:

- First... Second... Third...
- My first reason... My second reason...
- Above all, remember...
- The most important aspects are...

For example:

> The first step in building a fire pit is to design a pit that fits all your needs.

3
Internal Previews

As links, **internal previews** are like mini-introductions and look like detailed signposts. These statements tell the audience what will be covered next in the speech. Here are two examples:

> Let's look at how the NFL consists of 32 teams, two conferences, and four divisions.

> The United States has a major prescription drug cost problem. Let's look at how much drugs cost in the United States compared to other countries, what the pharmaceutical companies say about these high costs, and how we might regulate the cost of prescription drugs.

An internal preview is a great way to link your introduction and the body of your speech. It can act as the preview of your full speech, as in the last example above.

4
Internal Reviews

Internal reviews (also known as *internal summaries*) are like mini-conclusions. They summarize what you have just covered in the previous section of your speech. Here are a few internal review examples:

> Now that we understand the high cost of prescription drugs in the United States and what the industry suggests drives the higher costs, let's look at what we can do to bring those prices down.

> Knowledge, persistence, and charisma are what make a great salesperson.

> To review, you need an effective pit design, a good safe location, and the right materials to create an awesome fire pit.

Often, you will combine internal previews and internal reviews with a transition, as these examples do:

> Now that you have designed your fire pit, selected the right location, and gathered the necessary items for construction, it is time to build the pit.

> Now that we have discussed the evolution of football and the establishment of the NFL, we can move on to considering how the league is organized.

TIP: Effective Links

Creating your links ahead of time and placing them in the correct spots will help you remember to use them, and then you won't struggle for words during the delivery of the speech. You should write out the links completely on the preparation outline. You might also use an abbreviated version of your links in your delivery outline so that you remember to include them.

6.5 How Do You Cite Sources in Your Outline?

As discussed in Chapter 1, citing your sources—in speeches and in writing—is an ethical responsibility and the only way to prevent plagiarism. Whenever you borrow words or concepts, directly quote something, or paraphrase, you need to cite the source. If what you are discussing is not common knowledge for most of your audience, you need a citation. When in doubt, cite a source.

Most speech instructors will ask you to follow your style manual. However, the instructor may offer guidelines for how to handle citations unique to the public speaking forum. So be sure to check with your instructor. Some general guidelines are:

- Cite your sources within the outline, followed by a source page at the end of the outline.

- Incorporate citations into the text of the outline, record them parenthetically, or use a combination of both.

- Unless the citation is part of the outline text, place it at the end of a sentence and before the end punctuation.

- The information within the citation should point to the source listed on the source page at the end of your outline.

Your style manual offers detailed discussions on how to cite effectively; however, the table at the right offers a few general rules and examples for citing sources within your outline.

→ See pages 120–123 for details on how to cite sources orally.

MLA CITATIONS	**APA CITATIONS**
Use the author–page number method.	*Use the author–publication date method.*

One author, parenthetical citation:
". . . can help you save time and money" (Smith 345).

One author, parenthetical citation:
". . . can help you save time and money" (Smith, 2015).

One author, in-text citation:
According to Smith's article in the November issue of . . . (345).

One author, in-text citation:
According to Smith (2015), you can . . .

Two authors, parenthetical citation:
(Smith and Jones 456)

Two to six authors, parenthetical citation:
(Smith, Baker, & Jones, 2016)

Two authors, in-text citation:
According to Smith and Jones, the people agreed with the candidate (456).

Two to five authors, in-text citation:
Smith, Baker, and Jones (2016) found that the people agreed with the candidate.

Three or more authors:
(López et al. 85)

Six or more authors:
(López et al., 2014)

No author identified:
Begin with the first few words of the source on the source page (usually the title).
"Only 10 percent polled agreed" ("Politics Today" 45).

No author identified:
Begin with the first few words of the source on the source page (usually the title).
"Only 10 percent polled agreed" ("Politics Today," 2016).

Corporate or group authors:
The name of the group serves as the author.
(Food and Drug Administration 123)

Corporate or group authors:
The name of the group serves as the author.
(Food and Drug Administration, 2016)

No page number available:
(Food and Drug Administration)

No date available:
(Food and Drug Administration, n.d.)

PRACTICING ETHICS: Citations

Using proper citations in your outline will help you remember to cite your sources orally, preventing you from plagiarizing portions of your speech.

TIP: Web Pages

When citing web pages, you may not know the author, or the material may have been created by corporate or group authors.

6.6 How Do You Create a Source Page?

1 Follow the Overall Format Requirements

2 Create a Proper Entry for Each Source

As with citing sources within the text of your outline, your style manual will guide the creation of your source page. Again, you need to pay attention to any instructions given in class because an oral speech can have unique sources that your instructor may want included.

For example, APA style does not usually include personal communications (private letters, memos, e-mails, personal interviews, telephone conversations, etc.) on the source page. Many speech instructors, however, do want them cited formally on the outline and orally in the speech. In most cases, the speech instructor wants all sources. Don't forget to cite the sources for:

- Downloaded videos and music
- Internet documents
- Personal interviews
- Photos taken by others or from the Internet

In other public speaking situations, you may find that having a handout ready for distribution and including your source page will be helpful so that your audience can retain information better or do further investigation.

TIP: Help Your Credibility

Honesty about where you get your materials is the best policy and will build your credibility with your audience.

1

Follow the Overall Format Requirements

The following are general guidelines for creating the layout of the source page.

- Make sure you are using the most current and appropriate style manual for your class.

- If you are using MLA style, the source page uses the title "Works Cited," which is centered.

- If you are using APA style, the source page uses the title "References," which is centered.

- With either MLA or APA, your source page should:
  - Be double-spaced
  - Use a hanging indent
  - List sources in alphabetical order
  - Use the same font (style, color, and size) as the text of the outline
  - Use standard one-inch margins

The table on the following pages shows you—at a quick glance—some differences between these two styles. Check your style manual for a more detailed description for creating a source page.

2

Create a Proper Entry for Each Source

Each style manual gives detailed instructions on how to create the entries on the source page. You will want to refer often to your manual. The table on the following pages outlines the most common sources used in a speech, according to MLA or APA. The key to a successful source page is to select a style and stay with it consistently. Double-check for proper format if you are using software to create your source page. Software can make mistakes or be out of date.

> ### CHECKLIST for Creating an Outline
>
> ❑ Did I include the topic, specific purpose, and central idea?
>
> ❑ Did I use full sentences?
>
> ❑ Do I have only one sentence for each outline component? Does each sentence cover only one idea?
>
> ❑ Did I create a complete introduction and conclusion?
>
> ❑ Am I using correct outline format?
>
> • Am I using Roman numerals for the main points?
>
> • Am I using uppercase letters, numbers, and lowercase letters for the appropriate levels of subpoints?
>
> • Does each subpoint have at least two divisions?
>
> ❑ Are my main points equal?
>
> ❑ Do the components of my outline follow correct subordination?
>
> ❑ Did I include links?
>
> ❑ Did I include the in-text citations and a source page?

MLA AND APA AT A GLANCE

Book–MLA	Lee, Harper. *Go Set a Watchman*. HarperCollins, 2015.
Book–APA	Lee, H. (2015). *Go set a watchman*. New York, NY: HarperCollins.
Newspaper–MLA (print and database)	Nicholas, Peter, Laura Meckler, and Colleen McCain Nelson. "Clinton, Sanders Collide at Debate." *The Wall Street Journal*, 5 Feb. 2016, pp. A1+ Elias, Paul. "San Francisco Police Recite Pledge to Root Out Intolerance in Ranks." *Chico Enterprise-Record*, 31 Jan. 2016. *Lexis Nexis Academic*, www.lexisnexis.com/hottopics/Inacademic..
Newspaper–APA (print and database)	Nicholas, P., Meckler, L., & Nelson, C. M. (2016, February 5). Clinton, Sanders collide at debate. *The Wall Street Journal*, pp. A1, A5. Elias, A. (2016, January 31). San Francisco police recite pledge to root out intolerance. *Chico Enterprise-Record*. Retrieved from Lexis Nexis Academic.
Magazine–MLA (print and website)	Baden, Joel, and Candida Moss. "Can Hobby Lobby Buy the Bible?" *The Atlantic*, Jan-Feb. 2016, pp. 70-77. Baden, Joel, and Candida Moss. "Can Hobby Lobby Buy the Bible?" *The Atlantic*, Jan.-Feb. 2016, www.theatlantic.com/magazine/archive/2016/01/can-hobby-lobby-buy-the-bible/419088/.
Magazine–APA (print and website)	Baden, J., & Moss, C. (2016, January/February). Can Hobby Lobby buy the Bible? *The Atlantic*, 317(1), 70–77. Baden, J., & Moss, C. (2016, January/February). Can Hobby Lobby buy the Bible? *The Atlantic*, 317(1), 70–77. Retrieved from http://www.theatlantic.com/magazine/archive/2016/01/can-hobby-lobby-buy-the-bible/419088/

Web page– MLA (with government author)	United States, Department of Health and Human Services. "Vaccines for Children—A Guide for Parents and Caregivers." *U.S Food and Drug Administration,* Aug. 2015, www.fda.gov /BiologicsBloodVaccines/ResourcesforYou/Consumers /ucm345587.htm.
Web page– APA (with government author)	U.S. Department of Health and Human Services, U.S. Food and Drug Administration. (2015, August). *Vaccines for children—A guide for parents and caregivers.* Retrieved from http://www.fda.gov /BiologicsBloodVaccines/ResourcesforYou/Consumers/ucm345587 .htm
Interview conducted by speaker–MLA	Jones, Tammy. Personal interview. 1 Apr. 2016. Jones, Tammy. Telephone interview. 1 Apr. 2016. Jones, Tammy. E-mail interview. 1 Apr. 2016.
Interview conducted by speaker*–APA	**APA normally does not recognize undocumented sources such as interviews. Because speakers often use interviews as source material, your instructor may ask you to include them as shown below.* Jones, T. (2016, April 1). Personal interview. Jones, T. (2016, April 1). Telephone interview. Jones, T. (2016, April 1). E-mail interview.

> **TIP: Examples of APA and MLA**
> Looking at correct source pages can help you visualize how to put one together. The samples on pages 141 and 327 follow APA format, and the sample on page 385 follows MLA.

Chapter 6: Review

ASSESSING YOUR KNOWLEDGE

6.1 What Are the Parts of an Outline?

Objective 6.1: **IDENTIFY THE PARTS OF AN OUTLINE**

There are four main parts to an outline. They are:
- The introduction
- The body of the speech
- The conclusion
- The source page

→ See pages 128–129.

6.2 How Can You Create an Effective Outline?

Objective 6.2: **EXPLAIN HOW TO CREATE AN EFFECTIVE OUTLINE**

On your preparation outline, you should:
- Record the topic, specific purpose, and central idea. Make sure you include your instructor's specific requirements for identifying you and your speech.
- Use full sentences.
- Cover only one issue at a time.
- Develop the introduction and conclusion.
- Use correct outline format. Again, make sure you follow your instructor's requirements.
- Use balanced main points.
- Employ subordination.
- Plan out formal links.
- Use proper citations. Proper citations include citations within the outline and on a source page created according to MLA or APA style guidelines.

→ See pages 130–135.

6.3 What Are the Different Types of Outlines?

Objective 6.3: **DESCRIBE THE DIFFERENT TYPES OF OUTLINES**

- The working outline is usually a handwritten, rough outline you use through the early stages of the speech creation process.
- The preparation outline is a full-sentence, complete outline detailing your entire speech.
- The delivery outline maintains the tight structure you created in the preparation outline but eliminates much of the detail. It retains only the basics of what you need to deliver the speech and any delivery notes.

→ See pages 136–143.

6.4 What Can You Use to Link Your Speech Parts Together?

Objective 6.4: **LIST WHAT YOU CAN USE TO LINK YOUR SPEECH PARTS TOGETHER**

You can use transitions, signposts, internal previews, and internal reviews.
- Transitions are words or phrases signaling movement from one point to another as well as how points relate.
- Signposts are words or phrases that signal to the audience where they are with regard to related thoughts and/or what is important to remember.
- Internal previews are like mini-introductions and look like detailed signposts. They tell what will be covered next.
- Internal reviews are like mini-conclusions. They summarize what you have just covered.

→ See pages 144–145.

6.5 How Do You Cite Sources in Your Outline?

Objective 6.5: **ILLUSTRATE HOW TO CITE SOURCES IN YOUR OUTLINE**

- Follow the style manual required by the instructor (usually APA or MLA).
- Cite sources within the outline, followed by a source page at the end of the outline.
- Incorporate sources within the text of the outline, record as parenthetical citations, or use a combination of both.
- Unless the citation is part of the outline text, place it at the end of the sentence and before the end punctuation.
- The information within the outline citation should point to one of the sources listed on your source page.

→ See pages 146–147.

6.6 How Do You Create a Source Page?

Objective 6.6: **DEMONSTRATE HOW TO CREATE A SOURCE PAGE**

- Follow the overall format requirements determined by the style manual. Make sure you are using the correct edition and type of manual required for the course.
- Title your source page "Works Cited" if you use MLA or "References" if you use APA.
- Create a proper entry for each source you use.
- Remember to double-space the source page and use a hanging indent for each entry.

→ See pages 148–151.

TERMS TO REMEMBER

introduction (129)
body (129)
main points (129)
subpoints (129)
links (129)
conclusion (129)
standard of balance (134)
working outlines (136)
preparation outlines (137)
delivery outlines (142)
transitions (144)
signposts (145)
internal previews (145)
internal reviews (145)

7 ORGANIZING THE SPEECH BODY

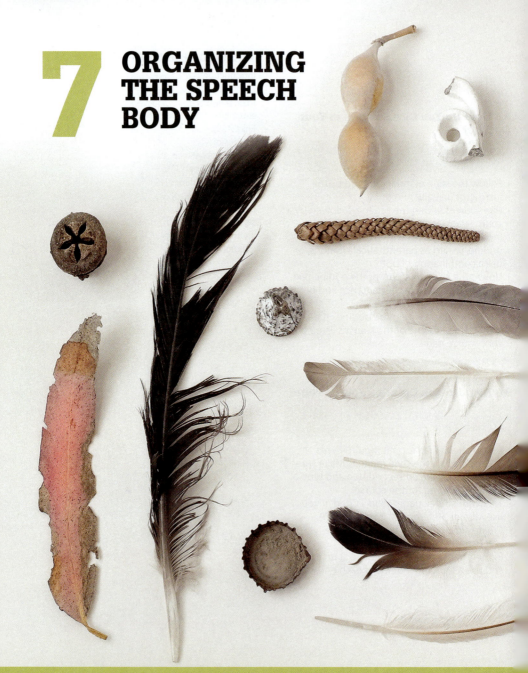

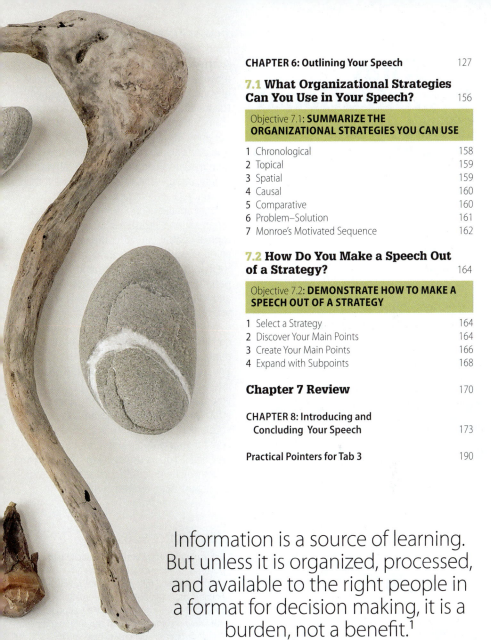

Information is a source of learning. But unless it is organized, processed, and available to the right people in a format for decision making, it is a burden, not a benefit.[1]

WILLIAM POLLARD

7.1 What Organizational Strategies Can You Use in Your Speech?

1 Chronological
2 Topical
3 Spatial
4 Causal
5 Comparative
6 Problem–Solution
7 Monroe's Motivated Sequence

A *strategy* is a plan designed to achieve a goal—in this case, your specific purpose of your speech. Strategy is concerned with the relationship and arrangement of your main points. In other words, your strategy is not about how you explain your main points (the content), but about how your main points relate to and follow each other (the organization)—to achieve your goal to inform, persuade, or accentuate a topic.

Most speakers choose from seven basic organizational strategies: chronological, topical, spatial, causal, comparative, problem–solution, and Monroe's motivated sequence.

Chapter 6 noted that there are three main parts to a speech: the introduction, the body, and the conclusion. Your strategy will help you organize the body of your speech.

When you select a strategy, you will consider which one works best with your general purpose, the topic, and the audience. Because these three elements are constantly interacting with and reacting to each other, you may find that you can use more than one strategy effectively—and that is fine. Trust your instincts to select one that seems the best for your purpose, topic, and audience, as well as for you as the speaker. The following pages will help you understand in greater detail how each strategy works.

CONFIDENCE BOOSTER

Selecting the right strategy and sticking to it is a powerful confidence booster. The time you spend making sure you follow the strategy will help you become more familiar with the details of your speech. A major contributor to low confidence is not knowing what your next thought might be. A well-organized speech will help you look and feel confident and trustworthy.

ORGANIZATIONAL STRATEGIES FOR SPEECHES

STRATEGY	WHAT IS IT?	WHEN MIGHT YOU USE IT?	WHAT TYPES OF SPEECH USE IT?
Chronological	Strategy based on moving through time or sequential steps	Useful for speeches about a process or development over time or plan of action	Informative Persuasive Special occasion
Topical	Strategy highlighting the natural subtopics or divisions within a speech topic	Ideal when your topic has inherent subtopics	Informative Persuasive Special occasion
Spatial	Strategy describing the arrangement of space related to an event, place, or object	Useful when you need to walk your audience through a space or setting	Informative Special occasion
Causal	Strategy based on cause-to-effect or effect-to-cause	Effective for speeches focusing on causes or consequences of something already present or possible	Informative Persuasive* Special occasion
Comparative	Strategy that explains or argues by comparing something to something else	Great when topics are abstract, technical, or difficult; beneficial for showing advantages	Informative Persuasive*
Problem–solution	Strategy demonstrating a problem and then explaining or advocating a solution	Useful when trying to change attitudes or when calling for a particular solution	Informative Persuasive*
Monroe's motivated sequence	A five-step strategy that motivates an audience to action based on their needs	Excellent strategy for a call-to-action speech	Persuasive*

*When you are giving a persuasive speech, these strategies often help create the strongest persuasive arguments.

1
Chronological

You will use the *chronological strategy* when you need to move through steps in a process or develop a timeline. Depending on the topic and your general purpose, you might move forward or backward through the process or timeline for effect. This type of arrangement is especially helpful when stressing the history of an event, person, or thing or when demonstrating a process.

For example, a process speech might look something like this:

Specific purpose: To inform my audience how to use a compost bin

Central idea: Composting is an easy way to save space in our landfills while growing great vegetables or flowers.

 I. There are many types of composting bins, making it important to select the right one for your needs and budget.

 II. Where you position your composting bin can make composting either effortless or grueling.

 III. A few simple steps will help you maintain a sweet-smelling, productive compost pile.

 IV. Using the "black gold" from your pile will supply you with a bounty of produce or flowers.

Here, each main point walks the listener through the major steps of composting. The subpoints should do the same.

A timeline example might look like this:

Specific purpose: To inform my audience about the evolution of the mobile phone

Central idea: The cell phone, which dates back only to 1973, has seen a great deal of development in a very short time.

 I. The first model, introduced in 1973 and eventually released in 1983, is now hardly recognizable as a portable phone.

 II. The flip phone, which was first seen in 1989 and changed significantly over the next decade, became the first truly mobile phone.

 III. The late 1990s introduced both "candy bar" style phones and phones with full keyboards.

 IV. Smartphone technology truly gathered steam in the 2000s.

In this example, each main point covers a major section of the mobile phone's historical timeline. This speech logically proceeds from oldest date to most recent. However, some chronological speech topics can also cover a timeline in reverse.

> **TIP: Demonstration Speeches**
>
> When you give a demonstration speech (a "how to do it" speech), you can use the chronological strategy to create a step-by-step organization.

2
Topical

You will use the **topical strategy** (also called the *categorical*) when there is a strong inherent or traditional division of subtopics within the main topic. If you give a speech about chocolate, for example, a natural topic division could be white, milk, and dark. For a topic such as taking a vacation to Orlando, you might divide the topic according to how people traditionally think about vacations—places to see, places to eat, and places to stay. Here's an example using the topical strategy to organize a speech on succeeding in school:

Specific purpose: To inform my audience about techniques to improve their schoolwork

Central idea: To succeed in school, you need to organize your life, carefully manage your time, and focus mentally.

I. Organization is the process of giving structure and order to your work.

II. Time management is controlling or directing time into useful chunks.

III. Mental focus is realizing what you have to do and concentrating hard on that single item.

Notice how each main point takes on a different subtopic—organization, time management, and mental focus. As individual subjects, these may seem unrelated, but in relation to the central idea and main topic, they are logically connected.

3
Spatial

A **spatial strategy** recognizes space as a way to arrange the speech. This strategy is useful when you want to discuss your topic in relationship to proximity, a physical setting, or a natural environment. Examples might be speaking about your tour through the White House, room by room; telling the new freshman class about your campus, building by building; or speaking about historical sites such as Gettysburg or Mount Vernon. A speaker can even arrange an informative speech about the human tooth spatially—by beginning at the outermost part, the enamel, and working in to the soft center, or dental pulp. Here's another example:

Specific purpose: To inform my audience about the Grand Canyon

Central idea: Carved by the Colorado River, more than 277 miles long, and more than a mile deep in places, the Grand Canyon National Park is like three parks in one when you visit the North Rim, the South Rim, and the Inner Canyon.

I. The North Rim has a much higher elevation than the South, making it cooler, with better views of the Canyon.

II. The South Rim is more accessible and has several historical sites.

III. The Inner Canyon is the unpredictable lifeline of the park.

The spatial strategy is often a useful way to deal with a setting as large as the Grand Canyon. It helps you divide the space (North Rim, South Rim, and Inner Rim) into more-manageable parts.

4
Causal

You will use the **causal strategy** when you want your audience to understand the cause and effect or consequences of something. With this strategy, you can either trace the path that leads up to a certain result or backtrack from the effect to the cause. Which way you go depends on what is most important to your specific purpose.

For example, explaining why young potential voters tend not to vote in U.S. elections would be a great candidate for this type of arrangement.

Specific purpose: To inform my Political Parties class about why young adults don't vote

Central idea: Feelings of powerlessness, irrelevance, and lack of connection are all reasons young U.S. citizens do not vote.

I. Most young potential voters believe that their votes won't make a difference.

II. Most young potential voters note that most politicians don't care about what concerns the younger generation.

III. Most young potential voters feel little sense of connection to what happens in their communities.

Depending on your topic, you may have one cause leading to a single effect, a single cause leading to several effects, or several causes leading to one effect.

5
Comparative

The **comparative strategy** uses the practice of compare and contrast. In an informative speech, you might use this strategy with new, abstract, technical, or difficult-to-comprehend topics. Here, you compare your topic to something the audience knows. This strategy only works when the two things you are comparing are comparable or analogous. For example:

Specific purpose: To inform new study-abroad students about what it is like to live in Florence, Italy

Central idea: Comparing what living in Florence might be like to your experience here in Columbus will help you anticipate the next year.

I. Your living arrangements will be unlike what you might experience now.

II. Your classroom experience will be unlike that in U.S. schools.

III. Your social life will be different.

This example uses the comparative strategy to inform, helping the audience understand and follow the speech by comparing the unknown (Florence) with the familiar (Columbus).

In a persuasive speech, this strategy can be used to convince an audience that one thing is better than another, by comparing the two. This is a common practice used by many salespersons and is often referred to as **comparative advantage.**

Don't get carried away with the number of comparisons you make, which can be confusing. In a short presentation, five or fewer comparisons will suffice.

6
Problem–Solution

You will use the ***problem–solution strategy*** when you want to show your audience how to solve a problem, making it an arrangement suited for a persuasive speech. With this strategy, your speech will have two main sections, dedicated to the "problem" and the "solution." For example:

Specific purpose: To convince my audience that artificial sweeteners are dangerous

Central idea: Artificial sweeteners are an easy alternative for the calorie conscious, but the toxic effects of their chemicals should prompt consumers to seek safer choices.

I. **(problem):** Artificial sweeteners such as sucralose, aspartame, and saccharin cause major side effects that can be potentially dangerous.

II. **(solution):** Gradually decreasing your intake of artificial sweeteners by drinking more water, unsweetened tea, or naturally flavored drinks is the solution for preventing future problems and improving your overall health.

TIP: Informative Speeches

The problem–solution strategy can be used with informative speeches when your audience is familiar with the problem and solution but not the reasons behind the decision. Here, you use the strategy simply to inform them.

Some persuasive speeches using the problem–solution format may need more than two main points. Why? First, you may need to expand your strategy when the problem and/or solution is so complex that you need more than one main point for either or both, to help your audience understand your position. Secondly, you may need to expand your points if you think your audience might be unwilling to accept the idea that there is a problem or that your proposed solution is the best.

Specific purpose: To convince my audience that there is a serious problem with the education system in our town

Central idea: As members of this community, we need to recognize the current problems with educating our children and to swiftly seek effective solutions to those problems.

I. **(problem):** The 2016 standardized test results show that our students at all levels are behind in math, reading, and writing skills.

II. **(problem):** At the high school level, we see a decline in the sciences as well.

III. **(problem):** Our high school dropout rate is one of the highest in the state.

IV. **(solution):** We need to implement a program to evaluate and update the curriculum in all these areas.

V. **(solution):** We need to attract more motivated and successful educators to our schools.

VI. **(solution):** We need to improve our class facilities.

7

Monroe's Motivated Sequence

Developed by Alan Monroe of Purdue University in the 1930s, **Monroe's motivated sequence** is really a more detailed problem–solution strategy. Basing the speech on what motivates the audience, the speaker convinces the audience that the speaker has the solution to their needs. If you remember the discussion about audience needs and motivations in Chapter 2, you should see the benefit of this strategy, which has five stages:

- Attention—During this stage, you begin to direct your audience's attention toward your topic.

  → See Chapter 8 for ideas on creating attention-grabbing devices.

- Need—Here, you demonstrate for your audience that they need a change by suggesting that a problem exists and they need to solve it.

- Satisfaction—At this stage, you propose the solution to the problem and support it as the best one, with the appropriate evidence. The audience must feel that your plan will work.

- Visualization—With the problem highlighted and the solution suggested, you now help the audience visualize how great the situation will be after they implement the plan. In other words, help them visualize the benefits.

- Action—Now, call them to action or tell them exactly what they must do to achieve the solution you have suggested.

The motivated sequence has an added benefit: Its stages correspond to all parts of a speech.

Speech Outline	Motivated Sequence
Introduction ←	Attention Stage
Body	
First main point ←	Need Stage
Second main point ←	Satisfaction Stage
Third main point ←	Visualization Stage
Conclusion ←	Action Stage

PRACTICING ETHICS: Using Monroe's Motivated Sequence

Monroe's motivated sequence, by its nature, is manipulative, and listeners' reactions to the manipulation can be based on emotion rather than logic. Be careful and ethical when you appeal to your audience's emotions to change their minds and to take action. There are always consequences with actions. Help your audience make ethical and safe choices.

Here's an example using this strategy.

Specific purpose: To convince my audience that we need to save the mountain gorilla

Central idea: The extinction of the mountain gorilla, who shares almost 98 percent of its genetic makeup with humans, could greatly cost humankind.

Introduction (attention stage): The mountain gorilla is one of the world's most endangered species, with only 880 remaining in Africa and none surviving in captivity (gorilladoctors.org).

I. **(need stage):** The mountain gorilla shares almost 98 percent of its genetic makeup with humans, so the diseases, the malnutrition, and the habitat concerns afflicting the gorillas could affect the human population as well.

II. **(satisfaction stage):** If this gorilla is to survive and the delicate balance of the ecosystem maintained, we must safeguard the gorillas of Rwanda, Uganda, and the Democratic Republic of the Congo.

III. **(visualization stage):** Since 1989, conservation groups like the Mountain Gorilla Veterinary Project have helped the mountain gorilla population rise by about 40 percent, making them the only species of great ape whose population is rising, not falling (Morrisanimalfoundation.org)

Conclusion (action stage): You can help save the mountain gorilla by supporting research and conservation efforts through donations to organizations such as the African Wildlife Foundation or the Dian Fossey Gorilla Fund International or by spreading awareness about the problem.

According to O. C. Ferrell and Michael Hartline in their book *Marketing Strategy*, marketers use a slightly different version of the motivated sequence—known by the acronym AIDA—when selling products or services, which you could use for a slightly different speech.

A – Awareness: Attract the attention of the customer.

I – Interest: Raise customer interest by focusing on advantages and benefits.

D – Desire: Convince customers that they want and desire the product or service.

A – Action: Lead customers toward taking action and/or purchasing.

TIP: When to Use AIDA

The AIDA strategy works best with audiences that are not negative or hostile about your topic or solution. Asking a negative or hostile audience to change their minds and take action on that change is often too much to ask. Using the problem–solution strategy would be better in this case.

7.2 How Do You Make a Speech Out of a Strategy?

1 Select a Strategy

2 Discover Your Main Points

3 Create Your Main Points

4 Expand with Subpoints

1
Select a Strategy

Most speeches can use more than one strategy. Consider your general purpose, topic, and audience when selecting the best strategy for your speech.

First, be sure the strategy will work for your general purpose (to inform, persuade, or accentuate). Some of the strategies work for all types of speeches, and some work only for informative or persuasive speeches.

Then, does your topic suggest a strategy? For example, a speech on the history of Mardi Gras calls for a strategy related to time (chronological).

Finally, what does your audience need to know, or what are your goals for them? For example, if you are explaining a complex topic, the comparative strategy may help your audience understand the topic by comparing and contrasting it to something they are familiar with.

2
Discover Your Main Points

As noted in Chapter 6, your main points are the major themes or thoughts you want to discuss about your topic. Sometimes the strategy you select to use for the speech will suggest the focus of the main points. For example, with the problem–solution strategy, you know you will have at least one main point for the problem and one for a solution. However, you may not be ready to select a strategy until you have discovered your main points. The best way to do this is to make a list of everything you want to convey in the speech. One common method is shown on the facing page.

CHECKLIST for Selecting an Organizational Strategy

❏ Does the strategy work for my general purpose?

❏ Does my topic suggest a strategy?

❏ What does my audience need to know? What strategies support my goals for them?

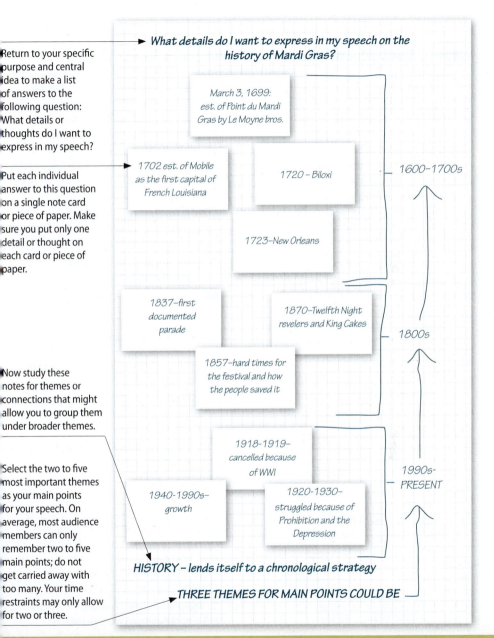

Return to your specific purpose and central idea to make a list of answers to the following question: What details or thoughts do I want to express in my speech?

Put each individual answer to this question on a single note card or piece of paper. Make sure you put only one detail or thought on each card or piece of paper.

Now study these notes for themes or connections that might allow you to group them under broader themes.

Select the two to five most important themes as your main points for your speech. On average, most audience members can only remember two to five main points; do not get carried away with too many. Your time restraints may only allow for two or three.

What details do I want to express in my speech on the history of Mardi Gras?

March 3, 1699: est. of Point du Mardi Gras by Le Moyne bros.

1702 est. of Mobile as the first capital of French Louisiana

1720 – Biloxi

1723–New Orleans

1837–first documented parade

1870–Twelfth Night revelers and King Cakes

1857–hard times for the festival and how the people saved it

1918-1919– cancelled because of WWI

1940-1990s– growth

1920-1930– struggled because of Prohibition and the Depression

1600–1700s

1800s

1990s– PRESENT

HISTORY – lends itself to a chronological strategy

THREE THEMES FOR MAIN POINTS COULD BE

3

Create Your Main Points

Effective main points will take some time to create. Doing so now will help you stay on track and save time. Aim for the following qualities to make your main points effective.

COMPLETE SENTENCES

Your main points should be complete thoughts, not only words or phrases. They should contain at least a noun and a verb.

Creating complete sentences will help you think in complete thoughts when you give the speech. Complete sentences will also help you be exact about what you want to say during each section of the speech.

For instance, the following incorrect example could be about anything related to candle making. You could be speaking about the history of candle making, the dangers of candle making, the mass production process, or the process of making candles at home.

INCORRECT:

I. Candle making

CORRECT:

I. The process of candle making is simple enough to do at home.

The correct example clarifies what you will speak about.

ONE IDEA IN EACH POINT

You should introduce only one idea in each main point. Watch for words such as *and*, *or*, or *but* connecting two independent issues in one sentence.

→ See page 131 for discussion of covering only one issue at a time.

DECLARATIVE SENTENCES

Write your main points in declarative sentences, which should not be difficult because you tend to write most of your papers, letters, and notes this way. A declarative sentence simply states fact or argument and does not ask your audience to respond or take action. It states the main point you are making. Declarative sentences never end in a question mark.

INCORRECT:

I. Are organic light-emitting diode (OLED) screens better than LCDs?

II. What are the pros and cons of an LCD and an OLED?

III. Which screen is cheaper?

CORRECT:

I. The positive qualities of current LCD screens make their purchase a better value than the purchase of an OLED screen.

II. Both types of televisions have potential negatives, but the LCD is the best fit for most homes.

III. The price difference cements the LCD as the better purchase.

COORDINATION

Your main points should adhere to coordination; that is, as much as possible, the main points are balanced or equal to each other in weight and level of ideas. They should not overtly relate to each other but should directly relate to your specific purpose.

For example, say your specific purpose is:

To inform my audience about a few of the most influential American women painters

In the following incorrect example, the main points relate back to the specific purpose, but they are unbalanced. You would spend most of the speech time on point one.

INCORRECT:

I. From the founding of this country through the mid-twentieth century, several American women painters influenced the art world.

II. Contemporary American women painters continue to set the new standard.

Instead, you might divide your main points into three significant periods of development. Doing so will allow you to coordinate and balance the amount of information about the artist highlighted. Plus, you will end with the most significant period of development for women painters. For example, few significant women artists in America were working prior to the 1800s, so your first main point could cover 1800–1874, marking the first significant period for female American painters. Your second main point could cover 1875–1974, and the last point could cover the new revolution of female painters from 1975 to the present.

CORRECT:

I. From 1800 to 1874, American women painters created genre art to appeal to the popular masses.

II. From 1875 to 1974, American women painters gained somewhat limited acceptance as professionals.

III. From 1975 to the present, American women painters have gained significant acceptance.

Within each main point, you would strive to select a similar number of influential painters to focus on and balance the information you have on each.

PARALLELISM

You use ***parallelism*** effectively when you arrange your words, phrases, or sentences in a similar pattern, which can help your main points stand out. For example, simply starting each main point with the same beginning pronoun can signal when you begin a new point and make it easier for your audience to remember the points.

I. Your classroom experience will be unlike that of high school.

II. Your social life will be different from what it was in high school.

III. Your everyday responsibilities will be different.

→ See pages 206–207 for further discussion on using parallelism throughout your speech.

At this point, you should have the best strategy and main points for your topic and audience. Now you can begin to give body or substance to your speech.

CONFIDENCE BOOSTER

Parallelism, like repetition or mnemonic devices, can help you remember your speech. If you use the devices, you will spend less time looking at your notes and you will have more confidence in remembering the key issues.

4
Expand with Subpoints

The subpoints are the filling or content that give your speech substance. Subpoints elaborate on each of the main points. Their job is to clarify, emphasize, or provide detail for the main point they support. In the subpoints, you will use your support materials (statistics, facts, testimony, examples, etc.). You can have multiple layers of subpoints. Your subpoints can also have subpoints. The number of subpoints and layers will vary depending on how much material you have to convey or need to use. Remember, adhering to proper outline format will help you see how your subpoints relate to the main points and to each other.

I. First main point

    A. First subpoint of I

        1. First subpoint of A

            a. First subpoint of 1

            b. Second subpoint of 1

        2. Second subpoint of A

    B. Second subpoint of I

II. Second main point

Related subpoints (indicated here by colors) should use consistent symbols and alignment.

→ See Chapter 6 for a more detailed discussion on outline format.

Follow these suggestions when creating your subpoints.

- Use full sentences.

- Introduce only one idea in each subpoint.

- Adhere to coordination and subordination. Subpoints on the same level should coordinate or be equal to each other. Subpoints directly below a main point or a subpoint should be subordinate, or secondary, to the point above them.

- Your subpoints do not need to follow the same organizational strategy you used for you main points. For example, suppose you use a problem–solution strategy to organize your speech's main points. You might then organize subpoints in the "problem" portion chronologically, while using a topical strategy for the subpoints in the "solution" portion. Subpoints could also be arranged as a formal argument.

→ See Tab 7 for more information on argumentation.

COMMON ORGANIZATIONAL PROBLEMS

If you follow the suggestions in Chapter 6 and this chapter, you should not have many, if any, organizational problems. However, it is smart to watch out for the more common ones.

COMMON ORGANIZATIONAL PROBLEM	PREVENTION/SOLUTION
Your selected organizational strategy does not fit the topic or audience.	• Before you commit to a strategy, always consider what your audience needs to know (or do) about your topic. • While you consider the audience's needs, keep your general purpose, specific purpose, and central idea in mind. • Then select the strategy that helps you best fulfill the audience's needs as well as your goal for the speech.
You stop adhering to the arrangement of the strategy at some point during the speech.	• Refer to this text several times during the process of creating your outline, to refresh your memory about the strategy you are using. • Set up an outline shell or template that mirrors the strategy before you start filling in support materials.
You have too many main points.	• Remember that most classroom speeches will only have time for two or three main points unless the strategy calls for more. • Longer speeches might make up to seven main points work, but your audience will have trouble remembering more than that. • If you feel like you need more main points, check your specific purpose. It may be too broad, or you may have strayed from it.
You do not have enough time for the body of the speech.	• Check to see if you are spending too much time on the introduction or conclusion. The approximate formula for breaking down your speech time is: Introduction: 15% Body: 80% Conclusion: 5%
You are spending too much time on one or two main points and cannot cover the rest efficiently.	• Maintain a standard of balance in your main points and in each level of subpoints. No one will be timing how long you stay on a point, but you do not want to shortchange a point.

Chapter 7: Review

ASSESSING YOUR KNOWLEDGE

7.1 What Organizational Strategies Can You Use in Your Speech?

Objective 7.1: **SUMMARIZE THE ORGANIZATIONAL STRATEGIES YOU CAN USE**

Seven of the most common organizational strategies are:
- **Chronological:** The chronological strategy moves through steps in a process or develops a timeline.
- **Topical:** The topical strategy highlights a strong inherent or traditional division of subtopics with the main speech topic.
- **Spatial:** The spatial strategy recognizes space as a way to arrange the speech.
- **Causal:** The causal strategy emphasizes the cause and effect or consequences of something.
- **Comparative:** The comparative strategy compares and contrasts your topic to something the audience understands.
- **Problem–solution:** The problem–solution strategy outlines a problem and then offers a solution.
- **Monroe's motivated sequence:** The strategy called Monroe's motivated sequence is a detailed problem–solution strategy with five stages: attention, need, satisfaction, visualization, and action.

➜ See pages 156–163.

7.2 How Do You Make a Speech Out of a Strategy?

Objective 7.2: **DEMONSTRATE HOW TO MAKE A SPEECH OUT OF A STRATEGY**

- Select a strategy that works with your general purpose, topic, and audience needs. The table to the right summarizes some helpful hints on when you might use a specific strategy.
- Discover the 3–5 main points for your speech. Return to your specific purpose and central idea to make a list of possible main points. Try to answer this question: What detail or thought do I want to express in my speech? Study your answers to this question, and note themes or connections that allow you to group thoughts together. Now, select 3–5 main points.
- Create your main points. They should be:
  – Complete sentences
  – Limited to one idea in each point
  – Declarative sentences
  – Coordinated
  – Parallel
- Expand on your main points with subpoints. The job of your subpoints is to clarify, emphasize, or provide detail for the main point they support. This is where you use most of the support material you have collected. You may have multiple layers of subpoints. Subpoints should be:
  – Full sentences
  – Limited to one idea in each subpoint
  – Coordinated and subordinate
  – In a logical order

➜ See pages 164–169.

STRATEGY	WHEN MIGHT YOU USE IT?
Chronological	Useful for speeches about a process or development over time or plan of action
Topical	Ideal when your topic has inherent subtopics
Spatial	Useful when you need to walk your audience through a space or setting
Causal	Effective for speeches focusing on causes or consequences of something already present or possible
Comparative	Great when topics are abstract, technical, or difficult; beneficial for showing advantages
Problem–solution	Useful when trying to change attitudes or when calling for a particular solution
Monroe's motivated sequence	Excellent strategy for a call-to-action speech

For persuasive speeches, the causal, comparative, problem–solution, and Monroe's motivated sequence strategies often create the strongest persuasive arguments.

TERMS TO REMEMBER

strategy (156)
chronological strategy (158)
topical strategy (159)
spatial strategy (159)
causal strategy (160)
comparative strategy (160)
comparative advantage (160)
problem–solution strategy (161)
Monroe's motivated sequence (162)
parallelism (167)

8 INTRODUCING AND CONCLUDING YOUR SPEECH

8.1 What Should Your Introduction Do?

1 Capture Your Audience's Attention

2 Build Your Credibility Early

3 Demonstrate Audience Relevance

4 Introduce the Topic and Preview the Speech

Many beginning speakers miss the importance of *launching* into their speech. The introduction should be one of the most exciting, moving, and interesting moments of the speech. What emotional and physical feelings do you have when you hear or say the word *launch*? That is exactly what your introduction should feel like.

1

Capture Your Audience's Attention

Think about the noise and distractions you hear as you enter a room of people, such as a classroom. People are talking about the weather, recent events, family issues, or dating or work problems. They are moving chairs, shuffling papers, texting, or checking messages. Their minds and bodies are wandering, and you have to get them to focus on you and your topic. As people who love fishing or the Texas Longhorns would say, you have to "hook 'em," or capture their attention.

This function of the introduction may be the most important—you have to get the audience's attention before you can do anything else with your speech. Good speakers spend a lot of time crafting their attention-getters.

Take a look at the following attention-getter used by Andalee, a student, for her speech on laundry skills.

> Classes have been in session a few weeks now, and I bet the laundry monster is about to bust out of your closet. You may not have a clean pair of socks or, worse yet, a clean outfit for your date tomorrow night. Maybe you did a load and everything white came out pink because you missed sorting out a red sock. Add in special laundry care instructions or a stain, and your stress level over how to do your laundry hits the top of the chart. How much bleach do you really need to use? Does liquid fabric softener go in before the rinse cycle or during? Should you use enzymes? Heck, what are enzymes?

Andalee uses anecdotes, questions, and other attention-grabbing tactics.

→ See "What Are Effective Attention-Getters?" on pages 176–179 for more details.

2
Build Your Credibility Early

Your introduction should begin to reveal your credibility as a speaker with ethical consideration for your audience and a relationship with the topic. As discussed in Chapter 1, Aristotle referred to the speaker's credibility as *ethos*. The audience needs to perceive you as kind, competent, caring, honest, and excited about your topic and speech event. You can start establishing ethos in the introduction by:

- Being confident—practice
- Demonstrating your knowledge of the topic early, which will influence your audience's perception of the rest of the speech
- Pointing out what you have in common with the audience or topic
- Making it evident that you are sincere and concerned for the audience's well-being

Building your credibility does not need to be complicated. In most speeches, employing an effective delivery style and using a simple sentence begins the process. You will continue to build credibility throughout the speech. Andalee drew on her experience:

> As a mother of a toddler and as a spouse, I wash laundry all the time! I have spent a lot of time researching the best and cheapest way to keep our clothes looking great.

TIP: Delivering the Introduction

Using an energetic delivery from the introduction of your speech onward can also build interest and get your audience excited about the topic.

3
Demonstrate Audience Relevance

Audiences want to know quickly why your speech is relevant to them. An early statement about what your topic has to offer can demonstrate that they have something to gain from listening to you. For example, Andalee used this statement:

> As a college student like you, I have to use time wisely and keep to a minimum the cost of replacing damaged clothes or purchasing expensive laundry aids.

The earlier you can convince your audience that your topic is important or interesting to them, the sooner they will be attentive and invested.

4
Introduce the Topic and Preview the Speech

After capturing your audience's attention, you need to give listeners a preview of what they can expect from your speech. This step moves the focus from you to the essence of your speech and usually consists of a single sentence or two, briefly outlining your speech. For example:

> Today, I want to help you see that doing the laundry doesn't have to be stressful or expensive. Actually, it can be quite easy if you take the time to properly sort your laundry, purchase a few basic cleaning items, and follow proper washer and dryer techniques.

In these two sentences, Andalee has given a quick preview of what her speech will cover.

8.2 What Are Effective Attention-Getters?

1 **Facts and Statistics**

2 **Stories, Narratives, Illustrations, or Anecdotes**

3 **Quotations**

4 **Humor**

5 **Questions**

6 **References**

An ***attention-getter*** is something you say, show, or do to get your audience to focus on you, your topic, and the goal of your speech. In most cases, it should be the first words spoken or the first images or actions shown. Attention-getters have a big job, so spend time crafting them, trying them out on someone else, and practicing them. Generally, you will use one of six creative tactics.

1
Facts and Statistics

Facts and statistics can help you point to a remarkable situation or problem. They can be very vivid or shocking even though they are condensed. For example:

> According to the Centers for Disease Control and Prevention in the online fact sheet titled "Impaired Driving: Get the Facts," updated November 24, 2015, "Every day, almost 30 people in the United States die in motor vehicle crashes that involve an alcohol-impaired driver. This amounts to one death every 51 minutes." Additionally, the CDC fact sheet notes, one-third of impaired drivers involved in fatal crashes are between 21 and 24 years of age.

Facts and statistics work best if they are unfamiliar to the audience; they can then have a shock value and engage the audience. In the example above, the facts and statistics about teen drinking and driving demonstrate how serious of an issue this has been and still is today.

2 Stories, Narratives, Illustrations, or Anecdotes

Stories, narratives, illustrations, and anecdotes are vivid accounts that can personalize your speech by helping the audience identify with the topic. The accounts should be interesting, evoking, and entertaining. You should not need to explain them. Be creative and selective. The accounts can be true or fictional, from your personal life or from broader arenas. Be careful if you are telling your own story because you may become too emotional or the audience may have such heightened empathy for you that it is hard for them to listen.

In a classroom speech, Albina told this story:

> Zohar is a nine-month-old boy. He does not have the comforts of growing up that you and I have. Zohar coughs violently. An IV pumps medicine into his shriveled arm—medicine that may soon run out. His ribs show clearly through his fragile skin. Zohar's parents hold his tiny hands and pray for his recovery, but Zohar has malaria and severe malnutrition. He is near death. Zohar is only one—one of thousands who will die, one of millions affected. Zohar was born in the region of Darfur, in a country called Sudan, on the continent of Africa, where children just like him are being forced out of their homes by violence as we speak. Journalist Emily Wax, in her 2004 *Washington Post* article "In Sudan, Death and Denial," introduces us to Zohar and his family.

This example has just enough emotional appeal to draw the audience in.

3 Quotations

Quotations are words or passages written or said by someone else. For an attention-getter, you want a succinct and interesting quotation from someone who will raise your credibility. You may use word-for-word quotations or paraphrases. The words or passage may come from a speech, novel, poem, short story, play, TV or movie dialogue, or another similar source. For example:

> "To stand at the edge of the sea, to sense the ebb and flow of the tides, to feel the breath of a mist moving over a great salt marsh, to watch the flight of shore birds that have swept up and down the surf lines of the continents for untold thousands of years, to see the running of the old eels and the young shad to the sea, is to have knowledge of things that are as nearly eternal as any earthly life can be," writes the famous environmental activist Rachel Carson, in her 1941 book *Under the Sea-Wind*.

TIP: Using Attention-Getters

- Facts and statistics are most effective if they are unknown to the audience and from a reliable source.

- Make sure you give the name of the person you are quoting and his or her qualifications or relationship to your topic. Include enough of an oral citation to direct your audience to the appropriate source.

- If the quotation is long—requiring you to read it—practice it over and over for dramatic effect. You want to maintain eye contact.

- If you are using pictures and video for illustration, practice with them to smoothly incorporate them into the speech.

4
Humor

Humor can build a positive relationship with your audience and lighten up a dry or complex topic. However, you must be careful when using humor if you want to be effective and ethical. Any use of humor should:

- Relate to you, your audience, topic, and/or occasion

- Be funny (try it out on someone else)

- Not be demeaning to a particular group of people

- Be understandable to your audience (be careful of using humor across cultures or subcultures that might not understand the joke)

For example, President Obama appropriately made fun of White House security in his 2015 White House Correspondents' Association Dinner speech. Knowing the audience would understand the references, Obama states:

> Meanwhile, back here in our nation's capital, we're always dealing with new challenges. I'm happy to report that the Secret Service, thanks to some excellent reporting by White House correspondents, they're really focusing on some of the issues that have come up. And they finally figured out a foolproof way to keep people off my lawn. *(Laughter.)* It works. And it's not just fence-jumpers. As some of you know, a few months ago, a drone crash-landed out back. That was pretty serious, but don't worry, we've installed a new, state-of-the-art security system. *(Laughter.)*

Like Obama, you might get a few laughs if your humor is relevant, understandable, and appropriate.

5
Questions

You can use a question or a series of questions to direct your audience's attention to your topic. The questions can be asked in a manner to get a direct response or posed as ***rhetorical questions*** when you do not want a response but simply want to focus audience attention. Here are some examples:

Response-evoking questions:

> By a show of hands, how many of you are not allowed by the university to bring a car to campus? (*wait*) How many of you had trouble finding a parking place on campus today? (*wait*) How many of you have had to park far away at night and then walk home alone? (*wait*)

Rhetorical questions:

> Are you tired of taking the bus to the mall or bumming a ride because the university won't allow you to bring a car to campus? Are you sick of being late to class because you can't find a parking place? Are you mad that you have to walk home from a faraway parking lot at night?

Both types of questions can have some problems that you need to be aware of and try to prevent. The response-evoking questions can take a lot of time, and they can sidetrack your audience too much; also, the answers to the questions may not be what you expect. Rhetorical questions can cause audience members to linger too long in the thoughts or feelings you evoked and miss the next part of your speech. Beginning speakers often perceive questions as the easiest method and rely too heavily on them, lessening their effectiveness. Use the best method, not the easiest.

6
References

You can also get your audience's attention by referring to yourself, the audience, or the occasion; historical or recent events; or a prior speech. In some cases, it might be necessary, if the speaking event is momentous.

For example, referencing the events of the day and the 9/11 attacks, President Obama begins his May 2, 2011, remarks on Osama Bin Laden with:

> Good evening. Tonight, I can report to the American people and to the world that the United States has conducted an operation that killed Osama bin Laden, the leader of al Qaeda and a terrorist who's responsible for the murder of thousands of innocent men, women, and children.

> It was nearly 10 years ago that a bright September day was darkened by the worst attack on the American people in our history. The images of 9/11 are seared into our national memory—hijacked planes cutting through a cloudless September sky; the Twin Towers collapsing to the ground; black smoke billowing up from the Pentagon; the wreckage of Flight 93 in Shanksville, Pennsylvania, where the actions of heroic citizens saved even more heartbreak and destruction.

TIP: Locating Attention-Getters on the Internet

STATISTICS:
www.gallup.com
www.census.gov
www.prb.org
www.data.gov
www.nationmaster.com
www.usa.gov/federal-agencies

QUOTATIONS:
www.bartleby.com
www.bemorecreative.com
www.famous-quotes-online.com
www.coolnsmart.com
www.brainyquote.com

STORIES:
www.inspirationpeak.com

HUMOR:
www.short-funny.com

HISTORICAL/RECENT EVENTS:
aad.archives.gov/aad

GREAT SPEECHES:
www.americanrhetoric.com/speechbank.htm

Yesterday, December 7th, 1941 — a date which will live in infamy — the United States of America was suddenly and deliberately attacked by naval and air forces of the Empire of Japan.[1]

FRANKLIN DELANO ROOSEVELT

8.3 How Do You Organize an Introduction?

Most speech instructors suggest creating the body of the speech before you write either the introduction or conclusion. You need to know the tone and content of your speech before you can introduce or conclude it.

Once you are ready to write your introduction, its major parts should correspond to the four functions discussed earlier in this chapter. Your introduction should be no more than 15 percent of the total speech time, so you usually have under a minute to carry out these functions.

Any introduction should start with a good attention-getter, but you can present the other parts in just about any order. Beginning speakers often have the impulse to introduce themselves first. However, if you will be introduced or if the audience already knows you, this step is not necessary. Remember that the first thing you do or say should be designed to grab the audience's attention.

The template below and the example on the next page suggest the two most common arrangements for the parts of an introduction.

INTRODUCTION

Attention-getter: ....
....

Credibility material: ....
....

Relevance to audience: ....
....

Preview of speech: ....
....

Jameel is creating a speech on compulsive shopping for his class assignment. After many drafts and revisions, his introduction looks like this:

INTRODUCTION

Attention-getter: Shopping—it's the American pastime. It gives us a temporary high and a feeling of enjoyment we can't find quite the same way in other activities. As Robert Coombs suggests in his 2004 book, the *Handbook of Addictive Disorders*, "Almost all of us have purchased goods at some time to cheer ourselves up, and many see money and material possessions as tangible signs of personal success. We use consumption to improve our image, self-esteem, or relationship with others." But the questions are how far is too far, and how much is too much? And should you consider yourself or a loved one a compulsive shopper?

Relevance to audience: In his 2015 book *Treatment Strategies for Substance and Process Addictions*, Robert L. Smith notes that about 6 percent of the U.S. population—roughly 17 million people—are compulsive shoppers. That means two of us in this room might be considered compulsive shoppers.

Credibility material: Personally, I enjoy the many highs of shopping and have at times spent more than I should on one trip to the mall. But does that make me a compulsive shopper?

Preview of speech: In this speech, I will explore compulsive shopping as an addictive disorder, who tends to have the disorder, and how it can be treated.

Jameel has correctly included all four parts of an introduction. What attention-getter tactics can you identify? How has Jameel applied some of those tactics to other parts of his introduction?

CHECKLIST for Your Introduction

- ❑ Do I have an effective attention-getter?
- ❑ Do I begin to establish my credibility?
- ❑ Do I establish relevance between my audience and the topic?
- ❑ Do I preview the speech?

CONFIDENCE BOOSTER

Most beginning speakers experience their strongest communication apprehension in the first few minutes of a speech. A solid and creative introduction can help you feel more comfortable. Never plan to just "wing" or improvise your introduction. Be prepared; practice the introduction completely and multiple times. Doing so will help you feel more relaxed.

8.4 What Should Your Conclusion Do?

1 Signal the Ending
2 Summarize
3 Elicit a Response
4 Create an Impact One Last Time

The best way to create a conclusion is to see it as almost the reverse of your introduction, or that they are very similar and frame your speech. You will use some of the same tactics in the conclusion that you did in the introduction. Although you usually will not need to demonstrate your credibility with the topic or show the relevance to the audience at this point in the speech, you do need to review what you have said, tell the audience what you want them to do, and "WOW" them one last time. Ultimately, your conclusion should provide closure, leaving your audience enlightened and satisfied.

Do not rush creating your conclusion or cut short the process because you think you can craft it as you give the speech. Your conclusion is the last moment you have to increase your audience's understanding and appreciation, persuade them, or entertain them. Take advantage of this significant moment.

The next few pages will help you harness the power of your conclusions.

1
Signal the Ending

This function is like the end of a good movie or book. Throughout, the viewer or reader has moved along a path that builds to one defining moment—the ending. In speeches, you need to signal that ending. The most common ways to signal that the end is near are:

- A vocal change, such as slowing down and beginning to lower your intensity
- A physical change, such as moving from behind the lectern (often accompanied by a vocal change)
- A language signal, such as "In conclusion…" or "Today, we have…"

Once you have signaled the conclusion, you should not bring up new information about your topic. Otherwise, you are taking your audience back to information that should be in the body of the speech, which is confusing.

2
Summarize

This is your last chance to tell your audience about your topic in a way that will help them remember it. This statement should effectively and concisely restate your speech's main points.

For example, a speech informing your audience about counterfeit medicines popping up for sale in places such as the Internet could have a summary statement like this one:

> We've learned a lot about counterfeit medicine today. However, what's important to remember is, first, counterfeit medicine is widespread; second, counterfeit medicine is difficult to contain; and third, there are steps you can take to protect yourself from counterfeits.

3
Elicit a Response

Ideally, you do not want your audience to come away from your speech as passive vessels—taking in your speech but doing nothing with it. Therefore, you need to elicit, or bring forth, the response you wish them to have in relation to your topic. In other words, tell the audience what you want them to do with the information you have just given them. For example:

> Now that you know that counterfeit medicines can be a problem, it is time for you to take action to protect yourself and your loved ones.

Or, as another example, at the end of a toast:

> Please join me in toasting our new mayor.

4
Create an Impact One Last Time

Finally, the very end of your speech should take one last moment to really make your speech memorable and leave your audience with an intense feeling. That feeling should almost compel them to clap enthusiastically. That is the "WOW" moment of a speech. Because this moment is important to the effectiveness of your conclusion, the next section of this book will help you craft an effective "WOW" statement.

8.5 What Can You Use as a "WOW" Statement?

1 **Stories, Narratives, Illustrations, or Anecdotes**
2 **Quotations**
3 **Humor**
4 **Rhetorical Questions**
5 **Challenges to the Audience**
6 **References Back to the Introduction**

1 Stories, Narratives, Illustrations, or Anecdotes

These devices help humanize your topic and can appeal one last time to your audience's emotions. You should not bring up new information but can use another brief story, narrative, illustration, or anecdote that directly relates to your central idea. In a conclusion, keep them as short as possible and try not to read them directly, which would lower their impact. For example:

> I would like to end with a story about my grandfather's service in World War II.

Emotional power (*pathos*) can be an effective way to help your audience remember your speech.

2 Quotations

When using a quotation to end a speech, the quotation may have a direct relationship with the topic or may be somewhat metaphorical in capturing the essence of the topic.

For example, for a speech related to the Apollo 11 landing or a speech motivating the audience to volunteer, you could end with:

> As Neil Armstrong said, "That's one small step for man; one giant leap for mankind."

TIP: Use Attention-Getter Techniques

The best way to think about a "WOW" statement is to treat it like the attention-getter in the introduction. Many of the techniques you can use to grab your audience's attention can dazzle them at the conclusion of the speech as well.

3

Humor

Laughter is a positive experience for most individuals and can ease an audience out of your speech. Remember to make sure any use of humor relates to your audience, topic, and/or occasion; test the material to see if it really is funny; avoid demeaning humor; and make sure your audience will understand the joke.

For example, you might end a speech on reducing stress with this bumper-sticker saying:

"Stress is when you wake up screaming and you realize you haven't fallen asleep yet."

4

Rhetorical Questions

A series of rhetorical questions can focus how you want your audience to consider your topic and the goal.

For example, in a speech to persuade college students to help in an after-school program, these questions could end the speech:

See these children? (*click to slide 5*) Do you want them to end up like other inner-city children? Do you want them to be another crime statistic?

This speaker pairs the rhetorical questions with an image to increase the effect.

5

Challenges to the Audience

Ending by challenging your audience to act in a certain way can focus their attention on that behavior.

For example, adding a few more questions to the previous example challenges the audience to make a proposed response.

See these children? (*click to slide 5*) Do you want them to end up like other inner-city children? Do you want them to be another crime statistic? Do you have 20 minutes a week that you could give toward changing the lives of these children? I do, and I hope you will join me in volunteering in the Glenwood after-school program.

6

References Back to the Introduction

This type of "WOW" statement creates a frame for your speech by referring back to the attention-getter you used in your introduction.

For example, if you use the first few lines of a poem to start a speech, you might end with more of the poem. Or, if you tell a story at the beginning, returning to that moment of emotional appeal and finishing the story can nicely frame your speech.

→ See page 187 for an illustration of this technique.

> **PRACTICING ETHICS: Using Humor**
>
> Be ethical when using humor. Many jokes and humorous stories can be inappropriate or derogatory. Review the discussion about the ethical use of humor in attention-getters (page 178) if necessary.

8.6 How Do You Organize a Conclusion?

Your conclusion should be approximately 5 percent of your speech time. This is not much time, and you do not want to leave your audience feeling either like you suddenly stopped speaking or you went on forever after you signaled the ending. So it is important to spend some time constructing your conclusion.

CONCLUSION

Summary statement: ....
....

Audience response statement: ....
....

WOW statement: ....
....

As in your introduction, the organization of your conclusion can vary; but generally, the above template and the example on the next page show the basic order. Remember to always end with a "WOW" statement.

For the end of her classroom speech about unrest in Darfur, Albina crafted this succinct and moving conclusion.

CONCLUSION

Summary statement: I hope my speech today has offered you some insight into the Darfur issues. We have discussed the history of Darfur, why the violence in the region continues to worsen, and how we can make an effort to bring about peace.

Audience response statement: My purpose in giving this speech is to persuade you that even as citizens of the United States, we can take action to save lives.

WOW statement: Remember nine-month-old Zohar from the beginning of my speech? Zohar did not make it—and he became one of the thousands who died. To his parents, Zohar was their only child. To the world, Zohar is a statistic. Your actions could make Zohar, a child and someone's son, one of the last to be a statistic.

Albina has correctly included all three parts of a conclusion. Notice how her "WOW" statement refers back to a story in her introduction and finishes that story, to end on a note of emotional appeal.

CHECKLIST for Your Conclusion

❏ Do I signal the ending of the speech?
❏ Do I end the speech soon after signaling the conclusion?
❏ Do I restate my main points?
❏ Do I challenge the audience?
❏ Do I have the best possible "WOW" statement ending my speech?
❏ Do I have the necessary oral citations, if any are needed?

Chapter 8: Review

ASSESSING YOUR KNOWLEDGE

8.1 What Should Your Introduction Do?

Objective 8.1: **RESTATE WHAT AN INTRODUCTION SHOULD DO**

- Capture your audience's attention.
- Build your credibility early in the speech.
- Demonstrate how your speech relates to the audience.
- Introduce your speech topic and preview the speech.

→ See pages 174–175.

8.2 What Are Effective Attention-Getters?

Objective 8.2: **EXPLAIN HOW TO CREATE AN EFFECTIVE ATTENTION-GETTER**

An attention-getter is something you say, show, or do to get your audience to focus on you, your topic, and the goal of your speech. The six most common attention-getting tactics are:
- Facts and statistics
- Stories, narratives, illustrations, or anecdotes
- Quotations
- Humor, when ethical and effective
- Questions
- References to yourself, the audience, or the occasion; historical or recent events; or a prior speech

→ See pages 176–179.

8.3 How Do You Organize an Introduction?

Objective 8.3: **SUMMARIZE HOW TO ORGANIZE AN INTRODUCTION**

Your introduction should contain an attention-getting device, your credibility material, a statement relating the speech to your audience, and a preview of the speech. Any introduction should start with an attention-getter, but you can present the other parts in just about any order. Your introduction should be no more than 15 percent of the total speech time.

→ See pages 180–181.

8.4 What Should Your Conclusion Do?

Objective 8.4: **RESTATE WHAT A CONCLUSION SHOULD DO**

- Signal the end of your speech.
- Summarize your speech.
- Elicit a response from your audience to your speech.
- Create an impact one last time with a "WOW" statement.

→ See pages 182–183.

TERMS TO REMEMBER

attention-getter (176)
quotations (177)
rhetorical questions (178)

8.5 What Can You Use as a "WOW" Statement?

Objective 8.5: **DESCRIBE WHAT YOU CAN USE AS A "WOW" STATEMENT**

• Stories, narratives, illustrations, or anecdotes
• Quotations
• Humor, when ethical and effective
• Rhetorical questions
• Challenges to the audience
• References back to the introduction

→ See pages 184–185.

8.6 How Do You Organize a Conclusion?

Objective 8.6: **SUMMARIZE HOW TO ORGANIZE A CONCLUSION**

As in your introduction, the organization of your conclusion can vary; but generally, the organizational order is first the summary statement, then the audience response statement, and finally the "WOW" statement. Your conclusion should be approximately 5 percent of the total speech time.

→ See pages 186–187.

Practical Pointers for Tab 3

FAQs

What are the most common outlining mistakes I should watch out for?

Students who struggle with outlining usually commit one of the following mistakes:

- They don't record the topic, specific purpose, or central idea.
- They don't use the correct outline format. Presentational outlines should not contain symbols such as bullets or asterisks.
- They don't include significant detail for each point in the outline.
- They don't use full sentences throughout.
- They don't cite sources within the text of the outline and/or don't include a source page.
- They don't follow MLA or APA format.

I'm confused about how to cite a website. Can I get more help with this?

Consulting the MLA or APA handbook or another current writing handbook is the best way to learn how to cite a particular source. Here are basic citations for an entire website:

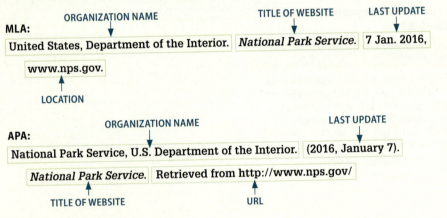

ADDITIONAL SUPPORT

If you are still struggling with outlining or citing sources, these resources might help:

- The Purdue Online Writing Lab (OWL), http://owl.english.purdue.edu
- Check the reference area of your library for current writing handbooks that might help.
- Make an appointment with your instructor or your institution's writing lab or center. Outlining a speech is very similar to outlining a paper.

TAB 4
Presenting

9

USING LANGUAGE SUCCESSFULLY

Neither your life nor the world you
live in just happens. You control the quality of
your lives and your communities. It is only in
giving to others that you can find meaning and
satisfaction in what you do.[1]

SONIA SOTOMAYOR

Ain't I a woman?[2]

SOJOURNER TRUTH

9.1 What Makes Language So Important?

1 Meaning
2 Culture
3 Power

1

Meaning

To understand how you use language, it is important to realize that *language* or, more precisely, *words* are symbols that you create, learn, and use to express your thoughts and feelings. Words are:

- **symbolic:** A word represents what it is referring to either by association, resemblance, or convention.

- **arbitrary:** The relationship between the word and what it stands for is random, subjective, or coincidental.

For example, think about the word *book*. Nothing about the letters that make up that word, or their arrangement, directly or logically relates to the thing you are reading from right now. That relationship is understood only when you learn to associate the word (*book*) with pages bound between two covers.

The movie *The Miracle Worker*, about the life of Helen Keller, features a scene in which Annie Sullivan teaches blind and deaf Helen the sign for water—a key breakthrough as Helen connects the word and the object together. At that moment, the word *water* became the symbol for that cold, wet substance Helen had felt for years; previously, she had no word or language to express it. The word now had meaning for Helen.

In their book, *The Meaning of Meaning*, Charles K. Ogden and Ivor A. Richards demonstrate how words (symbols) relate to the things they represent. Ogden and Richards created the "triangle of meaning," represented in the illustration on the next page.

THOUGHT

BAT ----- THING

WORD

Notice that the bottom of the triangle is broken, and no direct relationship connects the word (*bat*) to the thing (the animal). Instead, the word must go through your thought process to connect to the living animal. In your mind, if the word is familiar, you have two types of meanings that help you come up with a definition of the thing represented. They are the *denotative* and *connotative* meanings of a word.

DENOTATIVE MEANING

The **denotative meaning** of a word is the accepted meaning and is the one found in the dictionary. For example,

> bat—a small animal like a mouse with wings that flies at night (*Longman Dictionary of American English*)

Sometimes a word can have more than one denotative meaning. Then, you must pay attention to the context surrounding the word. For example, the word *bat* could refer not to the animal but to a piece of sporting equipment.

> bat—a long wooden stick used for hitting the ball in baseball (*Longman Dictionary of American English*)

CONNOTATIVE MEANING

The **connotative meaning** of a word is the emotional and personal reaction you might have to that word. Your reaction could be anywhere on a continuum from an emotional avalanche (a significant positive or negative response to a word) to an emotional famine (no real response at all). Let's return to the bat example.

What if you are highly afraid of bats (the mammal)? Some people exhibit fear at just the thought of the word. Nothing in the word itself or its denotative definition should elicit that kind of response, but those individuals have had an experience with or a knowledge of bats that adds a negative connotative meaning for them. For instance, maybe they were once attacked by a scared bat or they know that bats can carry rabies.

Conversely, what if you are a zoologist and your specialty is the study of the red bat? Your response to hearing the word would more likely be excitement and interest.

These differences in the emotional and personal reactions to a word add to your understanding and meaning of a word. The denotative and connotative meanings work in tandem to create your overall understanding and response to most words. As a speaker, you should always be aware that your audience may not have the same denotative or connotative meaning in mind for a word you use. For example, younger speakers often use *girl* with a positive intent when referring to any woman, but that word choice might have a negative connotative meaning for some older women. Slang in particular tends to be purely connotative, and we use it so often that we can be unaware of its influence on others.

2
Culture

Language is one of the means individuals use constantly to create, share, and transmit their cultural identity.

Culture is learned patterns of beliefs, values, attitudes, norms, practices, customs, and behaviors shared by a large group of people. These patterns often change and are shared through symbolic interaction (i.e., language).

The online and social networking cultures you may belong to are examples of how connected language and culture are to each other. Since the Internet explosion of the past century, cyberculture members have had to learn many new words, phrases, and grammatical conventions. Cybercultures tend to change almost daily, so their language is extremely dynamic. If you want to practice the proper norms, customs, and behavior, you have to stay on top of the current language—words and terms such as *blogging, texting, tweeting, hashtag, skype,* and *apps.*

Even the way you construct words and sentences in the "texting culture" is different. For example, this text is totally acceptable as "textese" but would not be in other interactions:

Had a gr8 time tnk for dinner C U @*$ 2mrw

Translated, it says:

I had a great time. Thanks for dinner. See you at Starbucks tomorrow.

As a speaker, you are part of multiple cultures that influence your language choices. However, none is more important to the public speaker than the cultures represented in the audience and connected to the speech topic. If you have the opportunity to give the same speech to different, diverse audiences, your language may be radically different.

The limits of my language mean the limits of my world.[3]

LUDWIG WITTGENSTEIN

PRACTICING ETHICS: Select Language Carefully

The words you choose to use can create meaning and cultural identity, influence feelings and attitudes, move people to action, or empower or break down individuals and groups. Carefully selecting your words is one of your most important ethical practices when giving a speech.

- Realize that your connotative meaning for a word may not be offensive, but to someone else the word could seem extremely inappropriate. Remember that listeners' interpretations of a word is part of the message being conveyed.
- Use emotionally rich language sparingly and when appropriate. Do not cloud your audience's judgment by using language that incites strong emotions that cannot be supported logically.
- Use appropriate language.

  → See the section "Be Appropriate" on page 200 for suggestions.

3

Power

Do you know the children's rhyme "Sticks and stones may break my bones, but words will never hurt me"? Parents often recite this to children when someone has called the child a hurtful name. Although the rhyme's intent is to teach a child to view words as powerless,

words are anything but powerless.

Here are some powers of language.

- Language helps you understand and create meaning, and through language, you create, share, and transmit cultural identity—and that is powerful.

- Language allows you to name experiences or things. For example, before Bill Wasik, senior editor for *Harper's Magazine*, staged the first "flash mob" in 2003, the term did not exist. You may now know that a flash mob is, as described by author Clay Shirky in *Here Comes Everybody*, "a group that engages in seemingly spontaneous but actually synchronized behavior" that is organized via e-mail, for example.

- Language can bring people together for a common cause. For example, once you understood the meaning of the term *flash mob*, you could then participate in one. This ability to gather or mobilize is powerful.

- Language can persuade you to act a certain way. Maybe you persuade a friend to join you in a flash mob. Persuasion is powerful.

- Unfortunately, language has the power to create and maintain inequality, to control, to hurt, and to disempower. This power can be conscious or unconscious, and history contains numerous examples. For instance, much of Adolf Hitler's power came from his persuasive speeches.

Or think about the current use of the word *terrorist*. What images come to mind when you say or hear the word? Which of these statements might you consider true?

James Holmes (Aurora movie theater shooting) is a terrorist.

Dylann Storm Roof (Charleston church shooting) is a terrorist.

Syed Rizwan Farook and Tashfeen Malik (San Bernardino shooting) are terrorists.

Terrorism is commonly defined as politically motivated actual or threatened violence. A terrorist's nationality or religion has nothing to do with being labeled a terrorist, but since 9/11, many people tend to associate the label with certain national or religious ties. Today, some people may not consider Holmes or Roof terrorists because they are non-Islamic U.S. citizens, even though their acts were seemingly politically motivated. Conversely, many might see any act of or attempt at mass destruction as terrorism.

- Fortunately, language creates equality and frees, heals, and empowers—listen to the language used by activists such as Robert Kennedy, Wangari Maathai, Mary Robinson, Bono, and Malala Yousafzai— and that is powerful.

9.2 How Can You Use Language Effectively?

1 Be Clear

2 Be Correct

3 Be Specific

4 Be Conversational

5 Be Appropriate

6 Be Distinctive

1

Be Clear

Always use language your audience will recognize and understand. Keeping your language clear and familiar is highly contingent on knowing your audience.

→ See Chapter 2 for details on getting to know your audience.

These guidelines will help keep your language clear and familiar:

- Select a style and level of language appropriate to your audience.

- Be cautious with ***jargon***, or specialized or technical language, which might be confusing. If you use it, do so sparingly and define words that could be unfamiliar.

- Be cautious with abbreviations and acronyms, which can be confusing to a listener. An ***abbreviation*** is the shortening of a word to stand as the whole word. For example:

  limo = limousine

  An ***acronym*** is a word formed from the initials or other parts of several words.

  NRA = National Rifle Association or National Recovery Administration

Use abbreviations and acronyms sparingly, if at all, and always explain them the first time you use them in a speech.

TIP: Intercultural Audiences

Jargon, abbreviations, and acronyms can be unfamiliar and confusing to intercultural audiences. Be especially sensitive to language with diverse audiences.

2

Be Correct

Your language should be free, as much as possible, of interpretation error and should adhere to certain standards. Using language incorrectly often leads to misunderstanding and low speaker ethos (credibility). When speakers use language incorrectly, they tend to use the wrong word, mispronounce words, or use incorrect grammar.

→ See page 216 for more on pronunciation.

Although you can be somewhat less formal with your grammar in an oral presentation, you still want to adhere to correct grammar rules. Do not equate informal with incorrect. Here are four common errors.

ERROR #1: MISPLACED MODIFIER

This error occurs when you place a modifier too far away from what it is modifying.

INCORRECT:
The man caught a bass wearing a purple hat.

CORRECT:
The man wearing a purple hat caught a bass.

ERROR #2: PRONOUNS

There are three common pronoun errors. First, make sure your pronouns are in agreement (plural vs. singular) with the nouns they refer to.

INCORRECT:
Everyone wants their own piece of the pie.

CORRECT:
Everyone wants his or her own piece of the pie.

Second, make sure you use the correct form of a pronoun for its function in the sentence. Use pronouns such as *I*, *she*, and *he* as subjects; use forms such as *me*, *her,* and *him* as objects.

INCORRECT:
Him and me are best friends.

CORRECT:
He and I are best friends.

He and *I* are subjects in the above examples. Below, *her* and *me* are objects, receiving the action of Mom's yelling.

INCORRECT:
Mom yelled at she and I.

CORRECT:
Mom yelled at her and me.

Third, if you are using third-person singular pronouns (*he*, *she*, *one*, and *it*), use *doesn't*, *does not*, or *does*. For all other pronouns (*I, you, we*, and *they*), use *don't*, *do not*, or *do*.

INCORRECT:
She don't want to go.

CORRECT:
She doesn't want to go.

ERROR #3: *WENT VERSUS GONE*

When using a helping verb (such as *has* or *have*), use the past participle form of a verb.

INCORRECT:
I should have went to the party.

CORRECT:
I should have gone to the party.

ERROR #4: SUBJECT/VERB AGREEMENT

A singular noun in the present tense uses a singular verb. Plural nouns use plural verbs. The following sentence refers to only one of many coats; the noun is singular and the verb should be, too.

INCORRECT:
One of these coats are mine.

CORRECT:
One of these coats is mine.

3

Be Specific

Getting your message across in a straightforward manner is necessary in a speech. Recall the most difficult book or article you have ever read. Then recall how many times you reread passages to understand them—or completely started over. Your audience cannot do that during your speech. They hear things once, maybe twice if you repeat something. In an instant, they must interpret your message and formulate a response and/or commit it to memory. Here are some steps that will help you stay specific.

- Be concrete. Concrete words create precision, clarity, and vividness. They focus on a person, object, action, or behavior and help listeners create a complete and, hopefully, accurate image. For example:

ABSTRACT:
The person saved the dog.

CONCRETE:
Firefighter Bradley saved the husky from the frozen pond.

- Eliminate unnecessary words. For example:

WORDY:
Assigning students assignments that are not related to the class is not something Professor Miller would do.

MORE CONCISE:
Professor Miller would not give unrelated assignments.

- Speak primarily in the active voice. In the active voice, the subject is doing the action stated in the verb. In the passive voice, the subject is the receiver of the action.

ACTIVE:
The truck hit the car.

PASSIVE:
The car was hit by the truck.

Occasionally, passive voice can be effective when you want to emphasize the receiver of the action more than the doer. But use it sparingly. This example from the Declaration of Independence uses passive voice for effect.

We hold these truths to be self-evident, that all men are created equal, that they are endowed by their Creator with certain unalienable Rights, that among these are Life, Liberty, and the pursuit of Happiness.

- Avoid clichés. **Clichés** are overused words or phrases that have lost their effect. Some examples:

Live and learn	Needless to say
A matter of time	To tell the truth
Before I knew it	Cut to the chase
Fit as a fiddle	Without a doubt

- Avoid fillers. **Fillers** are sounds, words, or phrases that serve no purpose and do not help your audience understand the message. Often, you can find a more concise way to say something, or you can eliminate the word or phrase. Some examples:

INSTEAD OF	SAY
a number of	several
due to the fact that	because

AVOID FILLERS SUCH AS
ah, um, like, you know, or actually

4

Be Conversational

If you have ever read a transcript of an oral conversation, you know that the way people speak is radically different from the way they write. Likewise, if you have ever heard someone read a paper aloud, you know that this format is much harder to follow than a conversational delivery and requires greater concentration on the part of the listener.

When you give a speech, you want to use an oral style rather than a written style. In oral style, you use more everyday language, personal pronouns such as *we* or *you*, contractions, and shorter sentences that put the subjects and verbs closer together. For example:

WRITTEN STYLE:

Calling the jungles of Central and South America home, Bradypus variegatus is a slow-moving, leaf-, shoots-, and fruit-eating mammal in the order Pilosa.

ORAL STYLE:

Three-toed sloths, or Bradypus variegatus, call the jungles of Central and South America home. These slow-moving mammals eat leaves, shoots, and fruit. All sloths are relatives of ant-eaters, in the animal order Pilosa.

The table below summarizes the major differences between written and oral styles.

CHARACTERISTICS OF ORAL STYLE	CHARACTERISTICS OF WRITTEN STYLE
Informal language	Formal language
Animated language	Technical language
Simple sentence structure	Complex sentence structure
Personally tailored messages	Impersonal messages
Repetition and restatement	Detailed and complex thoughts

CHECKLIST for Using an Oral Style

❏ Am I using language known to my audience or words that have fewer syllables than I might use in a written style?

❏ Am I using short sentences?

❏ Am I employing a variety of communication signals—gestures, intonation, inflection, volume, pitch, pauses, and movement?

❏ Am I focusing on what needs to be said and not bogging my audience down in details and complexity?

❏ Am I using pronouns such as *I, you, we*, and *me* to make the message more personal and to form a relationship with the audience?

❏ Am I using repetition, restatement, and other such devices to help others remember my message?

5

Be Appropriate

The type of language you use should suit you, your audience, and the situation. Always remember that you are cocreating your message with your listeners. Their denotative and connotative definitions of a word may or may not be the same as yours. Your success depends on selecting appropriate language that is constructive, not destructive.

USE CULTURALLY APPROPRIATE AND UNBIASED LANGUAGE

- Avoid singling out personal traits or characteristics (such as age, disability, race, sex, sexual orientation, and so on) when they do not relate to the subject at hand. For example:

  INCORRECT: The gay student had coffee.

  The student's sexual orientation has nothing to do with the consumption of coffee.
- Use the name for an individual or group that they prefer, such as:

  African American or black; Asian or Asian American; indigenous or Native; white or Caucasian; Hispanic, Latino, or Chicano; gay, lesbian, bisexual, or transgendered (avoid *homosexual*); a person with Down Syndrome; a person who uses a wheelchair
- Avoid language that promotes stereotypes. For example:

  AVOID: woman driver, Mr. Mom, redneck

USE GENDER-NEUTRAL LANGUAGE

AVOID	USE INSTEAD
man and wife	husband and wife, couple, partners, spouses
chairman or chairwoman; fireman; congressman; councilwoman	chair or chairperson, firefighter, congressperson, councilmember
housewife	homemaker, parent, or caregiver
pronoun *he* to represent both male and female or situations generally viewed as masculine (such as sports) pronoun *she* in situations generally viewed as female	the plural *they*, or replace with *one*, *you*, or *he or she* You can also reword to avoid using pronouns: "On average, each nurse was disappointed with the raise." or "On average, nurses were disappointed with their raises."
girl or boy (over the age of 18)	woman or young woman, man or young man
Miss and Mrs.	Ms. to refer to married and unmarried women (as you would use Mr.)

6

Be Distinctive

As these segments from a speech given by retired U.S. Marine Corps Cpl. Aaron Mankin demonstrate, the right language can paint an emotional picture in the minds of those listening. Mankin is speaking at the Iraq and Afghanistan Veterans of America Sixth Annual Heroes Gala, November 13, 2012. Read the excerpts aloud or, better yet, search the Internet for a video of Mankin delivering the speech for the full effect of the language's distinctive style.

> I was a combat correspondent, a journalist, for the Marine Corps, a camera in one hand and a rifle in the other. And a storyteller's worst nightmare is becoming the story....
>
> So, there I was, one fateful day in May, when an improvised explosive device tore through a 26-ton vehicle filled with Marines, chow, ammunition, throwing us 10 feet into the air. Six men to my right, some fathers, all sons, gave their lives. How I didn't make seven, God only knows.

> And I believe that it is for this purpose, so that I may share with you the things that I have witnessed so that you will know the things that you demand of us and we gladly provide.... I get to share these stories with you, things that all of us should know. I'm blessed.
>
> There are things in my life now, blessings I can count that may have never existed. I can connect with fellow warriors in ways that others can't because I understand what it means to transition home, how difficult it can be.
>
> But in all respects, my transition has been easy, because you see my scars. I wear my uniform everywhere I go.
>
> But there are those among us in our community, in our families, who have scars that are never seen. And I hurt for them, as you should. It's not easy. And that is the burden we carry for our country.

The next section of this chapter offers you strategies and examples for how to make your language distinctive.

CHECKLIST for Using Language Effectively

❏ Is my language correct?

❏ Is my language clear? Do I avoid jargon?

❏ Is my language specific? Do I use concrete words and active voice?

❏ Is my language appropriate? Do I avoid biased words?

❏ Do I use a conversational, oral style?

❏ Is my language distinctive?

CONFIDENCE BOOSTER

Building your vocabulary will help you feel more comfortable speaking. Here are a few suggestions to build your vocabulary.

1. Read more.
2. Actively pursue words. Look them up when you do not know them.
3. Make a habit of learning a new word every day.
4. Play word puzzles and games.
5. Read a dictionary or a thesaurus.

9.3 How Can You Boost Your Distinctiveness?

1 Use Vivid Language
2 Use Speech Devices

1

Use Vivid Language

When you think of something being vivid, you think of it as bright, glowing, vibrant, colorful, dramatic, and flamboyant. Vivid language is everything you can imagine that is contradictory to dull, uninteresting, dry, lifeless, or lackluster.

You can bring life and vividness to your speech by using language that appeals to your audience's senses or by enhancing your words so that they are remarkable and memorable.

APPEAL TO THE SENSES

Senses are the physiological methods humans use to perceive things around them. Attributed to Aristotle, in his *De Anima*, the traditional classifications for human senses are seeing, hearing, smelling, tasting, and touching. More recently, movement and bodily tension have been added.

When you develop your speech, using language that evokes or appeals to one or more of these senses can be a powerful tool—to bring an object to life, vividly explain a technique, invoke passion, or simply entertain. Although you will not want every sentence to use a sensory appeal and you will not use every appeal in one speech, you will want to use enough appeals to keep the audience interested and listening. So experiment with turning an ordinary statement into a sensory image. Use the table on the next page to help you.

SENSES	WHY MIGHT I APPEAL TO THIS PARTICULAR SENSE?	EXAMPLES
Sight (visual)	To make a visual comparison between things or to restore a visual image memory	"His eyes sparkled with anticipation." "The closet was pitch black."
Sound (auditory)	To help the listener understand how something sounds or to evoke a sound memory	"As the wind blew, you could hear the cracking and splitting of the tree limbs." "The screeching of the tires tore through me like fingernails on a chalkboard."
Smell (olfactory)	To take a person back to a place, time, or feeling, as people often associate smell with a memory	"Many people remember the smell of cookies or turkey baking when they think of great Christmas memories, but I don't. My favorite memory is the cool, leathery smell of the brand-new football my Dad gave me when I was eight." "The aroma of popcorn filled the theater."
Taste (gustatory)	To associate the taste of something with something known or to restore taste memory	"It tastes like chicken." "The sweet rolls were chewy and buttery, with a hint of almond."
Touch (tactile)	To create the feel of something or evoke a relationship/feeling between the person and the object touched	"Think about the last time you really played a video game and how the controller warmed to your intensity and vibrated softly as you fought your battle." "The puppies' ears were like velvet."
Movement (kinetic)	To create speed or direction or to evoke the sense of how something moves	"You can experience no better feeling than the graceful motion of your body at an insanely fast speed, crisscrossing down a mountain on a snowboard."
Tension (kinesthetic)	To create/evoke bodily tension or lack thereof	"As she reacted to her anger, you could see her jaw and fists clench." "As he fell to sleep, his body became a rag doll."

ENHANCE YOUR LANGUAGE

Just as you can decorate, rejuvenate, or beautify your home, your appearance, and even your car, you can enhance your words. However, when you enrich words to enhance a speech, you are doing more than just making them fancier. You are making them more remarkable and memorable. Read this section from the end of President Ronald Reagan's address given the night of the *Challenger* tragedy, January 28, 1986. Read it aloud or watch the video (search for it online) for the full effect.

> There's a coincidence today. On this day three hundred and ninety years ago, the great explorer Sir Francis Drake died aboard ship off the coast of Panama. In his lifetime the great frontiers were the oceans, and a historian later said, "He lived by the sea, died on it, and was buried in it." Well, today, we can say of the *Challenger* crew: Their dedication was, like Drake's, complete.
>
> The crew of the space shuttle *Challenger* honored us by the manner in which they lived their lives. We will never forget them, nor the last time we saw them, this morning, as they prepared for their journey and waved goodbye and "slipped the surly bonds of earth" to "touch the face of God."

Reagan uses vivid and other evocative language choices, making the speech as a whole remarkable, memorable, and appropriate for the somber occasion.

Speaking of freedom, in his Second Inaugural Address, President George W. Bush uses metaphor when comparing freedom to fire. He states:

> … And as hope kindles hope, millions more will find it. By our efforts, we have lit a fire as well—a fire in the minds of men. It warms those who feel its power, it burns those who fight its progress, and one day this untamed fire of freedom will reach the darkest corners of our world.

As you can see from these segments, the language grabs listeners' attention and directs them to the denotative and connotative meanings the speakers wished to convey.

Often, you can combine an appeal to senses with enhanced language to boost the effectiveness of your message, as this student did in a speech about traveling to the Bahamas. Look at how Gwenn revised her description of water:

LESS DISTINCTIVE:
The water was an amazing color.

MORE DISTINCTIVE:
The color of the water was like a fusion of the blue in a bright sky and the green of a lush meadow.

Gwenn is appealing to sight by describing a past memory as well as to movement (kinetic) in the fusion (a joining together). She tops off those appeals by explicitly comparing the color of the water to the sky and a meadow (simile).

You can use techniques called **_tropes_** to transform ordinary words. Based on Edward Corbett and Robert Connors, _Classical Rhetoric for the Modern Student_, this table explains the most common tropes.

TROPE	WHAT IS IT?	EXAMPLES
Simile	An explicit comparison between two things, using _like_ or _as_	"The car seat was hard as a rock." "After applying the motion sickness patch, my mouth was dry as a bone."
Metaphor	An implied comparison	"Creating the icing is a breeze." "Your home is your castle." "That debate was a train wreck."
Personification	Giving human traits to an object, idea, or animal	"Opportunity knocked." "Snow had blanketed the city." "This boat is a beauty."
Oxymoron	Connecting two ordinarily contradictory words together	Hell's Angels, jumbo shrimp, Led Zeppelin, Iron Butterfly, found missing, deafening silence, unbiased opinion, original copies, almost exactly, Great Depression
Hyperbole	The use of exaggeration for emphasis	"I told you a million times to clean your room." "After the race, my legs weighed a ton." "My sister will buy anything that is on sale."
Irony	The use of words to convey a meaning that is the opposite of its literal meaning	"I am overjoyed at the thought of going to the dentist." "I am so brilliant that I locked myself out of my car."
Onomatopoeia	Words that imitate the sounds they represent	achoo, ahem, baa, bah, bang, bark, beep, boink, boo, buzz, chatter, chirp, clang, clap, click, ding-dong, fizz, smack
Rhetorical questions	Asking a question, but not for the purpose of receiving an answer	"Do you consume a lot of diet soda daily? Do you think it is healthier than regular soda? Do you think it helps people lose weight?"
Metonymy	The use of a related word or phrase to stand in for another	"We need boots on the ground." "Let me give you a hand."

2

Use Speech Devices

Like enhancing your words, the techniques of finessing word order—known as **_schemes_**—can help you create distinctive language. Here, you can repeat sounds, words, phrases, sentences, and grammatical patterns. You can juxtapose contrasting ideas, change word order, or omit words to create a rhyme that appeals to the ear and makes your words unforgettable.

Consider the nursery rhymes you learned as a child. They were fun to say and hear as well as easy to remember because they contained speech devices. Many of them used devices of repetition, like this one.

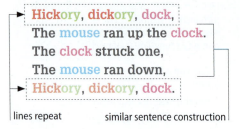

Hickory, dickory, dock,
The mouse ran up the clock.
The clock struck one,
The mouse ran down,
Hickory, dickory, dock.

lines repeat   similar sentence construction

Repetition is only one type of device, or scheme, that you can utilize. The table on page 207, based on Corbett and Conners, explains common speech devices used by speakers today.

At the beginning of his speech after the 2016 Iowa caucus, Senator Marco Rubio used repetition and parallelism several times to build the intensity of the moment. Note the bold-faced phrases in this passage:

> So, this is the moment they said would never happen. **For months, for months they told us we had no chance. For months they told us** because we offered too much optimism in a time of anger **we had no chance. For months, they told us** because we didn't have the right endorsements or the right political connections, **we had no chance. They told me that we had no chance** because my hair wasn't gray enough and my boots were too high. **They told me** I needed to wait my turn. That I needed to wait in line.

SCHEME	WHAT IS IT?	EXAMPLES
Repetition	Replicating the same words, phrases, or sentences for emphasis	"… And on that path to freedom, Harriett Tubman had one piece of advice. **If you** hear the dogs, **keep going. If you** see the torches in the woods, **keep going.** If they're shouting after you, **keep going.** Don't ever stop. **Keep going. If you** want a taste of freedom, **keep going.** Even in the darkest of moments, ordinary Americans have found the faith to **keep going.**" —Hillary Rodham Clinton, 2008 DNC speech
Assonance	Repeating a similar vowel sound	"**We need** to **meet** and **greet.**" "… the **odious apparatus** of Nazi rule." —Winston Churchill
Alliteration	Repetition of initial consonants in two or more words in close proximity	"Already American vessels have been **searched, seized,** and **sunk.** —John F. Kennedy, *Profiles in Courage* "She placed the **cold, clammy cloth** on his forehead."
Parallelism	Duplicating the same grammatical patterns	"We have seen the state of our Union in the endurance of rescuers, working past exhaustion. We've seen **the unfurling of flags, the lighting of candles, the giving of blood, the saying of prayers**—in English, Hebrew, and Arabic." —George W. Bush, address to Congress, 2001 "**Tell me and I forget. Teach me and I may remember. Involve me and I will learn.**" —Benjamin Franklin
Antithesis	Juxtaposition of contrasting ideas, often in parallel structure	"That's one small step for **man**, one giant leap for **mankind.**" —Neil Armstrong, July 21, 1969 "We have found ourselves **rich in goods**, but **ragged in spirit.**" —Richard Nixon, first inaugural speech
Anastrophe	Reversing expected word order to gain attention	"Cold and damp was the wind." "Ask not what your country can do for you; ask what you can do for your country." —John F. Kennedy, inaugural speech
Asyndeton	Deliberately omitting conjunctions	"I think tonight of the 'Greatest Generation.' We look back and marvel at their courage—**overcoming the Great Depression, fighting Nazi tyranny, standing up for freedom around the world.**" —Chris Christie, 2012 RNC speech "**I came, I saw, I conquered!**" (Veni, Vidi, Vici!) —reportedly written by Julius Caesar

Chapter 9: Review

ASSESSING YOUR KNOWLEDGE

9.1 What Makes Language So Important?

Objective 9.1: **ARTICULATE WHAT MAKES LANGUAGE SO IMPORTANT**

Language is important because it is the tool we use to create meaning and culture and to influence others.

- *Language* or, more precisely, *words* are symbols you create, learn, and use to express your thoughts and feelings. Words are symbolic in that they represent what they are referring to either by association, resemblance, or convention. Words are arbitrary because the relationship between the word and what it stands for is random, subjective, or coincidental. Words can have a denotative and a connotative meaning.
- Language is one of the means individuals use constantly to create, share, and transmit their cultural identity. Culture is learned patterns of beliefs, values, attitudes, norms, practices, customs, and behavior shared by a large group of people.
- Language is powerful in that it informs our minds, creates and helps us express feelings or thoughts, helps us transmit our identity, brings us together or divides us, and is persuasive. Language can create equality, freedom, and empowerment. Unfortunately, it can do the opposite as well.

→ See pages 192–195.

9.2 How Can You Use Language Effectively?

Objective 9.2: **EXPLAIN HOW TO USE LANGUAGE EFFECTIVELY**

- Be clear. Be cautious of your use of jargon, abbreviations, and acronyms. Explain them when necessary. They can be especially difficult for intercultural audiences to understand.
- Be correct. Make sure you are using the correct words, pronouncing words correctly, and using correct grammar.
- Be specific. Use concrete language and avoid abstraction, clichés, and fillers. Use active voice in your speech whenever possible. Use passive voice only to emphasize the receiver of an action when that is more important.
- Be conversational. Compared to written style, conversational (or oral) style is
  - Less formal
  - More animated
  - Simpler in sentence structure and language
  - Tailored more toward the personal
  - More repetitive
- Be appropriate. Your language should suit you, your audience, and the situation. Remember to use culturally appropriate and unbiased language.
- Be distinctive. Carefully select and craft your language for maximum effect.

→ See pages 196–201.

9.3 How Can You Boost Your Distinctiveness?

Objective 9.3: **DESCRIBE HOW TO BOOST YOUR DISTINCTIVENESS**

- Use vivid language by appealing to the senses or enhancing words with tropes. Common tropes are simile, metaphor, personification, oxymoron, hyperbole, irony, onomatopoeia, rhetorical questions, and metonymy.
- Use speech devices, or schemes, to create distinctive language. Common schemes are repetition, assonance, alliteration, parallelism, antithesis, anastrophe, and asyndeton.

→ See pages 202–207.

TERMS TO REMEMBER

symbolic (192)
arbitrary (192)
denotative meaning (193)
connotative meaning (193)
culture (194)
jargon (196)
abbreviation (196)
acronym (196)
clichés (198)
fillers (198)
tropes (205)
schemes (206)

10 DELIVERING YOUR SPEECH

10.1 What Are the Elements of Vocal Delivery?

1 **Pitch**
2 **Volume**
3 **Rate**
4 **Pause**
5 **Variety**
6 **Pronunciation**
7 **Articulation**
8 **Dialect**

1

Pitch

Pitch is how high and low your voice is in frequency and is determined by how fast or slow your vocal cords vibrate. The greater the number of vibrations per second your cords move, the higher the pitch. Two aspects determine how fast your cords will vibrate.

The first is the length and thickness of the vocal cords. For example, in general, women's vocal cords tend to be short and thin, allowing the cords to vibrate fast. Therefore, their voices are usually higher in pitch than men's.

The second aspect is how relaxed or stressed your body is. When you are excited, tense, or frightened, the muscles around your voice box (larynx) unconsciously tighten, raising the pitch of your voice. To demonstrate how this works, say this phrase calmly: "The tree is falling." Now, imagine your friends are standing near the tree and you must save them by yelling, "The tree is falling!" During the second demonstration, your voice is clearly louder—but it is also higher in pitch, signaling your friends to the danger.

You already know from Chapter 1 that former British Prime Minister Margaret Thatcher trained her high feminine voice to be lower. Pitch is something you can work on if your voice is extremely high or low; and, as with many elements in your speech, variety in pitch is important. A constant pitch, known as ***monotone***, is distracting and boring. Varying your pitch (***inflection***) will help you demonstrate enthusiasm, excitement, concern, and dedication to the topic.

2
Volume

Like your stereo volume, your vocal **volume** is how loud or soft your voice is. Some speech instructors would say the appropriate volume is slightly louder than your normal speaking voice. However, you need to consider the size of the room and audience, the level of environmental noise, and whether you must project on your own or will be using a microphone.

Aim for a volume that can vary and still be heard in the back row of the audience when you are at your softest—and not hurt you at your loudest. If you speak in a perpetually soft voice that can just barely be heard, your audience may think you are unsure or timid. Not varying the volume can sound boring or apathetic. A loud voice can make your audience stop listening and can damage your vocal cords.

Pay attention to the cues your audience sends you about your volume. They may lean forward if you are too quiet and turn their heads slightly to hear you better. If you are too loud, they may lean back, lower their chins slightly, and frown.

If you are from a culture where speaking softly is more acceptable, you might have trouble recognizing when you are too quiet. Practice your speech with someone who will tell you to keep raising your voice until you reach a good volume, and then rehearse at that level several times. You may feel like you are yelling; that's normal. Relax and practice the new level until it seems more comfortable.

3
Rate

Your vocal **rate** is the speed at which you speak. The average rate is between 120 and 150 words per minute. In parts of the country, people may speak faster (e.g., New York City) or slower (e.g., some southern states). You can vary your rate to add excitement, exhilaration, or urgency to your speech. The best way to find a good overall rate is to pay attention to your audience. If your audience seems bored, speeding up may help. If the topic is difficult and they appear confused, slowing down would be helpful. If you feel out of breath during your speech, that is a good indication that you are talking too fast. Slow down, let your audience catch up, and allow yourself to breathe.

TIP: Using a Microphone

If a room or audience is very large, the acoustics are poor, or you are physically unable to project your voice, you will need to use a microphone.

- If possible, practice your complete speech with the sound system, to uncover problems.
- Perform a second sound check 30 minutes or so before the event starts.
- Periodically, pay attention to the sound person, if there is one. He or she may signal you when an issue arises (for example, if you forget to turn on the microphone).
- Determine the type of microphone and how close to or far away from it you need to be.
- Beware of making distracting vocal sounds (popping sharp consonants or heavy breathing) or nonverbal sounds (hitting the lectern) that might be amplified by the system.
- Be careful not to make side or private comments that might be heard over an open microphone. Always assume that the microphone is on, until you are a safe distance from it.

4

Pause

A vocal *pause* can be used for more than just slowing down your speaking rate. Pauses can allow your audience to linger on a thought in order to apply meaning or gauge significance. Also, pauses can be used as a tool for enhancing or emphasizing a point, and they can draw your audience's attention to a point you are about to make.

Maybe you once had an elementary school teacher who used this technique to get your class under control. Your teacher stood at the front of the room with hands on hips or arms crossed and yelled out, "Class!" He or she then waited. Eventually each child realized that the silence had a significant meaning: The class was to get a time-out.

At the end of his inaugural address on January 20, 1961, John F. Kennedy provided an excellent example of how pauses can focus an audience's attention on the message and evoke a major reaction. Each line break represents a pause (capitalization indicates increased volume); you can listen to the speech on YouTube.

> And so, my fellow Americans,
> ask NOT
> what your country can do for you;
> ask what you can do for your country.
>
> My fellow citizens of the world,
> ask NOT
> what America will do for you,
> but what together we can do
> for the freedom of man.

REMOVING VOCAL FILLERS

Do not be afraid to use pauses to help avoid using vocal fillers. As you learned in Chapter 9, fillers are extraneous sounds and words such as *ah*, *um*, *like*, or *you know*. Most pauses that are uncomfortable for a speaker are not significant to the audience, but the fillers become distracting.

The process of removing vocal fillers from your speech will take time and a lot of patience. In the end, it will be worth it, and you will appear and feel much more confident.

- Practicing your speech numerous times will help you become familiar with your topic, which will decrease the time it takes you to recall what to say next. Speakers tend to use vocal fillers when struggling for their next word or sentence. But make sure to use enough natural pauses that you do not speed through your speech.

- Realize that removing vocal fillers is a process. The first step is to make a conscious effort to recognize that you are using fillers. Then, you must work to recognize when and why you use them. The next step is to preempt the usage, which takes time, dedication, and patience.

- Having a friend or family member signal you each time you use a filler during a rehearsal might be beneficial.

- Record your speech and listen to it. Hearing how fillers detract from your delivery can inspire you to use them less.

5
Variety

German writer Jean Paul Richter once noted that the "variety of mere nothings gives more pleasure than the uniformity of something." Although "mere nothings" are never effective in a speech, Richter's point does have some merit. As the previous discussion of volume, pitch, rate, and pause suggests, vocal variety is a necessity if you want to give an effective speech. You use vocal **variety** when you fluctuate, change, or adjust your volume, pitch, rate, and pauses. To do so brings your voice and, therefore, your words to life, filling them with expression and animation. To be an effective speaker, you must employ vocal variety.

To understand what vocal variety can do for your speech, locate a video clip of a famous speech. AmericanRhetoric.com and YouTube have several, such as former President Ronald Reagan's "tear down this wall" speech—remarks delivered in front of Brandenburg Gate in Germany on June 12, 1987.

Here is the basic text of the most famous portion of the speech:

> General Secretary Gorbachev, if you seek peace, if you seek prosperity for the Soviet Union and Eastern Europe, if you seek liberalization: Come here to this gate! Mr. Gorbachev, open this gate! Mr. Gorbachev, Mr. Gorbachev, tear down this wall!

As Reagan speaks these now-famous words, his voice deepens, slows at times, and rises in volume to punch the ending. If written poetically to simulate the vocal variety President Reagan used, this same section would look like the following. End-of-line breaks represent longer pauses or breaks, added spaces between words represent short pauses, and capitalization represents increased volume and intensity in his delivery.

> General Secretary Gorbachev,
> if YOU seek peace,
> if you seek prosperity for the Soviet Union
> and Eastern Europe,
> if YOU seek liberalization:
> Come   here   to THIS gate!
> Mr. Gorbachev,
> open   THIS   gate! (applause)
> Mr. Gorbachev,
> MR. GORBACHEV,
> TEAR   DOWN   THIS   WALL!

His effective delivery inspired listeners around the world. Listen to a recording for yourself and see if you, too, can feel the energy when he speaks.

6
Pronunciation

Correct **pronunciation** is the standard or commonly accepted way to make a word sound. For example, do you know someone who incorrectly says the word *picture* like the word *pitcher*? The word *picture* should be pronounced "pik-chure," and *pitcher* should be pronounced "pit-chure."

Poor pronunciation can, at the very least, slow down your audience's listening skills as they try to figure out what you intend or, in the worst case, cause complete misunderstanding.

Recognizing when you mispronounce a word can be difficult, as you may not know you are doing it. Ask your friends and family to pay attention and tell you when you mispronounce a word. If you are unsure of how to pronounce a new word, look it up or ask someone who should know. Many online dictionaries allow you to play sound recordings of correct pronunciations.

Not knowing how to correctly pronounce words can also significantly lower your ethos. Be diligent and find out the correct way to pronounce the words you plan to use in your speech.

SOME COMMON MISPRONUNCIATIONS

CORRECT SPELLING	MISPRONUNCIATION	CORRECT PRONUNCIATION
asked	aks	askt
clōthes	close	clōthes
especially	ex-pecially	es-pecially
February	Feb-u-ary	Feb-ru-ary
hierarchy	hi-archy	hi-er-archy
jewelry	jew-le-ry	jew-el-ry
library	li-berry	li-brer-y
nuclear	nu-cu-lar	nu-cle-ar
theater (or theatre)	the-ate-er	the-uh-ter

We are what we repeatedly do; excellence, then, is not an act but a habit.[1]

WILL DURANT,
summarizing Aristotle

7
Articulation

Articulation is how completely and clearly you utter a word—for example, saying "morning" instead of "mornin'." Closely linked, and often used synonymously with *articulation*, is **enunciation**, or the distinctiveness and clarity of linked whole words—for example, saying, "Did you eat yet?" instead of "Jeat yet?"

Speaking fast, mumbling, running words together, and dropping vowels or consonants (as in "drinkin'") are all considered poor articulation or enunciation—commonly referred to as "lazy speech." Audiences may view these habits as inappropriate for a public speech, which can harm your ethos.

Mumbling is a common problem for beginning speakers. If you have this habit, make a conscious effort to eliminate it. Warming up your mouth can help. Before entering the speech location, open your mouth wide several times, stretching your jaw muscles (be careful if you have medical issues with your jaw), then hum as you rapidly vibrate your lips together. Like an athlete stretches legs or arms, you need to warm up your mouth's muscles.

8
Dialect

All cultures and cocultures have unique elements in their speech, known as dialects. A **dialect** is how a particular group of people pronounces and uses language. Dialects can be regional (e.g., the South) or ethnic (e.g., Jewish English).

Dialects are important for establishing and maintaining cultural identity, so you do not automatically need to avoid using dialect. However, if your dialect is significantly different from that of your audience, it can distract them and decrease your effectiveness.

When a dialect interferes with communication, it is usually because grammar and vocabulary cause the misunderstanding. For example, in the Boston area, you might hear a water fountain called a bubbler or a rubber band called an elastic.

When speaking outside of your region or culture, use the more standard vocabulary. Doing so will help you prevent misunderstanding and distraction, while maintaining your individual identity.

CHECKLIST for Vocal Delivery

❏ Is my volume appropriate for this space and the audience size? Do I need to use a microphone?

❏ Am I using both low and high pitches? Do I need to regulate my natural pitch?

❏ Is my rate too fast or too slow?

❏ Am I using pauses effectively?

❏ Do I use enough vocal variety?

❏ Am I pronouncing all my words correctly?

❏ Am I mumbling, running my words together quickly, or clipping consonants or vowels?

10.2 What Are the Elements of Physical Delivery?

1 Appearance
2 Eye Contact
3 Facial Expression
4 Gestures
5 Movement
6 Posture

1

Appearance

If you know of her, two things come to mind when you think of Lady Gaga—her music and her appearance. Although her appearance is not what makes her a good singer, it is part of the persona she wishes to create, helping her stand out and be memorable.

Similarly, you should acknowledge the influence your appearance can have on your speech. *Appearance* includes your dress and grooming choices. Once you walk into a room, the people around you begin to form first impressions about you. Unlike Lady Gaga, you should rarely, if ever, draw attention to your appearance because you want your audience to focus on your message. Your appearance should improve your ethos and support your message. Here are some guidelines:

- Always be well groomed.
- Dress for the occasion. You want to dress a bit better than what is expected for the occasion and the audience.
- Consider environmental issues. Wearing black on a hot, sunny day may make you sweat and appear more nervous.
- Use your appearance to support, not detract from, your topic. (For example, wearing a suit for a speech on changing motor oil in a car will seem odd.)
- Think about the mood, attitude, or image you want to project.
- Avoid wearing distracting items such as flashy colors or jewelry.

2

Eye Contact

If there is one piece of advice effective speakers understand, it is to make eye contact. You must establish and maintain eye contact with your audience if you want them to stay focused on you and your message and view you as trustworthy. In addition, eye contact enables you to obtain feedback during the speech.

Although cultural norms differ, Western culture prefers **direct eye contact**, or briefly looking straight into the eyes of the other person. During a public speaking occasion, you can accommodate this cultural preference by randomly selecting several people in the audience to make direct eye contact with. Choosing those audience members who are actively listening to your speech and smiling will help boost your confidence as well.

Direct eye contact

Choose several audience members to make direct eye contact with. As an audience member, help the speaker by being an active listener and maintaining eye contact with him or her.

The beginning speaker often uses ineffective eye contact. Familiarize yourself with the ineffective practices in the table below. If you recognize yourself in any of these categories, try to self-regulate the behavior or ask a friend to watch you during your speech.

INEFFECTIVE EYE CONTACT	WHAT IS IT?	EFFECTIVE SOLUTION
The Bobber	A speaker who bobs up and down rhythmically from notes to audience	Practice the speech so you don't rely on your notes so much, or shorten your delivery outline.
The Stargazer	A speaker who looks above and beyond the audience	Don't be afraid to look at your audience. Most audiences are friendly.
The Obsessor	A speaker who looks at only one or two audience members during the whole speech	Use more of the space in front of the audience, forcing you to look at more people, and practice including most of the audience.
The Obliterator	A speaker who tends to look at only one side of the audience and forgets the rest	Prior to the speech, familiarize yourself with the edges of the audience in all directions. Move around and use more of the space in front of the audience during the speech.

3
Facial Expression

Facial expressions are the use of facial muscles to convey your internal thoughts or feelings. Many animals use facial expressions, but humans seem to be the masters of this form of communication. Although you have thousands of different expressions, only six seem to be universal.

UNIVERSAL EXPRESSION	HOW DO YOU MAKE IT?
Happiness	Raise mouth corners into a smile
Fear	Raise brows, open eyes fully, and open mouth slightly
Surprise	Arch brows, open eyes wide to expose more white, and drop jaw open slightly
Disgust	Raise upper lip and wrinkle nose bridge (which raises cheeks)
Anger	Lower brows, press lips together firmly, and bulge eyes
Sadness	Lower mouth corners and raise inner portion of brows

Here are some tips for using effective facial expressions.

- Match your expressions to your verbal message.
- Keep your expressions natural. Avoid overdoing or exaggerating them.
- When speaking across cultures, consider the universality of your expressions.

4
Gestures

You use *gestures* when you use your body or parts of it (hands, arms, eyes, or head) to convey a message and feelings during your speech. The gestures used during a speech are usually either emblems or illustrators.

Emblems are speech-independent and culturally learned gestures that have a direct verbal translation. When you shrug your shoulders to convey "I don't know" or form a circle with your thumb and index finger on the same hand to communicate a feeling of "OK," you are using emblems. Winking, nodding yes, waving hello, and rolling your eyes are emblems, too. An emblem may not mean the same thing in another culture, so be careful.

Illustrators are speech dependent and closely linked to what is being said. They help you demonstrate words or messages in a speech. For example, if you put up one finger as you say, "my first point," you are using an illustrator.

Effective gestures should:

- Vary, so that they do not become rhythmic and distracting
- Be appropriate to the speech, audience, and occasion
- Be purposefully used and add to your message

5
Movement

Movement refers to your use of motion and space during the speech. How to use space depends, as with other aspects, on your needs, the topic, the audience, and the occasion.

If the topic and the event are extremely formal, such as a graduation ceremony, standing to the side of the lectern or moving around on the stage is less acceptable. However, most speech events will allow some flexibility with movement and will be better if you use it. Standing completely still can make you seem rigid or unapproachable and can cause any nervous tension in your body to intensify.

Lecterns (especially with microphones) are useful tools but can be a barrier between you and your audience. If you want to build a friendlier and more approachable relationship, avoid using a lectern. If possible, stand to the side or move around periodically. You should avoid pacing, however. Just remember to make your movement purposeful, not distracting, and consistent with your verbal message. If a microphone is necessary, try to use a lapel or wireless one.

6
Posture

Posture is the position of your body during your speech and, like your facial expressions, can convey inner thoughts and feelings you have about yourself, your audience, the topic, and the situation. If you are nervous, your body might be rigid and straight. If you are very relaxed, depressed, or tired, your shoulders might droop or you might lean against the table or lectern. If you close off your body by hiding behind a lectern or crossing your arms, you appear less approachable.

Conversely, if you are somewhat at ease and excited about your speech, your body will be open (front of the body visible), mostly relaxed but energized, and straight but not stiff. This posture is more natural and inviting to the audience. It conveys that you are enthusiastic and comfortable with your audience, topic, and situation. Your posture can significantly influence your ethos.

Bad posture
Crossing your arms or leaning against the lectern

Good posture
More natural and inviting to the audience

CHECKLIST for Physical Delivery

❏ Is my appearance well groomed and appropriate?
❏ Am I employing good direct eye contact?
❏ Am I varying my facial expressions, gestures, and movements? Are they natural?
❏ Does my posture convey enthusiasm for my topic, the audience, and the occasion?

10.3 What Are the Methods of Delivery?

1 **Extemporaneous Speaking**
2 **Manuscript Speaking**
3 **Memorized Speaking**
4 **Impromptu Speaking**

1

Extemporaneous Speaking

Extemporaneous speaking is considered the most acceptable contemporary method of delivery. Here, you plan out, rehearse, and deliver the speech from an outline consisting of key words, phrases, and delivery notes.

WHEN SHOULD YOU USE IT?

This type of delivery is more audience centered than others because it is speaking "with" your audience and not "at" them. When your goal is to give an audience-centered speech, this is the method to use. In fact, you should try to use this method most of the time. Most classroom speeches require extemporaneous delivery.

DELIVERY TECHNIQUES

With the extemporaneous style, you will expand on the brief notes you have in front of you as you speak. You have rehearsed the speech so that you are not scrambling for something to say, which allows you to adapt to the audience and to sound more natural. Preparing the speech effectively and rehearsing it enough to become very comfortable with the topic are essential to this type of delivery.

→ See also "How Do You Prepare for an Extemporaneous Speech?" on pages 224–227.

2
Manuscript Speaking

Manuscript speaking occurs when you read word for word from a copy of the speech.

WHEN SHOULD YOU USE IT?
This form of delivery is used when you must present the speech exactly as planned, so that you do not omit important details or misstate critical information.

DELIVERY TECHNIQUES
Make as much eye contact as possible, keep your gestures high and not hidden by the lectern or prompter, and keep your voice dynamic. Rehearse until you are comfortable with your delivery and message. Mark delivery tips on the manuscript.

3
Memorized Speaking

Memorized speaking means you rehearse the speech so much that you commit the full text to memory.

WHEN SHOULD YOU USE IT?
Some speakers employ memorized delivery when accuracy and the appearance of spontaneity are equally important. This method works well for brief speeches, such as toasts.

DELIVERY TECHNIQUES
The key to an effective memorized speech is to rehearse it a lot and make it sound fresh. Keep your excitement high, and use effective verbal and nonverbal delivery techniques.

4
Impromptu Speaking

Impromptu speaking is the only method of delivery that has very little, if any, preparation or rehearsal. If any outline is used, it is simply notes jotted down quickly.

WHEN SHOULD YOU USE IT?
Even though this type of speech is the least prepared, often uses a very basic organizational strategy, lacks solid evidence, and uses simplistic language, impromptu speaking is the delivery we use the most in our everyday lives and careers. You use this type of delivery when answering a question in a public forum (such as the classroom), when you need to offer information or dispute an issue during a meeting, and when you are asked to address an audience at a moment's notice.

DELIVERY TECHNIQUES
The best technique is to always be prepared with appropriate knowledge and information. You will almost always be asked to respond about something you should or do know. These steps will help you put your thoughts together:

- Pay close attention during the event.
- If you have time, write down key words or ideas and think about a logical order.
- Limit your remarks to two or three points.
- Think about what evidence you can offer to support your points.

PRACTICING ETHICS: On the Spot
Sometimes impromptu speaking will make you feel like you are being "put on the spot" or asked to speak without preparation. Never make up information to sound good or to get through the moment.

10.4 How Do You Prepare for an Extemporaneous Speech?

1 **Read Aloud the Preparation Outline**

2 **Consider Your Support Materials**

3 **Prepare Your Delivery Outline**

4 **Prepare Your Presentation Aids**

5 **Practice Multiple Times**

6 **Do a Final "Dress Rehearsal"**

7 **Prepare for Questions**

8 **Prepare for the Day of the Speech**

1 Read Aloud the Preparation Outline

At this step in the rehearsal process, you want to read aloud the preparation outline several times. Pay attention to the order of your points, how much support material you are using, and the order of the support materials. Include your links as well, to see if they smoothly transition between points and parts of the speech. Read aloud the introduction and conclusion to see if they are interesting and flow well. Read the preparation outline one more time, at a reasonable pace, and time yourself. Make changes where necessary to correct issues or to adhere to the time limit. At this point, you should be under the time limit, because you have not added verbal and nonverbal techniques or presentation aids that will take up time during your speech.

There is no magical formula for how many times you need to rehearse your speech at each of the following steps. This is the key: as many times as you need to move successfully to the next step. If you read your preparation outline aloud two times and feel you are ready to make the delivery outline, then do so.

TIP: Preparation Outline

You should have your preparation outline finished at least two days before the speech event or in the time frame required by your instructor. Most speakers need to practice over the course of several days to make a speech sound conversational, so give yourself time to spend with your finished preparation outline.

2
Consider Your Support Materials

Delivery techniques can make or break a segment of great support material. Beginning speakers can unwittingly fall into poor delivery habits when they use support materials, particularly extended examples, narratives, or statistics. However, good delivery can bring your support materials to life.

Here are a few techniques and suggestions:

- Understand your materials—and deliver them in a way that shows you do.

- Practice saying aloud the entire support material segment, especially if the material is a long narrative or example. Become so familiar with the words that they seem like your own. Practice statistics to the point that you do not need to look at your notes to remember them.

- Employ dramatic effect. Speak with enthusiasm that is appropriate for your topic and the occasion. Use dramatic pauses, stress important words, and vary the pace of your words to help access the emotional potential of the materials. If you are bored or unexcited about your material, your audience will be, too.

- Use repetition and/or restatement to help your audience understand and remember your support materials.

- Consider using presentation aids to reinforce what you are saying. Presentation aids are exceptionally helpful when presenting statistical information. Conversely, refrain from putting extended examples on a visual aid and simply reading them to your audience.

3
Prepare Your Delivery Outline

Now, you want to reduce your preparation outline to only key words, phrases, and important quotations, statistics, or details. Try not to include too much of the introduction or the conclusion. You will tend to read it if you do, and direct eye contact is crucial. After you have what you think is the final delivery outline, add delivery cues where you think you might need them. Also note cues for presentation aids. If you are struggling to remember details when using the delivery outline, back up a step. Check your logic, and read the preparation outline aloud again.

→ See Chapter 6 for more help creating a delivery outline.

4
Prepare Your Presentation Aids

Next, prepare the presentation aids exactly as you will use them in the speech event. Do not cut corners here. You want to practice with the finished aids to discover any problems and to make them seem a natural part of your speech.

→ See Chapter 11 for more on using and creating presentation aids.

TIP: Delivery Outline

If your hands tend to shake when you give a presentation, use stiff paper, note cards, or something like a file folder or clipboard to support your delivery outline. This will allow you to feel comfortable when picking up your notes or not using a lectern.

5
Practice Multiple Times

Now it is time to put your speech on its feet. Practice your speech exactly as you plan to give it. Here are some hints:

- At this stage, always practice from the delivery outline. If you are struggling with any part, read over the preparation outline and then return to practicing with the delivery outline.

- Practice a few times in front of a mirror or record your speech. Watch for distracting behavior. Is your posture appropriate, and are you using effective gestures? Audio or video recording a rehearsal will allow you to focus on vocal quality. Video recording will also help you pay attention to your body language and eye contact.

- Do not assume that if your friend can give a speech with only two rehearsals, so can you.

- Time yourself several times while using your finished presentation aids and necessary equipment, if any. You want to get as close as possible to the time limit.

- Practice with a rehearsal audience. Ask family members, friends, or classmates to play the role of audience and to offer feedback.

- Evaluate what you have learned from the rehearsal audience and from watching and listening to yourself. Change the speech message or your delivery style when necessary. Rehearse again, incorporating these changes. Even an excellent speech has room for improvement.

→ See Chapter 13 for help with evaluating your speech.

6
Do a Final "Dress Rehearsal"

The last step in the rehearsal process is to do what actors call a "dress rehearsal." With this rehearsal, you want to simulate as closely as possible the exact event when you will give the speech. So it is important to:

- Rehearse in the space (or a close alternative) where you will give the speech.

- Use the exact delivery outline you will use during the speech. Make sure you number the pages or cards to prevent a mix-up the day of the speech.

- Use the exact presentation aids and necessary equipment.

- Try to rehearse at the exact time, to consider possible issues with noise, lighting, temperature, and so on.

- Rehearse standing or sitting as you will during the speech.

- Wear the clothing you plan to wear, to see if it is appropriate and makes you feel confident.

- Ask a friend or colleague to watch your dress rehearsal and offer comments.

- Rehearse until you are as comfortable as possible, but do not wear yourself out. You will need energy for your speech event.

CONFIDENCE BOOSTER

- The more you practice with your delivery outline and presentation aids, the lower your apprehension will be.
- During the speech, avoid apologizing or calling attention to your shortcomings. Your audience may not notice any. Don't dwell on them, or you'll lose your concentration and audience focus.

7
Prepare for Questions

Not all speaking situations will have an opportunity for an audience question-and-answer (Q and A) session. Like some impromptu speeches, a Q and A session may happen spontaneously, so be prepared:

- Anticipate questions you might get, and plan answers. Think about and consider questions you hope for—or dread.

- Practice your answers.

- If your topic is complex, prepare a "Facts Sheet" with details that you can consult during the Q and A session.

- Remain calm, confident, and professional with aggressive or difficult questioners.

- Repeat the question if it was hard for the rest of the audience to hear.

- Confirm that you answered the question effectively. Ask: "Does that answer your question?" "Does that make sense?"

- Be honest if you do not know the answer. "I don't know" is an acceptable answer if you have demonstrated your knowledge in other ways. Offer to look for an answer and get back to the audience member if the situation allows you to do so.

- Give your speech to a practice audience and have them ask you questions.

- If you are giving a mediated presentation, use Twitter, instant messaging, or another mediated method for question-and-answer interaction with a distant audience.

8
Prepare for the Day of the Speech

THE DAY BEFORE THE SPEECH

- Avoid activities that will stress your voice, mind, and body. Get a good night's sleep (eight hours), eat right, keep hydrated, and limit your caffeine and alcohol consumption. Avoid taking drugs such as antihistamines and expectorants before you speak.

- Prepare what you will wear.

- Practice at least once so that you can go to sleep that night feeling confident.

THE DAY OF THE SPEECH

- Don't forget to eat. If your body doesn't have the fuel it needs, nervousness may intensify and your memory will decrease. If your speech is within an hour of a meal, avoid eating foods that can irritate your throat, such as ice cream, milk, and chocolate.

- Get to the speech event early so that you are not rushed.

- Check all necessary equipment and deal with any issues you discover.

- If you will be speaking for a long period of time, keep water handy.

- Try to be by yourself just before the speech and prepare yourself mentally. Do vocal or physical activities to warm up and lessen your apprehension.

- Look over your notes one more time to make sure they are in the right order.

- Finally, walk to the front of the room with confidence.

10.5 How Do You Prepare for a Mediated Presentation?

1 Establish the Type of Presentation
2 Analyze Your Audience
3 Learn to Use the Technology
4 Prepare and Practice
5 Deliver the Presentation

Increasingly, you may be asked to deliver a mediated speech. ***Mediated presentations*** use technology as a channel outside of the speaker or audience to exchange a message. For example, if you video record your speech and your instructor or classmates watch the video at another time, you are giving a mediated presentation. Likewise, if your boss asks you to give a presentation during a web-based virtual meeting or you give an opinion segment on the radio, you are giving a mediated presentation. Depending on the situation and technology available, you might need to give a mediated presentation using only a video recording device, or online mediated tools such as podcasts, webinars, screencasts, slide narrations, or hangouts (interactive group video chats).

Much of what you have learned about public speaking will assist you with a mediated presentation. However, the fact that your audience can be more of an unknown and may be in another place, viewing or listening to you at a different time and through a different channel, changes the dynamics of the process.

If you are asked to give a mediated presentation in speech class, it is most often a prerecorded video shared electronically. However, a speech delivered with audience interaction via online tools, such as GoToMeeting, WebEx, or Google Hangouts is becoming more common. In the professional world, live, recorded, and hybrid presentations (combination of live and recorded) are common.

1

Establish the Type of Presentation

The first step in creating a mediated presentation is to determine the type of mediated presentation you are required to give or that would be best for your speech situation. Online education scholars typically classify mediating tools as supporting either **asynchronous engagements** or **synchronous engagements**. Often your audiences will be more complex and the mediating tools will assist you in **hybrid engagements**. See the table below.

To determine the type, ask:

- Will this be a single-speaker event, an interview, or a panel discussion? How will the interview members or panel and the audience interact?

- What tools are readily available for me to use? What do I know how to use? Which would be best for my speech situation and topic?

- Do I need to record the speech and electronically share it with the audience?

- Will my entire audience view the speech from a shared prerecorded video?

- Will a portion of my audience be either present in the room or able to interact via an online or other mediating tool?

Some online speech courses require you to locate a specified number of adult audience members to be present as you record or give the speech. In this case, you know a portion of your audience is interacting in real time and the rest is not.

TYPE OF MEDIATED PRESENTATION	ENGAGEMENT STYLES	EXAMPLES
Recorded	**Asynchronous engagements** occur when the speaker and audience interaction is not in real time.	Sharing prerecorded video or audio—on YouTube or Pearson's MediaShare, for example—where the audience is not present when the presentation is recorded (e.g., narrated slide shows or product demonstrations)
Live	**Synchronous engagements** occur when the speaker and the audience interact in real time via some sort of mediation.	Video or web conferencing or teleconferencing (e.g., real-time WebEx or Skype meetings where the entire audience is mediated)
Hybrid	**Hybrid engagements** occur when part of your audience is interacting in real time and a subset of the audience is not.	This could be a speech with some combination of a physically present audience interacting in real time, a mediated audience not in real time, and/or a mediated audience interacting in real time.

2
Analyze Your Audience

When considering the mediated audience, conduct audience analysis just as you do with any speech. Try to find out as much as you can about their attitudes, beliefs, values, traits (personal, psychological, and social), and even why they are attending or viewing your presentation.

Because you may not have direct contact with some or all the audience, it is important to discover as much as possible about them to predict their needs and responses and know how to engage them. In some cases, you may have an audience present in the room with you and another portion viewing the speech from a distance or at a later time. In this situation, you might be tempted to analyze only those you know will be present in the room with you, but be careful of falling prey to this habit. Always consider those viewing the speech via mediation as well. If you are recording a speech for a class and are required to have a small audience present in the room with you, it is best to select that audience to mirror the composition of the audience viewing the mediated video.

Likewise, you might find yourself in a situation where you don't know who the mediated audience will be over time. For example, think of your favorite TED Talk or seek out and watch a TED Talk that might interest you at ted.com. The TED speaker really doesn't know who will watch that recorded presentation—when it is new or in the future—or attend the TED conference in person. The TED speaker has to gauge the audience based on the current cultural climate, be more generally inclusive, be unique, and realize the viewer is likely choosing to watch the video because of the topic description or a requirement. The TED speaker may do some research and note that data on Alexa.com suggests that women with one or more college degrees are more likely to visit ted.com. Although that gives the TED speaker a bit of insight into the probable audience, it is still very general.

→ See Chapter 2 if you need help with analyzing your audience.

TIP: Engaging the Mediated Audience

Because mediated presentations can feel impersonal or distant, and listeners will often be distracted, be sure to involve and connect with your audience by using:
- Image-rich and evocative language
- Personal examples
- Shared experiences of your audience

3
Learn to Use the Technology

As should be obvious by now, mediated presentations require that you learn and use some sort of video equipment and online tools to share your speech with others. Video conferencing, screen sharing, and communication platforms like WebEx, GoToMeeting, and Google Hangouts are popular workforce platforms for sharing videos and communicating with others. Platforms like these are computer driven and may require you to obtain a membership, download software to your computer, and have a connected webcam. In some cases, you are limited in how many people you can connect with.

For class purposes, you will likely be asked to video record your speech with a quality digital camera and upload it to a video sharing site such as YouTube, Blackboard, Pearson's MediaShare, or Vimeo. It is extremely important that you learn to use the equipment and software prior to recording the speech and making the mediated connection with your audience.

Your instructor will likely provide specific instructions on what to use and how to distribute the recorded speech. If you search online with such search phrases as "How to use WebEx," "How to use Google Hangouts," "How to use GoToMeeting," or "How to upload videos to YouTube," you will discover numerous official sites, tutorials, and videos that will help you learn the appropriate technology. See the Tip box below.

Play around with the technology and make sure you understand what it has to offer and what specific buttons are for. Don't assume that what one platform does, others do as well. For example, Google Hangouts has a microphone icon with a line through it. In most computer applications, that means your microphone is muted. However, here it means the mic is live and you need to select the icon to mute it.

The key to effective mediated communication is to learn the technology before you are ready to go live with your interaction with others and to seek out help when necessary. Explore the technology before you need to really use it.

> **TIP: Tutorial/Help Sites**
>
> Here are a few websites that might be useful for mediated interactions:
> - www.webex.com/support/getting-started.html
> - www.webex.com/how-to/
> - support.google.com/hangouts#topic=
> - www.gotomeeting.com/meeting/online
>   -meeting-support
> - free.gotomeeting.com/help
> - support.google.com/youtube#topic=

4
Prepare and Practice

PREPARING

- Familiarize yourself early on with the equipment and tools.

- Select equipment that will produce a quality product. Follow your instructor's guidelines. For example, some instructors might feel smartphones don't produce the best audio or video. You might need to use a moderate-quality video camera or newer camcorder with the ability to upload to the Internet. A tripod for your phone or camera will also help you produce the best video. Your speech can only be as good as the production quality—poor video or audio makes a speech ineffective no matter the content or delivery.

- Try to keep your message short when not adhering to a regulated length.

- Plan interactivity with your audience or presentation aids, if appropriate and possible, to keep the audience focused.

- Use a neutral background or one that will not compete with you. Make sure you are well lit, with the light in front of you. Consider what is directly behind or above you. You don't want something inappropriate and distracting behind you or "growing" out of the top of your head.

- Coordinate your clothing. Muted colors often work well. Stay away from patterns, stripes, and flashy ornamentation. Be wrinkle-free and don't wear tinted glasses. Look professional.

PRACTICING

Practice at least one time by creating exactly what will happen the day of the speech. This includes recording, having a local audience (if required and possible), wearing what you plan to, doing and using what you plan to, and running through the entire speech. This should be a rehearsal of the event rather than a practice of a few parts. As you do this, consider the following:

- Keep your hair out of your eyes.

- Use some movement, especially with your hands. Try to keep hands in the lower portion of the video image but not out of sight if you are gesturing. Relax your shoulders. Stand, if possible. Keep your feet flat and about six inches apart. If you sit, try to sit slightly forward and straight.

- Use vocal variety, speaking as though you are telling an exciting story.

- If you won't be visible (e.g., speaking over a screencast), vocal delivery and interactivity are even more important.

- Know your speech well. This will free you to focus on using the technology to its best potential and handle problems.

- Practice displaying presentation aids for the camera so they are viewable and readable in the recording.

- Time your speech using all the equipment and adjust as needed.

- Review your recorded practice video and make adjustments.

- Consider what might go wrong and prepare a multilmodal backup plan.

5

Deliver the Presentation

RECORDING

- On the day of the event, test and practice with the equipment one last time.
- Prevent interferences. Turn off cell phones, calendar updates, Google Chat, or other notifications. Post a "Do Not Disturb" sign on the door.
- Always be aware that the technology could be on and recording you.
- Set up any presentation aids.
- Check the lighting to ensure you and your aids are visible.
- Avoid focusing the camera on your face. If possible, keep half to three-fourths of your body in view. If you use a lectern, make sure part of it is visible.
- Make eye contact with the camera and the audience in the room. Ignoring the camera could signal to the mediated audience that you don't care or can't be trusted. Visualizing the camera as one of your friends will help you interact with it as a person.
- If your assignment requires the audience to be visible in the video, include them in a way that you are not blocked. Children and pets should not be part of the audience.
- Make sure the camera is steady during the entire speech. A tripod will help.
- Remember to speak loudly enough for the microphone to pick up your voice.
- Check your finished recording to be sure it works properly.

DELIVERING THE FINAL VIDEO

- After recording the speech, review the video for audio or video problems. Assessment of your speech depends on what your instructor can see and hear. If you have problems, rerecord the entire speech. For a class, editing a speech is unethical, and you should never do it unless so instructed.
- If you are not using a video conferencing platform, you will need to upload the video via an Internet-based platform (such as Blackboard, Pearson's MediaShare, YouTube, or Vimeo) for distributing the video to the audience.
- Check your recording again, after uploading, to be sure it works properly.

SYNCHRONOUS ENGAGEMENTS

A few reminders:

- Keep the focus simple and segments of the engagement short.
- If possible, have everyone log in early to check connectivity and to resolve unexpected issues.
- Pay close attention to interactions with audience members. Include a question-and-answer session and consider using chat functions if available. Having someone besides the main speaker facilitate the questions can be helpful.
- As a participant, remember that you are in a virtual presentation or meeting. Stay focused. You might mute your line to prevent distractions until time for interactions.

Chapter 10: Review

ASSESSING YOUR KNOWLEDGE

10.1 What Are the Elements of Vocal Delivery?

- *Pitch* is how high or low your voice is in frequency.
- *Volume* is how loud or soft your voice is.
- *Rate* is the speed at which you speak.
- *Pause* is when you stop speaking or slow your speaking rate for effect. Pausing can help you prevent the use of vocal fillers.
- *Variety* is the fluctuation, change, or adjustment of your volume, pitch, rate, and pauses for effect.
- *Pronunciation* is the standard or commonly accepted way to make a word sound.
- *Articulation* is how completely and clearly you utter a word; *enunciation* is how distinctively you say linked whole words.
- *Dialect* is how a particular group of people pronounces or uses language.

→ See pages 212–217.

10.2 What Are the Elements of Physical Delivery?

There are six physical elements to consider when delivering a speech. You should:
- Consider your appearance.
- Make eye contact with your audience.
- Match your facial expressions with your verbal message, look natural, and consider expressions that work well across cultures.
- Incorporate gestures for emphasis.
- Use motion and space during your speech.
- Employ effective posture.

→ See pages 218–221.

10.3 What Are the Methods of Delivery?

- Extemporaneous speaking is when the speaker plans out, rehearses, and delivers the speech from a key-word/phrase outline in a conversational manner. This is considered the most appropriate contemporary method of delivery and is the one most accepted in a speech class.
- Manuscript speaking occurs when you read word for word from a copy of the speech.
- Memorized speaking means you rehearse the speech so much that you commit the full text to memory.
- Impromptu speaking is where the speaker has little or no preparation or rehearsal prior to giving the speech.

→ See pages 222–223.

10.4 How Do You Prepare for an Extemporaneous Speech?

- Read aloud the preparation outline.
- Consider your support materials.
- Prepare your delivery outline.
- Prepare your presentation aids.
- Practice multiple times.
- Do a final "dress rehearsal."
- Prepare for questions.
- Prepare for the day of the speech.

→ See pages 224–227.

10.5 How Do You Prepare for a Mediated Presentation?

Objective 10.5: **ILLUSTRATE HOW TO PREPARE FOR A MEDIATED PRESENTATION**

Mediated presentations use technology as a channel outside of the speaker or audience to exchange a message. Mediated presentations can be classified as asynchronous, synchronous, or hybrid engagements.

When preparing to give a mediated presentation, you need to:

- Remember to consider everything you have learned about public speaking in general.
- Establish the type of presentation. You will give either a recorded, live, or hybrid mediated presentation.
- Analyze your audience, including those who will be in the room with you and those viewing via mediation.
- Learn to use the appropriate technology.
- Prepare everything you need for your presentation and practice the speech as you will give it. Practice with the equipment and technology, including any presentation aids or interactive features, until you feel comfortable with it and confident about using it for the speech event.
- Deliver the presentation. Record it if required or, if it is live, follow guidelines for synchronous engagements. Check any recording before and after uploading, to be sure it works properly.

→ See pages 228–233.

TERMS TO REMEMBER

pitch (212)
monotone (212)
inflection (212)
volume (213)
rate (213)
pause (214)
variety (215)
pronunciation (216)
articulation (217)
enunciation (217)
dialect (217)
appearance (218)
direct eye contact (219)
facial expressions (220)
gestures (220)
emblems (220)
illustrators (220)
movement (221)
posture (221)
extemporaneous speaking (222)
manuscript speaking (223)
memorized speaking (223)
impromptu speaking (223)
mediated presentations (228)
asynchronous engagements (229)
synchronous engagements (229)
hybrid engagements (229)

11

USING PRESENTATION AIDS

11.1 What Are the Types of Presentation Aids?

1 **Actual Items**
2 **Models**
3 **Photographs**
4 **Drawings**
5 **Charts and Tables**
6 **Graphs**
7 **Media**

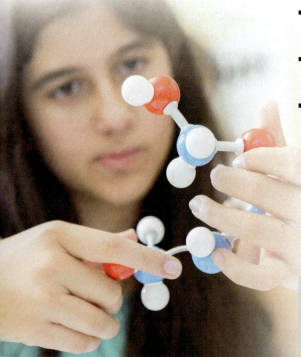

Presentation aids are two- or three-dimensional visual items, video footage, audio recordings, and/or multimedia segments that support and enhance your speech.

Presentation aids can:

- Make it easier for your audience to understand your topic by illustrating a concept or providing condensed information.

- Grab and maintain audience interest by being vivid and dramatic.

- Assist with retention. Your audience will remember more information if you not only tell them, but also show them.

- Improve your credibility, or ethos, if they are well made, used appropriately, and not distracting.

- Help you cross a cultural divide by supplementing your words for a diverse audience.

- Convey emotion. Visual images and audio recordings can be effective ways to create an emotional audience response.

- Help you maintain an extemporaneous delivery. Proper use of presentation aids forces you to know your speech well enough to venture away from your delivery outline to incorporate and explain the aid.

PRACTICING ETHICS: Types of Aids

Do not use dangerous, illegal, or prohibited presentation aids. If an aid could be harmful to you or your audience, use a model or picture instead.

1

Actual Items

You can use people, animals, or objects when they are the actual items you are talking about or relate to the topic of your speech and help relay your message. For example, if you are planning to give a demonstration speech on how to uniquely wrap a gift, you might wrap different boxes in distinct ways.

Advantages

- Can get your audience's attention
- Can demonstrate, illustrate, exemplify, or emphasize your topic
- Can be simple to add to your speech if you do not need to create them
- Can help the audience visualize persuasive issues

Disadvantages

- Can be scary, dangerous, inappropriate or illegal for the occasion or location of the speech (e.g., live spiders or snakes, guns, anything with a flame, cats if people are allergic, etc.). Get your instructor's approval if the item is unusual for the classroom.
- Can be too small to see or too large to bring
- Can distract the audience from the message

2

Models

Models are three-dimensional representations. Models are usually scaled to size—often smaller than the real thing, such as a model car, but sometimes larger, such as a model of a molecule.

Advantages

- Are great alternatives when you cannot bring the actual items
- Can get your audience's attention
- Can demonstrate, illustrate, exemplify, or emphasize your topic
- Can be simple to add to your speech when you do not need to create them
- Can help you visually compare and contrast

Disadvantages

- Can be hard to locate and expensive
- Can be too small for everyone to see
- Can be unpredictable if they have working parts
- Can distract the audience from the message

3
Photographs

Photographs are two-dimensional representations of places, concepts, people, animals, or objects. They can be original photographs displayed on a document camera, posters of photographic images, or other types of print display.

Advantages

- Can be as effective as an object or model
- Can condense a lot of material onto one aid
- Can create a sense of authenticity
- Can help you compare and contrast
- Can appeal to the audience's emotions
- Can help you explain an abstract concept

Disadvantages

- Can be hard for the entire audience to see
- Can be less effective than an actual item or a model
- Can be overused if they are stock photographs, making them less effective than photographs created for your speech

4
Drawings

Drawings are maps, sketches, diagrams, plans, or other nonphotographic representations of places, concepts, people, animals, or objects. They may show a whole area or part of one, or dissect the parts or workings of something.

Advantages

- Can be very helpful when objects or models are not practical or available
- Can visually demonstrate how something works, operates, or is constructed
- Can sometimes be located ready-made
- Can show detail, processes, relationships, or arrangements
- Can be used to emphasize location, geography, or topography (especially maps)

Disadvantages

- Can be hard to locate or create
- Can be hard for the entire audience to see
- Can have too much detail
- Can lower your credibility if sloppy

5
Charts and Tables

Charts are visual summaries of complex or large quantities of information. Two common charts are flowcharts and organizational charts. ***Flowcharts*** (see example below) diagram step-by-step development through a procedure, relationship, or process. ***Organizational charts*** illustrate the structure or chain of command in an organization. ***Tables*** consist of numbers or words arranged in rows, columns, or lists.

Advantages

- Can make the complex understandable
- Can summarize a lot of information
- Can show relationships and potential cause-and-effect issues
- Can help an audience think through hypothetical situations (especially charts)
- Can help the audience quickly understand exact numbers or information

Disadvantages

- Can be less memorable than other visuals
- Can require a lot of time to explain
- Can be confusing if too detailed
- Can be hard for the entire audience to see

→ See pages 18–19 for a larger, expanded version of this flowchart.

6
Graphs

Whereas charts and tables simply organize numbers and words, ***graphs*** are visual representations of numerical (statistical) information that demonstrate relationships or differences between two or more variables. There are four common types: line graphs, bar graphs, pictographs, and pie graphs.

LINE GRAPHS

Line graphs contain numerical points plotted on a horizontal axis for one variable and on a vertical axis for another; you then connect the points to make a line. Be sure to clearly label horizontal and vertical axes so that your audience can see and understand them. See the example below.

Advantages

- Can simplify complex statistical information
- Can be extremely easy to read if created effectively

Disadvantages

- Can be less effective if you have more than three lines to plot
- Can require a projector

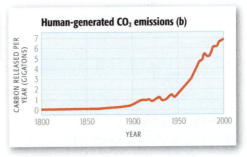

BAR GRAPHS

Bar graphs (also known as *bar charts*) are visuals consisting of vertical or horizontal bars that represent sets of data. Make sure your horizontal and vertical axes are clearly labeled.

Advantages

- Can be easy for your audience to interpret if created effectively
- Can demonstrate change over time at a glance

Disadvantages

- Can be less effective in black and white
- Can require a projector

PICTOGRAPHS

Pictographs (also known as *pictograms*) are bar graphs that use pictures instead of bars. Make sure to label the graph and assign a unit measure to the individual pictorial icons.

Advantages

- Can make statistical information more interesting
- Can be easy for your audience to interpret if created effectively

Disadvantages

- Can take time to locate appropriate pictures or icons to represent your data
- Can be unfamiliar to your audience
- Can be less effective in black and white
- Can require a projector

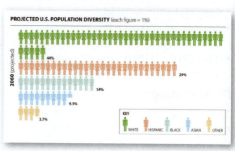

→ See page 34 for a larger version of this pictograph.

→ See page 34 for a larger version of this pictograph.

TIP: Showing Time

When creating a line or bar graph and time is a variable, always put time on the horizontal axis.

TIP: Finding Icons

These sites offer icons and graphics that might be helpful when creating a pictograph:
www.coolarchive.com
www.freegraphics.com
www.findicons.com

PIE GRAPHS

Pie graphs (also known as *circle graphs* or *pie charts*) are circular graphs with sections representing a percentage of a given quantity. It is best to limit your segments to seven or fewer. You can combine the smallest ones if you have more than seven. Always make sure your pie adds up to exactly 100 percent. Labels should be brief and outside the segments if needed. Pie and bar graphs tend to illustrate the same types of data, but you should use a pie graph when comparing segments of a whole.

Advantages

- Can help your audience quickly visualize the divisions of the whole item you are discussing
- Can effectively graph up to seven variables at once

Disadvantages

- Can be difficult to clearly and visibly label the segments
- Should be in color

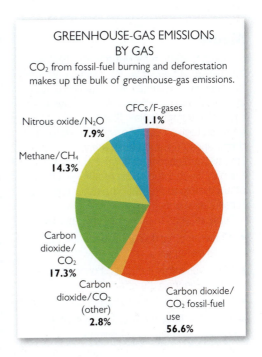

GREENHOUSE-GAS EMISSIONS BY GAS

CO_2 from fossil-fuel burning and deforestation makes up the bulk of greenhouse-gas emissions.

CFCs/F-gases 1.1%
Nitrous oxide/N_2O 7.9%
Methane/CH_4 14.3%
Carbon dioxide/CO_2 17.3%
Carbon dioxide/CO_2 (other) 2.8%
Carbon dioxide/CO_2 fossil-fuel use 56.6%

When to Use Graphs	Line Graph	Bar Graph	Pictograph	Pie Graph
Informing and persuading	●	●	●	●
Demonstrating change over time or comparing two or more items	●	●	●	
Showing frequency, distribution, and correlations	●	●		
Comparing percentages related to one whole thing				●

7

Media

Sometimes static two- or three-dimensional images are not effective. For example, Whitney is a college basketball player helping conduct a high school basketball camp, and she needs to teach a complex play. She decides to use game footage so that she will be able to slow down, speed up, and pause the video to make sure her audience understands the essence of the play. Such information would be difficult or impossible to present with other types of presentation aids.

Some reasons to consider using media:

- When the topic demands more auditory and visual examples
- When you know it might be difficult to keep your audience's attention
- When you know your message really needs it
- When you have the right equipment and software to make it professional
- When time and money to create the aids are not factors
- When you have practiced enough to make its use seem flawless

When you use mediated presentation aids, you might use video, audio, a combination, or a more complex multimedia format.

> Great presenters
> connect with their
> audience, speak naturally,
> and allow the [aids] to
> enhance their story.[1]
>
> NANCY DUARTE

VIDEO AND AUDIO

Audio and video clips can be effective presentation aids. ***Video clips*** are any footage you use from television, movies, or any other type of video. ***Audio clips*** are recordings of sound only. For example, you might have a recording of the sounds dolphins make, music, an interview, a radio program, or a famous speech.

Advantages

- Can grab attention and make a speech memorable by appealing to your audience through sight, sound, and movement
- Can illustrate a point
- Can be used with PowerPoint or Prezi
- Can increase your ethos when used properly

Disadvantages

- Can require special production skills
- Can require special equipment that might not be available at your speech event
- Can require a lot of practice with the equipment to smoothly incorporate the video and audio into the speech
- Can be time-consuming
- Should only be used for short durations so that they do not become the speech or compete with the speaker
- Can increase the potential for errors, bad timing, ineffective technology use, and equipment failure

MULTIMEDIA

Multimedia refers to the combination of multiple presentation aids (still images, graphs, text, sound, and video) into one choreographed production.

Advantages

- Can be very creative and appeals to almost all senses
- Can be very professional
- Can increase your ethos when used properly

Disadvantages

- If too flashy, can overpower the speech
- Can be costly and time-consuming to make
- Requires special equipment and skills
- Can be difficult to coordinate—especially in an unfamiliar space
- Should only be used for short durations so that the aids do not become the speech or compete with the speaker
- Can increase the potential for errors, bad timing, ineffective technology use, and equipment failure

PRACTICING ETHICS: Aid Sources

Remember to cite the sources for presentation aids that you did not create or the sources of information you put into an aid. For example, "This YouTube video, downloaded July 10, shows …" When using a search service such as Google Images, cite the website that owns the image, not Google Images.

It is often wise to add a written reference to a source on a visual you didn't create or collect the content for. This will help you remember an oral citation. Place it at the bottom in a font large enough to read, and include necessary citation information. Follow your instructor's suggestions.

➜ See pages 255–256 for examples.

11.2 How Do You Determine What Presentation Aids You Need to Use?

1 Establish Their Purpose
2 Select the Best Type
3 Consider How to Display Them

To determine which presentation aids to use, establish a purpose for each aid; select the best types for you, your topic, your audience, and the situation; and consider what options you have to display or produce the aids. For example, if you will be speaking to a large audience, a handwritten list of numbers on a flip chart will not do much to support your speech, whereas professionally created graphs can be helpful.

1

Establish Their Purpose

You should never use a presentation aid just because you can or to be glitzy. The important parts of any speech are you and the speech message. Your presentation aids should assist, support, and facilitate your message, not detract from or outshine it. Each aid you use needs a distinct purpose. You can establish the purpose by returning to your preparation outline and considering where in the outline you need to use an aid to:

- Grab attention or maintain interest.
- Promote understanding and clarity.
- Appeal to your audience's emotions.
- Help the audience remember key issues.
- Aid in intercultural communication.

TIP: Using Visuals Cross-Culturally

- Limit the number of words and, if possible, use the audience's language.
- Avoid words that might not translate well (technical words, jargon, slang, etc.).
- Avoid images that could be confusing or offensive.
- Consider cultural views of colors. For example, the color red symbolizes good luck in China, but in South Africa, it is the color of mourning.

2
Select the Best Type

You should select the type of presentation aids to use by considering yourself, your topic, your audience, and the situation.

FOR YOU

When considering yourself as a factor, think about the answers to questions such as these: What equipment am I comfortable with? What software do I need to create or present the aids? Am I familiar enough with that software to be effective? Which aids would I feel comfortable using? Which types will raise my credibility? Which presentation aids do I have time to create and practice with?

FOR YOUR TOPIC

When considering your topic, think about your speech goal: Is it informative or persuasive? If informative, how can your aids help the audience visualize your message, challenge what the audience already knows, or simplify information? If persuasive, think about how your aids can support an idea, evoke emotions, demonstrate fulfilling a need, call the audience to action, or show audience relevance. Ask yourself: How can each aid move through the speech to reach the conclusion?

FOR YOUR AUDIENCE

When considering your audience, reflect on their relationship with the topic and their ability to access the presentation aid. Ask yourself: What do they need to know about the topic, and which aids would be supportive? Will the information in the speech be difficult for the audience to understand? If so, which aids will best assist their understanding? Are there reasons why all or part of the audience would not be able to access a presentation aid? For example, are there factors that might prevent someone from reading or seeing visuals or hearing video/audio clips?

FOR THE SITUATION

Where, why, and when you are speaking could significantly influence which type of presentation aids you use. For example, many visual aids will not work outside, and even quality audio is challenging. Likewise, many special occasion speeches are given at events where certain presentation aids would seem strange. For example, a PowerPoint presentation might seem inappropriate during a eulogy or a wedding toast. However, displaying an object or pictures that relate to the person being eulogized or raising your glass to signal the wedding toast would be acceptable.

3
Consider How to Display Them

Finally, you must consider how the aids will be presented for the audience. Various methods are available to most speakers. Your decision will be determined by what you are comfortable with, the size of the audience, the availability of equipment, what will work in the speech environment, cost, and effectiveness. The next section will explain some options for displaying your presentation aids. Whichever method you select, remember to practice multiple times with that method as you rehearse your speech.

11.3 What Are the Common Methods for Displaying Aids?

1 **Chalkboards and Whiteboards**

2 **Posters**

3 **Handouts**

4 **Flip Charts**

5 **Advanced Technology**

1

Chalkboards and Whiteboards

Chalkboards and whiteboards are usually available in classroom settings and provide impromptu surfaces for writing (with chalk or special markers).

Advantages

- Are usually free and easy to use
- Can be used spontaneously
- Can easily be edited or corrected
- Can have few potential problems
- Can supplement other aids
- Can be a backup when advanced technology fails

Disadvantages

- Can be considered low tech and unprofessional
- Can do little to build ethos
- Can limit your eye contact with the audience
- Require good writing and spelling skills

When to Use Chalkboards and Whiteboards

- For impromptu explanations
- For brainstorming with the audience
- As a backup to other aids

Helpful Hints for Usage

- Use this type of aid sparingly.
- Locate an eraser, some chalk, or a working marker before starting the speech.
- Use upper- and lowercase letters and print legibly.

2

Posters

Posters are hand- or computer-created single-sheet visuals intended to be attached to a wall or displayed on an easel. They typically include text and visual elements but may be entirely visual or entirely textual.

Advantages

- Can grab attention
- Can be useful for condensing information
- Can be professionally prepared (although expensive to print)

Disadvantages

- Are less effective for large audiences
- Can look sloppy if created by hand
- Can be time-consuming and difficult to create

When to Use Posters

- When you do not have or do not trust electronic equipment
- To demonstrate a sequence or change over time by placing each step on a new poster. For example, if you want to demonstrate the evolution of Mickey Mouse, you might create several posters, each depicting one of Mickey's incarnations.
- For small group presentations

Helpful Hints for Usage

- Keep your posters simple, neat, and professional.
- Make them large enough to be seen.
- Proofread your posters or have someone else do it.
- Discreetly number multiple posters to keep track of their order.
- Plan out how to display your posters; never hold them.
- Practice with your posters.

Healthy Eating
12345

TIP: Creating and Printing Posters

You can create a poster with some presentation software if you have access to a printer that can print large sheets. However, printing can be costly. In the workplace, this is more common. To create a poster in PowerPoint, use a blank slide and change its size. Click on the Design tab, select Slide Size menu/Page Setup/Custom slide size, and specify the width and height; most posters range from 32" x 42" to the maximum, 56" x 42".

You can also use design websites. Piktochart.com and Canva.com are two free options for designing printable presentation aids.

3

Handouts

Handouts are standard-size printed pages designed to help you distribute new information that will summarize or reinforce your speech message. They typically include text and/or visual elements.

Advantages

- Can be convenient, easy to use, and inexpensive
- Can contain large amounts of information

Disadvantages

- Can be extremely distracting if given to the audience prior to or during the speech
- Can do little to aid your message or build your ethos if given after the speech
- Can be costly if long and/or for a very large audience

When to Use Handouts

- When details are too small to be effective on other types of presentation aids
- When audience retention is crucial
- To reiterate or summarize
- To provide a reading list
- To provide copies of your presentation
- As a backup to other aids

Helpful Hints for Usage

- Under most circumstances, handouts should be given after the speech to prevent distracting the audience.
- Only distribute handouts before giving the speech when it is absolutely necessary for your audience to follow you closely.
- Never distribute handouts during a speech.
- Include a title, the date, your name, and contact information.
- Make sure they look professionally made.
- Make about 10 percent more copies than you expect to hand out.

TIP: Printing Handouts

You can print handouts of your PowerPoint presentation directly from the software. Select the print option and select one of the standard handout layouts.

In Prezi, you will need to have the Pro version or save the presentation as a PDF and print from that format.

You can use Piktochart.com or Canva.com to create handouts not tied to a presentation software.

4
Flip Charts

A flip chart is a large pad of unlined or lined paper displayed on either a large free-standing or small tabletop easel.

Advantages
- Are convenient, easy to use, and inexpensive
- Do not require electricity
- Can be professionally prepared (but then expensive)

Disadvantages
- Do not work well for large groups (best for 10 or fewer audience members)
- Can be sloppy and time-consuming
- Can do little to build your ethos
- Require good writing and spelling skills

When to Use Flip Charts
- To appear spontaneous and involve audience
- For small group presentations

Helpful Hints for Usage
- Practice writing on and using the chart.
- Prepare the pages in advance or pre-write in light pencil.
- The first page should be blank or contain a title.
- Leave every other page blank for "silence" and to avoid having the next aid show through.
- Use no more than five words across and five lines down.
- Write only on the top two-thirds of the page.
- Print legibly; write letters at least three inches tall, and use upper- and lowercase.
- Use black and blue for text, and strong primary colors for emphasis or graphs, diagrams, and so on.
- Allow for extra writing time.
- Test your markers ahead of time.

5
Advanced Technology

CONTEMPORARY MEDIA

Along with the ability to easily transfer information, current media options offer you the ability to display information in ways that were unimaginable to an average person a few decades ago. Rarely will you speak in a professional venue that does not have some type of advanced media technology to assist you in conveying your message. One or more of these devices are in most classrooms, assisting you, your peers, and your instructor in the educational process.

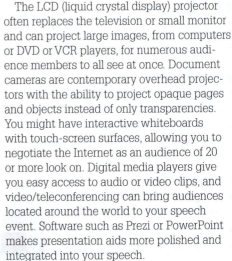

The LCD (liquid crystal display) projector often replaces the television or small monitor and can project large images, from computers or DVD or VCR players, for numerous audience members to all see at once. Document cameras are contemporary overhead projectors with the ability to project opaque pages and objects instead of only transparencies. You might have interactive whiteboards with touch-screen surfaces, allowing you to negotiate the Internet as an audience of 20 or more look on. Digital media players give you easy access to audio or video clips, and video/teleconferencing can bring audiences located around the world to your speech event. Software such as Prezi or PowerPoint makes presentation aids more polished and integrated into your speech.

Advantages

- Can be more professional-looking to use computer-generated and computer-controlled aids
- Can build speaker ethos
- Can often include Internet access
- Can appeal to multiple senses of the audience members
- Can be seen and heard by larger audiences

Disadvantages

- Can be less effective when you want to create an intimate approach
- Can upstage you
- Can be time-consuming to create the aids
- Can require special knowledge to create or run the aids

TRADITIONAL MEDIA

Although considered less effective and out of date, traditional media devices such as standalone CD players, DVD players, VCRs, overhead projectors, and slide projectors are helpful in some situations. They may be all you have available; the best solution for the size of audience (if it is small); best for the environment; or valuable as a backup plan.

Advantages

- Can be relatively easy to learn to use
- Can back up contemporary media devices
- Can have fewer problems than more-contemporary technologies
- Can be less expensive and therefore more commonly available

Disadvantages

- Can be viewed as less-advanced technologies and are therefore not as strong at building ethos
- Can be awkward and more difficult to integrate into a speech than are computer-aided and computer-generated aids

When to Use Advanced Technologies

- When you want aids that are more effective than other printed or handmade display options
- When you are comfortable enough to create an effective aid and can easily present it
- If the equipment is readily available

Helpful Hints for Usage

- Smoothly integrate the devices into your speech. The technology should not be an obstacle to the audience.
- Don't let the technology upstage you.
- Don't let technology give your speech for you. Your audience expects to hear you, not a long audio/video clip or automated presentation aid.
- Always check the equipment and know its limits. For example, will the room be dark enough for the LCD projector?
- Have a backup plan.
- Keep the presentation simple, neat, and clear. Do not get carried away with bells and whistles.

11.4 How Do You Craft an Effective Aid?

1 Follow Good Design Principles

2 Give Yourself Enough Time to Be Creative

1

Follow Good Design Principles

In *Slide:ology: The Art and Science of Creating Great Presentations*, Nancy Duarte writes, "To succeed as a presenter, you must think like a designer."

Communication educators might add that to be a good designer, you must think like an audience-centered communicator, always mindful of your audience. Every decision you make about a presentation aid's design should have the goal of relaying your message better and focusing on the audience's needs for understanding that message.

To meet this goal, you must follow good design principles and give yourself enough time to be creative.

Design principles relate to the arrangement and placement of various elements (color, text, line, images, space, etc.) for optimum effect. When you create two-dimensional presentation aids, think about the arrangement and placement of visual elements on the page, poster, slide, or canvas. Likewise, when you think about the relationship of all of your aids within a given speech, you need to consider arrangement and placement to allow the aids to nourish your verbal message. There are five design principles you should consider.

TIP: Plan Your Time

Plan your time carefully. You are better off starting early and having time left over to rehearse more—or to relax and feel confident about your preparation—than scrambling at the last minute and creating poor presentation aids.

UNITY

The principle of unity recognizes the need for the elements you use to relate to each other. If you use multiple aids, they should fit together as a unified whole to support your speech. For example, here are some aids for a speech about toucans.

Color unity
Make sure colors work well together and are complementary (opposite on the color wheel), analogous (colors that touch each other on the wheel), or monochromatic (variations of one color).

Color harmony
Use colors that are in harmony with the tone of your speech. Here, the color palette invokes the toucans' colors and surrounding environment.

Image unity
Images should relate to the text shown with them and to your verbal message at that moment.

PATTERN

The pattern principle recommends that you create a design format and use it consistently. Reusing patterns will help your audience quickly digest the material because the layout is familiar and not distracting. Keep your pattern simple.

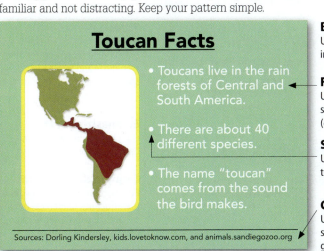

Backgrounds
Use consistent colors, textures, or images for background.

Fonts
Use the same types, colors, and sizes of fonts with related elements (e.g., format all titles the same).

Symbols
Use the same symbols (bullets, etc.) to establish related patterns.

Content
Use a consistent format for content such as source lines for text and graphics. Always cite sources.

BALANCE

Balance deals with equilibrium—a feeling of stability, symmetry, and calm. Balance in your aids will enhance your audience's feeling that your speech is balanced and organized.

Toucan Size

Largest:
Toco toucan

Smallest:
Aracari varieties

Source: Getty

Balanced fonts
Choose easy-to-read sans serif fonts (such as Tahoma or Arial), and use only one or two. Avoid using all caps.

Readable font size
Use a font size large enough to be seen by everyone in the room—44 points for titles and 24 points to 32 points for other text is a general guideline.

Effective balance
Balance the elements with each other and with the blank space.

EMPHASIS

You can use design elements to emphasize what is most important. Also, your complete arsenal of presentation aids for a speech should adhere to the principle of emphasis. Use only aids that stress the important aspects of your verbal message.

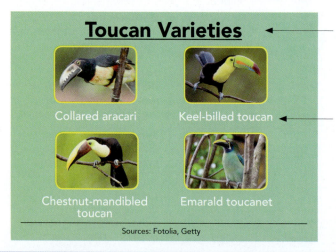

Toucan Varieties

Collared aracari

Keel-billed toucan

Chestnut-mandibled toucan

Emerald toucanet

Sources: Fotolia, Getty

Titles
Use titles for things such as lists, graphs, or areas of a poster. Titles emphasize and foreshadow your speech content.

Emphasizing text
Light text against a medium background projects the best.

Emphasizing elements
Bullets, color, images, text size, text structures (underline, bold, or italic), and music are ways to draw the eye or ear to what is important.

RHYTHM

Rhythm has to do with a real or imagined sense of movement. Just as you can create a sense of rhythm with your vocal quality, you create a visual sense of rhythm by emphasizing movement. Also, the pacing of your presentation aids throughout the speech can establish a rhythmic flow. Added animation and sound can create rhythm, but be careful that they do not distract from or compete with your speech message. Limit these and use them consistently—and for a meaningful purpose, not simply because they are available. Some easier ways for beginning speakers to use rhythm in aids are text placement and images that contain or suggest movement.

- **Text placement:** Using text or spacing that relates to each other, such as placing titles and source lines in the same position on each aid, creates one type of rhythm. For example, note how the titles and source lines in the toucan presentation aids are placed similarly throughout the series.

- **Movement:** Images that contain movement or move across or around the background can create a sense of rhythm. For example, look at the "Toucan Size" slide on the previous page. The photo of a toucan flying suggests movement.

TIP: Use an Idea Bank

Use the same idea-bank process you used to narrow your speech topic to focus in on your presentation aids (see Chapter 3). At the beginning of the process, consider anything an option and open your mind to wild ideas. One of your wild ideas just might become the best idea. That's the beauty of the creative process.

2
Give Yourself Enough Time to Be Creative

The time needed to be creative is difficult to predict because of so many variables. For example, can you easily come up with interesting ideas? Are you familiar with how to research and collect ideas? Are you comfortable with the method for producing your aid? The answers to these questions can drastically affect the time it takes to create your aids. For a general idea, Nancy Duarte offers a timeframe for creating an hour-long presentation with 30 slides. If you adapt her recommendations to an eight-minute speech with four to six slides, your creation time might be similar to the following timeline:

- **1 to 2 hours** for researching and collecting ideas/information
- **1 hour** to evaluate audience needs and to outline your ideas
- **2+ hours** to create the presentation aids
- **30 minutes to 1 hour** to rehearse with aids

4.5 to 6+ hours total

Keep in mind that this is an estimate and you are the only one who can predict how long it will take. Be honest with yourself. If you don't know how to use the software or tend to spend a lot of time on details, you will need more time. Likewise, if it only takes you 30 minutes to create your aids, are you being creative and supporting your speech the best way you can?

11.5 How Can You Use Presentation Software?

1 Create a Storyboard

2 Begin with Presentation Software Basics

Many software packages can help you create professional presentation aids incorporating text, images, charts, graphs, sound, and/or video. Two of the most common are Power-Point and Prezi.

PowerPoint is a Microsoft program for creating slide shows. Prezi is a cloud-based program that allows you to tell a story on a virtual canvas. Deciding which to use can depend on your preference and what works for your topic and audience. Very linear topics may work better in PowerPoint. If your audience is new to Prezi, they can get caught up in what it can do and miss the message.

Other great software options are Keynote, Google Slides, and Slides (slides.com).

Although software packages allow most anyone to create professional presentations, they have downsides as well.

- They are overused and often used poorly.
- They can steal the show so that your speech itself is ignored.
- They can turn the listeners off or destroy your credibility as a speaker.

Learn how to take advantage of presentation software without letting it have power over your speech. Creating computer-generated presentation aids takes time and knowledge.

> **TIP: Software Tutorials**
>
> Investing in a good tutorial might be wise if presentation software is something you will use often. Here are some potentially helpful sites:
>
> - support.office.com/en-us/article/PowerPoint
>   -training-40e8c930-cb0b-40d8-82c4
>   -bd53d3398787
> - support.office.com/en-us/powerpoint
> - prezi.com/support
>
> → See pages 260–263 for PowerPoint and Prezi basics.

1

Create a Storyboard

Storyboarding is similar to outlining a speech and is the act of sketching out the content and arranging the sequence of your aids. Storyboarding before you open your software frees you to see what you need, what order is best, and what will allow you to be most creative. Overall, your purpose should be to help the audience understand your message better. Your aids should not be talking points for you to read during the speech.

STEPS FOR STORYBOARDING

1. Locate unlined paper if possible. (Lined paper tends to make you wordy and not visual.) If you are using PowerPoint, draft each of your slides by hand on paper. For Prezi, write your topic in the middle of a page and circle it. From there, map out what your audience needs to know. Think of your map as a visual metaphor for your information. For example, if you want your audience to decide between two different options, your visual metaphor might be the intersection of two roads. Prezi has several predesigned templates for maps.

2. Let your introduction, main points, and conclusion guide the content of your slides or canvas. Try to limit your slides or path points to one or two per main point. You can place blank/blackout PowerPoint slides when you need to draw the focus back to you. In Prezi, you can do this by remaining zoomed in on your last frame.

3. Make a note to include source material where necessary.

4. Adhere to effective design principles.

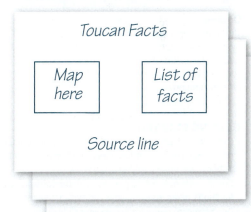

2
Begin with Presentation Software Basics

Although giving a complete tutorial on PowerPoint or Prezi here is not possible, the following pages highlight some of the basics. Don't be afraid to ask for help from a colleague or someone at a computer center.

POWERPOINT

PowerPoint is widely available and useful for a linear slide presentation. Make sure you learn the features of the version of PowerPoint you will be using. The example here shows PowerPoint for Mac 2016.

Tools
The toolbar allows you to do tasks such as choose fonts, insert text and images, select a design, and view your slide show.

Slide thumbnails
Here you can scroll through your slides, drag slides to change order, and click between slides to add one.

Design
This function includes built-in slide layouts as well as a blank slide if you want to build one from the ground up.

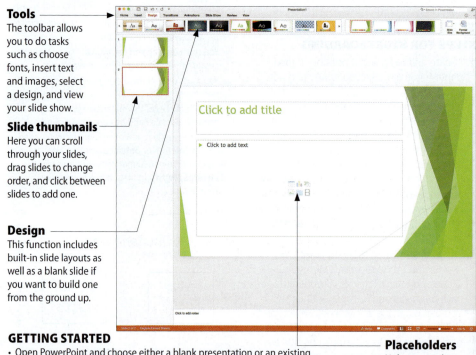

Placeholders
Unless you select a blank slide, borders will outline the preset placeholders for inserting images or text.

GETTING STARTED

- Open PowerPoint and choose either a blank presentation or an existing design. Each built-in design offers a unified theme of colors, fonts, and graphic options. Don't pick one that is too busy.
- Create a title slide first to practice with the software. Using the insert functions, begin inserting your text and/or images.
- Don't forget to periodically save your slide show.

As you create your slides, follow the design principles outlined on pages 254–257. PowerPoint offers many ways to incorporate text, visuals, video, audio, and animation, but the simpler you keep your aids, the more effective they can be.

Color

Limit your use of color and maintain consistency throughout. Ideally, use one background color or slide theme and two to three font colors, at the most, for titles, text, and emphasis. Medium colors are usually better than very dark ones.

Space

Using the preset slide layouts will show you how arranging and grouping together similar information and leaving space free of images or text can help you adhere to effective design principles. You do not want your audience to be overwhelmed visually or to feel the slides are out of balance (for example, top- or bottom-heavy).

Text

Clearly, text will be an important part of your slides. You will use titles and, in some cases, include several lines of text in the main part of a slide. Keep text brief and organized so that your audience can read it quickly. Lists and bulleted items work well. Select fonts that are easy to read. Limit your fonts to no more than two different ones on a single aid, and be consistent throughout the slides. Remember to avoid using all capitals (use both upper- and lowercase). Use italics, underlining, different-colored text, and boldface sparingly and for emphasis only. Titles and text size should be readable by everyone in the room. A general guideline is 44 points for titles and 24 to 32 points for other text.

Images and Sound

PowerPoint gives you several options for inserting visuals, audio, and video. The first rule for deciding whether to use inserts in your slides, and if so which ones, is to ask, How does this item help illustrate, support, or clarify my topic? If you don't have a solid answer to that question, you don't need the image, sound, or video. If the insert passes that test, it also must be:

- Large and clear enough to be seen
- A high-enough resolution to be projected on a large screen
- Clearly related to your topic and ethically appropriate
- Displayed with a title and, if needed, source information
- Smoothly integrated into the presentation

Keep in mind that simpler is often better.

TIP: Presenting PowerPoint Slides

- Have a backup plan in case the system fails.
- Check the order of your slides against your delivery outline.
- Know how to display the slides in slide-show view, not the normal view you used as you created them.
- Learn slide-show commands. For example, when in slide-show mode, press the *B* key for blackout and the *W* key to return to the visual. This will help you display slides only when you are referring to them in your speech.
- Rehearse using the slide show (in the speech event space, if possible).
- Make sure you have saved all of the slides, sound clips, and video for transportation to the event.
- Check the equipment the day of the speech.

PREZI

Prezi is a presentation tool that helps you translate your speech into a visual concept map combining words, images, links, and/or videos into a nonlinear aid. Instead of moving through a series of slides, Prezi lets you zoom in and out across a large area—known as a canvas—that uses movement and 2.5D visualization. You can create a public account for free at prezi.com. This allows you to use the public editor and save a few prezis to the cloud. Be careful; all prezis created with the public editor are available for anyone on the Internet to view.

Top menu
Options and menus on this bar allow you to do such tasks as preview the prezi, add numerous types of frames, change color themes, or insert images, media, or PowerPoint slides.

Left sidebar
Allows you to visualize the paths and navigate each as you create their content. Click on thumbnails to zoom in on them.

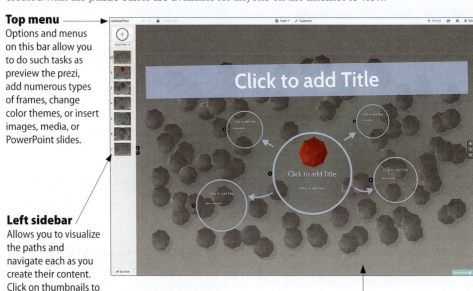

Zoomable canvas
The canvas is the interactive surface where you create the prezi. You can click directly on it to add text or right-click on it to change the background color.

GETTING STARTED

- Set up an account and choose "Create a new prezi."
- Select or create a canvas template. The program has a blank option as well as predesigned templates, such as the one shown above.
- Begin by filling in the overall theme or titles and path points by adding text, images, or video.
- Consider your best color choices for the background and text. You can customize your canvas.
- Edit the path you want the prezi to take by clicking on Edit Path, located on the left sidebar.
- Run the presentation and evaluate its effectiveness.

As you design your prezi, think about the story you want to tell and how to move your audience through that story effectively. Don't zoom in and out too much or spin around path points. That can confuse your audience and even cause motion sickness for some. Make your path flow easily from one point to another.

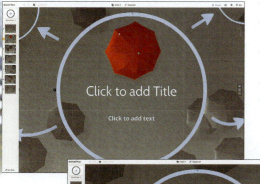

Questions to ask as you build a prezi:

- How can I use my canvas to better inform or persuade my audience?
- What are the specifics I want my audience to know by the end of the prezi?
- What visuals might I use for each key point?
- Am I using too much text? Am I being consistent with layout and visuals? Am I using good design principles?
- Does my prezi flow well as a presentation?
  - Does my prezi support my speech or does it do it all for me? (Your prezi should not distract your audience or outshine your speech message.)
  - Am I using effective visual and sound elements as suggested on page 261?

as suggested on page 261?

TIP: Presenting a Prezi

- Have a backup plan in case the system fails. If you won't have an Internet connection the day of your speech, you will need a downloaded, portable prezi to run on the computer. Remember, depending on how you embedded any YouTube videos, they may only play with an active Internet connection or might be blocked by the system the day of your speech. You also cannot edit a portable prezi.
- Check that your path through the prezi relates to your speech outline.
- Know how to run the prezi. (For example, pressing ESC exits full-screen mode; you can zoom in and out with a mouse wheel or the + or – tools on the right sidebar in presentation mode. You can show the prezi in full screen by clicking on the button in the bottom right corner.)
- Rehearse using the prezi (in the speech event space, if possible).
- Check the equipment the day of the speech.
- Don't rush though the presentation.

11.6 How Do You Use a Presentation Aid Successfully?

PROOFREAD, PREVIEW, AND PRACTICE

Always proofread your aids for spelling or other errors. Having someone else proofread them is often a good idea, to catch details that you might miss.

Preview any computer-generated aids in the room where you will give the speech, at or close to the time you will speak, and with the exact equipment if possible. Sunlight can wash out projected images, and some LCD projectors are not very bright. If you encounter such issues, you may need to change color schemes. Make sure the system will accept the medium (flash drive, CD, etc.) your presentation is stored on. Be sure to save all of the files associated with the presentation in the same folder on the medium you will take to the speaking event; a common error is to forget audio or video files. The software you use to create the presentation should be the same version as the one you will use to deliver the presentation.

Practice with all aids you plan to use, including people, objects, models, computer-generated aids, and others. Not knowing how to use an aid or fumbling with it—or the equipment used to project it—will lower your ethos and increase your communication apprehension. You should be comfortable with your aid and any equipment related to it.

CHECK THE EQUIPMENT

Always check that the equipment is present, working, and set how you want it. You do not want to be surprised by discovering that you did not turn on the equipment. You will need to pause or talk over the booting-up process, making you seem unprepared. Check the sound level of audio equipment. Even check for chalk, markers, and erasers, if there is any possibility you will need them.

KNOW WHEN TO DISPLAY AIDS

Display your aids as you need them, and then remove them from sight. The element of surprise helps draw your audience's attention to your topic as you display items and pulls attention back to you as you remove them. Turning the aid around or over, removing it from sight, or going to a blank slide/screen are all simple ways to achieve this.

DON'T PASS THE AIDS AROUND

If you have objects, items, pictures, or hand-outs, don't pass them around. This is distracting, and it is highly unlikely that everyone will get to see passed-around aids within the timeframe of your speech. If you think the handouts will help listeners understand as you go, give them to the audience before you begin and incorporate them into the speech. Focus the audience on where you are on the handout. If possible, it is best to give out all handouts after your speech.

USE THE TOUCH, TURN, TALK METHOD

The "Touch, Turn, Talk Method" refers to how you should relate to your presentation aid and the audience. The Touch stage happens as you point to, direct your eyes toward, move toward, and/or literally touch the aid you are using, drawing the focus completely to the aid. The Turn stage happens as you turn from the aid and regain eye contact with the audience. Then you move into Talk, where you explain the aid. The process should be a fluid back and forth between you, the aid, and the audience. You need to acknowledge the aid, return to the audience, and explain the content of the aid. Just displaying an aid or talking directly to the aid, instead of looking at the audience, is not effective.

PREPARE A BACKUP PLAN

Always have a backup plan. Be prepared for it to rain or snow the day of your speech, and have a way to keep your aids dry. Be prepared for equipment to be missing or to fail. If you have a plan, you will not be as stressed when something does go wrong, and you will still be able to give your speech effectively.

CHECKLIST for Presentation Aids

- ❏ Do my aids look professional?
- ❏ Do they support and enhance my speech?
- ❏ Are my aids appropriate for the topic, audience, and situation?
- ❏ Am I ethically representing information with my aids?
- ❏ Are my aids clear, simple, and understandable?
- ❏ Did I effectively design the aids?
- ❏ Do I cite sources in the speech and on the visuals?
- ❏ Do I effectively incorporate the aids in the speech?
- ❏ Do I balance my aids throughout the speech?

CONFIDENCE BOOSTER

Presentation aids can boost your confidence by:

- Helping you internalize your information as you create the aids
- Helping you organize your thoughts
- Serving as a way for you to present your message more professionally
- Giving you the opportunity to change your visual focus and/or physically move during the speech
- Offering you the opportunity to redirect your audience's eyes to something besides you

Chapter 11: Review

ASSESSING YOUR KNOWLEDGE

11.1 What Are the Types of Presentation Aids?

Objective 11.1: **LIST THE TYPES OF PRESENTATION AIDS**

Presentation aids are two- or three- dimensional visual items, video footage, audio recordings, and/or multimedia segments that support and enhance your speech.
- Actual items, such as people, animals, or objects
- Models
- Photographs
- Drawings, including maps, sketches, diagrams, plans, or other nonphotographic representations
- Charts and tables, such as flowcharts and organizational charts
- Graphs, including line graphs, bar graphs, pictographs, and pie graphs
- Media, including video, audio, and multimedia

→ See pages 238–245.

11.2 How Do You Determine What Presentation Aids You Need to Use?

Objective 11.2: **EXPLAIN HOW TO DETERMINE YOUR PRESENTATION AID NEEDS**

- Establish the purpose for each aid. It should assist, support, and facilitate your message, not detract from or outshine it.
- Select the best type of aids for you, your topic, your audience, and the situation.
- Consider how you will display your aids. Think about methods you are comfortable with, the size of the audience, the availability of equipment, what will work in the speech environment, cost, and effectiveness.

→ See pages 246–247.

11.3 What Are the Common Methods for Displaying Aids?

Objective 11.3: **SUMMARIZE COMMON METHODS FOR DISPLAYING AIDS**

- Chalkboards and whiteboards
- Posters
- Handouts
- Flip charts
- Advanced technology, including contemporary and traditional media

→ See pages 248–253.

11.4 How Do You Craft an Effective Aid?

Objective 11.4: **DESCRIBE HOW TO CRAFT AN EFFECTIVE AID**

- You should follow good design principles. Design principles relate to the arrangement and placement of various elements (color, text, line, images, and space). There are five main design principles:
  - Unity: the need for elements to relate to each other
  - Pattern: the use of a consistent design format
  - Balance: a feeling of equilibrium
  - Emphasis: highlighting what is most important
  - Rhythm: a real or imagined sense of movement
- Allow yourself enough time to be creative and to craft your aids. Consider factors such as how easily you come up with interesting ideas and how comfortable you are with the method for producing your aid.

→ See pages 254–257.

11.5 How Can You Use Presentation Software?

Objective 11.5: **SUMMARIZE HOW TO USE PRESENTATION SOFTWARE**

- Create storyboards for your aids. Storyboarding before you open your software frees you to see what you need, what order is best, and what will allow you to be most creative.
- Begin with the basics of your presentation software. The most common programs are PowerPoint and Prezi. PowerPoint is useful for a linear slide presentation. Prezi uses a visual concept map and lets you zoom in and out across a large area known as a canvas. Before you create your aids, get to know the features of the program you are using.

→ See pages 258–263.

11.6 How Do You Use a Presentation Aid Successfully?

Objective 11.6: **DESCRIBE HOW TO USE A PRESENTATION AID SUCCESSFULLY**

- Proofread, preview, and practice:
  - Proofread your aids to catch any errors.
  - Preview any computer-generated aids.
  - Practice with all aids you plan to use.
- Check your equipment to make sure it is working and set how you want it.
- Display the aids when you need them, and then remove them from sight.
- Don't pass any aids around. This will distract your audience.
- Use the Touch, Turn, Talk Method to relate to your aids and the audience.
- Always have a backup plan, so that if something goes wrong with the aids, you will still be able to give your speech effectively.

→ See pages 264–265.

TERMS TO REMEMBER

presentation aids (238)
models (239)
photographs (240)
drawings (240)
charts (241)
flowcharts (241)
organizational charts (241)
tables (241)
graphs (241)
line graphs (241)
bar graphs (242)
pictographs (242)
pie graphs (243)
video clips (244)
audio clips (244)
multimedia (245)
design principles (254)
storyboarding (259)

Practical Pointers for Tab 4

FAQs

How can I improve my language skills?

Improving your language skills takes effort, but it doesn't have to be time-consuming or boring. Here are some tips:

- Select three new words from a dictionary and try to use each of them in a sentence several times throughout the day when appropriate. Often, they will become part of your vocabulary. Repeat daily and keep a word diary of the words you learn. Read over it periodically.
- Play online word games such as "Words with Friends," or work other word puzzles.
- Use a dictionary and thesaurus as you read and write. Don't jump over words you don't know; look them up and use them correctly.
- Read every day. It can be a website, newspaper article, book, or magazine. Just read. The more you do, the better your language skills will be.
- Join a writing group or keep a detailed journal that pushes you to learn new words.
- Listen to the vocabulary of others.

I have trouble with mumbling. How can I fix that?

When someone tells you that you are mumbling, he or she is saying that you are not articulating all the necessary sounds that make language distinct and clear. A quick way to determine if you mumble is to record yourself speaking and then to play it back for someone, with the volume turned down so the listener is just able to hear what you are saying. If you mumble, it will be difficult for the listener to understand you.

To stop mumbling, you have to be motivated to do so. Work on it daily, in your normal speech. Consider all parts of the words, especially voiced consonants. Exercise your facial muscles (especially the lips). For example, do a big "toothy grin," hold it, and release. Then purse your lips, hold, and release. Repeat several times.

ADDITIONAL SUPPORT

For more on mediated presentations and presentation aids, consult the following:

www.masternewmedia.org

money.howstuffworks.com/business
-communications/how-online
-presentations-work.htm

blog.duarte.com/category/tips-2

www.presentationzen.com

www.danroam.com

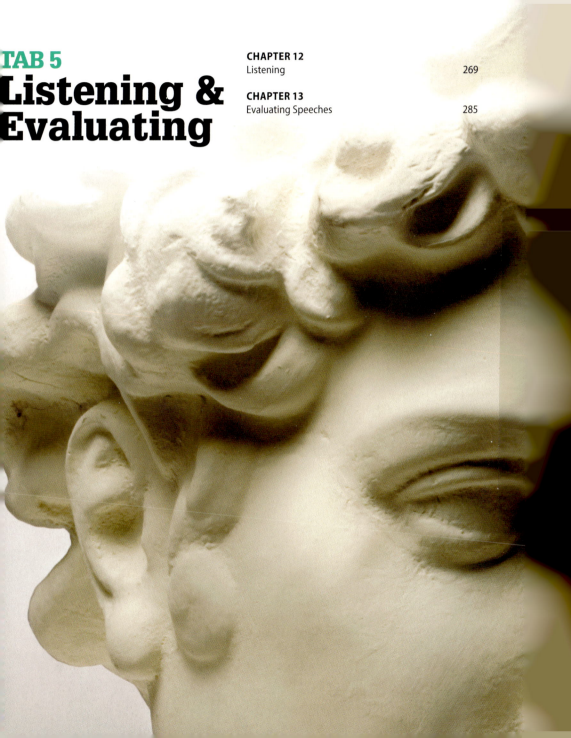

TAB 5
Listening &
Evaluating

12
LISTENING

The most basic and powerful way to connect to another person is to listen. Just listen. Perhaps the most important thing we ever give each other is our attention.[1]

RACHEL NAOMI REMEN, M.D.

12.1 Why Is Listening an Important Skill?

1 Your Knowledge Increases
2 You Build Better Relationships
3 You Fulfill Your Communicative Responsibility

1

Your Knowledge Increases

Michael is a pre-dental major struggling with his chemistry class. He frequently gets distracted, and his anxiety about understanding the information sometimes causes him to tune out the teacher as he focuses on his notes. Determined to learn the concepts, he decides he needs to listen more carefully to lectures and lab instructions. He starts by sitting in the front of the room, where it is easier to pay attention and to prevent his mind from wandering. Also, he begins to participate more in class discussion.

You may have found yourself in a situation like Michael's, whether in a math class when the instructor explained a new equation or at work when your manager explained a new job-related procedure.

Listening allows you to take in, process, and use information. Listening helps you develop your expertise or skill with a subject. It allows you to collect information to make your daily life easier and more enjoyable. Effective listening may prevent you from missing a professional opportunity, it may save you time and money, and it may advance your career. Many accomplished people believe listening is the key to success.

Listening also tells us about ourselves. For example, make a list of what really makes you sit up and listen. What topics can hold your attention for hours? What topics or people do you find easy to listen to? What types of music do you enjoy? The answers to these questions will feature what you value, agree with, or find interesting. Taking an inventory of what you listen to will begin to draw a picture of your self-identity.

2
You Build Better Relationships

Michael's changes in behavior during his chemistry class helped improve his relationship with his instructor. She saw him as a more dedicated student, determined to understand the subject.

Listening allows us to build and maintain healthy relationships with our families, significant others, friends, and coworkers. Just as listening can teach you about yourself, listening to others will help you know what is important to them. Their words will give you clues to their identity.

Through understanding how our identities interlock, you build relationships and strengthen them. Once you choose to maintain a relationship, listening allows you to deal with conflict or help the other person cope with or resolve a crisis in his or her life. Listening shows others that you value and care about them.

In a world where you can watch television, use a computer, send text messages and e-mail, or talk on a phone almost anywhere, listening doesn't seem to have a chance. If you often find yourself doing one of these activities and abruptly responding to others with "I'm listening," you are not listening effectively—and that is the message you are sending. Although this type of multitasking is acceptable sometimes, it should not be the norm. Know when it is not appropriate.

Good communication is vital in every stage of relationship development. The failure to communicate and listen in an interpersonal relationship will result in a languishing relationship at best and, more likely, an unhappy or negative relationship.

3
You Fulfill Your Communicative Responsibility

As you know from studying the communication process in Chapter 1 (pages 4–5), one of the major reasons scholars view the process as transactional is that the audience actively participates. The act of listening completes the transaction between the speaker and the audience. Each audience member becomes an active participant, not a passive vessel.

Audience members who believe that the speaker is entirely responsible for the effectiveness of the message are falling prey to *passivity syndrome*. For effective communication to occur, the speaker and the audience member are both responsible for completing and understanding the message. When Michael did not understand his instructor, he used nonverbal and verbal communication to signal his confusion and worked to pay closer attention. As a communication participant, Michael met the message head on. His instructor cannot listen to or remember a message for him; he must take that responsibility.

Finally, it is your duty to listen actively as a citizen in a democratic society dedicated to the freedom of speech. As journalist Walter Lippmann wrote, "While the right to talk may be the beginning of freedom, the necessity of listening is what makes the right important." In other words, what is said is only as valid as the listener's willingness to listen and ability to comprehend and evaluate what is said. Our duty is to listen and analyze a message, not simply take it as fact or reality regardless of the source.

12.2 What Is the Process of Listening?

Understanding the listening process begins with grasping the difference between hearing and listening. As this diagram suggests, ***hearing*** happens when sound waves strike the eardrum and spark a chain reaction that ends with the brain registering the sound. This is the physiological awareness of sound that most people are born with. People who are deaf or have severe hearing loss hear by watching via a language of gestural, facial, and body movements. Hearing is the first step in listening and is typically an automatic function. In contrast, you must choose to listen. ***Listening***, according to the International Listening Association, is the conscious learned act of paying attention, assigning meaning, and responding to a verbal and/or nonverbal message. The listening process has five phases: receiving, attending, understanding, responding, and remembering.

HEARING

is the physiological process of receiving sound.

ATTENDING
UNDERSTANDING
RESPONDING
REMEMBERING

LISTENING

is the act of paying attention and assigning meaning.

RECEIVING SOUND

Receiving is the physiological process of hearing. The ears collect the sound (or, if hearing is impaired, the eyes collect visual stimuli), converting and transmitting it to the brain.

Attending is the phase where you make your brain pay attention to a given sound or equivalent stimulus. For example, stop and listen to the sounds around you now. You may be able to hear birds outside, music, people talking next door, or the soft whoosh of air coming from the air conditioner or heater. Now, imagine a friend speaking in the middle of this symphony of sound, and pay attention to his or her words. If you are able to do so, you will no longer pay attention to some of those other sounds. The sounds do not go away; you are still hearing them, but not attending to them. If your hearing is impeded for any reason, you will attend only to the message you can see. In either case, you have chosen to concentrate on your friend's message and exclude others.

Understanding occurs when you apply meaning to what you are attending to— and is where communication really begins. You may hear a message and attend to it, but if you do not understand it, the communication was unsuccessful. If you enter a room where two students from Russia are speaking in their national language, you will hear it, if nothing prevents you from doing so. You may attend to their conversation if they are your friends and you are interested in what they may be discussing. But the understanding will not take place unless you know Russian.

Responding is the phase where you give feedback or a reply to the messages you have processed. Some communication scholars say the listening process ends with understanding because the communication was either successful or not. However, the communication process is transactional, and most listeners offer one of three different responses or some combination of these.

- *Verbal responses* are spoken or written feedback. Your verbal response might paraphrase the speaker's message, ask for further explanation, or simply answer a speaker's question.

- *Nonverbal responses* are visual cues offered by the listener (such as nodding yes or frowning when confused). They can be effective in their brevity but leave great room for misinterpretation.

- *Silence*, or no perceptible response, can also be a response. The listener may choose not to respond because that seems appropriate, or silence can suggest a problem between the speaker, listener, and/or message. Silence can also signal concentration. You often need other nonverbal cues to interpret silence properly.

Remembering, or retaining what you hear, is the final stage. Good listening skills often make use of a person's short-term and long-term memories. In the short term, you listen carefully for details to help you follow the speech's strategy and/or argument. The memory of those details helps you make sense of the speech in the moment but not necessarily remember it later. In the long term, you may commit to memory a broad understanding of the speech, as a means of retaining valuable information or maintaining a change in your attitudes, values, or beliefs.

12.3 What Are the Types of Listening?

1 Appreciative Listening
2 Empathic Listening
3 Informative Listening
4 Critical Listening

When you engage in the process of listening, you do so to achieve a goal. The four listening goals are to appreciate, empathize, comprehend, and be critical. You will always have one of these goals as your overarching reason for listening. However, listeners often use a combination to achieve the main goal. (For example, you may be listening for information but at the same time evaluating it critically for believability.) Each of these goals corresponds to a type of listening.

1
Appreciative Listening

Appreciative listening happens when you listen for recreation or enjoyment. Examples of appreciative listening are:

- Listening to a comedy show
- Listening to your favorite band
- Listening to water flowing in a stream and birds singing
- Listening to a speech that has the goal to entertain

2
Empathic Listening

Empathic listening occurs when your purpose is to give the speaker emotional support. Examples here could be:

- A religious leader listening to a congregation member
- A counselor listening to a patient
- A friend listening to another friend in need

This type of listening emphasizes carefully attending to the speaker; supporting the speaker by listening more than responding; and empathizing, or feeling as the other person feels.

3
Informative Listening

You engage in *informative listening* when you want to gain insight or comprehension. This approach to listening emphasizes concentrating on language, ideas, and details as well as remembering the knowledge.

In classes, you use informative listening when you pay attention to your professors. Other places where you might engage in informative listening could be:

- When a friend gives you directions to his new apartment
- At the hardware store as a sales associate tells you how to install tile
- When a doctor gives you medical instructions

In all of these examples, you listen for clarification of the language, you concentrate on the necessary details, and you engage in some sort of activity to help you remember (e.g., taking notes or memorizing).

TIP: Critical Listening

Critical listening takes time and practice. These tactics will help you:
- Listen carefully and ask questions.
- Avoid counterfeit questions, which mask a message as a question. "Are you finally off the computer?"
- Explore alternatives.
- Maintain a childlike curiosity—everything is interesting and possible.
- Be open-minded.

→ See page 281 for more on listening critically.

4
Critical Listening

Critical listening takes place when you listen carefully to a message in order to judge it as acceptable or not. This is the type of listening behavior you use when listening to:

- A presidential debate
- A salesperson trying to sell you a new sound system
- A friend when you are trying to decide if she is telling you the truth

Critical listening is the root of critical thinking. Theorists Brooke Moore and Richard Parker, in their book *Critical Thinking*, define *critical thinking* as "the careful, deliberate determination of whether one should accept, reject, or suspend judgment about a claim [or information] and the degree of confidence with which one accepts or rejects it." Astronomer Carl Sagan called this your "baloney-detection kit." Sagan's suggestion was to "equip yourself with a baloney-detection kit ... and be able to tell what is baloney and what is not."

You currently live in a time when informative and persuasive acts bombard you from all sides. They come at you from radio, television, the Internet, T-shirts, and even cereal boxes. You must be able and willing to ask such questions as: Why? Where did that information come from? How old is it? Who benefits from it? Who will get hurt? See the Tip box to the left for a few critical listening tactics.

12.4 What Can Prevent Effective Listening?

1 Internal Noise
2 External Noise

Most people would define noise as unpleasant sounds that might be loud, startling, irritating, or unwelcome. In the process of communicating (as shown on page 4), **noise** refers to the unwanted barriers that prevent you from listening effectively to the speaker. They can be pleasant or unpleasant things.

For example, you might find the deep, melodious voices of actors James Earl Jones and Morgan Freeman so pleasing that you focus more on the beauty of their voices than on their messages. Or you might feel that the harsh, nasal voices of actors Fran Drescher (as her character in *The Nanny*) and Gilbert Gottfried (comedian and the original voice of the AFLAC duck) are so annoying that you stop listening to the words spoken. Either of these vocal qualities could become a barrier and, therefore, noise preventing you from attending to what is important about the message.

As you learned in Chapter 2, noise is not always connected to the speaker; it can be something like a clock ticking, someone tapping a pencil, distracting thoughts, or hunger. Understanding what can become noise is the first step to preventing it from distracting you. There are two general categories of noise influencing communication: internal and external.

PRACTICING ETHICS: Unplugging

Electronic device distractions are plentiful and enticing these days. It is your ethical responsibility to ignore these devices when their use is inappropriate. Choose to be an attentive listener, and be "unplugged" when communicating face-to-face with others.

1

Internal Noise

Internal noise is any barrier to effective listening that originates within the body or mind of the listener. Internal noise can be either a physiological or a psychological barrier.

- *Physiological barriers* are bodily conditions that prevent or constrain your ability to process information.

- *Psychological barriers* are emotional conditions that prevent you from focusing on and absorbing a message. For example, your communication anxiety may prevent you from listening to the speech given just before yours, or your fear of a boss could prevent you from listening to his or her comments. A fight with your best friend or worries over how to make a car payment may preoccupy you. Perspective differences (seeing the message from different points of view) between a teenager and a parent can prevent listening when they do not share the same attitudes, values, beliefs, or expectations.

2

External Noise

External noise is any barrier to effective listening that originates outside of the listener's body and mind. External noise can be either an environmental or a linguistic barrier.

- *Environmental barriers* occur when something within the room or area where the speech is given interrupts your ability to concentrate.

- *Linguistic barriers* happen when the verbal and/or nonverbal messages from the speaker are unfamiliar to or misunderstood by the listener.

→ For advice on adapting to noise during a speech, see pages 42–43.

INTERNAL NOISE		EXTERNAL NOISE	
Physiological Barriers	Psychological Barriers	Environmental Barriers	Linguistic Barriers
Examples	*Examples*	*Examples*	*Examples*
Headache	Boredom	Environmental sounds	Jargon
Lack of sleep	Fear	Smells	Awkward sentence
Pain	Don't-care attitude	Disruptions	structure
Illness	Preoccupation	Bad ventilation	Difficult vocabulary
Hearing or visual	Anger	Room temperature	Unfamiliar or distracting
impairments	Anxiety	Uncomfortable seats	nonverbal delivery
	Frustration	Lighting	Poor organization
	Prejudice	Electronic devices	
	Perspective differences		

12.5 How Can You Help Your Audience Listen More Effectively?

Know your audience. Recognize your listeners' *egocentrism*, or the tendency for your audience to be interested in things that relate and matter to them. Be aware of barriers they might experience related to you, your topic, or the situation. If you know your audience will have a negative response to your topic or might have physiological or psychological issues preventing effective listening, recognizing and addressing these issues up front may help lessen their effects.

→ See Chapter 2 on getting to know your audience.

Create an effective message. Using an effective attention-getter, appropriate language, a sound organizational strategy, and exceptional supporting materials will help your audience stay connected to your speech. Difficult or obscure language will frustrate them. A poor organizational strategy will confuse them, and they will stop trying to follow you; good organization is key.

Be confident. Some audience members have trouble listening to messages delivered with low confidence because their empathy for the speaker overrides their focus on the content. Others may not give much weight to a speech when the speaker lacks confidence. Know your message well, and be self-assured and bold when you speak.

Control the environment. When you enter the speaking environment, change aspects that might reduce listening, if you can. For example, adjust temperature and lighting or remove any distracting noises.

Listen to your audience. As you speak, be attentive and responsive to verbal or nonverbal audience behavior that suggests they are confused, bored, or distracted.

Lend a helping hand across cultures. In our increasingly global society, you will likely speak to an audience that includes individuals from cultures different from yours. Take the time to learn what you can about their cultures. This table offers some suggestions for helping the cross-cultural audience member listen to and understand your speech.

HOW CAN YOU INCREASE EFFECTIVE LISTENING?	EXPLANATION
Get to know other cultures.	Try to know what cultures are in your audience, and learn about them. Study and interact with other cultures regularly so you are mindful of them. For example, some people from other cultures will nod in agreement to be polite when they do not understand.
Use a comprehensible oral delivery style.	Slow down, articulate and pronounce carefully, and use repetition and rephrasing.
Use nonverbal cues.	In the United States, smiling demonstrates your enthusiasm, and gesturing could highlight important points. Be careful not to use culturally specific nonverbal cues that might be misread.
Use presentation aids.	Presentation aids can help summarize or repeat information that might be difficult to remember or understand from oral delivery alone.
Be realistic and thorough in your message.	Take a little longer to discuss complex issues and do not use idioms, jokes, sarcasm, or exaggerations that might be confusing.
Listen to the audience's verbal and nonverbal feedback.	Watch for looks of confusion or blank expressions, side discussions that seem to be asking for clarification, shuffling through papers about the speech as if looking for clarification, or significant use of a translation dictionary or device as you speak. These are signals that someone is struggling with your message.

CONFIDENCE BOOSTER

- Dress for the occasion. Clothes make a difference.
- Stand tall.
- Try to minimize nervous behavior. If your hands shake, gesture with them.
- Captivate your audience with effective volume, tone, and articulation.
- Maintain eye contact with audience members.

CHECKLIST for Helping Your Audience Listen

❑ What do I know about my audience that might interfere with their ability to listen?
❑ Am I using the best means to grab and keep this audience's attention?
❑ How can my delivery and confidence level help?
❑ How can I control the environment better?
❑ What cues are the audience members sending me?

12.6 As an Audience Member, How Can You Listen More Effectively?

1 Listen Actively
2 Listen Critically

1

Listen Actively

Active listening is important if you are to be an effective consumer of information. Here are some steps to help you.

- Give your full attention. Do not watch the cars out the window, daydream, or think about the fight you had with someone before the speech.
- Listen for the main points.
- Take notes to help you remember.
- Respond to the speech. Nonverbal responses, such as nodding when you understand or looking confused when you do not, are always helpful. In some cases, the speaker or the situation will signal that you can be more verbally interactive, such as asking a question. Pay attention to what is appropriate.
- Participate in the question-and-answer session after the speech, if one is conducted.
- If you are a cross-cultural listener, work at building your vocabulary and knowledge of idioms or informal expressions. Pay attention to the speaker's body language (posture, gestures, intonation, expression, etc.). Let the speaker know when issues prevent understanding.

CHECKLIST for Listening Effectively

❏ Am I giving the speaker my full attention?
❏ Am I actively trying to comprehend the message?
❏ Am I signaling the speaker with the appropriate feedback?
❏ Am I listening critically?

2
Listen Critically

As human beings, our ability to think critically is one of the differences that distinguishes us from our furry and feathered friends as well as from machines. When you listen to a speech in a public forum, listening critically is important. Being an effective critical listener takes time and practice. Employing the following tactics will help you develop this skill.

- Listen carefully.
- Ask questions—especially the question "Why?" (either mentally asking yourself or, if appropriate, directly asking the speaker).
- Explore alternatives.
- Suspend judgment until details are given.
- Define criteria for making judgments but not at the expense of alternatives.
- Be open-minded and willing to adjust.
- Avoid nonproductive listening practices. The table below lists the most common ones.

You will find active and critical listening easier if you put yourself in the shoes of the person speaking. Just like an effective speaker must consider the audience's traits, an effective listener needs to empathize and identify with the speaker's feelings, thoughts, motives, interests, and attitudes. As you learned in Chapter 1, this act of empathizing and identifying is what theorist and philosopher Kenneth Burke called *identification*. Identification will prevent you from prematurely judging the speaker or topic, keep you from being resistant to new ideas or speaking styles, and hold you back from overreacting to "hot button" issues. Speaker and listener are coparticipants, equals, in the process of communication.

NONPRODUCTIVE LISTENING PRACTICE	WHAT IS IT?
Pseudolistening	Pretending to listen
Superficial listening	Paying attention to superficial things rather than the complex message
Selective listening	Tuning into only a part of the message or listening to only what you want to hear
Defensive listening	Taking comments as critical or hostile attacks
Multitasking	Although not a listening behavior, this behavior of attending to several things at once can negatively influence your skills.

Chapter 12: Review

ASSESSING YOUR KNOWLEDGE

12.1 Why Is Listening an Important Skill?

Objective 12.1: **EXPLAIN WHY LISTENING IS AN IMPORTANT SKILL**

- Listening increases your knowledge by allowing you to take in, process, and use information, which develops your expertise or skill with a subject. Listening also tells you about yourself.
- Listening helps you build better and healthier relationships.
- Listening helps you fulfill your communicative responsibility. You are falling prey to passivity syndrome if you believe it is entirely the speaker's responsibility to get a message across effectively. Active listening occurs when you pay close attention, attempt to understand the message, signal confusion or understanding, and engage in communication as a transaction.

→ See pages 270–271.

12.2 What Is the Process of Listening?

Objective 12.2: **DESCRIBE THE LISTENING PROCESS**

Hearing is physiological and only the first step of listening. Listening is the conscious learned act of paying attention, assigning meaning, and responding to a verbal and/or nonverbal message. Hearing is typically an automatic function. In contrast, you must *choose* to listen. The five phases of the listening process are:

- Receiving, or the physiological process of hearing
- Attending, or when your brain pays attention to a given sound or equivalent stimulus
- Understanding, or when you apply meaning to what you are attending to
- Responding, or when you give a formal response to the messages
- Remembering, or when you retain what you hear

→ See pages 272–273.

12.3 What Are the Types of Listening?

Objective 12.3: **IDENTIFY THE TYPES OF LISTENING**

- Appreciative listening happens when you listen for recreation or enjoyment.
- Empathic listening occurs when your purpose is to give the speaker emotional support.
- Informative listening transpires when you want to gain insight or comprehension.
- Critical listening takes place when you listen carefully to a message in order to judge it as acceptable or not. Critical listening is the root of critical thinking, or the "careful, deliberate determination of whether one should accept, reject, or suspend judgment about a claim [or information] and the degree of confidence with which one accepts or rejects it" (Moore and Parker).

→ See pages 274–275.

12.4 What Can Prevent Effective Listening?

Objective 12.4: **EXPLAIN THE BARRIERS TO EFFECTIVE LISTENING**

- Internal noise is any barrier to effective listening that originates within the body or mind of the listener. Internal noise can be physiological or psychological.
- External noise is any barrier to effective listening that originates outside of the listener's body and mind. External noise can be environmental or linguistic.

→ See pages 276–277.

12.5 How Can You Help Your Audience Listen More Effectively?

Objective 12.5: **SUMMARIZE HOW TO HELP YOUR AUDIENCE LISTEN MORE EFFECTIVELY**

- Know your audience.
- Create an effective message.
- Be confident.
- Control the environment.
- Listen to your audience.
- Lend a helping hand across cultures.

→ See pages 278–279.

12.6 As an Audience Member, How Can You Listen More Effectively?

Objective 12.6: **DESCRIBE HOW YOU CAN LISTEN MORE EFFECTIVELY AS AN AUDIENCE MEMBER**

- Listen actively. In other words, do not fake paying attention. Give the speaker your full attention, note the main points, and give feedback when appropriate.
- Listen critically. Don't judge too quickly, listen to details, ask questions, explore alternatives, be curious, be willing to adjust, and keep an open mind. Avoid nonproductive listening practices.

→ See pages 280–281.

TERMS TO REMEMBER

passivity syndrome (271)
hearing (272)
listening (272)
receiving (273)
attending (273)
understanding (273)
responding (273)
remembering (273)
appreciative listening (274)
empathic listening (274)
informative listening (275)
critical listening (275)
critical thinking (275)
noise (276)
internal noise (277)
physiological barriers (277)
psychological barriers (277)
external noise (277)
environmental barriers (277)
linguistic barriers (277)
egocentrism (278)

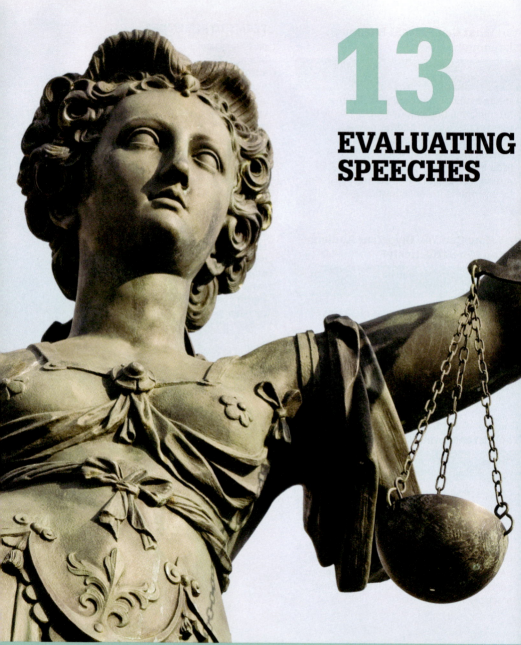

13

EVALUATING SPEECHES

Many receive advice, only
the wise profit from it.[1]

PUBLILIUS SYRUS

13.1 Why Is Evaluation Important to a Speech?

1 Evaluation Is a "Good Thing"

2 Evaluation Teaches Critical Thinking Skills

3 Evaluation Builds Your Confidence

4 Evaluation Makes You a Better Communicator

1

Evaluation Is a "Good Thing"

Oral evaluations are brief overviews, delivered in oral form, describing what the evaluator saw and felt about the speech. Oral evaluations may come either after an individual speech or at the end of a session of speeches. Formal oral evaluation of a speech in a public forum is rare.

Written evaluations are assessments given in written form, which tend to contain more-detailed descriptions and suggestions. The speaker may receive the evaluation just minutes after the speech or days later.

→ See page 291 for one example of a checklist that could be used as a written evaluation.

Evaluation is a good thing! Keep repeating this as your new mantra. Because, believe it or not, this statement is true, and the earlier you adopt it as your mantra for most things you do in life, the better you will do those things.

CHECKLIST for Effective Evaluation

❑ Did I describe for the speaker what I saw and heard?

❑ Did I offer an evaluation of whether the speech was effective or not?

❑ Did I explain my personal feeling on why it was effective or not?

❑ Did I support the evaluation with a rationale or related norm?

At its basic level, **evaluation** is description grounded in a justified judgment. In other words, evaluation is simply someone telling what he or she saw and heard, grounded in "why."

In their book *Performance Studies: The Interpretation of Aesthetic Texts*, Ron Pelias and Tracy Stephenson Shaffer break down the process of evaluation as *description, judgment, justification*, and *rationale*. Pelias and Shaffer are performance-studies scholars, and their discussion focuses on the evaluation of staged artistic performances; but because public speaking is a public event, their discussion applies here as well. Pelias and Shaffer argue that effective evaluation involves accurately describing a speech, fairly judging its worth, and logically justifying your view of it based on rational norms and reasons. For example:

DESCRIPTION
Your attention-getting device took us to the edge of the canyon and described the air.

Description answers "What did I see and hear?"

JUDGMENT
I really liked that.

Judgment answers "Was it good or not?"

JUSTIFICATION
The moment was so real, it gave me goose bumps. I was pulled into the speech, and I felt like I was there by the canyon.

Justification answers "Why was it good or not?"

RATIONALE
One of the major functions of the introduction is to grab the audience's attention and pull them into the speech. You achieved that goal by using emotive language and a great extended narrative.

Rationale answers "What is the logic or norm behind my justification?"

Note that nothing in the examples above talks about fault, censure, or disapproval. Evaluation is about describing what you see, making a judgment about how you feel about it, and then offering a sensible justification for what you think works or needs improvement. (Use the checklist on page 286 as a reminder.) Improvement does not mean tearing down or destroying; it means elevating to the next level of worth. If something about your speech is not quite working, then the message you intend to send may be misinterpreted or not received at all. Evaluation can help you adjust your speeches so that your messages are successful.

Nothing we do is perfect, and we can always strive to improve. When given appropriately and constructively, evaluation fosters growth and progress along the lifelong path to developing the great speaker and thinker that resides within you. View your speech as a diamond in the rough and evaluation as helping you carve a way to the beauty. Embrace evaluation; do not fear it. Evaluation is a good thing!

2

Evaluation Teaches Critical Thinking Skills

Think a moment about these questions.

- Are you being too trusting?
- Is that really the best buy?
- Can you learn from history?
- Are you thinking creatively?
- Can you think outside the box?

These are all questions that force us to think about our mindset and that of others. Such questions are designed to make us creators and participants in our own lives rather than passive vessels.

Imagine if Alexander Graham Bell had not wondered if there was a way to send our voices across vast spaces or if he had given up after the first experiments failed. You might still be sending messages only by mail or telegraph, and cell phones would not even be in our vocabulary, much less in our pockets. Imagine if your grandmother had never played around with her recipes to make them better. You would not have those special cookies or cakes to eat.

Critical thinking is important in our lives, and we must always strive to be better thinkers. Chapter 12 first introduced you to critical thinking as it relates to critical listening; here you should note that critical thinking is the mechanism for evaluation.

As detective Sherlock Holmes says in *The Hound of the Baskervilles*, "The world is full of obvious things which nobody by any chance ever observes." Holmes understands that chance observation teaches nothing and often passes us by. When you evaluate another speaker, your own speech, or a listener's evaluation of your speech, you are engaging and honing your critical thinking skills—observing detail and making a reasoned judgment about that detail.

Critical thinkers are always, like Holmes, seeking the answers to these questions: Who? What? When? Where? Why? To whom? Imagine if Macy, a student, gives a speech arguing that an electric toothbrush is better than a regular brush and she says:

Research shows that you will get better dental checkups if you use an electric toothbrush.

This statement may be true, but you as the listener should ask questions such as:

Who conducted and funded the research?

Who is reporting the research the speaker quotes?

Are there any studies refuting this?

Asking these questions allows you to seek alternative viewpoints and may give you reason to change your own.

PRACTICING ETHICS: Civility

A good critical thinker should also be an honorable one. Don't use your critical thinking skills to mislead, exploit, deceive, confuse, confound, aggravate, discourage, or harm. Great critical thinkers practice their skills with civility.

CONFIDENCE BOOSTER

Beginning speakers tend to focus their listening on what they consider "negative comments." Listen carefully to the whole evaluation. Assess what is important for you to work on in your next speech, and celebrate what was a success. Realize that striving for excellence in public speaking is an exciting, continually evolving process.

3
Evaluation Builds Your Confidence

Effective evaluation will build your confidence if you let it. Effective evaluation is not only about what needs to be improved; it also focuses on the successes.

As individuals, we are often hardest on ourselves and see only the negative. If evaluators listen carefully and do their job completely, they will describe the complete picture of your speech. Their evaluations will enrich your speech experience so that your next speech will be better and your confidence higher. Knowing what worked and what needs to be improved, and then taking the steps to work on those issues, will build your view of yourself as a good speaker. For example, Macy might respond negatively if someone gives her this response:

> Your evidence and logic were great. However, you need to work on keeping my attention during the detailed explanations and watch moving around aimlessly too much.

Yet this is really a nice comment if she listens carefully to it. First, having solid evidence and logic is one of the hardest things to do, and this listener has just stated that Macy excelled in that area. She should be very proud of that. Secondly, using language and delivery techniques to keep the audience's attention during detailed explanations might take a little work to master, but this is something even the beginning speaker can improve on quickly. Some of the new delivery techniques employed to keep the audience's attention might even keep Macy from moving around so much.

4
Evaluation Makes You a Better Communicator

No matter whether you are the one receiving the evaluation or giving it, participating in the act of evaluating will make you a better communicator. Most people learn better by watching and doing. The more you watch other speakers to learn where they succeed or need improvement—and then apply that knowledge to your own speeches—the more you will elevate your own skills.

So watch and listen to other speeches for ideas. As you observe a speech, ask yourself questions such as these:

- What type of support materials stood out as the most effective in this speech?
- What language choices worked well?
- What about this person's delivery was effective?
- What made the speaker appear extremely confident?
- How did the speaker use space?
- How did the speaker incorporate audience feedback?
- What "tricks of the trade" did the speaker use to keep your attention?

The list of questions you could ask is almost endless, and the skills and concepts you are learning throughout this book will guide you to what to look for in a successful speech. As you grow as a speaker as well as an audience member, you will ask better, more-detailed questions. You will notice the nuances of great communication.

13.2 What Should You Consider When Evaluating Speeches?

1 The Speech Message
2 The Speaker's Presentation

Unless you are competing or debating with someone else, most evaluators base their evaluations on established standards (often called *criterion-based evaluation*). This form of evaluation assesses speakers' abilities to meet set standards and does not compare them to others.

In the classroom, your instructor will explain the standards she or he deems important to the class objectives or the assignment. You can categorize most, if not all, of those standards under one of two headings: the speech message or the speaker's presentation.

1
The Speech Message

Evaluation standards related to the speech message focus on the effectiveness of the topic selection, the research, and the creation of the message. These standards correspond to the discussions in Tabs 1 through 3 of this book and to the first four sections (topic, introduction, body, and conclusion) in the brief listing of potential standards on the next page.

2
The Speaker's Presentation

Evaluation standards related to the speaker's presentation spotlight successful uses of language, delivery techniques, and presentation aids. These standards correspond to the discussion in Tab 4 and to the last section (presentation) of the list on the next page.

Remember, this form is only one sample; your instructor will use an evaluation that corresponds to your assignments.

TOPIC
- ☐ Speech accomplished purpose (to inform, to persuade, or to accentuate)
- ☐ Topic appropriate to speaker, audience, and occasion
- ☐ Interesting topic

The speech message

INTRODUCTION
- ☐ Gained attention and interest
- ☐ Established credibility
- ☐ Indicated relevance to audience
- ☐ Declared central idea
- ☐ Previewed speech

BODY
- ☐ Main points clear and obvious to the audience
- ☐ Points followed an appropriate organizational strategy
- ☐ Main points appropriately researched and supported
- ☐ Main points supported with appropriate presentation aids when necessary
- ☐ Oral citations included throughout speech
- ☐ Linked parts of speech

CONCLUSION
- ☐ Contained a summary statement
- ☐ Offered an audience response statement
- ☐ Effectively came to closure (WOW statement)

PRESENTATION
- ☐ Language was clear, concise, and appropriate
- ☐ Gestures/body movements were effective
- ☐ Consistent and effective eye contact
- ☐ Used vocal variety/emphasis/volume/rate
- ☐ Used appropriate delivery style
- ☐ Spoke with enthusiasm
- ☐ Spoke with conviction and sincerity
- ☐ Good use of delivery outline
- ☐ Presentation aids appropriate to speech topic (if applicable)
- ☐ Used presentation aids throughout entire speech (if applicable)
- ☐ Used professional presentation aids (if applicable)
- ☐ Speech met time requirements

The speaker's presentation

13.3 Who Evaluates Your Speech?

1 You

2 The Audience

3 The Instructor

4 Your Classroom Peers

1

You

Good evaluation begins with you, and you are already doing it as you create your speech. Tabs 1 through 4 of this book teach you how to make decisions along the path to creating a speech based on what works for you, your audience, and the speech situation. That is a form of evaluation.

However, your self-evaluation should not stop at the moment you begin or end your speech. As a speaker interested in effective communication, you should be reflexive after the speech as well. ***Reflexivity*** happens when you take a moment to consider yourself in relation to the speech and vice versa. Ask yourself questions such as:

- How did my actions or discussion in the speech affect the speech event?

- How did the speech event affect my actions?

- What could I improve on?

- How can I address areas needing improvement before my next speech?

Your instructor may formally require you to turn in a written self-evaluation as part of the class experience. With or without the class requirement, you should always self-evaluate your performance and effectiveness as a speaker.

2
The Audience

When an audience actively participates in your speech, they offer you feedback that can help you adjust your speech. So, in some sense, all audiences are offering you evaluation as you engage them in communication during your speech. They nod their heads in agreement, they lean forward when you draw them into the speech, they ask questions for clarification, and they sometimes struggle to stay focused or to understand a complex subject. These nonverbal and verbal responses are all clues to how effective you are being as the speaker.

Someone such as a teacher or boss may formally ask an audience to evaluate your speech afterwards. In most public settings, the evaluations are written comments that come from evaluation forms the audience fills out after the speech. These evaluations tend to be broad and focus more on the subject rather than the speaker, as this example demonstrates.

Session 1: New Documentation Policy
Presenters: Brian Bourke and Adelpha Kostas

Please complete a questionnaire after each session and return questionnaires to the drop box outside of the Human Resources office. Thank you for your input.

1. What information was the most beneficial?

2. How would you improve this session?

3. What benefits or problems do you see with implementing this new policy?

Other comments:

Such evaluations sometimes offer details that will help you become a better speaker, but you might find that asking a few people in the audience to give you specific suggestions to improve your speech is even more beneficial. It is never a bad idea to ask, "What can I do next time to make this presentation even more effective?"

In the public speaking classroom, your teacher might ask the other students to evaluate your speech, which can be very different from a public audience evaluation. The following pages will discuss this type of evaluation under the heading "Your Classroom Peers."

3
The Instructor

If you are in a speech class, as in any class, your instructor will evaluate you. In the public speaking class, evaluation is an essential part of the learning process. Most instructors use both oral and written evaluations to reinforce learning and the main principles taught in the class. When and how they evaluate, as well as the format they choose, can vary widely. Instructors will select the form that best represents their goals for students, their teaching style, and their teaching philosophy.

Keep in mind that your instructor is evaluating you within the frame of the class, and, just like the creative process, evaluation is not static. As the class progresses, the evaluations may become more detailed and expectations may increase. You should use each evaluation as a tool for improving your next speech. During the evaluation, ask questions of the evaluators and make comments. Actively engage in the evaluation process. Do not just glance at the evaluation once and forget it. Study the comments prior to creating your next speech and during the rehearsal stage of that speech. Let the previous evaluations be a guide to making that subsequent speech the best it can be.

CHECKLIST for Listening to Peer Speeches

❏ Am I giving the speaker my full attention?
❏ Am I actively trying to comprehend the message?
❏ Am I signaling the speaker with the appropriate feedback?
❏ Am I listening critically?

4
Your Classroom Peers

In the public speaking classroom, students will often evaluate speeches given by others in the class. Depending on your instructor's teaching practices, peer evaluation can be oral and/or written.

You do not need to be an expert in public speaking before you can offer a useful evaluation. However, the more you give speeches and evaluate others, the better and more helpful your evaluations will be.

- Your instructor will help you focus your evaluations.

- Reread "What Should You Consider When Evaluating Speeches?" on pages 290–291 before each evaluation session, to help you focus on what is important.

- Listen carefully to the speaker. Actively listen as if this is the first time you have heard him or her speak. Use the checklist on this page to review effective listening skills.

- Make notes on several things the speaker is doing well and what could be changed to have a stronger impact.

- Offer your feedback in the spirit of helping the speaker improve.

- Treat others the way you would like to be treated, and offer others the type of feedback that you would like to receive to help you improve.

- Construct your evaluations to offer a description of what you saw and heard, a judgment of what is effective or not, a justification for the judgment, and the rationale behind the judgment.

HOW CAN YOU EVALUATE A SPEECH?	EXPLANATION	EXAMPLES
Offer constructive feedback.	Instead of just offering a quick, unexplained response, include specifics. Answer the question "Why?"	INCORRECT: "It was good." CORRECT: "It was a good persuasive speech. The range of supporting evidence and its reliability was really convincing."
Be positive first.	Look for positive elements and offer them first, to frame your evaluation in an encouraging way. If you listen effectively, you will note something positive about the speech.	INCORRECT: "You had more than 45 'ums' in your speech." CORRECT: "Wow, this was a unique topic. I've read about victory gardens but didn't realize how important they were during the war. To improve your effectiveness, you might want to work on eliminating the vocal filler 'um.' You had a lot of these, and they became distracting."
Always offer improvement tips.	No speech is perfect. Always give speakers advice on what they might do to be even better next time.	INCORRECT: "It was a good speech. I didn't see anything that needed improvement." CORRECT: "I loved your use of presentation aids during the first half of the speech. It might be nice to carry that throughout the full speech by adding a few aids in the second half."
Avoid demeaning comments and attacks.	Humiliating the speaker or giving blunt negative responses about the speech is not helpful. Remember to describe, judge, justify, and rationalize your response.	INCORRECT: "This was a dumb topic for this audience." CORRECT: "As a college student, I had a bit of trouble staying with your topic of banning school uniforms in high schools because I am older. Is there a way to make this topic more appropriate to this audience?"
Be objective.	Evaluation is hard work, and personal feelings can cloud the goal. If you have issues with the topic or speaker or think either is "cool," do not base your evaluation on unrelated or superficial feelings.	INCORRECT: "You're so funny!" CORRECT: "This speech was very funny, and I loved it. I was really entertained. However, the purpose was to persuade me. I got caught up in the funny parts and forgot what you wanted me to do."

Chapter 13: Review

ASSESSING YOUR KNOWLEDGE

13.1 Why Is Evaluation Important to a Speech?

Objective 13.1: **RESTATE WHY EVALUATION IS IMPORTANT TO A SPEECH**

- Evaluation is a "good thing" and a positive experience if conducted effectively as a means for improvement. Evaluation is a description grounded in a justified judgment. The evaluation process breaks down into four parts: description, judgment, justification, and rationale.
- Your description answers "What did I see and hear?"
- Your judgment answers "Was it good or not?"
- Your justification answers "Why was it good or not?"
- Your rationale answers "What is the logic or norm behind my justification?"
- Evaluation teaches critical thinking skills. Critical thinkers ask Who? What? When? Where? Why? To whom? Critical thinking is a mechanism for evaluation.
- Evaluation builds your confidence. Effective evaluation should highlight your success and what needs to be improved. We often focus only on the negative and miss the effective aspects of our speeches.
- Evaluation makes you a better communicator. Most people learn by watching and doing. The more you watch other speakers to learn where they succeed or need improvement—and then apply that knowledge to your own speeches—the better you will be as a speaker.

→ See pages 286–289.

13.2 What Should You Consider When Evaluating Speeches?

Objective 13.2: **EXPLAIN WHAT YOU SHOULD CONSIDER WHEN EVALUATING A SPEECH**

- You should evaluate the speech message. Evaluation standards for a speech message focus on the effectiveness of the topic selection, the research, and the creation of the message.
- You should evaluate the speaker's presentation. Evaluation standards for the speaker's presentation relate to the use of language, delivery techniques, and presentation aids.

→ See pages 290–291.

13.3 Who Evaluates Your Speech?

Objective 13.3: **DESCRIBE WHO EVALUATES YOUR SPEECHES**

- You should be the first evaluator of your own speech. The decisions you make as you create your speech and deliver it are a form of self-evaluation. Even after you give the speech, you should be reflexive about the effectiveness of the event.
- Your audience will offer formal or informal feedback about your speech.
- Your instructor will evaluate your speech. Most instructors use both oral and written evaluation to reinforce learning. As the class progresses, the evaluation may become more detailed and expectations may increase.
- Your classroom peers often evaluate speeches. Peer evaluation can be oral and/or written.

When evaluating a speech, follow these guidelines:

- Always offer the speaker constructive feedback. Be specific about what works and what needs improvement.
- Begin your comments with a positive point, and then offer suggestions for improvements.
- Always offer ideas for something that could be improved.
- Be polite with your improvement tips, and don't offer demeaning comments or attacks. Remember that public speaking is a very personal process for the speaker.
- Be objective.

→ See pages 292–295.

Practical Pointers for Tab 5

FAQs

When I'm listening to a speech, how can I determine what is important to remember?

Focus on key parts such as the central idea, main points, and important support materials. To help you identify these, listen for links such as:

My first reason is …

Mentally note or write down the review statement in the introduction. That will help you identify the speaker's main points even before they are discussed.

Try to determine the speaker's organizational strategy early in the speech. For example, if the speaker is using a problem–solution strategy, you should focus on the problems presented and then the effectiveness of the solutions.

Realize that support materials are supporting the main points that the speaker views as important. Don't get caught up in all the small details of support materials.

Listen for clues. Speakers often give clues that signal important information, such as:

- Repeating information verbally more than once
- Offering information to the audience both verbally and visually. Speakers who effectively use presentation software may use the slides to support or repeat the important information or parts of their speech.

- Using hints such as:

  What's important here is …

- Using a physical or vocal delivery element to emphasize importance. For example, speakers may increase their volume, slow their pace, or move closer to the audience to stress importance.

When would I evaluate a speech outside of a class?

Because listening actively and critically should always be something you do as an audience member in any speaking situation, some evaluation will be present at every speech. You may not always give the speaker comments, however.

In your professional life, you will receive and give evaluations (performance reviews) of work and work behavior. Much of what you learn about evaluating a speech and receiving an evaluation can help you negotiate job-related reviews.

When you must give presentations and formal speeches in your personal, professional, and public life, you should always ask someone to evaluate your performance. You can't grow or improve as a speaker without evaluation.

→ See pages 438–439 in Chapter 18 for more on job-related reviews.

TAB 6

CHAPTER 14
The Informative Speech

299

Speaking to Inform

14

THE INFORMATIVE SPEECH

14.1 What Is Informative Speaking?

At its essence, speaking to inform is the act of *giving*. **Informative speaking** gives your audience *completely new* knowledge, skills, or understanding about your topic or increases their *current* knowledge, skills, or understanding.

The gift of information you give can range from a topic that seems indefinable, such as the origin of life, to a practical topic such as changing a tire. Whether you are the CEO of a large corporation, a local automotive salesperson, or a parent involved in the community's educational system, informative speaking is the bread and butter of our daily communication. We are constantly asked to describe, explain, demonstrate, or report on almost every aspect of our lives. You also use information in a persuasive speech (thus, it can feel informative), but informing and persuading differ in their goals. Persuasive speaking's goal is to create, stimulate, or change something in the audience.

→ Chapters 15 and 16 focus on persuasion.

PRACTICING ETHICS: Imparting Knowledge

The main benchmarks of great informative speaking are accuracy, unity, and inclusiveness. Ethically, these benchmarks translate into being:

- Truthful and reliable when selecting support materials
- Complete in your coverage of the topic, not simply relying on personal knowledge
- Organized enough to demonstrate how things "fit together" in the speech
- Evenhanded and unbiased when offering information
- Responsible in selecting an appropriate and legal topic for you, your audience, and the situation

You can categorize most informative speeches as speeches to describe, instruct, or explain. Normally, the topic—or what your audience needs to know about the topic—determines the type.

- A **speech to describe** usually describes an object, a person, an animal, a place, or an event.
- A **speech to instruct** teaches or demonstrates a process.
- A **speech to explain** clarifies a concept or issue.
- In some speaking situations, you might be required to give an informative **speech to report**, which is an oral report or briefing. You will most often give this type of speech when you are part of a group or organization, including the workplace, and need to report on the progress of something.

→ See pages 430–435 in Chapter 18 for more information on a speech to report.

The following table lists each type of informative speech, its corresponding topic labels, and examples of a speech topic for each.

TYPE OF INFORMATIVE SPEECH	TOPIC LABEL	SAMPLE SPEECH TOPICS
To describe	Object	To describe the features of a GoPro To describe the significance of the U.S. flag
	Person	To describe the events of Rosa Parks's life To describe the highlights of Odetta's music
	Animal	To describe the life cycle of the butterfly
	Place	To describe the Great Barrier Reef To describe the historical development of Gettysburg, Pennsylvania
	Event	To describe what happens at the Indianapolis 500 time trials To describe the significance of Veterans Day
To instruct	Process	To instruct about (demonstrate) creative ways to wrap a gift
To explain	Concept	To explain the basic principles of Islam
	Issue	To explain current issues related to illegal immigration
To report	Oral report or briefing	To report recent findings related to student parking needs on campus

14.2 What Is the Creative Process for Informative Speaking?

The first five tabs in this book outline the steps in the process of creating a successful speech. The next four will help you see how to use this process or parts of it for specific types of speeches and speaking situations. In this chapter, you will use the public speaking process to build an informative speech. The first column of the table to the right briefly reviews the five basic activities you will use to create an effective informative speech. Remember, the process is dynamic. Allow yourself to move creatively back and forth between each activity as you fashion your speech.

The last column of the table follows the example of how Laura, a college student in the Midwest, created her informative speech about trout. Spring break is around the corner, and Laura lives in northwestern Arkansas, where many of the rivers offer some of the nation's best trout-fishing opportunities. Although Laura's college is close to Arkansas, it is not in an area with many trout rivers. She surveyed her audience about their knowledge of fishing in general and discovered that most have some fishing knowledge and are very open to a fishing trip. Few of her classmates, however, knew there were different types of trout or how to fish for trout.

CONFIDENCE BOOSTER

This chapter will take you step-by-step through the process as it relates to the informative speech. Remember the Jesse Jackson quotation from Chapter 1. You can conceive a great speech a step at a time. You can believe in yourself. You can achieve it. Relax and be confident that you can create a successful informative speech.

THE CREATIVE PROCESS		INFORMATIVE EXAMPLE
1 STARTING	**HOW DO YOU CHOOSE A FOCUSED INFORMATIVE TOPIC?** → See page 304	Laura created an idea bank, surveyed her audience, and created this central idea: **Many midwestern states offer an exciting opportunity to catch varieties of trout that differ in appearance, habitat, and population.**
2 RESEARCHING	**HOW DO YOU RESEARCH THE INFORMATIVE SPEECH?** → See page 312	Laura searched fishing websites, found books on trout at the county library, and interviewed a local conservation officer.
3 CREATING	**HOW DO YOU OUTLINE AND ORGANIZE AN INFORMATIVE SPEECH?** → See page 314	Laura constructed her main points around the four types of trout (a topical strategy). She ordered the main points by largest population to smallest, to mirror the Midwest population trends. I. **Rainbow trout are found in most states.** II. **Brown trout are found coast to coast, except for a few southern states.** III. **Cutthroat trout were originally native to only western North America.** IV. **Brook trout are native to the eastern United States and Canada.** In her introduction and conclusion, Laura used personal narrative to paint a picture of what it is like to trout fish.
4 PRESENTING	**WHAT SHOULD YOU CONSIDER WHEN PREPARING TO PRESENT AN INFORMATIVE SPEECH?** → See page 328	Laura created her delivery outline on note cards, putting only enough key words to jog her memory. She also included delivery and presentation aid notes. Laura practiced several times before her speech date.
5 LISTENING & EVALUATING	**HOW DO YOU EVALUATE AN INFORMATIVE SPEECH?** → See page 330	Laura's classmates and instructor offered constructive advice about her speech. She noted, for instance, that she should work on gesturing more for her next speech.

OBJECTIVE 14.2: **EXPLAIN THE CREATIVE PROCESS FOR INFORMATIVE SPEAKING** 303

14.3 How Do You Choose a Focused Informative Topic?

1 **Get to Know the Audience and Situation**

2 **Create an Informative Idea Bank**

3 **Select and Narrow Your Informative Topic**

4 **Identify Your Specific Purpose**

5 **Confirm the Best Type of Informative Speech**

6 **Identify Your Central Idea**

7 **Create a Working Outline**

1

Get to Know the Audience and Situation

As you prepare an informative speech, your analysis of the audience and situation should help you to determine:

- Your topic choice and even the type of informative speech most appropriate for this audience

- What information you need to give this audience during this situation

- How to make your speech relevant to this audience

- How to select effective and interesting support material for this audience

For example, if you work for a research lab and must present findings to the board of the company funding your research, you would give a speech to report. The situation dictates that you need to speak about your research and not another topic. However, you might give the same information in a different format, a speech to explain, at a conference related to your field. The board members might not be entirely knowledgeable, and your peers at the conference might be experts; therefore, your speech's content, language, and delivery would change. For example, you would need simpler language and definitions for the nonexpert audience and more technical or highly detailed material for the experts.

Let's review what to consider when analyzing the audience and situation and apply it to the process of creating an informative speech.

THE AUDIENCE

Chapter 2 highlighted the need to know your audience's attitudes, beliefs, and values—as well as their psychological, personal, and social traits. These attributes might seem more important when persuading, but they are also essential to informing. Remember, the goal of an informative speech is to give the audience completely new knowledge, skills, or understanding about your topic or to increase their current knowledge, skills, or understanding. To do that you must:

- Understand what this audience distinctively knows or does not know about potential topics.
- Understand their attitudes, beliefs, and values about potential topics.
- Understand how their age, race, income, needs, group affiliations, and other traits will influence the information you should offer.

For example, if you are preparing to give an informational session on the latest iPhone to a group of college students and you know that most of them own a previous or similar model, your speech can focus on what makes this model unique. This audience will likely respond favorably to how the new phone will maintain their social and self-esteem needs. In contrast, an audience at a retirement center will more likely have a predisposed attitude toward a simpler model and how it might keep them safe. Even with the subject of trout, Laura determined how to organize her speech based on her audience analysis. She used a topical strategy, beginning with the trout found closest to where the majority of the audience lived.

THE SITUATION

Like the audience, the speaking situation (place, audience size, time, and occasion) can significantly influence your informative speech. For example, if the reason for your audience to gather at either the college or the retirement community is to learn new ways to stay safe following a major catastrophe, such as Hurricane Sandy in 2012, the situation will change the content and urgency of your delivery. Safety is now the key motivation for listening to and learning from your speech. Or, if you are asked to demonstrate a craft to Girl Scouts at a local park in an outdoor shelter, you should avoid selecting a craft that has a lot of small detail that will be difficult to see or lightweight parts that might blow in the wind.

Review Chapter 2 and the checklist below to help you analyze your audience and situation. As you move through the creative process for informative speaking, return often to these questions to reevaluate your audience and situation.

CHECKLIST for Analyzing the Informative Speech Audience and Situation

❏ What are the attitudes, beliefs, values, and traits of my audience? How will these affect my choices?

❏ What do they know about topics I am considering? What do they want or need to know?

❏ How can my topic ideas be unique and fascinating to this audience?

❏ Why is the audience here, and are there significant events to consider?

❏ What do I need to know about the situation, and how will it influence my choices?

2
Create an Informative Idea Bank

In Chapter 3 you learned, in general, how to create an idea bank. Modifying how you organize your informative idea bank can help you produce informative topic options. Notice how the steps below organize your idea bank around the types of informative speeches. This can help you generate general topics. However, keep in mind that some topics can lead to related topics that require a different type of informative speech. For example, a speech about the breed of dog known as a puli is a speech to *describe*, and a speech on how to groom a puli is a process speech to *instruct*. Don't let the types stifle your free association; let them increase your opportunities. Follow these steps:

1. Remember to use a sheet of paper—free-associating can be difficult on a computer.

2. Evaluate your speech assignment or speaking event for clues.

3. Make three columns titled Describe, Instruct, and Explain. In each column, list topics related to each type of speech. Be sure to include anything that comes to mind at this point.

If you are having trouble filling the columns, jump-start your creative spirit by looking through magazines, newspapers, news apps, or online news sites—or just look around your room or house for ideas. For example: What's the history of the Coke bottle shape? How was bubble gum invented? How can you make a pie out of Tang?

Below is one example of an informative idea bank.

Informative Idea Bank

Describe
Tree frogs
Crocodiles
Panama Canal

National parks
↓
Boundary Waters
Ansel Adams
Yosemite

Instruct
How to clean fish
How to pack a day pack
How to make candles
How to travel abroad on a small budget

Explain
Current concerns about overpopulation of deer

3
Select and Narrow Your Informative Topic

With an informative idea bank filled with possible topics, it is time to narrow in on the topic that fits you, your audience, and the situation. Here are some suggestions for narrowing the informative topic:

- Cross off topics that, after reconsideration, you discover aren't really informative.
- Cross off topics that you aren't enthusiastic about or would not feel comfortable giving a speech on.
- Cross off topics that are not appropriate for the audience or situation.

Now consider what is left, and these factors:

- Which topics might give completely new knowledge to your audience, or which ones do they need to know more about?
- Which topics might they find unique and interesting?

Suppose you created the idea bank on the previous page for class and, below, are narrowing your selections. You focus on the Panama Canal, as many people like to travel, it has historical relevance, and you recently traveled there.

This topic is still broad, but you can narrow it further later. For now, do some preliminary research to see if you can find quality information on the topic. If researching it seems difficult, you may want to revisit your idea bank for another topic or change the angle of this one.

→ See pages 48–55 in Chapter 3 if you need help selecting and narrowing a topic.

Informative Idea Bank

Describe

Tree frogs

Crocodiles

~~Panama Canal~~ (circled/highlighted)

National parks
↓
Boundary Waters

~~Ansel Adams~~

Yosemite

Instruct

~~How to clean fish~~

How to pack a day pack

How to make candles

How to travel abroad on a small budget

Explain

~~Current concerns about overpopulation of deer~~

4
Identify Your Specific Purpose

As you know from Chapter 3, the specific purpose is a single statement merging together your general purpose, your audience, and your objective for the speech. This may seem like an obvious and unnecessary step given that you already know you are informing your audience. But remember that it is the specific purpose that officially connects your audience to the objective of your speech. Here are some examples of informative specific purposes:

To inform the sales force about the new Fitbit

To inform my political science class about the political career of Paul Ryan

To inform the elementary school students about red-tailed hawks

Without the mental connections between the general purpose, audience, and objective, an informative speech on the Fitbit, Paul Ryan, or the red-tailed hawk could take many paths.

For your Panama Canal speech, when you merge your general purpose with your audience and objective, your specific purpose would look like this:

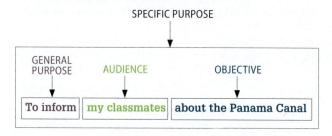

This specific purpose will help you keep your general purpose (to inform) and your audience (college students) connected to the objective of your speech (telling about the Panama Canal). From this point on, anything you include in the speech should inform a college-student audience with little knowledge of the canal.

→ See pages 56–57 in Chapter 3 if you need more help with creating a specific purpose.

5

Confirm the Best Type of Informative Speech

Before you move on to creating the central idea, you should reconsider your audience and determine the best type of informative speech you need to give to them. Your broad topic might be categorized on your idea bank under a speech to instruct, but that type might not be best for conveying what your audience wants or needs to know. Or you may find you need a different angle. For example, if your topic is baseball gloves and your audience consists of baseball players, they probably know how to take care of a glove. Therefore, a process speech (to instruct) on cleaning a glove might not interest them unless you have unique information. However, they may not know how a glove is made (a different process topic) or the history of the glove (an object topic, for a speech to describe).

If you are unsure what type of informative speech is best to give to your audience, use the table below to help you make that decision.

TO DESCRIBE	TO INSTRUCT	TO EXPLAIN
• Does your topic focus on describing concrete or tangible things that are human or nonhuman (e.g., the human mouth, Norwegian forest cats, Monument Valley, the 2013 presidential inauguration, Frederick Douglass, or tablet computers)?	• Does your topic explain the steps to create something, for how to do something, or for how something occurs (e.g., how animated films are made, how to repair a bike tire, or how tsunamis form)?	• Does your topic focus on abstract and/or complicated concepts and issues (e.g., freedom of speech, Hinduism, constructivism, global warming, immigration, or homophobia)?
• It is impossible to discuss everything related to an object, person, animal, place, or event. So can you narrow your topic enough to describe it effectively to the audience?	• Is your topic demonstrating or illustrating how something is made, is done, or works?	• Is the topic not too complex, so that you can explain it in the time allotted for this audience and situation?
• Can you describe something about your topic that will resonate and seem important to the audience? Can you describe information they don't already know about the topic?	• Is this a process that your audience needs to understand or to learn how to do?	• Speeches to explain often include qualities of speeches to describe and instruct. Would it be better to give one of those types of speeches related to your broad topic? For example, you might need to describe global warming and the process that creates it.
	• Do they have enough experience and knowledge that the process will make sense?	
	• Is your topic really something you could demonstrate or illustrate in the classroom?	

6
Identify Your Central Idea

Now you are ready to formulate your central idea (also called the *thesis statement*), or the concise one-sentence summary or preview of exactly what you want to say in your informative speech. This is how you will achieve the objective of your specific purpose.

Below are two examples of how the specific purpose of your Panama Canal speech can become a central idea. The objective of the specific purpose is shown in blue type.

If Your Specific Purpose Is ...

To inform my classmates about the Panama Canal

Your Central Idea Could Be ...

The Panama Canal is more than an old human-made waterway; it is one of the new Wonders of the World.

or

The Panama Canal is more than an old human-made waterway; it has an amazing history, it is an engineering marvel, and it is still growing.

Both could be acceptable. Some speech instructors like the simpler form of the first, and others like the central idea to reflect your main points, as the second example does. For some speeches, it might be difficult to establish the exact main ideas prior to doing research. You can always refine that part of the central idea as you begin to create your preparation outline.

→ See pages 58–61 in Chapter 3 if you need more help formulating your central idea.

CHECKLIST for Evaluating an Informative Central Idea

❏ Does my central idea describe, instruct, explain, or report?

❏ Is my central idea written as a complete statement?

❏ Does the statement use clear and concise language?

❏ Does my central idea focus on one speech topic?

❏ Will this informative central idea offer my audience new information and be worth their time?

TIP: Build on Your Central Idea

As you build your speech, you should always return to your central idea and use it as a test for how appropriate your support materials are to the speech. Always ask: Does this material directly relate to my speech objective? Will my audience see my reason for including this material as support for a main point? How can I clearly show them?

7
Create a Working Outline

At this stage, you should take a few minutes to map out a working outline (using the techniques you learned in Chapters 3 and 6), to guide your research. As you collect support materials for your speech, add what you find to this working outline. This will help you see where you need more information or when you need to change something.

Remember that your working main points might be questions you think need to be answered or simply phrases that relate to subtopics. As with your central idea, your main points will continue to evolve and become more defined as you create your speech. Think about what information your audience needs and how to incorporate that into three to five working points. Things to remember about an informative speech working outline:

- Try to limit your points as much as possible. You don't want to overload your audience's ability to remember.

- Try to make your working points unique, such as new or novel information. This will help you gain and keep your audience's attention.

- Be flexible. The working points may change significantly as you discover new and innovative material better suited to teaching your audience about your topic. Also, in the preparation outline stage of creating your speech, you want your main points to be concise and complete declarative sentences, not questions.

TOPIC: *The Panama Canal*

SPECIFIC PURPOSE: *To inform my classmates about the Panama Canal*

CENTRAL IDEA: *The Panama Canal is more than an old human-made waterway; it has an amazing history, it is an engineering marvel, and it is still growing.*

I. *What is the history of the canal?*
II. *How was it built?*
III. *What is the future for the canal?*

Remember, you may use questions for the main points in your working outline, but you should use declarative sentences in your preparation outline.

14.4 How Do You Research the Informative Speech?

As noted in Chapters 4 and 5, a variety of acceptable support materials is important to any speech. If you plan to describe, instruct, explain, or report in your informative speech, you need material that is unique, accurate, and inclusive enough to fulfill the informative goal. As a reminder, you can locate this type of information on websites; in books, newspapers, magazines, newsletters, journals, government resources, and reference works; and through firsthand personal knowledge. You may locate these items on the Internet, in the library, and through surveys and interviews.

Explore different possibilities, and don't rely on one research tool, such as only the Internet. For example, in addition to the Panama Canal Authority website, where you can find current information, there are books, related websites, and articles offering more canal history and facts. You might even know someone who served in the U.S. military and was stationed there. Be creative.

→ See Tab 2 if you need help with research.

CHECKLIST for Informative Support Materials

❏ Are the materials accurate, current, complete, trustworthy, and suitable?

❏ Will my support materials make my audience want to listen and learn?

❏ Will my support materials help my audience learn something new?

❏ If my topic is difficult, do I have multiple ways of approaching the topic?

❏ Are the support materials unique for my audience?

❏ Do I have a variety of source types?

❏ Do I have complete citation information for each source?

Here are some suggestions for researching the informative speech.

- As mentioned, don't rely on one research tool (for example, only the Internet).
- To inform, you must rely heavily on facts, definitions, testimony, and examples. Although you might use statistics, they should be used only to describe, explain, or report (not to persuade).
- Government websites and pamphlets are often good resources for demonstration processes.
- Locate materials that will make your audience want to listen and learn. So, constantly think about your audience and their relationship with the information you are collecting. The best ways to do this are:
  - Find materials that will interest your audience because they are relevant, unique, current, entertaining, and easy to understand.
  - If your topic is complex, make sure you use material from multiple perspectives and means. Try to relate complex or abstract information to things the audience already understands, or use analogies when the topic is difficult to understand.
    → See page 119 in Chapter 5 for more on the use of analogy.
  - Look for material that will help you inform people with a variety of learning styles. Education scholars Neil Fleming, Colleen Mills, and Howard Gardner suggest that most people learn via different styles—or a combination of them. Based on research by Fleming, Mills, and Gardner, the following table explains five styles most relevant to public speaking and offers tools for teaching each style.

WHAT LEARNING STYLES MIGHT YOU ENCOUNTER IN AN AUDIENCE?	WHAT CAN YOU USE TO APPEAL TO THESE LEARNING STYLES?
Visual learners obtain and process information visually.	Maps, diagrams, charts, photos, objects, video, spatial organizational strategy, visual imagery, or design principles (such as white space, patterns, shapes, or different formats to highlight important information)
Auditory learners learn best by listening and through effective use of sound.	Lecture, verbal involvement, verbal devices such as repetition or rhythm, group discussion, or debate
Read/write learners learn best when information is transmitted via effective use of words and, often, visual representations of words.	Formal definitions, handouts, lists, stories, personal narrative, or quotations
Logical learners learn best when they have to reason or think conceptually and abstractly.	A strong logical/sequential or problem–solution presentational strategy; also puzzles, games, statistical data, tables or charts, or visual or word patterns
Kinesthetic learners learn best by experiencing or touching.	Demonstrations, simulations, physical involvement such as role-playing, and effective speaker body language

14.5 How Do You Outline and Organize an Informative Speech?

1 **Start with Basic, Effective Outlining**
2 **Commit to a Strategy**
3 **Construct Main Points**
4 **Organize Support Materials**
5 **Compose Your Introduction and Conclusion**

1

Start with Basic, Effective Outlining

Tab 3 taught you the basics for how to outline a speech. Creating an informative speech outline is no different. You need an appropriate organizational strategy that unites the information you are presenting in a way that will help your audience understand and remember the content. Most of your instructors will ask you to complete a preparation outline at this point in the process. Remember, this outline is highly structured and at the minimum it should:

- Include necessary header information.
- Contain an introduction, the body of the speech, and a conclusion.
- Use complete sentences.
- Contain source citations within the outline and include a source page (use the citation style your instructor requires).

Use the format sample shown on the next page to create your informative preparation outline, or use the one suggested by your instructor.

→ See Tab 3 if you need more help outlining.

Student name   Class
Date   Instructor name

Topic: The Panama Canal

Specific purpose: To inform my classmates about the Panama Canal

Central idea: The Panama Canal is more than an old human-made
                    waterway: it has an amazing history, it is an
                    engineering marvel, and it is still growing.

INTRODUCTION
    Attention-getter
    Credibility material
    Relevance to audience
    Preview of speech

(Link from introduction to first main point)

BODY
    I.   The conception of the Panama Canal has a long and arduous
         history.
         A. Subpoint
         B. Subpoint
             1. Subpoint of B
             2. Subpoint of B
             3. Subpoint of B

(Link between first and second main points)

    II. Second main point
         A. Subpoint
         B. Subpoint
             1. Subpoint of B
             2. Subpoint of B
         C. Subpoint

(Link: Now that we understand the history behind the making of the
         canal, let's look at how it works.

    III. Third main point

         A. Subpoint
             1. Subpoint of A
                 a. Subpoint of 1
                 b. Subpoint of 1
             2. Subpoint of A
         B. Subpoint
         C. Subpoint

(Link to conclusion)

CONCLUSION
    Summary statement
    Audience response statement
    WOW statement

                    Works Cited (or References)

This example shows
how you would
begin to use the
template to create
your Panama Canal
speech.

Begin filling in main
points as you have
them written. Use
only one sentence
per each outline
symbol, whether it
is a main point or a
subpoint. You must
have two or more
subpoints.

Be sure to formally
write out your links.
In an informative
speech, the links help
your audience group
information for
better understanding
and retention.

The introduction
and conclusion are
extremely important
to the effectiveness
of your speech.
Spend time on them.
A section later in this
chapter will help you.

2
Commit to a Strategy

Informative speeches can utilize a chronological, topical, spatial, comparative, problem–solution, or causal strategy. Knowing which types of informative speech these strategies fit with most comfortably should begin to help you recognize which strategy you want. Use the table on the next page as a guide.

The lines between objects, people, animals, places, events, concepts, issues, and processes can blur. Often it is difficult to speak about a process without defining some objects or to speak about people without placing them at events. Who could talk about the 1960s singer Janis Joplin without placing her at the Monterey Jazz Festival or Woodstock? To understand her and her music, you must talk about those events in music history. Therefore, many topics can fit into one or more strategies. The important thing is that you select one and stay with it.

For example, in your Panama Canal speech, you want to talk about the canal's history, how it was built, and its future. These are natural subtopics, which lend themselves well to the topical strategy.

If your audience was somewhat familiar with the historical beginnings of the canal but not how it works or what is in its future, you would have different main ideas and use different strategies. For instance, if you decided to focus just on how it works, you would use a chronological strategy. If you decided to focus on the future and the new locks that are being built, you might use chronological, topical, or, potentially, causal to demonstrate what is causing the need for new locks.

The best way to stay committed to a strategy is to choose one as you begin to construct your main points and focus on what you need to tell your audience. As mentioned previously, this process is not linear. You cannot finalize main points before selecting the strategy; and some strategies will not work for certain speech goals because you cannot create or support the main points necessary to use that strategy.

→ See Chapter 7 if you need help selecting an organizational strategy.

Knowledge is power. Information is liberating.[1]
KOFI ANNAN

STRATEGY	WHAT TYPES OF INFORMATIVE SPEECH DOES IT FIT?	WHEN MIGHT YOU USE IT?	SAMPLE SPEECH TOPICS
Chronological	To describe To instruct	When giving a speech related to time or history, or when you need to teach a sequence/process	• To describe the history of Savannah, Georgia • To instruct on the proper way to wax skis • To demonstrate how to make jerky
Topical	To describe To explain	With any informative speech that has natural, inherent subtopics	• To describe different types of butterflies in the West • To explain basic color theory
Spatial	To describe	To describe a place, event, or object based on its relationship to space	• To describe a film festival based on the different venues around town • To describe the human tooth from the inside out
Comparative	To describe To explain	To compare a complex topic to something your audience knows better	• To explain Islam by comparing it to Christianity
Problem–solution	To explain To report	When a solution has been implemented and you need to explain why	• To explain next year's tuition increase
Causal	To describe To explain	To describe or explain something based on how it is caused (or the reverse)	• To explain how secondhand smoke causes asthma

3

Construct Main Points

If you return to your working outline, you can see the basis of your main points in the questions you wrote. However, final main points cannot be questions, so these need some work.

> I. What is the history of the canal?
>
> II. How was it built?
>
> III. What is the future for the canal?

Form is incorrect for a preparation outline

Main points need to be complete declarative sentences, written in a parallel structure, and balanced with each other. The working main points above could be rewritten as:

I. The conception of the Panama Canal has a long and arduous history.

II. According to Sriram Balu in the web entry titled "The Panama Canal: A Man-Made Engineering Marvel," the Panama Canal is an engineering wonder.

III. To stay competitive and effective in the future, the Panama Canal needs an upgrade.

Notice how, at the core, these three points are parallel ("the Panama Canal has a long and arduous history," "the Panama Canal is an engineering wonder," and "the Panama Canal needs an upgrade"). Paired with being complete sentences, the repetition and structure will help the main points stand out and assist your audience in remembering what you thought was important.

→ See pages 164–167 in Chapter 7 if you need help with constructing main points.

TIP: Main Points

Remember, most classroom speeches are too short for more than five solid points. Three or four main points are most common in the average classroom speech. With any informative speech, keeping it as short as possible will facilitate audience learning and memory.

4
Organize Support Materials

Proper outlining requires you to demonstrate how your subpoints containing the support materials are subordinate to your main points and to any subpoints that precede them. For example, if you have your first main point of the Panama Canal speech and have located appropriate support materials, you will be able to add the next level of the outline.

I. **The conception of the Panama Canal has a long and arduous history.**

    A. **According to Elizabeth Nix on an August 14, 2014, web page titled "7 Fascinating Facts about the Panama Canal" on History.com, the idea for a canal crossing Panama dates back to 1513 when Spanish explorer Vasco Núñez de Balboa discovered the Isthmus of Panama.**

    B. **The French took up the project in 1881, as noted by the History Channel (History.com).**

    C. **On June 26, 1902, the U.S. Senate passed the Spooner Act by a vote of 259 to 8.**

Indenting the three subpoints demonstrates that they must relate back to the first main point

As you add the next level of support material detail, your outline will start to fill out even more. Here is how subpoint B might look with its developing subordinate points.

    B. **The French took up the project in 1881, as noted by the History Channel (History.com).**

        1. **The Suez Canal engineer Ferdinand de Lesseps won the honor to dig the canal for France.**

            a. **As noted by historian David McCullough in his 1977 book *The Path Between the Seas*, Lesseps's workers began digging "the great trench" on Friday, January 20, 1882 (147).**

            b. **Lesseps's plan was to build the canal at sea level without locks (59).**

How you organize the material under each point or subpoint depends on the strategy you are using and/or what you see as the best order. For example, the Panama Canal speech can use a topical strategy at the main point level but will need to be chronological at most other levels to make sense.

Try to anticipate what your audience needs to know or might have trouble understanding. Don't assume they have knowledge of even small important details. For example, if you are demonstrating a recipe and it calls for a pinch of salt or a large onion, someone may not know what those measurements mean. Don't forget steps that seem logical to you—they might not be logical to others.

5

Compose Your Introduction and Conclusion

Like a good movie, a speech should grab the audience's attention at the beginning and end by gradually leading up to a "WOW" moment. The introduction and conclusion of your speech can make or break its success. So spend some quality time crafting both, and use some of your best support materials to make them sing. Here's a review of what they should include.

GATUN LOCKS
PANAMA CANAL
1913
CANAL DE PANAMÁ

LAUNCH YOUR SPEECH

Don't forget the importance of literally *launching* into your speech. Your introduction should be one of the most exciting, moving, and interesting moments of your speech. An introduction for an informative speech should "pitch" your speech to your audience. It should tell them why they need to learn more about your topic or at least amuse them in some creative way about the topic.

END YOUR SPEECH

The conclusion of a speech is almost the reverse of the introduction, minus the need to demonstrate your credibility (your speech should do that). The informative speech conclusion should leave your audience hungry for more knowledge about your topic. Your ultimate goal is to inspire them so much that they go out on their own to find more information about the topic.

See the Tip box for guidance on how long your introduction and conclusion should be in relationship to the rest of your speech.

→ See Chapter 8 for more details on writing introductions and conclusions.

TIP: Length

- Your introduction should be less than 15 percent of your total speech time.
- Your conclusion should be less than 5 percent of your total speech time.

INTRODUCTION

ATTENTION-GETTER: It cost $350 million to build a hundred years ago. It took some 2.3 million cubic meters of concrete and 240 million cubic yards of rock and dirt. It was recognized as one of the seven wonders of the modern world in 1994 and is still in use daily today. These amazing statistics are from the 2016 web page "Panama Canal" on History.com, and they are just a few facts about the marvelous Panama Canal.

This should be an exciting or unique moment in your speech.

CREDIBILITY MATERIAL: A recent trip through the canal and my interest in engineering have led me to look closely at the magnificence of this human-made waterway.

State why you should give this speech.

RELEVANCE TO AUDIENCE: We have a lot of ways to move things quickly from place to place these days, but we still depend on traditional means such as boats. With the Panama Canal, those boats have shorter trips and use way less fuel to influence our atmosphere, and shipment costs are less. All of these factors are important to much of what we buy—especially some foods. It is likely that some of the fruits and vegetables you consume took a ride through the canal.

Give them a reason to listen.

PREVIEW OF SPEECH: So, let's explore an overview of the events leading up to building Panama Canal, how it operates, and what is in the canal's future.

Give them a road map to your speech.

CONCLUSION

SUMMARY STATEMENT: In conclusion, the story of the Panama Canal started centuries ago and has not yet come to a close. Through the efforts of all those who fought to build it, the engineers who designed a workhorse that has tested time, and the need to adapt to modern demands, this wonder of engineering is guaranteed a place of value for the foreseeable future.

What should your audience remember?

AUDIENCE RESPONSE STATEMENT: If the Panama Canal still feels like something best left in your junior high history book, then don't think of it as history, or even as a waterway. Think of it instead as the ongoing proof of what a vision, a plan, and good old-fashioned effort can accomplish—a modern wonder.

What do you want them to do with that information?

WOW STATEMENT: And if something as monumental as the Panama Canal can be accomplished despite hardships, what else can we do? What else, when we share a vision and put in the work, can we build? What will be the next modern wonder?

Dazzle them one more time.

PREPARATION OUTLINE FOR AN INFORMATIVE SPEECH

Your name   Class

Date   Instructor's name

> This outline is only one example. Be sure to follow your instructor's guidelines.

Topic: The Panama Canal

Specific purpose: To inform my classmates about the Panama Canal

Central idea: The Panama Canal is more than an old human-made waterway: it has an amazing history, it is an engineering marvel, and it is still growing.

INTRODUCTION

Attention-getter: It cost $350 million to build a hundred years ago. It took some 2.3 million cubic meters of concrete and 240 million cubic yards of rock and dirt. It was recognized as one of the seven wonders of the modern world in 1994 and is still in use daily today. These amazing statistics are from the 2016 web page "Panama Canal" on History.com, and they are just a few facts about the marvelous Panama Canal.

> Using unique and somewhat startling statistics can grab your listeners' interest.

Credibility material: A recent trip through the canal and my interest in engineering have led me to look closely at the magnificence of this human-made waterway.

Relevance to audience: We have a lot of ways to move things quickly from place to place these days, but we still depend on traditional means such as boats. With the Panama Canal, those boats have shorter trips and use way less fuel to influence our atmosphere, and shipment costs are less. All of these factors are important to much of what we buy—especially some foods. It is likely that some of the fruits and vegetables you consume took a ride through the canal.

Preview of speech: So, let's explore an overview of the events leading up to building Panama Canal, how it operates, and what is in the canal's future.

(**Link:** Let's begin with the canal's early evolution.)

BODY

I. The conception of the Panama Canal has a long and arduous history.

    A. According to Elizabeth Nix on an August 14, 2014, web page titled "7 Fascinating Facts about the Panama Canal" on History.com, the idea for a canal crossing Panama dates back to 1513 when Spanish explorer Vasco Núñez de Balboa discovered the Isthmus of Panama.

        1. Balboa discovered that Panama was a slim land bridge separating the Atlantic from the Pacific, which sparked an interest in locating a natural waterway between the two oceans.

        2. In 1534, when they hadn't located a natural waterway, Charles V, the Holy Roman Emperor, ordered a survey of Panama to determine if a waterway could be built and where.

            a. This canal would be a cheaper trade route.

            b. However, nothing came of these early surveys for centuries to come.

    B. The French took up the project in 1881, as noted by the History Channel (History.com).

        1. The Suez Canal engineer Ferdinand de Lesseps won the honor to dig the canal for France.

            a. As noted by historian David McCullough in his 1977 book *The Path Between the Seas*, Lesseps's workers began digging "the great trench" on Friday, January 20, 1882 (147).

            b. Lesseps's plan was to build the canal at sea level without locks (59).

            c. Poor planning, engineering problems, diseases, and accidents plagued the process (20,000 workers died during this time), according to "7 Fascinating Facts about the Panama Canal" by Nix.

Oral citations should include the author, date of the source, and where you found it if possible. This establishes the source's credibility and currency and helps the audience locate it if they choose.

Including your oral citations on the outline will help you remember them during the speech and prevent you from committing plagiarism.

2. McCullough writes that in 1887, Lesseps announced the hiring of the Eiffel Tower engineer, Alexandre Gustave Eiffel, to design and build a lock system instead and to save the project (194).

3. However, Lesseps's company went bankrupt in 1889; Lesseps and Eiffel were convicted of fraud (known as the Panama Affair) in 1893 (which was eventually overturned), and Lesseps died in 1894, ending the canal dream for France (203, 233–234).

C. On June 26, 1902, the U.S. Senate passed the Spooner Act by a vote of 259 to 8.

1. Roosevelt signed it two days later and the U.S. entered the canal business (328).

2. However, McCullough notes, a Panamanian revolt to fight for independence from Columbia forced a rejection of the Treaty and pushed the U.S. to offer military assistance in 1903 (333–344).

3. The United States purchased the rights for $40 million and took control in 1904.

4. The first ocean-going boat, the *Cristobal*, passed through on August 15, 1914, with little fanfare because World War I began in July (609).

5. The Panama Canal Authority assumed full control of the canal in 1999 (History.com).

(**Link**: Now that we understand the history behind the making of the canal, let's look at how it works.)

> Include your links in the outline, and use them where you need to guide your audience to the next thought (usually between parts of the speech and the main points).

II. According to Sriram Balu in the web entry titled "The Panama Canal: A Man-Made Engineering Marvel," the Panama Canal is an engineering wonder.

A. The landmass between the Atlantic and Pacific Oceans at that point is slightly above sea level.

1. That was the reason Lesseps's sea-level canal rather than a lock system didn't work.
2. Bright Hub notes that sea vessels must be lifted 26 meters (or 85 feet) above the mean sea level and then dropped back down to mean sea level on the other side.

B. The canal is made up of two sets of locks, a watershed that helps fill an artificial lake, and locomotive mules for safety.
   1. There are two sets of three locks on each ocean side, as this diagram from Bright Hub illustrates (Brighthubengineering.com).
   2. Each lock has two chambers for two-way traffic.
   3. Small locomotive cars called mules help guide and center the vessels in the locks.
   4. The old locks limit the size of the vessels that can navigate through to 294.1 meters, or just a bit under 965 feet, in length, by 32.3 meters, or almost 106 feet, in width.

C. The artificial Gatun Lake sits between the locks, feeding the water into the locks and allowing the vessels to move across the isthmus to the other set of locks that lowers them back down.
   1. It takes 26,700,000 gallons of water over 10 minutes to raise or lower the vessel to the next section.
   2. None of that water is recycled.

Interesting detailed facts and statistics support the main point about engineering. Details such as these offer a great opportunity for appealing to the visual learners in the class. Remember to include graphs, charts, and pictures when possible.

(**Link**: The large water consumption and relatively small-sized vessels are what brings us to our third and final point—the future of the Panama Canal.)

III. To stay competitive and effective in the future, the Panama Canal needs an upgrade.
   A. According to the July 24, 2015, article "Expanding the Panama Canal" by Alan Taylor in *The Atlantic*, the Panamanians approved a referendum to expand the canal in 2006 (theatlantic.com).
   B. A major portion of the project is the creation of a third set of bigger and more efficient locks.

1. This will double the canal capacity, allowing larger cargo and cruise ships to transit the canal.
2. The new locks will use 7% less water than the old locks and reuse 60% of the water required for each transit, according to "The Panama Canal Expansion Program" document produced by the Panama Canal Authority in October 2012 (7).
3. The Authority notes that the new locks will offer shorter maintenance times at a lower cost as well.

C. The dredging part of the program will improve channel access and raise Gatun Lake's maximum operating level, improving water supply and how deep boats can go or draft (2).

D. The Panama Canal Authority states that it will take eight years and $5.25 billion dollars to complete by 2016 (3).

CONCLUSION

Summary statement: In conclusion, the story of the Panama Canal started centuries ago and has not yet come to a close. Through the efforts of all those who fought to build it, the engineers who designed a workhorse that has tested time, and the need to adapt to modern demands, this wonder of engineering is guaranteed a place of value for the foreseeable future.

Audience response statement: If the Panama Canal still feels like something best left in your junior high history book, then don't think of it as history, or even as a waterway. Think of it instead as the ongoing proof of what a vision, a plan, and good old-fashioned effort can accomplish—a modern wonder.

WOW statement: And if something as monumental as the Panama Canal can be accomplished despite hardships, what else can we do? What else, when we share a vision and put in the work, can we build? What will be the next modern wonder?

Signal the conclusion with your language and vocal delivery.

Like the attention getter, the WOW statement should be strong and unique. It should end your speech with a bang.

References

Balu, S. (2012, January 24). The Panama Canal: A man-made engineering marvel. *Bright Hub Engineering*. Retrieved from http://www.brighthubengineering.com/naval-architecture/35713-the-panama-canal-a-man-made-engineering-marvel/

McCullough, D. (1977). *The Path Between the Seas*. New York, NY: Simon & Schuster.

Nix, E. (2014, August 15). Seven fascinating facts about the Panama Canal. *History.com*. Retrieved from http://www.history.com/news/7-fascinating-facts-about-the-panama-canal

Panama Canal. (n.d.). *History.com*. Retrieved from http://www.history.com/topics/panama-canal

Panama Canal Authority. (2012, October). Panama Canal expansion program. Retrieved from https://www.pancanal.com/eng/expansion/rpts/informes-de-avance/expansion-report-201210.pdf

Taylor, A. (2015, June 24). Expanding the Panama Canal. *The Atlantic*. Retrieved from http://www.theatlantic.com/photo/2015/06/expanding-the-panama-canal/396716/

Include only sources cited in the speech, and format them according to an acceptable style manual (APA style is shown).

14.6 What Should You Consider When Preparing to Present an Informative Speech?

1 Language

2 Delivery

3 Presentation Aids

1

Language

Because you are always considering your audience, your situation, and yourself throughout the process of creating your speech, you have been working on language already. However, as you move to the delivery stage, you need to pay special attention to the final language choices you make. Chapter 9 highlighted the importance of language and how you can use it better in general. Your language should be accurate, appropriate, distinctive, and conversational.

When selecting language for an informative speech in particular, try to:

- Make selections that will assist in the learning process by being simple and clear, yet are unique enough to be educational—that will teach something new.
- Use *we* and *you* to help the audience feel included in the informative process.
- Avoid jargon, acronyms, and unfamiliar references as much as possible. If you use them, explain them.
- Use vivid and evocative language that creates a picture or engages the audience. Simile, metaphor, analogy, and rhetorical questions work best.
- Use personification, onomatopoeia, repetition, assonance, or parallelism to assist in understanding and memory.
- When giving a speech to instruct, use links to signal where you are in the process
- Use previews and reviews to help with complex topics and memory.
- → See Chapter 9 for detailed help with using effective language.

2
Delivery

The extemporaneous speaking style is often more central to the informative speech than to many other speeches. For example, imagine demonstrating a process while reading a manuscript. As Chapter 10 notes, speaking extemporaneously allows you to be more natural, able to connect with your audience, and able to adapt when they don't understand.

Rehearsal guidelines for an informative speech are similar to those for other speeches. You want to:

- Practice with the preparation outline a few times until you know details of the speech.
- Create a delivery outline.
- Practice with that outline and any presentation aids several times before the speech.

For an informative speech, you should also:

- Consider how to use your voice and nonverbal communication to assist your audience's understanding. Use a vocal rate, volume, and posture that convey positive enthusiasm, but speak slowly enough for listeners to absorb the information.
- Remember to make eye contact as often as possible, especially when giving a speech to instruct.
- Consider ways to include audience participation if appropriate and time allows.

→ See Chapter 6 for help creating a delivery outline and Chapter 10 for help with your delivery.

3
Presentation Aids

Presentation aids are not necessary in every speech, but they can be very beneficial to an informative speech. As noted on page 313, different people learn through different methods—by doing, seeing, listening, reading/writing, reasoning, experiencing, or a combination of these. In the informative speech, a presentation aid can help:

- Build redundancy, which will help your audience remember information
- Gain and keep your audience's attention
- Summarize large portions of information
- Build your credibility

When explaining or illustrating a process, presentation aids are almost always necessary.

When you use presentation aids, they should be professional but simple, used throughout the speech, and used effectively and appropriately. Practice repeatedly with them to make sure they work and are incorporated smoothly into the speech. And always have a backup plan in case equipment or aids fail to work.

→ See Chapter 11 for help with presentation aids.

show slide 1   **1**

Attention-getter:
- $350 million to build
- 2.3 million cubic meters of concrete
- 240 million cu
- Seven wonder
- (2016 web pa

PAUSE

show slide 2   **2**

I. The conception of the Panama Canal
   A. Dates back to 1513 (Nix, "7 Fascinating Facts," History.com)
      1. Balboa discovered a slim land bridge
      2. In 1534, Charles V survey

14.7 How Do You Evaluate an Informative Speech?

1 **Listen Effectively**
2 **Evaluate the Speech Message**
3 **Evaluate the Presentation**

1
Listen Effectively

Whether you are the speaker or an audience member, listening is crucial if the information in a speech is to be understood and retained.

If you are the speaker, think about how you can help your audience understand and retain information, and pay attention to their feedback during your speech. Many of the language, delivery, and presentational techniques mentioned in the previous section will help them listen effectively and want to listen. Be willing to adapt or adjust.

If you are an audience member, strive to make sense of and remember the information. Take notes if appropriate. Offer the speaker appropriate feedback during the speech. Listen critically by evaluating the information. Do you understand it? Is it believable? Is it complete?

2
Evaluate the Speech Message

The informative speech should never lose sight of the informative goal: to give the audience new knowledge, skill, or understanding relating to the speech topic or to increase current knowledge, skill, or understanding. Evaluate the message for clarity, accuracy, and organization. Does the speech inform (and not persuade)? Is it interesting? Does it relate to audience needs? Does it neither overestimate nor underestimate the audience's knowledge? Evaluate the appropriateness of the topic, the quality of support materials, and the citation of sources.

3

Evaluate the Presentation

Even a solid speech message cannot stand on its own without an effective presentation. Evaluating yourself and other speakers will help you improve your own techniques. Because effective techniques tend to go unnoticed, you need to keep a critical eye out for what works and what does not. Successful speakers emulate vocal and physical traits that are comfortable to them and that inspire their audience to listen and remember. They are prepared, energetic, natural, and audience-centered and present information honestly and ethically.

→ See Tab 5 if you need help with critically listening to and evaluating speeches.

Use this checklist, or guidelines provided by your instructor, to evaluate informative speeches. This list can also help guide you as you create and practice a speech.

CHECKLIST FOR EVALUATING THE INFORMATIVE SPEECH

TOPIC
.... Speech accomplished purpose to inform
.... Topic appropriate to speaker, audience, and occasion
.... Interesting topic

INTRODUCTION
.... Gained attention and interest
.... Established credibility
.... Indicated relevance to audience
.... Declared central idea
.... Previewed speech

BODY
.... Main points clear and obvious to the audience
.... Points followed an appropriate organizational strategy
.... Main points appropriately researched and supported
.... Main points supported with appropriate presentation aids when necessary
.... Oral citations included throughout speech
.... Linked parts of speech

CONCLUSION
.... Contained a summary statement
.... Offered an audience response statement
.... Effectively came to closure (WOW statement)

PRESENTATION
.... Language was clear, concise, and appropriate
.... Gestures/body movements were effective
.... Consistent and effective eye contact
.... Used vocal variety/emphasis/volume/rate
.... Used appropriate delivery style
.... Spoke with enthusiasm
.... Spoke with conviction and sincerity
.... Good use of delivery outline
.... Presentation aids appropriate to speech topic (if applicable)
.... Used presentation aids throughout entire speech (if applicable)
.... Used professional presentation aids (if applicable)
.... Speech met time requirements

Chapter 14: Review

ASSESSING YOUR KNOWLEDGE

14.1 What Is Informative Speaking?

Objective 14.1: **DEFINE INFORMATIVE SPEAKING**

Informative speaking gives your audience completely new knowledge, skills, or understanding about your topic or increases their current knowledge, skills, or understanding. There are four types:

- A *speech to describe* usually describes an object, person, animal, place, or event.
- A *speech to instruct* teaches or demonstrates a process.
- A *speech to explain* clarifies a concept or issue.
- A *speech to report* is an oral report or briefing.

→ See pages 300–301.

14.2 What Is the Creative Process for Informative Speaking?

Objective 14.2: **EXPLAIN THE CREATIVE PROCESS FOR INFORMATIVE SPEAKING**

Informative speaking follows the general speech creative process—starting, researching, creating, presenting, and listening and evaluating—but emphasizes being aware of what your audience knows and what you would like your audience to learn.

→ See pages 302–303.

14.3 How Do You Choose a Focused Informative Topic?

Objective 14.3: **DESCRIBE HOW TO CHOOSE A FOCUSED INFORMATIVE TOPIC**

- Get to know the audience and situation.
- Create an informative idea bank based on informative speech types.
- Select and narrow your informative topic. Choose one that can give new knowledge or spark interest.

- Identify your specific purpose.
- Confirm the best type of informative speech.
- Identify your central idea.
- Create a working outline.

→ See pages 304–311.

14.4 How Do You Research the Informative Speech?

Objective 14.4: **EXPLORE HOW TO RESEARCH THE INFORMATIVE SPEECH**

Seek out informative support material from a wide variety of sources and perspectives. Rely heavily on facts, definitions, testimony, and examples. Locate materials that will make your audience want to listen and learn. Look for materials that appeal to visual, auditory, read/write, logical, and kinesthetic learning styles.

→ See pages 312–313.

14.5 How Do You Outline and Organize an Informative Speech?

Objective 14.5: **DISCUSS HOW TO OUTLINE AND ORGANIZE AN INFORMATIVE SPEECH**

- Start with basic, effective outlining. Be sure your outline includes necessary header information, an introduction, the body of the speech, and a conclusion; uses complete sentences; contains source citations within the outline; and includes a source page.
- Commit to an appropriate informative strategy. Informative speeches can utilize a chronological, topical, spatial, comparative, problem–solution, or causal strategy.
- Construct your main points. Use elements such as parallelism and repetition to help your audience learn and remember.

- Organize your support materials. Anticipate what your audience needs to know or might have trouble understanding.
- Compose your introduction and conclusion. The introduction should include an attention-getter, credibility material, relevance to audience, and a preview. In an informative speech, it should "pitch" your speech to your audience. The conclusion should include summary, audience response, and "WOW" statements. It should inspire your audience to want to learn more.

→ See pages 314–327.

14.6 What Should You Consider When Preparing to Present an Informative Speech?

Objective 14.6: **EXPLORE HOW TO PRESENT AN INFORMATIVE SPEECH**

Language, delivery, and presentation aids (if any) should be crafted based on how they can help an audience learn and retain information.

→ See pages 328–329.

14.7 How Do You Evaluate an Informative Speech?

Objective 14.7: **DEMONSTRATE HOW TO EVALUATE AN INFORMATIVE SPEECH**

Listen effectively. Evaluate the speech message for how clearly and accurately it informs. Evaluate the presentation for techniques that inspire an audience to listen.

→ See pages 330–331.

TERMS TO REMEMBER

informative speaking (300)
speech to describe (301)
speech to instruct (301)
speech to explain (301)
speech to report (301)
visual learners (313)
auditory learners (313)
read/write learners (313)
logical learners (313)
kinesthetic learners (313)

Practical Pointers for Tab 6

FAQs

If I am giving an informative speech about something I know, do I need sources?

It would be a rare situation when you would give an informative speech about something you are not familiar with. However, familiarity is not an excuse to ignore the value of quality support material. You should always seek out material to support what you know and to increase your knowledge. Additionally, using support material from credible sources will always improve your ethos. Your audience will view you as more of an expert and will see how others support the information you are offering. When giving more mundane speeches (e.g., "How to creatively wrap a gift"), you might need to be a bit more imaginative about sources and material. Look for creative quotations you can use in the introduction and conclusion. Interview experts at a local crafts store. Compare and contrast ideas in magazines or how-to books. Use instructions from other sources. There are always other sources, to support any topic.

If I am giving a speech to instruct about a process, do I always need presentation aids?

To give an effective speech to instruct, you need to actually guide the audience through the process. The best way to do that is to do the process, or as much of it as possible, so that they can understand it. For example, cooking shows on television walk through the steps and illustrate the ones that would take too long to complete during the segment. We may not see them dry the beef jerky, but they illustrate how to do it. At the very least, each major part of the process should be supported with a presentation aid.

ADDITIONAL SUPPORT

If you will be demonstrating something:

- Try to collect tidbits of information to offer during longer moments of mixing, cutting, or building. For example, tell your audience about the origin of ramen noodles as you prepare the lettuce for a salad using the noodles. Cite the source of that information.
- Create a pamphlet or card containing the tools, steps, and other resources. Distribute the handout at the end of your speech.
- To save time, have ready before your speech event a premade example for each step, so you don't have to completely finish each during the speech before moving on to the next step.

TAB 7
Speaking to Persuade

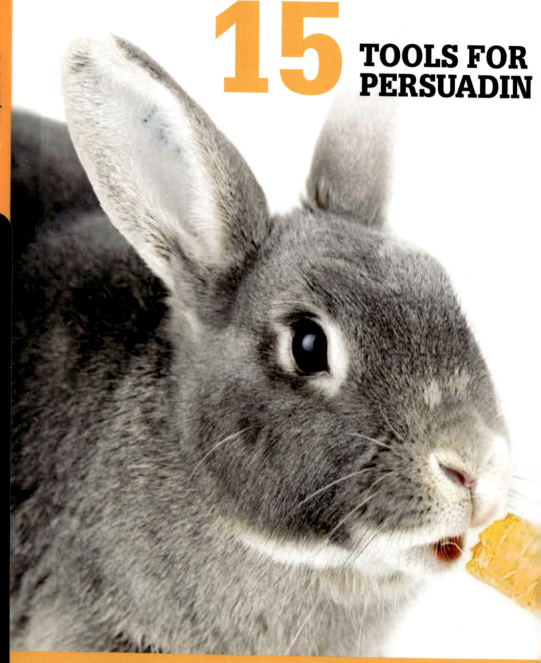

15 TOOLS FOR PERSUADIN

15.1 What Is Persuasive Speaking?

Persuasion is a deliberate attempt by the speaker to create, reinforce, or change the attitudes, beliefs, values, and/or behaviors of the listener. Persuasion can occur between two individuals or between a speaker and a larger audience. When you create a formal speech with the general purpose to persuade, you are engaging in **persuasive speaking**. Considering the definition of *persuasion* in smaller parts will help you understand its complexities.

A DELIBERATE ATTEMPT...

This portion of the definition connects back to our earlier discussion of the process of communication. If you remember the communication model, you know that the act of communication has its basis in the speaker and the speaker's deliberate attempt to send a message to the audience. For a communicative act to be persuasive, the speaker's intent or general purpose must be to persuade. The speaker is responsible for initiating the message..

→ See pages 4–5 in Chapter 1 for the explanation of the process of communication.

PRACTICING ETHICS: Coercion

Persuasion is not coercion! *Coercion* is forcing somebody, via threats or intimidation, to do something against his or her will. Persuasion gives the person the necessary knowledge to change or act differently via her or his own free will.

... TO CREATE, REINFORCE, OR CHANGE ATTITUDES, BELIEFS, VALUES, AND/OR BEHAVIORS

In Chapter 2, you learned that attitudes, beliefs, and values make up your audience's identity. Along with the behaviors your audience members engage in, these audience attributes are what you deliberately plan to create, reinforce, or change when you persuade. Let's review each.

- *Attitudes* are learned and persistent psychological responses, predispositions, or inclinations to act one way or feel a given way toward something, according to Martin Fishbein and Icek Ajzen in their book *Belief, Attitude, Intention, and Behavior: An Introduction to Theory and Research*. For example, you may not like the color pink and therefore do not respond favorably to anything pink. There is nothing wrong with the color—you just do not care for it. Attitudes are often, but not always, the easiest of the audience attributes to change.

- *Beliefs* are anything people have learned to accept as plausible based on interpretation and judgment. According to Ann Bainbridge Frymier and Marjorie Keeshan Nadler in *Persuasion: Integrating Theory, Research, and Practice*, you create a belief when you connect the object of your belief to an attribute. For instance, you believe water (object) is wet (attribute). Beliefs tend to be peripheral, or not central, to the person holding them because they are not closely related to the person's sense of self and identity in the world. They can be—although not always—more unstable or changeable than values. For example, you may believe today but not a month from now that red high-tops are cool.

- *Values* are enduring principles related to worth or what a person sees as right or wrong, important or unimportant. Frymier and Nadler indicate that values are closely linked to the core of our personalities and self-identities. Values are hard to change, and they support our attitudes and beliefs. For example, you may value a conservative ideology, higher education, or the Christian faith.

- *Behaviors* are unconcealed actions or reactions people have, often in response to some sort of stimuli. The ways people behave generally relate to their attitudes, beliefs, and values.

When an audience does not have the knowledge to hold a set attitude, belief, or value, or to understand why to behave a particular way, you persuade the audience to *create* or *adopt* the attitude, belief, value, or behavior you are advocating.

If the audience already agrees with you, you *reinforce* that attitude, belief, value, or behavior.

At other times, you motivate your audience to *change* existing attitudes, beliefs, values, and behaviors.

Persuasion is a complex process and a powerful practice that you must not take lightly. You must use the highest ethical standards when your intent is to persuade someone to think or act in a proposed way.

15.2 What Should a Persuasive Speech Do?

1 **Focus Listeners' Options**
2 **Appeal to a Particular Response**
3 **Support a Proposition of Fact, Value, or Policy**

1
Focus Listeners' Options

Persuasive speaking is like offering guidance to your listeners when they have several options to choose from and need your help to determine which is the best one. The job of the ethical persuasive speaker is to determine the best and safest option, support that decision logically, and offer information to the audience in a manner that allows them to make a wise decision. So persuasive speaking helps an audience focus their options and make a wise choice.

2
Appeal to a Particular Response

In the persuasive speech, you have an audience response in mind. That audience response determines which of the three types of persuasive speeches you will give.

- When you want to create a new or change an existing attitude, belief, value, or behavior for your audience, you are creating a *speech to convince*.
- When you seek to overcome apathy in your audience or reinforce an existing attitude, belief, value, or behavior, you are creating a *speech to stimulate*.
- When you ask your audience to take action, you are giving a *speech to actuate*.

You motivate your audience through what are known as appeals. **Appeals** (also called *proofs*) are the means by which you prove or establish the argument you are making. Pages 340–347 explain common traditional and contemporary appeals.

3

Support a Proposition of Fact, Value, or Policy

When you create a persuasive speech, you have an overarching argument (the body of the speech) that supports the assertion you are making in your central idea. The assertion you are making in your central idea is a proposition of fact, value, or policy.

For example, if your central idea is

> **Foods marked organic are not necessarily healthier than conventional foods.**

then the proposition you are supporting with this central idea is:

> **Organic foods are not healthier than conventional foods.**

And once you have identified your proposition, you can determine if it is a proposition of fact, value, or policy. Let's look at each category:

- ***Proposition of fact:*** Seeks to prove something factual and answers the question "What is accurate or not?" For example:

> **Vaping is not safe.**

> **Airbags are safe.**

> **Genetically altered vegetables are not healthy.**

- ***Proposition of value:*** Seeks to make a value judgment and answers "What has worth or importance? What is good, wise, ethical, or beautiful?" For example:

> **Funding after-school programs is a good use of tax dollars.**

> **Mandatory drug testing violates privacy rights.**

> **Plagiarism is unacceptable.**

- ***Proposition of policy:*** Seeks to prove a need for a new or different policy and answers "What procedures, plans, or courses of action need to be terminated and/or implemented?" This type of proposition can ask the audience to immediately act (To persuade my audience to volunteer to clean the city) or to simply agree (To persuade my audience that the city should outlaw smoking in public buildings). Other propositions of policy include:

> **All homeowners should be required to recycle.**

> **The City of Jonestown should not implement a tax on pet owners.**

> **The recreation center should be open 24 hours a day.**

> **The state needs stiffer laws related to child abuse crimes.**

In your organic foods speech, your proposition looks at the *accuracy* of the assertion that organic foods are not necessarily healthier than conventional foods. Therefore, your central idea seeks to support a *proposition of fact*.

Knowing the type of proposition your central idea supports will help you select an organizational strategy for creating the body of the speech, which will be made up of smaller arguments. These arguments will ultimately sustain your central idea—for instance, that organic is not necessarily healthier than conventional.

→ Page 368 in Chapter 16 further discusses the relationship between your proposition and your central idea.

15.3 What Are the Traditional Appeals Used to Persuade?

1 Appeal to Pathos
2 Appeal to Mythos
3 Appeal to Ethos
4 Appeal to Logos

In the fourth century BCE, Aristotle wrote in his *Rhetoric* about persuasion. As you learned in Chapter 1, Aristotle determined that you persuade others by three main appeals (pathos, ethos, and logos). In the *Poetics*, Aristotle introduced the concept of mythos, and other scholars—such as Michael, Suzanne, and Randall Osborn—reference it as another appeal.

1

Appeal to Pathos

An appeal to *pathos* deals with the listener's emotions. In other words, you can use your audience's sympathy and imagination to affect their attitudes, values, beliefs, or behaviors.

Eliciting your audience's emotions is a conjuring process and not a command. You must use vivid description and emotive language to stir your audience's sense of fear, sympathy, empathy, happiness, or anger.

Vivid description, especially by trusted experts who have firsthand knowledge, can be very moving. For example, on April 23, 1995, President Bill Clinton ended his speech at the Oklahoma City bombing prayer service with this emotional plea.

Yesterday, Hillary and I had the privilege of speaking with some children of other federal employees—children like those who were lost here. And one little girl said something we will never forget. She said, "We should all plant a tree in memory of the children." So this morning before we got on the plane to come here, at the White House, we planted that tree in honor of the children of Oklahoma. It was a dogwood with its wonderful spring flower and its deep, enduring roots. It embodies the lesson of the Psalms that the life of a good person is like a tree whose leaf does not wither.

My fellow Americans, a tree takes a long time to grow, and wounds take a long time to heal. But we must begin. Those who are lost now belong to God. Some day we will be with them. But until that happens, their legacy must be our lives.

Six years later, President George W. Bush invoked pathos with these remarks during his address on September 11.

> Tonight, I ask for your prayers for all those who grieve, for the children whose worlds have been shattered, for all whose sense of safety and security has been threatened. And I pray they will be comforted by a Power greater than any of us, spoken through the ages in Psalm 23: *Even though I walk through the valley of the shadow of death, I fear no evil, for you are with me.*

Both men, as trusted leaders, were called to speak during extraordinary times; both evoked powerful emotional images punctuated with a Bible verse.

Although it may seem unethical to play with your audience's emotions, philosophers and rhetoricians have long argued that logic may not be enough to get people to act. Appeals to emotions should rarely be used alone; but depending on the topic and your audience's relationship with that topic, you may need emotional appeals to put your audience in a mood to accept your logical argument, or you might need the logical argument to frame the appeal to their emotions.

For example, in a class speech on donating to the Red Cross, you would use statistics and facts, but that might not be enough to motivate your audience to donate. You might move them by presenting the human side of a recent disaster, such as using short narratives and photographs to illustrate individual struggles related to Hurricane Sandy in 2012. Giving a human face to your call for donation is often an effective way to advance a cause.

2
Appeal to Mythos

The appeal to mythos is often fueled by emotion and not always viewed as a noteworthy appeal. **Mythos** relates to a sense of one's history in the larger culture and the need to be a member of that culture. For example, our sense of what it means to be a woman or a man evolves from a community-accepted understanding of what is valued in women and men.

Other aspects of our cultural identity have a mythic appeal as well. In the United States, patriotism, nationalism, faith, pride, and valor are strong traditions and values. For example, you could appeal to mythos in a speech advocating buying American:

> In conclusion, we have seen that American-made products tend to be safer because we have stricter regulations and that buying them keeps our people employed and puts money back into local economies. So, be an American—buy American!

Most cultures create and perpetuate their mythic identity in the stories they weave into legends, folktales, music, and poetry. When you appeal to mythos in a speech, you often use narratives (stories) to create a strong sense of cultural identity, which, in turn, moves your audience to a change in belief, attitude, value, or behavior. For instance, you might use mythos in a speech about increasing taxes to fund local schools:

> Determination and knowledge are what built this great country, and we need to support our country by supporting our schools.

A downside to mythos is that it can promote **ethnocentrism**, or the notion that one's culture or viewpoint is superior to that of others.

3
Appeal to Ethos

Ethos is the credibility inspired by the speaker's character, or what Aristotle called *moral character*. You can have a strong argument and emotional appeal, but if the audience questions your character, you will have trouble persuading them.

The key to using your credibility effectively is to realize that it resides in *how your audience views you* and not in how you view yourself or your intentions. Aristotle claimed that the speaker's credibility evolved from *competency* and *character*. In modern times, a third trait, *charisma*, has been recognized.

- **Competency** is the audience's perception of how knowledgeable you are about your topic. Mentioning your related experience or education, citing a variety of support materials from credible sources, and presenting a polished speech will help demonstrate your competency.

- **Character** is the audience's perception of your intentions and of the concern you have for the audience. Do they see you as trustworthy, objective, honest, and similar to them? Finding ways to connect with the audience, demonstrating that you have investigated alternatives and challenges to your positions, and emphasizing your concern for the audience (rather than just for yourself) will build your character.

- **Charisma** is the audience's perception of your personality. Do they see you as energetic, friendly, approachable, and vocally as well as physically pleasing? Be confident and assertive in a positive manner. Use language and gestures to demonstrate your dynamic personality and excitement about the topic.

Your ethos will progress through three levels. The table below, based on *An Introduction to Rhetorical Communication* by James McCroskey, explains each level.

LEVELS OF ETHOS	INFLUENCING FACTORS
Initial ethos: your audience's perception of you before your speech starts	• If the audience has preconceived feelings about you • How you are introduced • The reason for the event • Prior speeches
Derived ethos: the credibility your audience assigns you during your speech	• Speech content • Reliability and credibility of your sources • Delivery aspects • Overall speech effectiveness
Terminal ethos: your audience's perception of you after you finish your speech	• Your ability to handle questions • Your exiting behavior • Follow-up comments

→ See Tab 2 for a discussion of source credibility and citations.

4

Appeal to Logos

The human ability to use logic can be a powerful persuasive tool. When you appeal to logic, or *logos*, in a speech, you appeal to the listener's ability to reason through statistics, facts, and expert testimony to reach a conclusion. Therefore, you engage in **reasoning**—the rational thinking humans do to reach conclusions or to justify beliefs or acts. You build arguments to influence your audience's beliefs, values, attitudes, and behaviors. The rest of this chapter will explain arguments in more detail, but here is the basic format of an argument:

1. Make a statement.
2. Offer support materials related to the statement as evidence.
3. Draw your conclusion.

For example, Katie is a student in a state that is considering a ban on cell phone use while driving. Katie, whose best friend died in a crash while driving and using her phone, will argue in her speech for supporting the ban. She creates her first argument using the basic format.

STATEMENT:	Cell phone use while driving is pervasive.
EVIDENCE:	As of August 2015, 92% of adults in America own cell phones. This is up from 53% in 2000 (Pew Research Center).
EVIDENCE:	According to the National Highway Traffic Safety Administration's "Traffic Safety Facts" (September 2015), at any given moment in 2014, 587,632 drivers were using cell phones or electronic devices while behind the wheel.
CONCLUSION:	Given these statistics, it would be difficult to drive anywhere and not meet someone using a cell phone.

Katie's next argument uses the same format and continues to support her overall purpose.

STATEMENT:	Cell phone use while driving is dangerous.
EVIDENCE:	The NHTSA's fact sheet (April 2015) states that ten percent of all fatal crashes, 18 percent of injury crashes, and 16 percent of all police-reported motor vehicle traffic crashes in 2013 were reported as distraction-affected crashes. Fourteen percent of the fatal distraction-affected crashes involved the use of a cell phone.
EVIDENCE:	Drivers talking on cell phones took 18 percent longer to react to an emergency braking situation (Drive-safely.net).
EVIDENCE:	Distraction.gov notes that engaging in tasks like texting that require your visual and manual attention triples the risk of getting into a crash.
CONCLUSION:	Numerous studies suggest that cell phone usage while driving is dangerous.

This material is only a part of Katie's speech, but you can begin to see how she logically leads her audience to the same conclusions she has reached.

15.4 What Are the Modern Appeals Used to Persuade?

1 Appeal to Need
2 Appeal to Harmony
3 Appeal to Gain
4 Appeal to Commitment

Although much of how you persuade relies on the classical appeals of logic, credibility, emotions, and cultural identity, the modern speaker can use other types of motivational appeals. Modern theorists argue that motivation to change can be grounded less in the logical and more in the psychological. In other words, people are motivated by such psychological appeals as meeting their needs, creating a sense of harmony, gaining something, or acting out of commitment.

1

Appeal to Need

This modern method of persuasion recognizes that your audience members have needs they see as important and necessary to fulfill. Demonstrating, when possible, how your topic will help your audience fulfill a need can be an effective motivator.

In Chapter 2, you learned about Abraham Maslow's hierarchy-of-needs theory, which states that humans have a set of needs that must be met. The pyramid diagram to the right illustrates the five hierarchical levels of needs. Appealing to your audience's needs makes for an effective persuasive speech. For example, persuading an audience to get a flu shot could appeal to good health, or the safety need.

In Chapter 7, you were introduced to Alan Monroe's motivated sequence as a classic organizational strategy using an appeal to need. To the right of the pyramid here, a flowchart demonstrates—in the highlighted second, third, and fourth stages of the sequence—how you thoughtfully and intentionally demonstrate to your audience that they have a need (to stay well); propose a solution to them that will satisfy the need (get a flu shot); and then help them visualize the benefits (visualize their good health, while numerous others fall ill).

This appeal relies on your knowing the audience's needs and paying attention to the hierarchy. For example, during a year following a light flu season, motivation might be difficult.

THE HIERARCHY OF NEEDS

Self-actualization needs relate to the need to reach your highest goal or potential.

Self-esteem needs relate to the need for respect or being viewed by others as important, which leads to feeling good about oneself.

Social needs relate to the need to belong or to be in lasting relationships, such as intimate partnerships, friendships, families, and social groups.

Safety needs are needs for overall security and protection, such as a sense of safety in your home, relationships, shelter, or good health.

Physiological needs are needs for food, water, air, general comfort, and sex.

MONROE'S MOTIVATED SEQUENCE

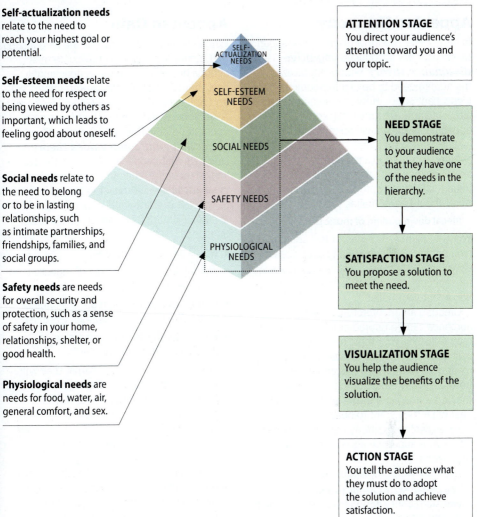

ATTENTION STAGE
You direct your audience's attention toward you and your topic.

NEED STAGE
You demonstrate to your audience that they have one of the needs in the hierarchy.

SATISFACTION STAGE
You propose a solution to meet the need.

VISUALIZATION STAGE
You help the audience visualize the benefits of the solution.

ACTION STAGE
You tell the audience what they must do to adopt the solution and achieve satisfaction.

Pyramid labels: SELF-ACTUALIZATION NEEDS, SELF-ESTEEM NEEDS, SOCIAL NEEDS, SAFETY NEEDS, PHYSIOLOGICAL NEEDS

➔ See Chapter 7 (pages 162–163) and Chapter 16 for more on using Monroe's motivated sequence to structure a persuasive speech.

2

Appeal to Harmony

In his book *A Theory of Cognitive Dissonance*, Leon Festinger introduced **cognitive dissonance theory**, which emphasizes the human need to be in a harmonious state (consonant state). However, sometimes there are conflicting attitudes, values, beliefs, ideas, or behaviors that cause an inharmonious feeling (dissonant state).

When listening to a persuasive speech, an audience may feel this sort of dissonance. Read the following proposition of value and think about how it makes you feel:

Illegal downloading of music is stealing.

You could agree, disagree, or feel apathetic (you don't care). If you don't think illegal downloading of music is stealing, the speaker must offer strong evidence to make you feel bad about your belief.

Creating an uncomfortable feeling in your audience can be unpredictable, especially if their beliefs in your topic are deeply seated. Just because you create dissonance does not mean your audience will accept your solution. They may discredit you or your sources, they may stop listening, or they may simply hear what they want to hear.

An appeal to harmony can also be used when your audience agrees with your proposition.

Let's say your proposition is:

The United States needs to adopt an emissions policy designed to help control the greenhouse effect.

If your audience agrees with the need to control the greenhouse effect, your goal now is to create a dissonance related to not acting upon their belief.

3

Appeal to Gain

When you appeal to gain, you are recognizing that most people weigh or evaluate their actions based on what the actions might cost them. In *Belief, Attitude, Intention, and Behavior*, Martin Fishbein and Icek Ajzen formulated a theory that helps you understand how this appeal works. Their **expectancy-outcome values theory** suggests that people will evaluate the cost, benefit, or value related to making a change in an attitude, value, belief, or behavior to decide if it is worthwhile or not. People in such a situation will ask these kinds of questions:

- Is this a good or bad idea?
- Will my family, friends, or colleagues approve or disapprove?
- If they disapprove, what are the ramifications? Are those ramifications worth it?
- Will my family, friends, or colleagues think better of me if I do this?

People will try to determine what they will gain or lose by changing. During a persuasive speech, if you can demonstrate to your audience that what you are asking to change or do will be a gain and not a loss, you may be able to motivate them to agree.

For example, if you are trying to convince a group of college students that they should engage in community service or sign up for an internship because future potential employers like to see these activities on résumés, you are appealing to the students' need to gain something more important than the time it will take to participate in the service or internship.

4

Appeal to Commitment

Another appeal recognizes how audience members might interpret your message, depending upon their commitment to critical thinking and involvement. The **elaboration likelihood model (ELM)**, presented by Richard Petty and John Cacioppo in *Communication and Persuasion*, argues that people will process your message by one of two ways: **central processing** or **peripheral processing**.

PROCESSING TYPE	WHAT IS IT?
Central processing	Being motivated to listen and think critically
Peripheral processing	Not paying close attention to an argument; or superficially accepting an argument

Think about how often you buy something because it has a logo on it, such as one for Tommy Hilfiger, Under Armour, Gucci, an NFL team, or Nike. Did you consider if there was something of equal quality for a lower price from another company? In this case, you don't critically think about how the item compares to others; you are peripherally processing. Think about how you listen in a class you do not find interesting. Then think about how you listen in your favorite class. In the less interesting course, your listening may be shallow—just enough to get the facts to pass the test (peripheral processing). In your favorite course, you may take notes, read before class, and participate in discussion (central processing). The level of your commitment and involvement makes you process differently.

As a speaker, you can use this knowledge to create a message relevant to the majority of your audience's interests. The challenge with using an appeal to commitment is that you need to know your audience and what they will process centrally. This heightens the significance of conducting effective audience analysis.

→ See Chapter 2 for more information about audience analysis.

For example, think about your feelings related to this proposition of value:

Texting while driving should be illegal.

Many students think texting while driving is harmless because they are careful. If you are giving this speech to a young adult audience, you have to be prepared for them to peripherally process it. They may ignore your facts, statistics, and examples even though your evidence is correct, plentiful, and logical. The audience reaction is based on their personal belief that they are careful but the people in your speech were not. Such audiences often refuse to listen critically. That's why, for a topic like this, some schools bring in spokespersons or simulators to demonstrate what can go wrong (in this case, when texting while driving).

At a basic level, the ELM theory should signal a need to consider issues such as your appearance, your delivery, and the completeness of your message when giving any speech. For example, this theory explains why you might not want to wear a body piercing to a job interview. The interviewer might peripherally judge you as a bad candidate because of his or her feelings toward body piercing instead of centrally evaluating your excellent qualifications.

15.5 What Are the Parts of an Argument?

1 Claim

2 Evidence

3 Warrants

An *argument* is a reason or a series of reasons you give to support an assertion. You use arguments to support your persuasive speech proposition and central idea. In his book *The Uses of Argument*, Stephen Toulmin notes that an argument has three main parts: a claim, evidence, and warrants.

One way to understand an argument is to think of it as a bridge you need to build so that you can convince an audience to cross to the other side of a vast river. The claim or conclusion of your argument is like the roadbed of the bridge. The evidence is the material making up the piers, which holds the roadbed in place; and the fact that the piers are made of concrete and metal is the warrant that makes the audience believe it is safe to cross. If your audience does not see the bridge as strong, they will not cross the bridge.

Let's look at each part of an argument in more detail.

> At the end of
> reasons comes
> persuasion.[1]
> LUDWIG WITTGENSTEIN

1

Claim

Earlier, you learned that all persuasive speeches support a proposition of fact, value, or policy and that your central idea summarizes or previews what you specifically want to assert. Now you can start to see how arguments work. When you make a smaller argument within the body of the speech, you will have a claim that acts just as your central idea does for the whole speech. The **claim** of an argument is the assertion you are making; it will be a claim of fact, value, or policy. Each claim should be a single, concise sentence. For example:

CLAIM OF FACT: People who wear seat belts tend to take better care of their health.

CLAIM OF FACT: Too much fluoride in our drinking water can be dangerous.

CLAIM OF VALUE: Owning a gun is wrong.

CLAIM OF VALUE: You should always adopt an animal from a shelter.

CLAIM OF POLICY: All public buildings should be smoke-free.

CLAIM OF POLICY: The city should change the current city ordinance to allow citizens to own a small flock of hens within the city limits.

Rarely, if ever, can you prove that a claim is 100 percent correct. Claims can be qualified as "possible," "probable," or "beyond doubt." If the qualification assigned to the claim has solid reasoning and enough evidence to support it at the level you are arguing, then the claim is sound and your audience is more likely to believe it. Clearly, if you wish to argue "beyond doubt," your reasoning and evidence have to be strong.

2

Evidence

When you make a claim, you have to support it. Here you ask, "What proof do I have to support this claim?" In this step, the support materials you have gathered become ***evidence***, or the information that proves your claim. Evidence comes in the form of examples, facts, definitions, testimony, and statistics.

Let's say your speech is on the change-of-policy claim about chickens:

CLAIM OF POLICY: The city should change the current city ordinance to allow citizens to own a small flock of hens within the city limits.

To support your claim, you consult books such as *Keep Chickens! Tending Small Flocks in Cities, Suburbs, and Other Small Spaces* by Barbara Kilarski and *Chickens in Your Backyard: A Beginner's Guide* by Rick and Gail Luttmann. There you discover the following potential evidence:

- Chickens and their eggs are great sources of protein.

- Naturally raised chickens and eggs have a better nutrient value than that provided by factory-farmed chickens.

- Chickens can reduce solid waste by eating table scraps.

- During hard economic times, raising your own chickens can be cheaper than buying the meat and eggs from a grocery store.

- Raising your own food puts you in control of what goes into your body.

- The practice of raising chickens in our backyards is more humane than supporting corporate chicken farms.

3
Warrants

Just presenting evidence will not necessarily demonstrate that your claim is accurate. You also need **warrants**, or assumptions that act as links between the evidence and the claim. This step is where you help your audience draw a conclusion about your claim and the evidence provided.

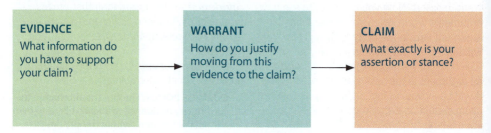

EVIDENCE
What information do you have to support your claim?

WARRANT
How do you justify moving from this evidence to the claim?

CLAIM
What exactly is your assertion or stance?

Staying with your topic of urban chickens, if you take two bits of information—one about the health benefits of chicken in general and one about how naturally raised chickens tend to be more nutritious than chickens raised on factory farms—you could support your claim like this:

EVIDENCE
Chicken is a great source of protein. Naturally raised chickens have a better nutrient value than those raised on factory farms.

WARRANT
Anyone raising his or her own chickens has access to a more nutrient-enriched form of protein.

CLAIM
Local citizens should be allowed to raise chickens.

Toulmin identified three ancillary elements to an argument as well. They are backing, reservation, and qualifier. In the examples below, note how the italicized phrases each relate to one of Toulmin's elements.

Backing is additional support to prove the warrant.

For example, *many studies support* the benefits of lean protein.

Reservation notes that a claim may not be true all the time.

Chickens raised in factory farms *usually produce an inferior-quality protein.*

Qualifiers soften the effect of reservations on a claim.

Local citizens should be allowed to raise chickens because *this poultry will likely yield better food.*

There are three types of warrants: *authoritative*, *motivational*, and *substantive*. Here is another example, related to the need for calcium in most men's diets, to demonstrate the three types of warrants.

1.
Authoritative warrants

link the evidence to the claim by assuming that the claim is accurate based on the credibility of the source of the support materials. For example, look at this outline of an argument:

EVIDENCE:
Doctors at the Mayo Clinic say calcium is necessary for men.

WARRANT:
The Mayo Clinic doctors are viewed as an extremely reliable source.

CLAIM:
Men need calcium.

2.
Motivational warrants

link the evidence to the claim based on the speaker's and audience's needs and values. For example:

EVIDENCE:
Men need calcium to prevent brittle-bone issues late in life.

WARRANT:
Men's happiness and quality of life in later years is dependent on healthy bones.

CLAIM:
Men need calcium.

3.
Substantive warrants

link the evidence to the claim based on the reliability of the support materials. In other words, are there enough examples and/or data to be convincing? Are the support materials representative?

EVIDENCE:
Several studies have found that many men are getting insufficient levels of calcium and suggest that this deficiency begins to negatively influence their bodies and lives in their later years.

WARRANT:
Enough evidence exists to support the fact that some men are not getting enough calcium and that this can have serious effects.

CLAIM:
Men need calcium.

In the urban chickens example on the previous page, the warrant is motivational, based on the values of healthy eating.

Warrants can be expressed or unexpressed, but in order for your argument to work, your audience must either intuitively understand or be shown the connection.

> **CHECKLIST for Creating an Argument**
> ❑ Is my claim a concise, declarative sentence?
> ❑ Do I have enough quality evidence to support my claim?
> ❑ What are my warrants or justifications for moving from the evidence to the claim?

15.6 What Are the Different Types of Arguments?

1 Argument by Deduction
2 Argument by Induction
3 Argument by Analogy
4 Argument by Cause
5 Argument by Authority

The differences between types of arguments relate to how they are constructed after you create your claim. Remember, a claim is a concise sentence stating what you want to prove. For example:

All dolphins, whales, and porpoises are mammals.

Once you know what you want your audience to accept, you need to decide what type of argument you want to construct. There are five types of arguments.

1

Argument by Deduction

Argument by deduction (also known as *reasoning by deduction*) constructs a series of general statements (known as *premises*) that together prove correct the claim/conclusion.

When arguing by deduction, you can use one of two formats: a *syllogism* or an *enthymeme*. The **syllogism** is the classical form of deductive reasoning, with this structure:

MAJOR PREMISE
All mammals feed their young milk via mammary glands located on the female of the species.
— Includes a generally accepted statement

MINOR PREMISE
All female dolphins, whales, and porpoises feed their young milk produced by mammary glands on the female.
— Includes a specific observation

CONCLUSION
Therefore, all dolphins, whales, and porpoises are mammals.
— Includes a statement that ties the major and minor premises together

When you use deductive arguments in a speech, you will not usually be so methodical in how you phrase the argument. This same syllogism might be presented as:

According to scientists, there are several characteristics that define mammals, but the most significant is how they feed their young. All mammals have the ability to feed their young through mammary glands located on the body of the female of the species. **MAJOR PREMISE**

Dolphins, whales, and porpoises all have this unique ability to allow their offspring to suckle. **MINOR PREMISE**

We consider dolphins, whales, and porpoises to be marine mammals. **CONCLUSION**

Sometimes, one of your premises will be obvious or common knowledge and you will not need to state it; this type of truncated syllogism is an **enthymeme**. In the example below, you would drop the obvious minor premise—that Jimmy Fallon is a human—and jump to the conclusion.

MAJOR PREMISE
All humans are mortal.

CONCLUSION
Therefore, Jimmy Fallon is mortal.

PRACTICING ETHICS: Ethical Arguments

Previously, you learned not to coerce your audience and, in Chapter 16, you will discover how to prevent faulty arguments. However, it is important to always use persuasive argument for the good.

- Don't conceal your true intentions.
- Don't represent yourself as an expert unless you are.
- Don't distort, mislead, pretend certainty, or fail to support your arguments.
- Don't exaggerate to manipulate.

Deductive reasoning must present a sound argument. To be sound, the major and minor premises as well as the conclusion must be factual; if they are not, the result is a **faulty syllogism**. For example:

MAJOR PREMISE
All environmentalists are vegetarians.

MINOR PREMISE
Yeon is an environmentalist.

CONCLUSION
Therefore, Yeon is a vegetarian.

FAULTY SYLLOGISM

The major premise here is false because many environmentalists are not vegetarians. Yeon may be an environmentalist, but that does not necessarily mean Yeon is a vegetarian. Likewise, Yeon may be an environmentalist and a vegetarian, but being a vegetarian may have nothing to do with being an environmentalist. To make a sound deductive argument, you want to ask: "Can I prove the major and minor premises are true? Is the conclusion reasonable, given the two premises?"

2

Argument by Induction

Whereas deduction deals with certainty, induction predicts probability. When you construct an **argument by induction** (also known as *reasoning by induction*), you will argue from specific cases to a general statement suggesting something to be likely based on the specific cases. We often use this type of reasoning in our everyday lives.

For example, if you buy a box of assorted chocolates and you eat three or four pieces in the box only to discover they are stale, you do not keep eating and assume the next one will not be stale. Instead, you reason that if the first three or four pieces (the specific) are stale, the whole box (the general) is stale. Likewise, if you check out gas prices at 9 or 10 gas stations in your city and they are all $1.79, you reason that gas in your town will probably cost $1.79 everywhere.

The reliability of these claims resides in the quantity and quality of the specific cases. The same is true for a speech using argument by induction. The induction can be based on examples, statistics, facts, or testimony.

This diagram demonstrates how you might reason through specific cases to support the claim "ZZtravel.com has the best rates for a variety of travel needs."

SPECIFIC CASE #1
Student A purchased airline tickets and hotel reservations to Cancún from ZZtravel.com because the service was the cheapest.

↓

SPECIFIC CASE #2
Student B rented a car and made hotel reservations for a trip to Orlando from the same online service because it was the cheapest she found.

↓

SPECIFIC CASE #3
Student C purchased airline tickets to make a trip back home to Oregon from the same online service because it was the cheapest.

↓

SPECIFIC CASE #4
Student D purchased airline tickets and a Eurail pass for a trip to Germany from the same online service because it was the cheapest he found.

↓

CLAIM
ZZtravel.com has the best rates for a variety of travel needs.

TIP: Inductive Arguments

Inductive arguments are useful when you know your audience is against what you are about to claim.

3
Argument by Analogy

When you create an **argument by analogy** (also known as *reasoning by analogy*), you conclude that something will be accurate for one case if it is true for another similar case. In other words, if it is true for A, it is true for B because they are so similar.

For example, many people who argue for a universal health care plan in the United States do so by making a comparison to Canada. Their claim based on an argument of analogy might be something like this:

> **Because the United States and Canada are so similar and a universal plan works in Canada, then universal health care will work in the United States.**

As in this example, you will most often use an argument by analogy when giving a persuasive speech on a proposition of policy.

As discussed in Chapter 5, there are two types of analogies: literal and figurative. An argument based on literal analogies (the comparison of two similar things) works better. Rarely will a figurative analogy (a metaphorical comparison of dissimilar things) prove a claim, and most of the time, a figurative analogy ends in faulty reasoning.

TIP: Faulty Arguments

When a speaker creates an argument, she or he can unintentionally or intentionally create a faulty argument or error in logic known as a fallacy. Chapter 16 will introduce you to some of the most common fallacies. Familiarize yourself with them, and always evaluate your arguments for such faulty reasoning. As an audience member, you should do the same for other persuasive speakers.

→ See pages 389–393 for more on fallacies.

4
Argument by Cause

Argument by cause (also known as *reasoning by cause*) attempts to demonstrate a relationship between two events or factors in which one of the events or factors causes the other. This form of reasoning may take an effect-to-cause or cause-to-effect form. Here are two claims suggesting this type of argument.

> **The increase in violence in our public schools is the effect of increased violence in the entertainment world.**

EFFECT-TO-CAUSE

> **Procrastinating on your assignments will cause you to get lower grades.**

CAUSE-TO-EFFECT

5
Argument by Authority

Argument by authority (also known as *reasoning by authority*) locates its power in the ethos of the testimony of others you might use to support your claim. When you use this type of argument, you collect testimony from individuals the audience will perceive as experts on the topic.

Argument by authority works only if the audience perceives the experts as credible and unbiased. For example, if you wanted to support the claim that stoplight cameras decrease accidents and save lives, you might consider quoting the chiefs of police in towns and cities already using these devices. For maximum effect, you should quote your sources directly, and you should always give their credentials.

Chapter 15: Review

ASSESSING YOUR KNOWLEDGE

15.1 What Is Persuasive Speaking?

Objective 15.1: **DEFINE PERSUASIVE SPEAKING**

Persuasion is a deliberate attempt by the speaker to create, reinforce, or change the attitudes, beliefs, values, and/or behaviors of the listener. When you create a formal speech with the goal to persuade, you are engaging in persuasive speaking. Remember that persuasion is not coercion, which is forcing someone, via threats or intimidation, to do something against his or her will.

→ See pages 336–337.

15.2 What Should a Persuasive Speech Do?

Objective 15.2: **DESCRIBE WHAT A PERSUASIVE SPEECH SHOULD DO**

An effective persuasive speech will:
- Focus the listeners' options through ethical and logical methods, so that they can make a choice.
- Appeal to a particular response from the audience by using traditional or modern appeals, or proofs.
- Support a proposition of fact, value, or policy.
  - A proposition of fact seeks to prove something factual and answers the question "What is accurate or not?"
  - A proposition of value seeks to make a value judgment and answers "What has worth or importance?"
  - A proposition of policy seeks to prove a need for a new or different policy and answers "What procedures, plans, or courses of action need to be terminated or implemented?"

→ See pages 338–339.

15.3 What Are the Traditional Appeals Used to Persuade?

Objective 15.3: **IDENTIFY THE TRADITIONAL APPEALS USED TO PERSUADE**

Appeals are the means by which you prove or establish the argument you are making. The traditional appeals are pathos, mythos, ethos, and logos. You use pathos when appealing to your audience's emotions. You use mythos when appealing to your audience's need for group membership and connection to the group's traditions, identity, and values. You use ethos when you demonstrate to the audience that you and your support material are reliable. You use logos when you appeal to your audience's ability to reason or work through your ideas logically.

→ See pages 340–343.

15.4 What Are the Modern Appeals Used to Persuade?

Objective 15.4: **IDENTIFY THE MODERN APPEALS USED TO PERSUADE**

The modern appeals are appeal to need, appeal to harmony, appeal to gain, and appeal to commitment. When you appeal to need, you focus your argument on helping the audience fulfill needs they may have. When you appeal to harmony, you demonstrate how your argument will help the audience create a pleasant or an agreeable state. When you appeal to gain, you recognize that most people base their actions on what it might cost them or give them. When you appeal to commitment, you shape your argument based on the level of involvement and willingness the audience has to engage with your topic.

→ See pages 344–347.

15.5 What Are the Parts of An Argument?

Objective 15.5: **SUMMARIZE THE PARTS OF AN ARGUMENT**

An argument is a reason or a series of reasons (known as reasoning) you give to support an assertion. According to Toulmin, arguments have three parts: a claim, evidence, and warrants. The claim is the assertion you are making. The evidence is the information that proves the claim. The warrants are the assumptions that act as links between the evidence and the claim.

Three ancillary elements to an argument are backing (additional support), reservation (why a claim may not be true all the time), and qualifiers (to soften the reservations).

→ See pages 348–351.

15.6 What Are the Different Types of Arguments?

Objective 15.6: **EXPLAIN THE DIFFERENT TYPES OF ARGUMENTS**

The types of arguments are:
- Arguments by deduction, or a series of general statements that together prove the claim
- Argument by induction, or a series of specific cases that lead to a general statement that something is likely
- Argument by analogy, or concluding something will be accurate for one case if it is true for another similar case
- Argument by cause, or demonstrating how one event or factor causes another
- Argument by authority, or supporting a claim via the ethos of testimony offered by others who are regarded as highly credible

→ See pages 352–355.

TERMS TO REMEMBER

persuasion (336)
persuasive speaking (336)
coercion (336)
speech to convince (338)
speech to stimulate (338)
apeech to actuate (338)
appeals (338)
proposition of fact (339)
proposition of value (339)
proposition of policy (339)
mythos (341)
ethnocentrism (341)
competency (342)
character (342)
charisma (342)
initial ethos (342)
derived ethos (342)
terminal ethos (342)
reasoning (343)
cognitive dissonance theory (346)
expectancy-outcome values theory (346)
elaboration likelihood model (ELM) (347)
central processing (347)
peripheral processing (347)
argument (348)
claim (349)
evidence (349)
warrants (350)
backing (350)
reservation (350)
qualifiers (350)
argument by deduction (352)
syllogism (352)
enthymeme (353)
faulty syllogism (353)
argument by induction (354)
argument by analogy (355)
argument by cause (355)
argument by authority (355)

16 THE PERSUASIVE SPEECH

Thaw with his gentle persuasion is more powerful than Thor with his hammer. The one melts, the other but breaks in pieces.[1]

HENRY DAVID THOREAU

16.1 What Is the Creative Process for Persuasive Speaking?

Influencing others through a persuasive speech is a remarkable task that requires you to be diligent and ethical in some ways that are different from those used in informative speaking. The table to the right briefly reviews the five basic activities you use to create an effective persuasive speech. Remember, being creative is not a linear process, so move back and forth between each activity as you mold your speech.

In the example at the far right, Maria, a student from Brazil, is studying in the United States. In an environmental class, she recently became aware of the staggering volume of plastic pollution in the United States.

After her environmental class ended, Maria joined the Clean Cities program in her college town. Now, she needs to give a speech about recycling to fellow students who live off campus. Maria will give her speech at a Saturday workshop held once a month to bring off-campus students together to build community and to show them how to be better consumers and citizens. Maria has been a part of the group for some time, so she knows many of her audience members, making her audience analysis relatively easy.

She develops a working outline with four main points:

Main point #1: What is plastic?

Main point #2: How do we use it?

Main point #3: How is it influencing our environment?

Main point #4: What is the solution?

Maria decides it will be important to use all the traditional appeals throughout her speech and will use arguments by induction and authority.

THE CREATIVE PROCESS	PERSUASIVE EXAMPLE

1 STARTING

HOW DO YOU CHOOSE A FOCUSED PERSUASIVE TOPIC?

→ See page 362

Maria creates this central idea:

> The amount of plastics thrown away daily is a serious problem, but a few simple steps on our part will lower plastic's impact on our future.

2 RESEARCHING

HOW DO YOU RESEARCH THE PERSUASIVE SPEECH?

→ See page 370

Using questions related to a proposition of policy to guide her, she conducts her research online and in the local public library. She also interviews a professor who specializes in waste management.

3 CREATING

HOW DO YOU OUTLINE AND ORGANIZE A PERSUASIVE SPEECH?

→ See page 372

Maria selects the problem–solution strategy for her speech and creates main points to fit that strategy.

Problem:
  I. Plastics are made from problematic raw materials.
  II. Plastics cause major environmental issues.

Solution:
  III. There are alternative forms of plastics and substitute materials.
  IV. There are alternative ways of using plastics.

She uses the environmental artwork of Chris Jordon to grab attention in the introduction and ends with startling statistics for her WOW statement.

4 PRESENTING

WHAT SHOULD YOU CONSIDER WHEN PREPARING TO PRESENT A PERSUASIVE SPEECH?

→ See page 386

Maria adjusts her language to clarify her arguments and to be more interesting. She creates her delivery outline and her Prezi presentation aids. Maria practices several times, including twice in the event space.

5 LISTENING & EVALUATING

HOW DO YOU EVALUATE A PERSUASIVE SPEECH?

→ See page 388

After the speech, Maria asks the audience to fill out a short survey of their experience, and she asks close friends for comments about her speech.

16.2 How Do You Choose a Focused Persuasive Topic?

1 Get to Know the Audience and Situation

2 Create a Persuasive Idea Bank

3 Select and Narrow Your Persuasive Topic

4 Confirm the Best Type of Persuasive Speech

5 Identify Your Specific Purpose

6 Identify Your Central Idea

7 Create a Working Outline

1

Get to Know the Audience and Situation

You already know from Chapter 2 that it is important to know your audience's attitudes, beliefs, and values as well as their psychological, personal, and social traits. Think about the definition of persuasive speaking offered in Chapter 15. If you are giving a persuasive speech, you are attempting to change, influence, or reinforce the attitudes, beliefs, values and/or behaviors of an audience. Being audience centered is crucial to the persuasive speech because you are asking the audience to agree with you on something. If you are successful, the audience members will agree to evolve in some significant way. If you do not know where your audience stands on your topic or what their needs are, you cannot expect to persuade them.

For example, imagine how difficult it might be as a manager to inspire employees to continue working hard on a project just after the company's CEO announces the need to eliminate some departments. You know most of your employees have had positive attitudes toward their jobs, but the timing of this announcement greatly influences your speaking situation.

Understanding who is in your audience and what the situation is will help you appeal to the target audience, a key component of the persuasive speech. The **target audience** is the primary group of people you are aiming to persuade; it is the subset of the audience that you most want to engage. Focusing in on this subset begins with understanding your audience as a whole and the situation.

For example, Megan is enrolled in a public speaking class, and her next speech must be a persuasive one. It is the end of the semester, and she is giving one of the last speeches in the class. She knows many of her audience members from outside of class and feels confident that she knows enough about the others just from interaction in the class. Before she started to brainstorm a topic, she wrote down some basic thoughts about the audience and situation. Megan then surveyed half of the class about what their biggest concern is right now. This information should help her narrow in on a topic. Once she has a better idea of her potential topic, she will return to analyzing the audience and situation, to help her further focus in on the target audience and to predict what she needs to say in her speech.

The checklist below helped Megan create notes about her audience and situation in general and move her focus toward the target audience as her speech developed.

CHECKLIST for Persuasive Audience and Situation Analysis

❑ What are the attitudes, beliefs, values, and traits of my audience?

❑ What topics might the audience be concerned with or find controversial? What do they potentially know about those topics, or what might be their views on them?

❑ Why is the audience here?

❑ What are the event details (location, time, etc.)?

❑ What are the audience's expectations because of the occasion? Are there external factors related to the situation that might influence my audience or suggest a controversial topic?

❑ How do any of these factors influence the type of persuasive speech I might give?

❑ How do any of these factors influence who my target audience is?

MY AUDIENCE AND THE SITUATION:

• 18 students and 1 female instructor

• 8 men and 10 women

• Age range 18 to 40ish—mostly 18–20

• 10 Caucasians (not sure of all of their ethnicities), 4 African Americans, 3 Koreans, 1 South African

• 11 of the students live on campus

• From previous discussion, the majority seems to lean toward the liberal side

• Most of the U.S. students are from within a 100-mile radius of campus

• Class is at 12:30 on Tuesday/Thursday

• My speech will be given between Thanksgiving and Christmas

• Biggest concern for several students seems to be finals—coming up in a few weeks

2

Create a Persuasive Idea Bank

If you do not have an assigned or predetermined persuasive topic, your next step is to find one. For a persuasive speech, the topic should be controversial or debatable—in other words, there are two or more different opinions people may hold about the topic.

Beginning speakers often have trouble getting started because they want to pinpoint the perfect "be all, end all" topic right from the beginning. Relax, consider a wide variety of topics at first, and let your mind wander. Databases such as EBSCOhost (shown below), CQ (Congressional Quarterly) Researcher, CQ Weekly, and Opposing Viewpoints Resource Center, or newspapers and magazines such as the *New York Times*, your local newspaper, *Time* magazine, and *The Week* are all great places to locate current persuasive topics. As you scroll through the databases or browse other sources, note topics that seem interesting. Let your brain free-associate other ideas. As you can see from the idea bank on page 365, Megan let her audience and situation notes guide her free association. When creating a persuasive idea bank, it is best to use phrases noting a side to an issue (e.g., "everyone should"). This allows you to consider multiple points of view and related topics.

In EBSCOhost, you can search databases using a general key word such as "controversy" or, as the example below does, a specific category such as "Supreme Court Cases." Then a review of the articles will often help you populate an idea bank.

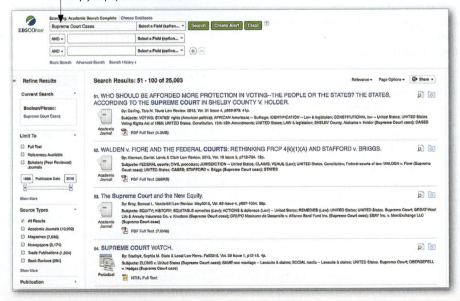

3
Select and Narrow Your Persuasive Topic

Now you are ready to narrow your ideas to a viewpoint or your stance on a debatable topic. If you are still unsure of which general topic you want to use, return to analyzing the audience and situation. Consider these questions:

- Are there topics that are just not persuasive enough? Is there any way to make them persuasive?
- Will the audience be neutral, negative, or positive? Will they have an extreme reaction? Which topic will appeal to a solid target audience?
- Are there situational issues that will help you determine the best topic?

Before you commit to a topic, do some preliminary research. If locating current quality information on the topic is difficult, you may want to select another topic or change the viewpoint of the one you are researching.

After reconsidering her audience and the situation of a speech class right before finals, Megan started to focus in on her ideas related to finals. Recently, she read an article about college students using "study drugs" and heard some students discussing their use. Viewing that as highly controversial, Megan decided this was a great topic and set out to do more preliminary research.

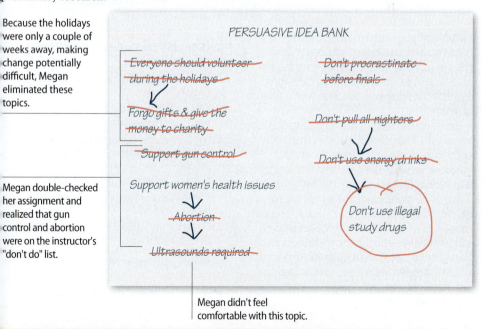

Because the holidays were only a couple of weeks away, making change potentially difficult, Megan eliminated these topics.

Megan double-checked her assignment and realized that gun control and abortion were on the instructor's "don't do" list.

PERSUASIVE IDEA BANK

Everyone should volunteer during the holidays

Forgo gifts & give the money to charity

Support gun control

Support women's health issues

Abortion

Ultrasounds required

Don't procrastinate before finals

Don't pull all-nighters

Don't use energy drinks

Don't use illegal study drugs

Megan didn't feel comfortable with this topic.

4

Confirm the Best Type of Persuasive Speech

Before moving on to create your central idea, it is important to confirm the type of persuasive speech you should give. A persuasive speech will be a speech to convince, stimulate, or actuate. Knowing the type of persuasive speech will help you determine your organizational strategy and focus on the response you want your target audience to have.

TYPE OF PERSUASIVE SPEECH	DESIRED AUDIENCE RESPONSE	EXAMPLES
To convince	To convince my audience to change their attitudes, values, beliefs, or behaviors	A speech arguing that outsourcing harms the U.S. economy, presented to a group of CEOs
To stimulate	To stimulate the existing attitudes, values, beliefs, or behaviors of my audience	A speech arguing that animal theme parks are cruel, presented to an animal rights group
To actuate	To move my audience to action	A speech arguing to vote for medical marijuana use, at a rally supporting a medical marijuana initiative

Given that you need to understand the exact audience response you desire from the speech, you need to define your target audience in relationship to your new topic. Use the checklist here to refine your audience analysis.

For example, Megan knows that younger members of her audience might try to cut corners in studying by doing things that could be harmful. Her preliminary research shows that the use of prescription drugs as a study aid is significant. She's heard some talk on campus about study-drug usage. Megan's biggest concern is for the students who might not have enough knowledge about the harmful effects to hold an opinion one way or the other. She decides to give a speech to convince her younger classmates not to use illegal study drugs.

> **CHECKLIST for Defining Your Target Audience**
>
> ❑ What *does* my audience know about my topic?
> ❑ What are their attitudes, beliefs, values, needs, and behaviors toward my topic?
> ❑ Will they agree, somewhat disagree, significantly disagree, or not have an opinion?
> ❑ Therefore, will I primarily be creating, reinforcing, or changing attitudes, values, beliefs, or behaviors?
> ❑ Do I want my audience to passively agree or to take action?

5

Identify Your Specific Purpose

To review, the specific purpose is a single statement connecting your general purpose, your audience (the target audience in this speech), and your objective. It needs to be clear and limited to only one topic. Let's see how Megan created her specific purpose.

You already know that her topic relates to the illegal use of prescription medication as a study aid. She personally believes that this behavior, especially using ADHD drugs illegally, is extremely dangerous, and she wants to convince her audience to believe the same thing.

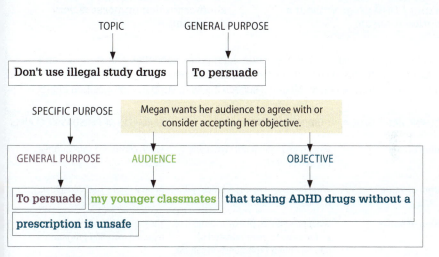

TOPIC | GENERAL PURPOSE

Don't use illegal study drugs | **To persuade**

SPECIFIC PURPOSE | Megan wants her audience to agree with or consider accepting her objective.

GENERAL PURPOSE | AUDIENCE | OBJECTIVE

To persuade | **my younger classmates** | **that taking ADHD drugs without a prescription is unsafe**

This specific purpose will help Megan keep to her general purpose (to persuade) and focus the attention of her target audience (the 18- to 20-year-old students because preliminary research demonstrated they are more likely to take illegal study drugs) on her objective (don't use ADHD drugs as illegal study drugs).

➜ See pages 56–57 in Chapter 3 if you need more help with creating a specific purpose.

6
Identify Your Central Idea

Now you and Megan are ready to formulate your persuasive central ideas. As you know from Chapter 3, the central idea (or thesis statement) is one concise sentence summarizing or previewing exactly what you are going to claim. Megan's looked like this:

Megan's Specific Purpose:
To persuade my younger classmates that taking ADHD drugs without a prescription is unsafe

Megan's Central Idea:
The use of ADHD drugs for nonprescription purposes is very dangerous.

At this point, it should be easy to see the overarching proposition that your speech—and Megan's speech—is trying to answer. Remember, all persuasive speeches support a proposition of fact, value, or policy. Megan's speech seeks to support a proposition of fact.

OVERARCHING PROPOSITION	GUIDING QUESTIONS	EXAMPLES OF PERSUASIVE CLAIMS
Proposition of fact	What is accurate or not? What will happen or not?	When consumed safely, coffee can be beneficial.
Proposition of value	What has worth or importance? What is good, wise, ethical, or beautiful?	Animal theme parks are cruel.
Proposition of policy	What procedures, plans, or courses of action need to be terminated or implemented? (This question can ask the audience to just agree or to act.)	The city should not implement a required recycling program.

→ See pages 58–61 in Chapter 3 if you need more help formulating a central idea.

CHECKLIST for Evaluating a Persuasive Central Idea

❑ Is the central idea persuasive in nature? Is it reinforcing or changing attitudes, beliefs, values, and/or behaviors?

❑ Does it support a proposition of fact, value, or policy?

❑ Is it a complete clear and concise statement?

❑ Can I cover this central idea in the time allotted?

❑ Is it unique?

❑ Is it worth persuading the target audience of this and worth their time?

7
Create a Working Outline

Before embarking on your major research, it is helpful to create a working outline to guide you. To review: Your working main points might be questions you think need to be answered, or they could simply be phrases that relate to subtopics. Later, when you get to your preparation outline stage, you want your main points to be concise and complete declarative sentences, not questions.

Your central idea might hint at possible main points. Also, your target audience and your preliminary research should offer some insights and ideas.

Megan's central idea did not offer insight into her main points. However, the article she read a few weeks ago and her preliminary research helped her start to formulate working points. She noticed discussions about who was taking ADHD drugs as study drugs, what drugs students were using, and the side effects. Megan knows the temptation to cut corners when stress is high and thinks it might be smart to end the speech with alternative solutions to the use of study drugs. She created five working main points (see below) that would eventually lead to her final main points and potential strategy.

Remember, you may use questions for the main points in the working outline but should use declarative sentences for your main points in the preparation outline.

Working outline for "Don't Use Illegal Study Drugs"

TOPIC: The illegal use of ADHD drugs

GENERAL PURPOSE: To persuade

SPECIFIC PURPOSE: To persuade my younger classmates that taking ADHD drugs without a prescription is unsafe

CENTRAL IDEA: The use of ADHD drugs for nonprescription purposes is very dangerous.

I. What are ADHD drugs?

II. What are the side effects of ADHD drugs?

III. Who is taking the drugs illegally?

IV. Why are they taking them?

V. What are some alternative solutions to study drugs?

16.3 How Do You Research the Persuasive Speech?

You know from Chapters 4 and 5 that the support materials you use are important. As the person crafting a persuasive message, you have a responsibility and an ethical duty to prevent either accidental or intentional deception, and just "saying so" does not prove a point. You must use a variety of support materials and demonstrate to the audience that the materials are accurate, current, complete, trustworthy, suitable, and from ethical sources.

Depending on your topic, your central idea, your proposition, or the arguments you are using to support your claim, different types of support materials will be more effective than others. Research as many angles as possible.

Remember to collect citation information for each source as you research. Consult resources such as plagiarism.org if you still have plagiarism concerns.

→ See Tab 2 if you need help with research.

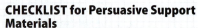

CHECKLIST for Persuasive Support Materials

❏ Are my support materials verifiable? Am I using the material as it was originally intended (not twisting it for effect)?

❏ Is the material the most current (up to the time of the speech, if possible)?

❏ Do I have enough material to make my argument? Does it give a complete picture? Did I consider all alternatives, including opposing ones?

❏ Can I trust the evidence and sources? Are they unbiased? Can my audience accept the sources as trustworthy?

❏ Is my material suitable for the topic, audience, and occasion?

❏ Do I have complete citation information?

Most debatable topics have more than two issues, solutions, or viewpoints. Your job is to understand as much as you can about them and present the viewpoint or solution you think is best. Complex topics require good detective work, and you will not find all the answers in one place.

Early in your research, you might start by considering the type of proposition you will support. The table below offers questions to help guide you. Keep in mind that this table is not exhaustive for each proposition.

TYPE OF PROPOSITION	QUESTIONS TO GUIDE YOUR RESEARCH
Proposition of fact	• Can you find multiple, varied, and reliable sources that verify your proposition of fact? • Are there reputable sources that support or dispute the fact (argument by authority)? What information can you find about their arguments? • Are there common myths or misconceptions about the topic that you need to dispel before your audience can be persuaded? • Are there verifiable cases that can support your proposition of fact (argument by induction)? • Is there a strong analogy (argument by analogy) you might make to predict future facts?
Proposition of value	• What groups or individuals can you find who may agree with the value behind your argument? Which ones will your audience consider reputable or influential (argument by authority)? • Who may disagree with the value behind your argument? What can you find out about why they disagree? • What material can you locate to support the guiding principles that justify the value judgment (argument by deduction)?
Proposition of policy	• Has the policy or plan of action you propose been implemented (or terminated) before? If so, what information can you find about the results? • Are there verifiable cases that can support your proposition of policy (argument by induction)? • Is there a strong analogy (argument by analogy) you might make to predict policy issues? • Is there material to support your proposition of policy based on what the policy will cause or what effects will result (argument by cause)? • If you want your audience to take an action, what details will you need to locate and give them in order for them to do so?

16.4 How Do You Outline and Organize a Persuasive Speech?

1 Start with Basic, Effective Outlining

2 Commit to a Strategy

3 Construct Main Points

4 Organize Support Materials into Arguments

5 Compose Your Introduction and Conclusion

1

Start with Basic, Effective Outlining

Constructing an effective preparation outline helps you create a persuasive speech that your audience can follow, that you can follow as you speak, and that can persuade others. Your audience needs to follow every detail of the argument you are presenting, so your organization must be appropriate to the topic and precise down to the smallest detail.

Revisit Tab 3 for a general review of outline creation if you still feel unsure. Remember that a successful preparation outline will:

- Include necessary header information.
- Contain an introduction, the body of the speech, and a conclusion.
- Use complete sentences.
- Cover only one issue at a time.
- Use balanced main points.
- Employ subordination.
- Plan out formal links.
- Use proper citations within the outline and include a source page (use the citation style your instructor requires).

As you create your persuasive outline, evaluating the strength of your argument will be easier the more detailed you are. Although important to any speech, strictly following these qualities for your persuasive speech will help you create a strong, effective argument that your audience can follow in the oral presentation. Your outline should adhere to either a format similar to the one on the next page or a format your instructor suggests.

→ See Tab 3 if you need more help outlining.

Student name   Class
Date   Instructor name

Topic: Illegal use of study drugs
Specific purpose: To persuade my younger classmates that taking
                               ADHD drugs without a prescription is unsafe
Central idea: The use of ADHD drugs for nonprescription pupposes
                               is dangerous, illegal, and not a good study-aid
                               solution.

INTRODUCTION
    Attention-getter
    Credibility material
    Relevance to audience
    Preview of speech

(Link from introduction to first main point)

BODY
    I.   Taking nonprescribed ADHD drugs is dangerous.
        A.   Subpoint
        B.   Subpoint
            1.   Subpoint of B
            2.   Subpoint of B
            3.   Subpoint of B

(Link between first and second main points)

    II.   Second main point
        A.   Subpoint
        B.   Subpoint
            1.   Subpoint of B
            2.   Subpoint of B
         C.   Subpoint

(Link between second and third main points)

    III. Third main point
        A.   Subpoint
            1.   Subpoint of A
               a. Subpoint of 1
               b. Subpoint of 1
            2.   Subpoint of A
         B.   Subpoint
        C.   Subpoint

(Link between third and fourth main points)

    IV. Fourth main point
        A.   Subpoint
            1.   Subpoint of A
               a. Subpoint of 1
               b. Subpoint of 1
            2.   Subpoint of A
         B.   Subpoint
        C.   Subpoint

(Link to conclusion)

CONCLUSION
    Summary statement
    Audience response statement
    WOW statement

                    Works Cited (or References)

After conducting research and selecting a strategy, Megan reworked her central idea to include a preview of her (now three) main points. Note the differences from the one on page 369.

Megan begins to fill in her main points, making sure they are full declarative sentences and cover only one idea at a time. She will make sure to have only one sentence per outline symbol and fill in the support materials.

Megan doesn't know yet how many subpoints each of her main points will have. For now, she leaves a variety of subpoint placeholders in her outline.

Although this template shows four main points, Megan's speech will only have three, and you could have three to five. Short speeches are usually best, with three or four main points.

2

Commit to a Strategy

Select the best strategy for your type of persuasive speech and your overarching proposition, and strictly adhere to that strategy. For a beginning speaker, it is easy to stray from the point or randomly string thoughts together, so be sure to write your main points so that they stick to the strategy. Periodically, you should return to Chapter 7—where the strategies are explained in detail, with examples—and make sure you are following your strategy.

WHAT FACTORS SHOULD YOU CONSIDER WHEN SELECTING A STRATEGY?	STRATEGIES
Speech to stimulate	
Audience viewpoint needs reinforcement	Monroe's motivated sequence, problem–solution, topical,* or chronological*
Speech to convince	
Audience is apathetic or uninformed and needs to create a viewpoint	Problem–solution, comparative, Monroe's motivated sequence, causal, topical,* or chronological*
Audience viewpoint needs to change because they disagree or are conflicted	Comparative, problem–solution, or causal
Speech to actuate	
Audience needs motivation to act	Most of the strategies work for this type, but Monroe's motivated sequence is often the best
Overarching proposition for your speech	
Proposition of fact	Causal, problem–solution, Monroe's motivated sequence, topical,* or chronological*
Proposition of value	Comparative, causal, comparative, or topical*
Proposition of policy	Problem–solution, comparative, causal, Monroe's motivated sequence, or topical*

*Remember, topical and chronological strategies are generally weaker persuasive strategies. They should only be used when nothing else works.

Megan selected and committed to the problem–solution strategy. She will spend most of her speech outlining the problems (the drugs are dangerous and illegal), and then she will offer alternative solutions to studying-related problems.

→ See Chapter 7 for a detailed explanation of these strategies.

3
Construct Main Points

Depending on how you constructed your central idea or which strategy you selected, one or both of these components might suggest the main points you will need to cover in the speech. If your central idea has evolved since the working outline, study it again for three or four possible subtopics, or study the strategy you want to use and how it might influence your main points. Strategies such as Monroe's motivated sequence have certain steps that become main points and determine the focus of those main points. If your central idea or strategy does not help determine main points, make a list of what you want to convey in the speech, group items that relate to each other, and create main points from those groups. Select the three or four most important ideas. Remember that your main points need to be complete declarative sentences, written in a parallel structure, and balanced with each other, and they should cover only one idea per point.

After conducting research, Megan reconsidered her central idea and focused it more to preview her main points. Megan committed to three main points.

I. Taking nonprescribed ADHD drugs is dangerous.

II. Taking nonprescribed ADHD drugs is illegal.

III. Taking nonprescribed ADHD drugs is not the solution.

→ See pages 164–167 in Chapter 7 if you need help with constructing main points.

4
Organize Support Materials into Arguments

Your arguments will become the subpoints supporting your main points. So it is time to decide which appeals to use, which types of arguments best fit your speech, and how to arrange the arguments. Make these decisions based on what you want to accomplish, your audience's relationship to the speech, and the needs of the organizational strategy. Once you have your arguments, you need to put them in a logical order. For example, Megan arranges the subpoints under her first main point using *induction*. She will offer facts about the physical problems caused by taking nonprescribed ADHD drugs and then end with her claim that it is dangerous. Two additional models can help you decide how to arrange arguments:

- The ***primacy model*** suggests that you should put your strongest arguments first because you are more likely to persuade if you win over your audience early. This method is best if your audience opposes your viewpoint.

- The ***recency model*** is the reverse of primacy. Here, you begin with the weakest argument and end with the strongest. If your audience is unfamiliar with your topic, is apathetic, or already agrees with you, this method is best.

There is no set way to approach creating arguments, and the more you do it, the better you will get.

5

Compose Your Introduction and Conclusion

Even though the body of a persuasive speech takes a bit more time and thought to develop than that of other speeches, you must still create a strong introduction and conclusion. Make sure you allow yourself plenty of time by starting early on the persuasive speech.

LAUNCH YOUR SPEECH

Keep your introduction stimulating, poignant, and fascinating. Megan uses a narrative, from a student who abused ADHD drugs, to grab her audience's attention and to appeal to pathos (the fear of what the drugs can do).

An introduction for a persuasive speech should focus your audience's attention on what you intend to claim about your topic. Megan cites statistics to logically demonstrate relevance to the audience. She then previews the proposition and main points of her speech.

Your audience will tend to wander off subject if you let them. So don't take too long to get to your point.

YOUR SPEECH'S FINALE

The persuasive speech's conclusion should leave your audience knowing your viewpoint and give them one more push to accept it or be influenced by it. Keep your specific purpose in mind as you construct the conclusion. In Megan's conclusion, notice how she specifies a response, summarizes, and "WOWs" her audience one last time.

See the Tip box for how long your introduction and conclusion should be.

→ See Chapter 8 for more details on writing introductions and conclusions.

TIP: Length

- Your introduction should be less than 15 percent of your total speech time.
- Your conclusion should be less than 5 percent of your total speech time.

INTRODUCTION

This should be an exciting moment in your speech.

ATTENTION-GETTER: "My use of Adderall as a study aid, 20 mg every so often, quickly escalated into 100 mg+ daily doses within 6 months of meeting a student who'd sell me his entire script for $60 each month. Amphetamine tolerance builds very quickly, and soon I wasn't able to obtain the energy and focus for which I came to depend upon amphetamines. I finally got help for my addiction, but I had to take time off of school to heal the damage I'd done to my brain chemistry."—Female student, 20, Pittsburgh (Schwarz)

State why you should give this speech.

CREDIBILITY MATERIAL: Recently, in my psychology class, we conducted research related to college students' use of ADHD drugs (such as Adderall, Vyvanse, Concerta, Focalin, and Ritalin). I was shocked to learn how prevalent this usage is nationwide and even on our campus.

Give them a reason to listen.

RELEVANCE TO AUDIENCE: Citing a study conducted by researchers at the University of Kentucky, Aaron Cooper, in the September 2011 article "College Students Take ADHD Drugs for Better Grades," reports that these drugs are more abused than marijuana. Thirty percent of students at UK have reported use. A survey conducted at our three local campuses suggests we are no different. Odds are six of you are using some type of study drug this semester.

Give them a road map to your speech.

PREVIEW OF SPEECH: We can't ignore this problem any longer. Today, I would like to persuade you not to use ADHD medications as study drugs. The use of ADHD drugs for nonprescription purposes is dangerous, illegal, and not a good solution for your study needs.

CONCLUSION

What should your audience remember?

AUDIENCE RESPONSE STATEMENT: Clearly, the decision to work a little harder to achieve one's goals and to be smart about it is far better than succumbing to the usage of nonprescribed drugs. I urge you all to opt for alternative solutions to cope with the stress of school and outside activities. These options are simple, safe, and legal. These options are what the successful students take—not a drug.

What do you want them to do with that information?

SUMMARY STATEMENT: Using ADHD drugs as nonprescribed study drugs is dangerous, even life threatening. Using ADHD drugs as nonprescribed study drugs is illegal, with potential fines and prison time, and may influence what you can do with your future. It is a felony!

Dazzle them one more time.

WOW STATEMENT: Make smarter choices to be a better student by preparing each day. As an African proverb states, "For tomorrow belongs to the people who are prepared for it today" ("Future").

PREPARATION OUTLINE FOR A PERSUASIVE SPEECH

Megan Kramer   COMM 110
12 March 2013   Dr. Dailey

Topic: Illegal use of study drugs

Specific purpose: To persuade my younger classmates that taking ADHD drugs without a prescription is unsafe

Central idea: The use of ADHD drugs for nonprescription purposes is dangerous, illegal, and not a good study-aid solution.

INTRODUCTION

Attention-getter: "My use of Adderall as a study aid, 20 mg every so often, quickly escalated into 100 mg+ daily doses within 6 months of meeting a student who'd sell me his entire script for $60 each month. Amphetamine tolerance builds very quickly, and soon I wasn't able to obtain the energy and focus for which I came to depend upon amphetamines. I finally got help for my addiction, but I had to take time off of school to heal the damage I'd done to my brain chemistry." —Female student, 20, Pittsburgh (Schwarz)

Credibility material: Recently, in my psychology class, we conducted research related to college students' use of ADHD drugs (such as Adderall, Vyvanse, Concerta, Focalin, and Ritalin). I was shocked to learn how prevalent this usage is nationwide and even on our campus.

Relevance to audience: Citing a study conducted by researchers at the University of Kentucky, Aaron Cooper, in the September 2011 article "College Students Take ADHD Drugs for Better Grades," reports that these drugs are more abused than marijuana. Thirty percent of students at UK have reported use. A survey conducted at our three local campuses

Megan uses a student's personal narrative to appeal to the audience's pathos.

She starts with general national statistics and then narrows the scope to highlight the relevance to this particular audience.

suggests we are no different. Odds are six of you are using some type of study drug this semester.

Preview of speech: We can't ignore this problem any longer. Today, I would like to persuade you not to use ADHD medications as study drugs. The use of ADHD drugs for nonprescription purposes is dangerous, illegal, and not a good solution for your study needs.

(**Link:** First, let's explore the problem with taking these drugs without a prescription.)

Megan uses a series of specific facts and other information to inductively support her claim at the end of this main point.

BODY

I. Taking nonprescribed ADHD drugs is dangerous. ◄

　A. This chart from the June 9, 2012, *New York Times* denotes that the common ADHD drugs used as illegal study drugs are either amphetamines or methylphenidates.

　　1. Adderall and Vyvanse are amphetamines.

　　2. Concerta, Focalin, and Ritalin are methylphenidates.

　　3. Both classifications of drugs are powerful central nervous system stimulants.

When possible, she uses material from highly credible sources.

　B. Their intended use is to treat attention deficit hyperactivity disorder (ADHD).

　　1. According to the National Institute of Mental Health, ADHD is a common childhood disorder that can continue through adulthood.

　　2. The specific cause is unknown.

　　3. Symptoms of ADHD are difficulty staying focused and paying attention, difficulty controlling behavior, and hyperactivity.

　C. Each of these drugs has potentially harmful side effects noted by the manufacturers.

1. After researching each drug on Drugs.com or Livestrong.com, I discovered that each can have similar side effects (show list).
   a. Serious side effects across many of these drugs include seizures, fast or uneven heart rate, blurred vision, unusual behavior, twitching or tics, and extreme high blood pressure.
   b. Less serious side effects can be insomnia; loss of appetite; headaches; stomach and intestinal issues; feeling restless, anxious, or jittery; and extreme dry mouth.
2. Adderall and Ritalin tend to be the most common study drugs, so let's look at their side effects specifically.
   a. Adderall has major serious and less serious side effects.
      i. Adderall's known serious side effects are fast or uneven heartbeats; pain or burning when urinating; talking more than usual; feelings of extreme happiness or sadness; tremors, hallucinations, unusual behavior, or motor tics; and dangerously high blood pressure ("Adderall").
      ii. Adderall's less serious side effects are insomnia; stomach pain, nausea, or vomiting; loss of appetite; vision problems, dizziness, or mild headache; sweating; mild skin rash; numbness, tingling, or cold hands or feet; and weight loss ("Adderall").
   b. Ritalin has major serious and less serious side effects as well.
      i. Ritalin's known serious side effects are fast or uneven heartbeats; feeling like you might pass out; fever, sore throat, and headache, with a severe blistering, peeling, and red skin rash; aggression; restlessness; hallucinations, unusual behavior, or motor tics; and dangerously high blood pressure ("Ritalin").
      ii. Ritalin's less serious side effects are stomach pain, nausea, or vomiting; loss of appetite; vision problems,

After discussing all ADHD drugs used as study drugs, Megan then focuses in on the drugs most commonly used as study drugs.

Note how Megan uses proper outline symbols and only one sentence per outline point.

dizziness, or mild headache; sweating; mild skin rash; numbness, tingling, or cold hands or feet; insomnia; and weight loss ("Ritalin").

3. Without a doctor determining if you should take these drugs or monitoring your health as you do, you are taking your life into your own hands.

   a. Quoting the Substance Abuse & Mental Health Services Administration in her Feb. 10, 2013, article, Morris notes that "emergency room visits tied to use of an ADHD stimulant rose from 13,379 in 2005 to 31,244 just five years later."

   b. "The portion of those visits caused by nonprescribed use of the stimulants rose to half."

4. Our lackadaisical view on the nonprescribed use of these drugs begins early.

   a. Morris states that a survey conducted by the Partnership for a Drug-Free America discovered that "40 percent of teens think prescription drugs are 'much safer' to use than illegal drugs."

   b. "29 percent think prescription drugs are not addictive."

5. Because of these dangerous side effects, each drug requires a prescription.

6. The bottom line: Taking ADHD drugs without a prescription and supervision of a doctor is downright dangerous.

(**Link:** Now, let's consider the legal problems with taking these drugs without a prescription as well as the practice of selling them.)

II. Taking nonprescribed ADHD drugs is illegal.

   A. According to NOLO.com (March 2013), a site dedicated to helping consumers and small business with everyday legal questions,

---

Here, Megan appeals to logic with current facts. Note that she uses quotation marks when directly quoting from the article.

Megan unequivocally states her first claim.

the legality of a drug is inherently tied to its use and who has the right to use it.

B. A prescription drug being used by someone without a prescription in the state of Missouri is considered the illegal possession of a controlled dangerous substance (CDS), as stated on CriminalDefenseLawyer.com, March 2013. ◄

When citing her source, Megan includes the date to demonstrate currency.

1. "It is a class C felony in our state to possess CDS without a valid medical prescription" (Steiner "Possession").

2. "Penalties for possession include a fine of up to $5000; and either up to a year in jail, or at the sentencing judge's discretion, at least two (and up to seven) years in prison" (Steiner "Possession").

C. Selling or distributing a CDS is a serious offense that can vary depending on the substance, amount, and if crossing state lines.

1. Illegal CDS sale or possession with intent to sell, in this case as a study drug, "is a class B felony."

2. In this case, a class B felony is "punishable with at least five (and up to 15) years in prison" (Steiner "Missouri Sale").

D. The course of your future can change; possessing or selling ADHD drugs as illegal study drugs is a felony, which, if you are convicted of, can keep you from pursuing your career choice.

(**Link:** Even though it may seem safe because "everyone does it," taking ADHD drugs as a study aid is dangerous and not legal. Now that we have outlined the problem, let's look for better solutions.)

III. All students experience pressure and stress, but taking nonprescribed ADHD drugs is not the solution.

Megan wrote this main point in such a way as to signal the problem–solution organizational strategy and to alert the audience to where she is in the strategy.

A. When asked, students give numerous reasons for taking illegal study drugs.

1. Their parents have high expectations.
2. They commit to too much.
3. Getting into and staying in college is harder than ever.
4. They don't have the skills necessary to cope with stress.
5. Their peers pressure them to take the drugs, so they have more time to play. (Cooper, Morris, Schwarz, "Study Drugs")

B. The solution is better overall habits.

1. Dr. Crawford, the director of our student counseling service, offered this advice.

   a. Don't procrastinate and wait until the last minute to start that big project or study for a test.

   b. Don't take on more than you can manage.

   c. Be smart with your time.

      i. Do the homework first and use an outing with friends as a reward.

      ii. Use a calendar to help you manage your time and to break down large projects or study sessions into chunks.

      iii. Make exercise part of your routine.

      iv. Get enough sleep and make the time as routine as possible.

      v. Seek professional help from the counseling service to help you manage your time and deal with your anxieties.

2. StudentHacks.org, a site dedicated to productivity tips to help students study smarter, offers these suggestions.

   a. Eat frequent, small meals instead of large ones or starving yourself.

   b. Study when you're at your sharpest.

      i. Listen to your body clock, not to everyone else, about when you should study.

      ii. The morning is often the best time.

Megan knew many of the students trust and admire the director of the campus counseling service. So, she interviewed her for the speech.

    c. Drink water often and caffeine only in moderation.

    d. Prepare your study site for comfort and with only the things you need.

    e. Take a short break every hour.

        i. Set a time—it is important to take the break before you realize you are tired.

       ii. Stretch during the break.

      iii. Study at the same time and place—a place that is dedicated to only studying.

(**Link:** Clearly, the decision to work a little harder to achieve one's goals and to be smart about it is far better than succumbing to the usage of non-prescribed drugs.)

CONCLUSION

Audience response statement: Clearly, the decision to work a little harder to achieve one's goals and to be smart about it is far better than succumbing to the usage of nonprescribed drugs. I urge you all to opt for alternative solutions to cope with the stress of school and outside activities. These options are simple, safe, and legal. These options are what the successful students take—not a drug.

Summary statement: Using ADHD drugs as nonprescribed study drugs is dangerous, even life threatening. Using ADHD drugs as nonprescribed study drugs is illegal, with potential fines and prison time, and may influence what you can do with your future. It is a felony!

WOW statement: Make smarter choices to be a better student by preparing each day. As an African proverb states, "For tomorrow belongs to the people who are prepared for it today" ("Future").

Megan uses repetition and parallelism stylistically here, to highlight her language. She ends the summary with a pathos appeal to fear of what the drugs can do. This mirrors her introduction.

Works Cited

"Adderall." *Drugs.com*, 2013, www.drugs.com/adderall.html. Accessed 10 Mar. 2013.

"Concerta Side Effects." *Livestrong.com*, 9 Dec. 2009, www.livestrong.com.

Cooper, Aaron. "College Students Take ADHD Drugs for Better Grades." *CNN*, 1 Sept. 2011, www.cnn.com/2011/09/01/health/drugs-adderall-concentration/.

Crawford, Julie. Personal interview. 3 Mar. 2013.

"Drug Laws and Drug Crimes." *NOLO*, 2013, www.nolo.com/legal-encyclopedia /drug-laws-drug-crimes-32252.html. Accessed 10 Mar. 2013.

"Focalin." *Drugs.com*, 2013, www.drugs.com/focalin.html. Accessed 10 Mar. 2013.

"Future." *ThinkExist.com*, 2013, thinkexist.com. Accessed 10 Mar. 2013.

"How to Study Effectively—8 Concentration Strategies." *StudentHacks.org*, 2007, StudentHacks.org. Accessed 10 Mar. 2013.

Morris, Caitlin. "More College Students Abusing ADHD Drugs." *The Record* [Troy], 10 Feb. 2013, www.troyrecord.com/article/TR/20130210/NEWS/302109994.

National Institute of Mental Health (NIMH). *Attention Deficit Hyperactivity Disorder* (ADHD). NIH Publication no. 08-3572, NIMH, 2008.

"Ritalin." *Drugs.com*, 2013, www.drugs.com/ritalin.html. Accessed 10 Mar. 2013.

Rose, Gianna. "Vyvanse Negative Side Effects." *Livestrong.com*, 31 Mar. 2011, www .livestrong.com/article/163897-vyvanse-negative-side-effects/.

Schwarz, Alan. "In Their Own Words: 'Study Drugs.'" *The New York Times*, 9 June 2012, www.nytimes.com/interactive/2012/06/10/education/stimulants-student-voices .html?_r=0.

Steiner, Monica. "Missouri Sale of a Controlled Substance Laws." *Criminal Defense Lawyer*, NOLO, 2013, www.criminaldefenselawyer.com/resources/criminal-defense /drug-charges/sale-controlled-substance-missouri. Accessed 10 Mar. 2013.

---. "Possession of a Controlled Substance in Missouri." *Criminal Defense Lawyer*, NOLO, 2013, www.criminaldefenselawyer.com/resources/criminal-defense /drug-charges/missouri-drug-possession-laws. Accessed 10 Mar. 2013.

"'Study Drugs' Popular Among High School Students." *The New York Times*, 9 June 2012, www.nytimes.com/interactive/2012/06/10/education/study-drugs-popular -among-high-school-students.html.

On her source page, Megan follows proper MLA style for each citation and for the overall format of the page. She uses hanging indents, alphabetizes the entries, double-spaces, and makes sure each entry is correct.

Even though Megan's class assignment required a minimum of only three sources, she used many more to effectively persuade her audience.

16.5 What Should You Consider When Preparing to Present a Persuasive Speech?

1 Language

2 Delivery

3 Presentation Aids

1

Language

Effective language is a must if you intend to persuade. Emotive and stylistic language helps your audience follow and remember your arguments and be emotionally moved. Remember, language is grounded in culture, is extremely powerful, and creates meaning. Select your language carefully and purposefully. To review, your language should be:

- Accurate—correct, familiar, and concrete
- Appropriate—suitable to you, your audience, and the situation
- Conversational—in word choice, sentence structure, and delivery aspects
- Distinctive—vivid language and unique speech devices

Think about how your use of transitions such as *therefore* and *as a result of* might clearly signal the bridge between two steps in an argument, or how you can use language ethically to stir the emotions of your audience. For example, instead of using common phrases in his 2013 State of the Union address, President Barack Obama used these:

> **Together, we have cleared away the rubble of crisis . . .**

> **It is our generation's task, then, to reignite the true engine of America's economic growth—a rising, thriving middle class.**

He also utilized repetition of key phrases such as these:

> **They deserve a vote.**

> **. . . the way we're made.**

→ See Chapter 9 for detailed help with using effective language.

2
Delivery

If you want to persuade an audience to agree with you, your delivery must be powerful and direct. Your voice and body language should suggest a high level of confidence and trust. You want an enthusiastic and varying vocal quality as well as good eye contact. Your posture should be lively and energetic. Your voice and body should be saying, "I believe what I am saying with my heart and soul. This is exciting!"

Remember to create a delivery outline containing just enough words, phrases, and delivery notes to jog your memory. Practice from the preparation outline the first few times, but then use the delivery outline. Rehearse your speech until you know it well, so that you won't rely on your notes and can make better eye contact with your audience. Also, prepare yourself the day of the speech by dressing appropriately. Often, you need to dress in business causal or more professional attire to help bolster your persuasive ethos. Prior to the speech, check out the space and necessary equipment, review your delivery outline, and inspect your presentation aids.

→ See pages 142–143 in Chapter 6 for a sample delivery outline and Chapter 10 for more delivery hints.

3
Presentation Aids

Presentation aids are frequently necessary for a persuasive speech, to help your audience understand facts and figures or follow the logic of an argument. Likewise, aids can be very emotionally provocative and persuasive in their own right. They are often a great addition to speeches when calling for action, when your audience is apathetic about your topic, or if you are arguing a proposition of value. Keep in mind that aids should support your speech; don't add them on just because you can.

Megan planned a slideshow for her speech. During the introduction, she will use a brief video highlighting how study-drug usage destroyed three young adults' lives. During the body of the speech, she will use slides with tables, quotations, and photos.

Megan practiced with her slideshow several times and made a checklist for inspecting the equipment the day of her speech.

→ See Chapter 11 for help with presentation aids.

1

INTRODUCTION

ATTENTION-GETTER: *(slide)* "My use of Adderall as a study aid, 20 mg every so often, quickly escalated into 100 mg+ daily doses …" –Female student, 20, Pittsburgh (Schwarz)

CREDIBILITY MATERIAL: my psychology class's research

RELEVANCE TO AU
more abused than
30% report usage
our survey: 6 of y

PREVIEW OF SPEE
(Link: First, let's ex
prescription.)

2

BODY

I. **Taking nonprescribed ADHD drugs is dangerous.**

   A. *(Show chart)* amphetamines or methylphenidates powerful central nervous system stimulants (remember source)

   B. Their intended use is to treat attention deficit hyperactivity disorder (ADHD).

      1. National Institute of Mental Health: ADHD is a childhood disorder

      2. cause is unknown

      3. symptoms of ADHD

OBJECTIVE 16.6: **DEMONSTRATE HOW TO EVALUATE A PERSUASIVE SPEECH**

16.6 How Do You Evaluate a Persuasive Speech?

1 **Listen Effectively**
2 **Evaluate the Speech Message**
3 **Evaluate for Fallacies**
4 **Evaluate the Presentation**

1

Listen Effectively

As the transactional model of communication from Chapter 1 indicates, speaker and audience are equally responsible for engaging in the process of communicating. Listening is essential to fulfill that responsibility. As a speaker, you need to work at helping your audience listen effectively; and as an audience member, it is your responsibility to listen actively and critically. When persuasion is the goal, critical listening is even more important.

For example, suppose you already agree with Megan. You should still question the believability of her facts and statistics. For example, is it possible that 30 percent of college students take nonprescribed study drugs? If you don't agree with Megan's preview in the introduction, can you suspend your judgment to consider the facts in her presentation?

> **CONFIDENCE BOOSTER**
>
> Critically listening to the persuasive speeches and arguments created by others will help you learn how to create stronger arguments and recognize your own faulty arguments. These skills will give you confidence to be an effective creator and consumer of persuasive messages.

388 **CHAPTER 16** THE PERSUASIVE SPEECH

2

Evaluate the Speech Message

Evaluate the message for clarity, accuracy, and overall organization.

- Is the topic persuasive?
- Is the speech designed to speak to a particular target audience?
- Is the evidence effective and appropriate?
- Are the sources credible and current?
- Is the information presented believable? If not, did the speaker attempt to help the audience view it as believable?

A persuasive speech should never lose sight of its central idea, its proposition, its target audience, and what it is trying to change or reinforce in the audience.

For example, Megan outlined the problem and argued for a preferred solution. On the Internet, Megan had located a *New York Times* article that included student interviews telling how ADHD drugs had influenced their lives, as well as persuasive legal material related to her state. The use of this support material allowed Megan to focus her message for her target audience (younger adult students in her state).

→ See the checklist on page 395 for a detailed evaluation format, or follow your instructor's guidelines.

3

Evaluate for Fallacies

One of the main ways a persuasive speech differs from other speeches is the reliance on effective arguments within the speech.

As noted in Chapter 15, when a speaker creates an argument, she or he can unintentionally or intentionally create a faulty argument or error in logic known as a ***fallacy***. Fallacies occur when you use evidence incorrectly or your interpretation of the evidence is incorrect.

Whether you are the speaker or an audience member, you need to be able to recognize when an argument falls apart or does not make sense, making it a bad argument.

There are numerous fallacies, but the table on the following pages explains some of the most common. For detailed discussions of these and additional fallacies, you can seek out books such as *Classical Rhetoric for the Modern Student* by Edward Corbett and Robert Connors and *An Introduction to Reasoning* by Stephen Toulmin, Richard Rieke, and Allan Janik. You can also locate more types and descriptions online by searching with the term "fallacies."

→ See pages 390–393 for a list of the most common fallacies.

PRACTICING ETHICS: Ask Questions

As a member of a democratic society, and one that bombards you with multiple messages daily, you must be willing to ask the hard questions to ensure your safety and the safety of others: Is this true? Who stands to gain? Are these sources unbiased? This is true whether you are a speaker or an audience member—or a media consumer.

FALLACY	WHAT IS IT?	EXAMPLES
Non sequitur	Not connecting an argument's conclusion to the premises (*Non sequitur* is Latin for "it does not follow.")	"If you do not buy this for me, you do not love me."
Hasty generalization	Drawing a general conclusion without sufficient support materials	"Two of my friends bought that album and hated it. That band is horrible."
Faulty use of authority	Using information or testimony from someone who is not a legitimate authority on the subject	Actors or athletes endorsing a product as the best when they are not experts on that product Using testimony from individuals who are not experts but are convenient; for example: "My roommate agrees that the tuition increase is too high."
Post hoc ergo propter hoc	Assuming that because one event comes after another, the first event caused the second (*Post hoc ergo propter hoc* is Latin for "after this, therefore because of this.")	"Last month, the city council passed an ordinance banning smoking in public places. The ordinance caused two pub to go bankrupt."
Ad hominem	Attacking the person instead of challenging an argument (*Ad hominem* is Latin for "to or against the person.")	"Who are *you* to question my decision? You didn't finish school." "That candidate would be a bad president. The National Organization for Women supports him."
Appeal to tradition	Assuming something is best or correct because it is traditional	"My grandfather bought a Ford, my father bought a Ford, so Ford must be best."

HOW OR WHY MIGHT IT HAPPEN?	WHAT EFFECTS COULD IT HAVE?	HOW CAN YOU AVOID IT?
You use faulty deductive reasoning in which your conclusion doesn't follow from your argument.	Your conclusion may be true or false, but you will confuse your audience because you haven't connected the dots.	Be sure every step of your argument leads to the next and connects to the claim.
You use faulty inductive reasoning (specific cases to the general claim), or jump to your point too quickly or without substance.	Your audience will not believe you. Even if your claim may be true, you haven't proven it.	Use a significant number of current and quality cases to argue from the specific to the general.
The source has insufficient expertise or is not an expert in the area under discussion. The area of expertise is not a legitimate discipline or area. Most other experts disagree with this expert. The expert is biased. The speaker does not identify the source's qualifications.	You may unethically persuade your audience, or they may view your argument as weak.	Make sure the person is a recognized expert related to the topic, and note her or his expertise during the speech.
You use faulty causal reasoning by drawing a conclusion when sequence alone is not enough to support the claim. Or, the events have no actual relationship.	You could create a false argument by saying that one thing causes something else to happen when it doesn't.	Verify with valid support materials that one event causes the other. Spend time during your speech helping your audience see how the two events relate.
Speakers divert the audience's attention from the real issue by attacking a person who is associated with a claim that presents a counterargument or by challenging that person's claim. This type of fallacy happens most often in debates or campaigns.	The fallacy distracts the audience or incites an aggressive emotional response that prevents them from engaging in logical reasoning.	Focus your argument on the issues being discussed and not the people discussing them. When you do discuss the people, only consider issues and traits related to the speech topic or claim.
This fallacy assumes older, traditional, or "that is always the way we do it" is best.	It prevents the audience from engaging in critical thinking by using only one criterion (tradition) to support a claim.	Base your claims on evidence such as facts, statistics, and testimony, and use tradition only to supplement that evidence.

FALLACY	WHAT IS IT?	EXAMPLES
False analogy	Comparing two things that are not similar or are dissimilar in a radical or important way related to the claim	Comparing campus life on a small liberal arts campus to that of a large state-university campus when trying to argue that they are really the same
Either-or fallacy	Considering only two options when there are more possible options	**"You are either for prayer in schools or you are an atheist."** In his 1968 presidential campaign, Eldridge Cleaver created this type of fallacy, to force voter choice, when he expressed the now-famous words, **"You're either part of the solution or part of the problem."**
Straw person	Ignoring the key components of a person's actual position and substituting it with a misrepresented version of his/her claim	**"Some senators want to give the wealthy all the tax breaks. They don't care about the poor and middle class.**
Ad populum	Arguing a claim is accurate because many people believe it or do it (*Ad populum* is Latin for "to the people.")	**"Most people in St. Louis voted for candidate A; the state of Missouri must be for candidate A."**
Faulty emotional appeal	Using only emotional appeal or unethically manipulating an audience's emotions to get them to accept a claim	A speech inducing fear that eating pork could transmit the H1N1 virus, rather than looking at the evidence that suggests transmission from pig to human is rare, would be a faulty appeal to fear.
Slippery slope	Arguing that a small event sets off a chain reaction to disaster	**"If you drop out of school, you will take drugs, become an alcoholic, and end up in jail."**

HOW OR WHY MIGHT IT HAPPEN?	WHAT EFFECTS COULD IT HAVE?	HOW CAN YOU AVOID IT?
This happens most often when the things being compared seem similar in superficial ways but in fact have important differences.	You might mislead your audience into believing two dissimilar things are similar, or fail to persuade because your audience realizes that the comparison is not equal.	Make sure that the two things being compared are similar, at least in the characteristics important to your claim.
The speaker fails to consider the range of options and tends to think in extremes. This fallacy can even occur when more than two choices are considered but the speaker still fails to offer other extremely viable options. This type of fallacy occurs often in arguments for changing a policy or offering a solution.	This can be a form of coercion. In any case, you are unethically limiting your audience's decision-making abilities.	The best solution is to never set up an either-or argument and to be as inclusive as possible when offering options.
When misrepresenting the other person's position, you might substitute a weaker, distorted, or exaggerated version. Basically, their claim is wrong or flimsy because you make it that way.	You might mislead your audience by distracting them from the truth of the argument.	To prevent this type of fallacy, always refute and state the other person's arguments as presented.
Also called *appeal to the masses* or *bandwagon fallacy*, this fallacy is similar to the faulty use of authority and the appeal to tradition.	This type of fallacy distracts the audience's attention from examining a claim.	Use popular opinion only to supplement other forms of evidence.
Faulty emotional appeals may manipulate a variety of emotions such as fear, wishful thinking, spite, and flattery. A speaker who stirs up an audience's feelings by strong provocation is a *demagogue*. For example, Adolf Hitler was a demagogue, preying on the fears of the people.	Unethical manipulation often evokes irrelevant emotions and draws attention away from logic or conceals something.	Use emotional appeals wisely, ethically, and sparingly—and always in conjunction with other forms of appeal.
You attempt to control via fear grounded in speculation. This is a form of faulty emotional appeal.	This fallacy avoids the main event by shifting attention to extreme hypothetical events.	Always consider the middle ground as a potential end result, and do not be overly dramatic.

4

Evaluate the Presentation

Successful delivery techniques rarely draw attention to themselves, but they help the audience stay interested in the speech while the speaker (you or another) builds ethos. Persuading an audience is difficult and will not happen if the speaker does not effectively use voice, gestures, and enthusiasm, or use an appropriate delivery style or presentation aids. If Megan's enthusiasm is low, or she doesn't make good eye contact, or she is too lighthearted or insincere, she will not convince those audience members who don't view taking study drugs as a problem. She needs to use a delivery style that supports the urgency and seriousness of the topic.

Critical listening and effective evaluation are key to the consumption of persuasive speeches. Here's a quick review of how to critically listen and offer an effective evaluation. Remember to offer a description, a judgment, a justification, and a rationale for what you hear and see.

DESCRIPTION
When you used that personal narrative by the student addicted to study drugs ...

JUDGMENT
That sort of scared me.

JUSTIFICATION
The moment was so real and it really made me stop and think about how stupid it might be to take these drugs.

RATIONALE
I think most students aren't really going to be logically persuaded. I think you have to use the appeal to emotions to scare them into believing that study drugs are dangerous and stupid.

The checklist on the next page, or guidelines provided by your instructor, will help you evaluate persuasive speeches.

→ See Tab 5 if you need more guidance on critically listening to and evaluating a speech.

> **TIP: Evaluating Persuasive Speaking**
>
> You know that the effectiveness of a persuasive speech relies on successful reasoning, quality evidence, and adhering to a strong strategy. As a listener and a critic offering advice, you may find it beneficial to take notes during the speech to diagram the logic for each main point.

CHECKLIST FOR EVALUATING THE PERSUASIVE SPEECH

TOPIC
.... Speech accomplished purpose to persuade
.... Topic appropriate to speaker, audience, and occasion
.... Interesting topic

INTRODUCTION
.... Gained attention and interest
.... Established credibility
.... Indicated relevance to audience
.... Declared central idea
.... Previewed speech

BODY
.... Main points clear and obvious to the audience
.... Points follow an appropriate organizational strategy
.... Main points appropriately researched and supported
.... Used effective proofs/arguments
.... Main points supported with appropriate presentation aids when necessary
.... Oral citations included throughout speech
.... Linked parts of speech

CONCLUSION
.... Contained a summary statement
.... Offered an audience response statement
.... Effectively comes to closure (WOW statement)

PRESENTATION
.... Language was clear, concise, and appropriate
.... Gestures/body movements were effective
.... Consistent and effective eye contact
.... Used vocal variety/emphasis/volume/rate
.... Used appropriate delivery style
.... Spoke with enthusiasm
.... Spoke with conviction and sincerity
.... Good use of delivery outline
.... Presentation aids appropriate to speech topic (if applicable)
.... Used presentation aids throughout entire speech (if applicable)
.... Used professional presentation aids (if applicable)
.... Speech met time requirements

Chapter 16: Review

ASSESSING YOUR KNOWLEDGE

16.1 What Is the Creative Process for Persuasive Speaking?

Objective 16.1: **EXPLAIN THE CREATIVE PROCESS FOR PERSUASIVE SPEAKING**

Persuasive speaking follows the general speech creative process—starting, researching, creating, presenting, and listening and evaluating—but emphasizes making a deliberate attempt to create, reinforce, or change your audience's attitudes, beliefs, values, or behaviors. Knowing where your audience stands on an issue, locating effective persuasive material, and putting together a strong argument are paramount.

→ See pages 360–361.

16.2 How Do You Choose a Focused Persuasive Topic?

Objective 16.2: **DESCRIBE HOW TO CHOOSE A FOCUSED PERSUASIVE TOPIC**

- Get to know the audience and situation.
- Create a persuasive idea bank of controversial or debatable topics.
- Select and narrow your persuasive topic.
- Confirm the best type of persuasive speech.
- Identify your specific purpose.
- Identify your central idea.
- Create a working outline.

→ See pages 362–369.

16.3 How Do You Research the Persuasive Speech?

Objective 16.3: **EXPLORE HOW TO RESEARCH THE PERSUASIVE SPEECH**

Seek out persuasive support material from a wide variety of sources and perspectives. Be extremely ethical and responsible by doing everything you can to prevent accidental or intentional deception, and to avoid just "saying so" because you believe something.

→ See pages 370–371.

16.4 How Do You Outline and Organize a Persuasive Speech?

Objective 16.4: **DISCUSS HOW TO OUTLINE AND ORGANIZE A PERSUASIVE SPEECH**

- Start with basic, effective outlining. Be sure your outline includes necessary header information, an introduction, the body of the speech, and a conclusion; uses complete sentences; contains source citations within the outline; and includes a source page. As you create your persuasive outline, evaluating the strength of your argument will be easier the more detailed you are.
- Commit to an appropriate persuasive strategy. You may potentially choose from all organizational strategies discussed in Chapter 7. The common and more effective persuasive strategies are causal, comparative, problem–solution, and Monroe's motivated sequence.
- Construct main points.
- Organize support materials into arguments.
- Compose your introduction and conclusion. The introduction should include an attention-getter, credibility material, relevance to audience, and a preview. In a persuasive speech, it should begin to focus your audience's attention on what your claim will be. The conclusion should include a summary, audience response, and WOW statement. It should inspire your audience one more time to create, reinforce, or change their attitudes, beliefs, values, or behaviors.

→ See pages 372–385.

16.5 What Should You Consider When Preparing to Present a Persuasive Speech?

Objective 16.5: **EXPLORE HOW TO PRESENT A PERSUASIVE SPEECH**

You should carefully consider your language, delivery, and need for presentation aids. Effective language is a must if you intend to persuade. Emotive and stylistic language helps your audience follow and remember your arguments and be emotionally moved. If you want to persuade an audience to agree with you, your delivery must be powerful and direct. Presentation aids are frequently necessary for a persuasive speech, to help your audience understand facts and figures or follow the logic of an argument. They can be very emotionally provocative and persuasive in their own right.

→ See pages 386–387.

16.6 How Do You Evaluate a Persuasive Speech?

Objective 16.6: **DEMONSTRATE HOW TO EVALUATE A PERSUASIVE SPEECH**

Listen effectively. Evaluate the speech message for how persuasive it is. Evaluate for fallacies, or errors in logic. Evaluate the presentation for techniques that help convince, stimulate, or actuate an audience.

→ See pages 388–395.

TERMS TO REMEMBER

target audience (362)
primacy model (375)
recency model (375)
fallacy (389)
non sequitur (390)
hasty generalization (390)
faulty use of authority (390)
post hoc ergo propter hoc (390)
ad hominem (390)
appeal to tradition (390)
false analogy (392)
either-or fallacy (392)
straw person (392)
ad populum (392)
faulty emotional appeal (392)
slippery slope (392)
demagogue (393)

Practical Pointers for Tab 7

FAQs

What kinds of topics are debatable?

For a topic to be persuasive, it must be debatable. In other words, it must be something that people can reasonably have differing opinions on. A debatable topic has more than one side to it (e.g., the abortion issue). It is not something generally agreed upon or accepted as fact by most people (e.g., traditional cars produce carbon dioxide). It is best to select a topic you can be passionate about or interested in. Here are a few examples to help you start brainstorming:

- Are hybrid vehicles better than nonhybrids?
- Should states implement voter ID requirements?
- Should all citizens be required to participate in community service?
- Can we reverse the effects of global warming?
- Should all students face mandatory drug testing?
- Is the No Child Left Behind Act working?
- Are 12-hour shifts for nurses safe?
- How should the United States prevent illegal immigration?
- Is the death penalty effective as a deterrent to serious crimes?
- Is homeschooling better than public schooling?
- Is online education effective?
- Are cell phones dangerous?
- Should the United States institute bilingual education?
- Should all employers offer birth control through health insurance?

What should I do if my audience resists my claim?

Trying to convince your audience to make big changes or serious moral decisions is difficult at best. It might be better to ask them to take a small step toward a big change rather than a momentous one. For example, asking your audience to walk to work once a week or turn off most electrical appliances for one evening hour a week might be more successful than persuading them to give up their car or electricity completely. Speeches arguing for abortion in cases of rape or incest, or speeches arguing for the death penalty for repeat offenders of very serious crimes, might work better than those arguing for pro-choice views or support for the death penalty in general.

If the audience verbally resists, stay calm, relaxed, and resolute; consider their points of view; and ask them simply to allow you to present your point of view. Keep in mind that they have a right to disagree with you.

ADDITIONAL SUPPORT

For more ideas for persuasive topics, browse these sites:

www.ereadingworksheets.com/writing /persuasive-essay-topics

www.speech-topics-help.com/persuasive -speech-ideas.html

For more tips on persuasive speaking, see:

blog.ted.com/2012/10/31/how-to-give -more-persuasive-presentations-a-qa -with-nancy-duarte

TAB 8
Speaking on Special Occasions

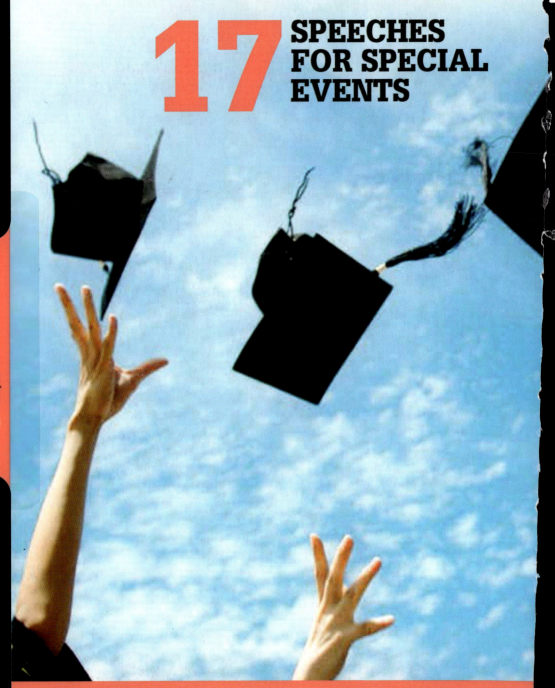

17 SPEECHES FOR SPECIAL EVENTS

17.1 What Are Special Occasion Speeches?

1 Speeches to Celebrate
2 Speeches to Commemorate
3 Speeches to Inspire
4 Speeches to Entertain

A ***special occasion speech*** has the general purpose to celebrate, commemorate, inspire, or entertain. The speaker's intent is to mark the occasion by making it a time to rejoice, honor, arouse, or amuse.

The special occasion speech is unique in that it often seems like it brings public speaking into the home or heart. It intertwines public speaking with your personal life, as wedding toasts do. For example, Andy has been best friends with Joe since grade school. Several months ago, Joe asked Stephanie to marry him and asked Andy to be his best man. When Andy told his dad, his father noted that Andy would be expected to give a toast at the wedding reception. Although you could be asked to give a special occasion speech because of who you are professionally, some aspect of the special occasion is usually tied to the daily lives of the speaker and the audience.

Special occasion speeches accentuate the extraordinary events in life, marking rites of passage, celebrating new beginnings, paying tribute to those you admire or love, and sometimes even entertaining your audience.

Let us celebrate the occasion with wine and sweet words.[1]

PLAUTUS

1
Speeches to Celebrate

Speeches to celebrate will honor or highlight a person, group, institution, place, or event. You may give a speech to celebrate at such events as weddings, anniversaries, retirements, banquets, welcome sessions, and birthdays. The speaker should praise the subject(s) of the special occasion and adhere to the expected customs of the group hosting the event. The tone of your speech should complement the personality of the person, group, institution, place, or event being celebrated.

2
Speeches to Commemorate

Speeches to commemorate pay tribute to or remember a person, group, institution, place, or event. Unlike the speech to celebrate, which honors the event of the moment (e.g., an eleventh birthday), speeches to commemorate reside more in the past or future, such as a speech marking the anniversary of the September 11 attacks or the death of Senator Ted Kennedy. In these examples, the events really being remembered are September 11, 2001, and the past life of Senator Kennedy. The focus of the speech to commemorate can touch thousands or be closer to home, as with the death of a local police officer or a family member. This type of speech should reflect the personality of the person or the tone of the group, institution, place, or event being commemorated, and it should consider the needs of the audience as well as the cultural expectations of the speaking event.

3
Speeches to Inspire

Speeches to inspire are created to motivate, stir, encourage, or arouse the audience. Commencement speeches, keynote addresses, inaugural speeches, sermons, and daily devotionals are often examples of speeches to inspire. Inspirational speeches may reflect the personality and professional status of the speaker, but the main considerations are the needs of the audience and the expectations of the speaking event.

4
Speeches to Entertain

Speeches to entertain have the general goal to amuse, delight, and engage the audience for the purpose of enjoyment, with a bit of wisdom or tribute thrown in, depending on the special occasion. Speeches given at banquets, award dinners, and roasts are often speeches to entertain. These speeches are expected to be cheery, playful, light, and usually optimistic, but they may have an underlying serious message that can be informative or persuasive.

PRACTICING ETHICS: Cultural Sensitivity

Special occasion speeches are very culturally specific and embedded. Make yourself aware of protocol and cultural expectations. Be audience centered.

17.2 What Is the Creative Process for Special Occasion Speaking?

Speeches for special occasions are some of the most creative you will ever present. They bring public speaking into your daily life to celebrate, commemorate, inspire, and entertain audiences during extraordinary times.

The table on the next page briefly reviews the five basic activities from Chapter 1 that you use to create an effective speech. Remember, being creative is not a linear process, so move back and forth between each activity as you mold your speech.

You can apply the process to any special occasion speech. The far right column in the table offers the example of Jeremy, who is the student president at his college. He has been asked to give a brief speech at the groundbreaking ceremony for a new student commons building. There will be several other speakers, so Jeremy decides he wants to focus specifically on inspiring students' pride in the new building.

THE CREATIVE PROCESS	SPECIAL OCCASION EXAMPLE

1 STARTING

DETERMINE THE PURPOSE AND TYPE OF SPEECH
➜ See page 404

Jeremy determines that he needs to give a speech to inspire.

ANALYZE THE AUDIENCE AND SITUATION
➜ See page 405

His speech will be outdoors, during homecoming. He will be one of seven speakers to speak for three minutes each.

FOCUS ON A CENTRAL IDEA
➜ See page 406

Jeremy wants to inspire pride and anticipation. His central idea is:

> This is the beginning of a special place for interaction, inspiration, and revitalization.

2 RESEARCHING

RESEARCH YOUR SPEECH
➜ See page 406

Jeremy served on the building's design committee, so he consults his notes to create a list of what the building will offer.

3 CREATING

OUTLINE AND ORGANIZE YOUR SPEECH
➜ See page 407

Introduction: This is the beginning…
I. A safe haven where study groups and friendships will grow.
II. A meeting place where important decisions will be made and explored.
III. A quiet corner to relax after a full day of study.
Conclusion: This is the beginning…this is a building we can call our own. Home.

4 PRESENTING

PRACTICE YOUR SPEECH
➜ See page 407

Jeremy will speak at a televised event with dignitaries, so he creates and practices with a manuscript.

5 LISTENING & EVALUATING

EVALUATE THE SPECIAL OCCASION SPEECH
➜ See page 407

Jeremy asks several classmates and professors to evaluate his speech. He also plans to watch the video later to self-evaluate.

17.3 How Do You Write a Special Occasion Speech?

1 **Determine the Purpose and Type of Speech**

2 **Analyze the Audience and Situation**

3 **Focus on a Central Idea**

4 **Research Your Speech**

5 **Outline and Organize Your Speech**

6 **Practice Your Speech**

7 **Evaluate the Special Occasion Speech**

1

Determine the Purpose and Type of Speech

You can create a special occasion speech much like you would an informative or persuasive speech. The primary difference is that this speech is determined by the occasion more than almost anything else. With most speeches, you first focus on understanding your audience. With the special occasion speech, you start by determining your purpose.

When you are invited to deliver the speech, ask about the purpose of the occasion. If the person inviting you is not able to answer your questions, seek out someone directly related to the occasion. Find out if you are speaking at a special meeting, conference, or ceremony. Knowing the focus or theme of the event can help you determine your topic. Does the event or its audience come with certain expectations or wishes? Should the speech celebrate, commemorate, inspire, or entertain? Know what the organizers expect. For example, for the speech about the new student commons building (page 403), Jeremy knew he would be speaking at a groundbreaking ceremony during the weeklong homecoming events at his college.

TIP: Clarifying the Speech Type

You should pay attention to how the person offering you the invitation to speak talks about the speech event. His or her description of the event or topic might give you clues to the type of speech expected.

Now you want to determine if you should give a speech to celebrate, commemorate, inspire, or entertain, and also establish the type of special occasion speech. In general, the type of speech you give will match up to one of the following general purposes.

GENERAL PURPOSE	TYPE OF SPEECH
Speech to celebrate	Toast or roast Introduction Award presentation or acceptance
Speech to commemorate	Eulogy or tribute
Speech to inspire	Speeches of inspiration, such as sermons, commencement addresses, or motivational talks
Speech to entertain	After-dinner speech

Although the lines between these purposes seem to blur, you will only have one purpose for each type of speech. For example, a eulogy is a speech to commemorate but can celebrate a life as well. Your general purpose is to commemorate; your speech's tone is celebratory.

→ See "What Are the Types of Special Occasion Speeches?" (pages 408–419) for more information on each.

2
Analyze the Audience and Situation

Understanding the exact special occasion tells you a lot about what you need to do in your speech, but you still need to analyze the audience and the details of the situation.

When considering your audience, ask:

Who will be in the audience?
Determine general characteristics, special needs, and size. For example, a college commencement speech included this:

> When I asked the staff to tell me about you, they told me that 65 percent of you graduating today are African American … I remembered that … most low-income and first-generation students, as well as students of color, are less likely to attend four-year institutions and persist through degree completion.
>
> Do you know how many U.S. residents hold a bachelor's degree as of 2011? According to the Census Bureau, just over 30 percent…. If you are black, that number drops to 19 percent, and 14.1 percent if you are Hispanic. Today, you will increase those numbers—you should be proud.

This speaker merged information from the staff with statistics from other sources.

When you are analyzing the situation, ask:

Where will I speak?
Ascertain the size of the room, if there will be a lectern and/or microphone, and other details.

Will someone introduce me? Will there be other speakers?
If so, coordinate with the persons involved.

How long should I speak?
Know what the organizers expect.

→ See Chapter 2 for more on audience and situation analysis.

3
Focus on a Central Idea

Central ideas for longer special occasion speeches, such as keynote addresses or nomination speeches, will be similar to those of informative or persuasive speeches. Shorter special occasion speeches, such as toasts or award acceptance speeches, will focus more on a theme. For example, if you return to Andy's wedding toast, his central idea is:

Special people deserve special people in their lives.

Jeremy's (from page 403) is:

This is the beginning of a special place for interaction, inspiration, and revitalization.

Although these central ideas do not tell you exactly what will be said, they establish themes. Both speakers are now ready to brainstorm main points.

If you are giving a longer special occasion speech, take the time to draft working main points to guide your research.

Later in this chapter are specific suggestions for what to include in each type of special occasion speech. For now, use these questions as you draft working main points:

- What ideas first came to mind when you were invited to give the speech?
- If you were invited because of your expertise or profession, how might that focus your content?
- What might the audience know about you that would help you focus?
- If you had to select three things for your audience to remember, consider, believe, or enjoy, what would they be?

→ See Chapter 3 for how to craft a central idea.

4
Research Your Speech

Depending on the type of special occasion speech, your research may be more personally reflective (from within your own experience) or you may need to do more formal research. For a wedding toast, you will use your own knowledge of and experience with the couple, but for an award presentation, you might need to research the history of the award and the recipient. In the example on page 403, Jeremy used the notes he took as a member of the building design committee to support his speech. Some speeches to inspire, such as a commencement speech, can require a lot of research, depending on the main points covered. Here are some questions that might guide your research.

- Are there special issues related to the occasion that require detailed understanding of a person, group, institution, place, or event? What do you need to know and tell your audience?
- What materials (quotations, statistics, facts, etc.) might you need to locate related to your *topic* to celebrate, commemorate, inspire, or entertain this audience?
- What materials (quotations, statistics, facts, etc.) related to your *audience* might you need to help them celebrate, commemorate, be inspired, or be entertained?

→ See Tab 2 for more on research.

PRACTICING ETHICS: Plagiarism

Examples of special occasion speeches are plentiful on the Internet. They can give you ideas, but it is inappropriate—and plagiarism—to use one of these as your own.

5 Outline and Organize Your Speech

Outlining is as important to the special occasion speech as it is to the informative or persuasive speech, to help you avoid rambling or forgetting important parts. Even the shortest special occasion speech will include an introduction, a body, and a conclusion. However, you may condense the parts into one, two, or three sentences. Use links to connect key points and to lead your audience through the speech. The chronological, topical, spatial, and comparative strategies are most common in special occasion speeches.

INTRODUCTION
 Attention-getter
 Credibility material
 Relevance to audience
 Preview of speech

Short speeches may incorporate all of these in one sentence.

BODY
 I. First main point
 II. Second main point
 III. Third main point

Very short speeches may have only one main point.

CONCLUSION
 Summary statement
 Audience response
  statement
 WOW statement

Should reflect the mood of your audience and speech.

Note Jeremy's outline on page 403. Jeremy uses only three points, because the speech will be very short. He focuses on creating a sense of new beginnings and home.

→ See Tab 3 for more on outlining and speech construction.

6 Practice Your Speech

Most special occasion speeches will contain celebratory or inspirational language and will be delivered extemporaneously because they are part of everyday life and need to come from the heart, not a piece of paper. However, for special situations like Jeremy's (speaking for television and with dignitaries) or longer speeches (such as commencement or keynote addresses), manuscripts are often better for adhering to time, details, and effective delivery. In either case, rehearse until your delivery sounds confident and natural.

7 Evaluate the Special Occasion Speech

Unless you are giving special occasion speeches as part of a class assignment, they are rarely formally evaluated. However, you still want to make sure you have covered the necessary parts, used appropriate organization, and crafted a speech appropriate to the audience, topic, and occasion.

CHECKLIST for Evaluating a Special Occasion Speech

❑ Does my speech include an introduction, relevant main points, and a conclusion?
❑ Am I using an appropriate organizational strategy?
❑ Is my language clear, vivid, and appropriate?
❑ Is the length of my speech appropriate?
❑ Is my delivery dynamic and enthusiastic?
❑ If appropriate, am I delivering the speech extemporaneously?
❑ Do I maintain eye contact?

17.4 What Are the Types of Special Occasion Speeches?

1 **Toast or Roast**

2 **Speech of Introduction**

3 **Speech of Award Presentation**

4 **Speech of Award Acceptance**

5 **Eulogy or Tribute**

6 **Speech of Inspiration**

7 **After-Dinner Speech**

1

Toast or Roast

A ***toast*** is a ritual expressing honor or goodwill to a person, group, institution, or event, punctuated by taking a drink. You may offer a toast at events such as New Year's Eve, weddings, birthdays, housewarmings, graduation dinners, and retirement parties. Toasts may be sentimental, appreciative, or congratulatory in content. Their tone can range from solemn to appropriately humorous.

A ***roast*** is a humorous tribute to a person and almost exclusively a U.S. cultural phenomenon. The event and the speech are both called a roast. The protocol involves a series of speakers, all joking or poking fun at the honoree, often with a few heartwarming moments. It is important that you ascertain the overall tone the event organizer wants to create. Some roasts lean toward the insulting or eccentric when the event organizers view that as appropriate for the person being roasted. Most roasts have a host or emcee. Coordinating your speech content and tone with the host's intent is very important as well.

In the 1970s, Dean Martin and Don Rickles were legendary at roasting. You can locate several appropriate examples on YouTube.

TIP: Responses from the Audience

As an audience member at a toast, if you pick up your glass at the beginning of the toast, don't put it down until the end. You should always raise your glass and sip some liquid, or you will appear impolite or seem to suggest that you don't agree with the toast.

SPECIAL GUIDELINES

- Reflect the tone and purpose of the event.
- Speak mostly about the honoree.
- Be positive, appropriate, and gracious.
- Mix your humor with heartfelt meaning. Avoid inside jokes in a toast or roast.
- Stand, if possible, when you offer a toast or roast.
- Know the protocol for the event (e.g., wedding toasts usually follow an order—father of the bride or host of the reception, best man, maid of honor, and then groom).
- Be brief and adhere to your time limit, especially at a roast. A toast should be three to five minutes or less.
- Toasts should almost always be given without notes. Giving a toast from notes on your phone is especially inappropriate and will cause you to look down too much.
- Praise, honor, and compliment. It is the honoree's day to shine and be happy.
- Tailor remarks to mirror the values, beliefs, and attitudes of the honoree and those close to him or her. Anything you say will be recorded in their memories and potentially on video.
- If possible, clearing your content with the event hosts in advance of a toast or roast might be wise.
- End the speech with a positive toast or blessing. Indicate the end of the toast verbally ("Here's to Jeff and Steve!" or "To Norm and Dylece!") and nonverbally (raise your glass).

EXAMPLE

Andy, the best man you met earlier, wrote this toast.

May I have your attention, please? Wow, what an amazing day and celebration. For those who don't know me, I'm Andy Cooper, Joe's shadow. We met in grade school and will leave this life as best friends. We have played ball, chased after quail, and hitchhiked across this great land together.

On one of our trips, I learned a lot about how calm, cool, and trainable Joe could be. We were camping out under the stars in the state of Washington when we awoke to a large female moose straddling Joe's body, literally, and staring straight into his eyes. I'm there in my sleeping bag, wondering what her breath smells like and if she will bite or lick his face. Joe had to be wondering what her plans were for him in that compromising position. He didn't move.

I didn't move. She checked us out for what seemed like an eternity and eventually sauntered off. We learned that day to stay calm and cool and let the ladies have their way.

Stephanie, you owe that moose a lot. Joe, you better be glad you saw Stephanie first. She is one special catch and deserves the best. Too bad for her, she saw you first. No, seriously, I wish you two many years of happiness and a lifetime of joy. Special people deserve special people in their lives. Today, two very special people begin a lifetime of happiness and joy together. Congratulations, Joe and Stephanie! (*toast*)

2
Speech of Introduction

A *speech of introduction* presents to the audience an event's next or main speaker. This type of speech might also set out to welcome the audience; establish the tone, mood, or climate of the event; and/or build a level of excitement.

SPECIAL GUIDELINES

- Research the background of the speaker so that you can give a brief overview of his or her accomplishments and credentials. Review the speaker's résumé if you can. You might also talk with the event organizer or conduct a mini-interview with the speaker prior to the introduction. Do not wait until the last minute to research. You need time to prepare, and the speaker needs the time before the speech to get ready as well.

- Briefly preview the speaker's speech title and topic if appropriate. You should work this out ahead of time with the speaker. Do not give your own speech on the topic.

- Introductions should be short. The audience has come to hear the featured speaker.

- Your final words should ask the audience to welcome the speaker and include his or her name. For example, "Please join me in welcoming the CEO of AirBound, Joyce English."

EXAMPLE

Anne Frank wrote in her diary, "No one has ever become poor by giving." If that is true, our next recipient is one of the richest women in the world. It is my honor tonight to introduce someone who has worked to help others and give them a voice when they could not help themselves or were voiceless. She has rolled up her sleeves to build homeless shelters and homes after a devastating tornado. She gave up a high-powered job to lead the local food bank through tough times and to create a buddy pack program for the children of our community. Please join me in giving a warm welcome to Laken Nell.

This introductory speaker starts with a quotation as an attention-getter and transition to the featured speaker. She then gives a brief preview of the featured speaker's accomplishments and connection to this audience before giving her title and name.

CONFIDENCE BOOSTER

Most special occasion speeches relate to affirmative topics, and their audiences usually want to listen. Even eulogies are positive in that they affirm the life of someone special to the audience, and you wouldn't be giving the eulogy if you weren't a positive part of that experience. Use that affirmative spirit to override your nervousness or lack of confidence. Decide beforehand to make your speech a powerful and positive experience for you and your audience.

3

Speech of Award Presentation

You will give a *speech of award presentation* when you are asked or are in a position to be the individual announcing the recipient(s) of an award, prize, or honor. This type of speech may be given at an award ceremony, banquet, party, business meeting, convention session, or the end of a long gathering for a particular purpose (e.g., a retreat).

SPECIAL GUIDELINES

- You should either set or mirror the tone of the proceedings.

- If it is not obvious to the audience, explain who you are and why you are giving the award. This should be very brief because the award is not about you.

- Explain the significance of the award.

- Compliment and recognize all of the nominees as a group.

- Highlight the achievements of the recipient(s) or explain why the individual or group is receiving the award.

- Be brief—no longer than five minutes and usually much shorter.

- If possible, physically hand the award to the recipient. In Western culture, it is common to hand the award with the left hand and shake hands with the right. Be sure to investigate, ask someone, or pay attention to others' behavior to determine the proper cultural procedure for shaking hands, as it can vary. Practice this maneuver so that it is not awkward.

EXAMPLE

It is my honor and privilege to present the fifth annual St. Vincent Award. Ester St. Vincent worked in our elementary schools for more than 40 years. Outside the classroom, she dedicated much of her life to civic duty.

She was a volunteer at the local soup kitchen and the hospital, taught adults to read, and took in countless animals until they could make it on their own. She led the cry to save this town after a major flood.

This award was established in 2006, to honor this extraordinary citizen. Each year, we give the award to a local community member who carries on Ms. St. Vincent's spirit and sense of civility and duty.

This year, we had several outstanding nominees, making the decision a tough one; we honor you all. However, after great scrutiny, one obvious candidate began to emerge.

This year's recipient grew up here, works as a nurse practitioner in our community, volunteers to maintain the city gardens, helps give medical care to the homeless, and has organized several successful fundraisers.

The 2016 recipient of the St. Vincent Award is Eliana Lee.

Notice how this speaker briefly explains the award, praises those candidates who did not receive it, and quickly highlights the important achievements of the award recipient just before announcing her name. This speech is to the point and builds the intensity of the moment.

4
Speech of Award Acceptance

A *speech of award acceptance* is the response you give when receiving an award, prize, or honor. You may give this type of speech after receiving an award or honor, or at an event marking a significant achievement in your life (e.g., a retirement reception, sports event, or contest).

SPECIAL GUIDELINES

- Be prepared if you know you will or might receive an award. The audience usually expects to hear from you.

- Be respectful of the event and give your speech from the heart. Unless the award ceremony is intended to entertain rather than to honor, you should respect the organizers' purpose to honor you. Be humble.

- Be appropriate to the event.

- Thank the person or group giving you the honor.

- Thank those close to you and/or those who have contributed greatly to your success. Limit this list to the most significant people, and avoid a long list (three to five works best).

- Show a little emotion or pride.

- Make the award meaningful for your audience or appeal to their emotions. For example, dedicate your award to someone or something appropriate to the occasion.

- Know when to stop. Do not go on and on. Be as brief as possible (usually three to five minutes). Pay attention to your audience.

EXAMPLE

Thank you, Mayor Craig, for your kind words and endless support. I would also like to thank the award committee and the other nominees. I am truly humbled by your recognition and company. Giving back to this community is my life and passion. Growing up here, I have loved this small town and its people—the people who made me who I am today. It took people like Ms. St. Vincent and my family to show me that I could be whatever I wanted, and I thank them for pushing and lifting me. They inspired me to do the same for others.

Almost every day when I would walk home from school or my dad's store, Ms. St. V, as we called her, would be on her way to help a cause. Or she would call me over to help take care of baby rabbits, a doe, or other animals someone had brought her to rehabilitate.

When my dad's store was wiped out by the flood, she was the first one there with a mop and bucket to help. No cause was too small or too large in Ms. St. V's eyes. Her motto was "Keep movin' forward and smile!" Thank you for this honor.

Here, the recipient of the award begins by thanking the appropriate people and graciously dedicates the speech to make a point about helping others.

5

Eulogy or Tribute

The word **eulogy** derives from the Greek word *eulogia*, meaning "praise" or "good word," and is a speech presented after a person's death, at ceremonies such as funerals.

A **tribute** commemorates lives or accomplishments of people, groups, institutions, or events and can be given with the recipient present or posthumously (after death). Tributes are often given at award ceremonies or dinners.

SPECIAL GUIDELINES

- Your focus should be to commemorate and celebrate the life of the honoree.
- Although eulogies and tributes should be brief (under 10 minutes), determine what is expected.
- For a eulogy, your purpose is to celebrate the deceased and to comfort the living. Pay attention to the needs of the audience.
  - Stay in control of your emotions. Using a manuscript can help.
  - Refer to the family or close friends and colleagues.
  - Focus on the person, not how he or she died.
  - Be positive and genuine.
- For a tribute, remember that your purpose is to honor the achievements of a person, group, institution, or event.
  - Vividly describe the accomplishments without overstating the facts.
  - Be genuine and informative.
  - Use those achievements to inspire and educate the audience.

EXAMPLE

On December 21, 2012, Senator Harry Reid eulogized Senator Daniel K. Inouye during a memorial service at the Washington National Cathedral. The eulogy first addresses the audience's struggle with death, followed by a celebration of Inouye's American story.

> **Ecclesiastes 3:2 tells us, "To everything there is a season, a time to every purpose under heaven: a time to be born, and a time to die." It was Daniel Inouye's time. Dan Inouye lived a full and productive life. ...**

> **He was a war hero—a decorated soldier who left the innocence of youth and most of his right arm on an Italian battlefield where he defended our nation's freedom even as that nation questioned the loyalty of patriots who looked like him. ... He was a legislative hero—a progressive Democrat who would never hesitate to collaborate with a Republican colleague for the good of this country.**

Reid paints a picture of the type of person Inouye was by using the word *hero* in this section and such words as *noble*, *dignity*, and *remarkable* later in the eulogy. In his conclusion, Reid returns to the earlier Bible quotation and ends with:

> **During his 1968 convention speech, Dan taught the nation that aloha doesn't just mean hello, and it doesn't just mean goodbye. It also means I love you. Aloha was Dan's last word. So I say to my friend in return: Daniel Ken Inouye, aloha. I love you. And goodbye until we meet again.**

To read the complete eulogy, visit democrats .senate.gov/2012/12/21/reid-eulogy-for -senator-daniel-inouye-to-everything-a -season/.

6
Speech of Inspiration

A **speech of inspiration** strives to fulfill a general purpose to motivate, encourage, move, or arouse an audience in a positive manner. Religious sermons, commencement addresses, motivational talks in the workplace or locker room, and nomination speeches at rallies, as well as keynote and welcoming addresses at conventions, are all speeches of inspiration. These speeches aim to awaken an audience's feelings, such as pride, perseverance, spirituality, and the search for excellence. The effectiveness of this type of speech is rooted in the speaker's ethos and his or her appeal to audience pathos. Vivid language and storytelling are often key, as demonstrated in this radio devotional given by the Rev. John Yonker.

> An old story tells about a teacher who held up a sheet of clean, white paper. "What do you see?" he asked the children. "A piece of paper," they told him. He then took a pen and drew a small black dot on the paper. "Now, what do you see?" he asked. "A dot," they all responded. "A dot?" he asked. "Why do you see the dot and not the rest of the paper?"
>
> Sometimes, life goes the same way. With each new sunrise, God gives us a clean sheet of paper, but we often let some small incident ruin it for us. A disagreement, a lost earring, an unkind word, a disruptive phone call—these trivialities become the dot we concentrate on instead of the rest of the paper.
>
> This is John Yonker at First Christian Church, reminding you to hang onto your perspective. Don't let one tiny ink spot blind you to a whole sheet of white paper!

SPECIAL GUIDELINES

- Select a topic, theme, or subject that reflects the expectations, mood, and tone of the speaking event.
- Know your audience and what would inspire them.
- Talk about something that inspires you. If you are not inspired, your audience will not be either. Let your passion be inspirational.
- Appeal to your audience's pathos via stories (especially true ones), extended examples, or anecdotes. Use strong examples of what is or could be.
- Use vivid language, repetition, alliteration, metaphor, and other speech devices, and focus on connotative (emotional) usage.

  → See Chapter 9 for more on effective language usage.

- Draw on the power of inspirational people by quoting them at key moments.
- Use a vocal flow and rhythm that builds in intensity. Rally the audience's emotions with your delivery style. Be very dynamic.
- End with a significant WOW moment.

EXAMPLE

This speech was given at a ceremony just before a college graduation. Kyra, the student speaker, was elected by her peers to speak at this symbolic ceremony marking the passage from member of the senior class to alumna of the institution.

Kyra draws attention to a large portion of the audience.

Let me begin by welcoming all of you to this wonderful tradition. I would especially like to welcome and thank those of you in the audience who supported us over the past few years. Without our parents, partners, professors, friends, and the administrative staff, this journey would not have been possible or, for that matter, as much fun. If it is not too presumptuous of me to speak for all of the seniors, I would like to thank all of you from the bottom of our hearts for your support and the sacrifices you have made so this event could happen. It is a glorious day and one that I—no, we—will remember for years to come.

She signals there will be five points in her speech.

As many of you know, I have been very involved in theatre during the past four years. As a member of the Elysium Players, I took my job of bringing theatre to life again on this campus very seriously. So today, as we prepare to celebrate our years of hard work and education, it seems only fitting that I take a few moments to share with you five life lessons I have learned from theatre and that I hope will guide your future personal and professional lives.

Lesson Number One—Passion

Agnes George de Mille, actor, dancer, and niece to the great Cecil B. de Mille, once said, "It takes great passion and great energy to do anything creative, especially in theatre. You have to care so much you can't sleep, you can't eat, you can't talk to people. It's got to be just right. You can't do it without passion." To excel in theatre, you must love it; because, if you don't, you won't be successful in it. You have to be willing to memorize pages and pages of text, which you will forget as soon as the show is over. You have to make it through the long, tiring rehearsals night after night for over three months straight. And, you WILL, but you definitely don't want to come back to the next rehearsal after spending a whole evening believing that at any moment the bats living in Launer Auditorium are going to attack. I can say from much experience that if you don't love theatre, the Launer bats will scare you away. In essence, the show can't go on without passion. Your future is the same. You must love life and be passionate about living it. If you live apathetically, never taking a stand, never pushing yourself, you won't enjoy living it and you won't succeed at even the small things. You must live your life with a passion strong enough to see past the mundane, the exhaustion of hard work, and the scary little unknown things. YOU MUST BE PASSIONATE!

Lesson Number Two—The Ensemble

As Kenneth Haigh once said, "You need three things in the theatre—the play, the actor[s], the audience—each must give something." All the parts of the play must work together in unison to make a successful production. This unity, or working together, is what we define as an ensemble, or a group of complementary parts that contribute to a single effect. In life, whether we are teachers, athletes, businessmen and women, lawyers, doctors, partners, or parents, we all have something to give and a role to play. That role cannot simply stand alone as a solo act; it must work toward achieving unity, balance, and technique. We must recognize that our roles touch, create, and complement the lives of those around us—our students, patients, clients, customers, loved ones, and children. The quality of our role balances and elevates theirs. We must remember to work together and not against each other, because life is an ensemble with the people we care about the most.

Lesson Number Three—A Supporting Role

Believe it or not, you don't always have to be center stage. There are times when you must choose to play a supportive role. Ninety-eight percent of what goes on in theatre productions happens before the audience even enters the auditorium—late-night rehearsals, set design and production, advertising, and costuming (just to name a few)—and although the star actor of the show may be a vital part, the show wouldn't go on without the rest. In life, we must know when to step back in the shadows and live life because we love it, and not because we want formal recognition for what we are doing. We must help others receive the recognition they deserve, and support them as they endure challenging and exciting times, just as so many have done for us during our four-year journey to this day. And, possibly most importantly, we must learn to support others and lift up those who lag a bit behind.

Lesson Number Four—"Criticism Is a Good Thang"

I will admit I still struggle with this lesson. A very wise professor and director once told me (actually, told me and all the other Elysium players a few

To draw attention to a new lesson, Kyra uses a famous quotation.

Kyra ends each lesson with an inspirational challenge.

hundred times), "criticism is growth." And although none of us likes to hear that we aren't doing everything as perfectly as we see it, she is right. A play looks very different from the point of view of the director or the audience, and actors on stage are often stuck in the small scene they are creating instead of seeing the whole picture. A performance is only as good as the image the actors create in the minds of others—not just within their own minds. We are not always perfect and can't always see things from the other perspective. Therefore, criticism is growth. Although at times it can be hard to swallow, criticism will only make us stronger and better if we choose to listen. We also need to be aware of ourselves as critics, that we offer criticism to those we care about, not in an effort to break them down, but rather to build them up—to feed their potential for growth. "Criticism is a good thang!"

Lesson Number Five—Stretch

Four years ago when I first walked through Rogers Gates, if someone had told me that if I stayed here I would someday be sitting center stage in Launer singing "Happy Birthday" to myself in a horrible southern accent in front of an audience of my peers, I would have laughed and then turned and run back to Colorado. Well, I did that 3 weeks ago. An actor can't grow on stage if she or he is not willing to stretch. And I firmly believe we can't grow in life if we aren't willing to step out of our comfort zones. The College, believe it or not just after finals week, has become a comfortable space for us and it is time to move on. I feel both excited and apprehensive of that move. However, I believe that it is time to brave the future. As Alan Alda once said, "Be brave enough to live life creatively. The creative is the place where no one else has ever been. You have to leave the city of your comfort and go into the wilderness of your intuition. You can't get there by bus, only hard work and risk and by not quite knowing what you're doing. What you'll discover will be wonderful. What you'll discover will be yourself."

As I close, I challenge you, as we enter the next phase of our lives, to live your life creatively. Step out, take risks, and force yourself to grow in ways you never imagined. Aristotle claimed happiness could be found in choosing well. I say, if theatre has taught us anything, it has taught us that happiness can be found in choosing creatively. Be bold. Discover yourself by living a life that is passionate, part of the ensemble, filled with supporting roles, healthy criticism, and stretching outside of the comfort zone! Live a life of theatre.

Moving into the last point, Kyra draws the speech back to the moment by referencing Rogers Gates, which are just behind her during the speech.

She follows the theatre metaphor through to the end of her speech and incorporates strong quotations in the last few seconds.

7

After-Dinner Speech

Despite the name, an ***after-dinner speech*** can be given any time you need to give a speech with the general purpose to entertain but with a relevant message. Most after-dinner speeches are lighthearted but contain a more serious element buried in the entertaining parts. This type of speech can occur before, during, or after meal gatherings; at professional and civic meetings; at events opening or closing campaigns; or at end-of-the-year events. After-dinner speeches tend to be longer than other special occasion speeches and are usually specific to the audience and/or the occasion.

SPECIAL GUIDELINES

- Start preparing the speech early. An after-dinner speech is one of the more difficult speeches to create because you are trying to entertain and deliver a relevant message at the same time.

- Tailor the speech to the occasion and the audience. Do not simply pull a canned speech out of your repertoire.

- Be appropriate. Do not offend. Analyze your audience and situation to learn what might be appropriate or expected.

- Be focused and structured. You still need an introduction, a body, and a conclusion. Decide if the relevant message is meant to inform or to persuade your audience.

- Be creative but avoid doing stand-up. You were asked to do a speech, not a comedy routine, and that is the expectation. Also, you probably are not a professional comedian, and although it might look simple, stand-up comedy takes years

to perfect. You can still use humor in a structured, well-organized, and purposeful speech—just avoid making the speech all about being comical.

- Be dynamic and cheerful. Your delivery should be extremely upbeat. If you aren't excited and having fun, the audience won't be either. Use a lot of eye contact and speak extemporaneously.

- Some presentation aids (e.g., video, images/pictures, or items) can help make the speech entertaining.

- Know your time limit and stick to it. Your audience will not expect a long speech. This type of speech can be as short as two to three minutes or as long as 10 to 15 minutes.

- Practice. When you are being creative and entertaining, effective timing and delivery are musts. Always rehearse this type of speech in front of an audience for feedback and editing hints.

PRACTICING ETHICS: Entertaining Ethically

- When your goal is to entertain, avoid using language, jokes, or examples that are potentially insensitive to religion, race, gender, ethnicity, sexual orientation, age, or even political persuasion. Such references will destroy your credibility, will offend your audience, and may provoke an undesired response.
- Do not make your audience feel alienated or uncomfortable for any reason.

EXAMPLE

The following excerpts are from a White House Correspondents' Dinner speech given by President Gerald Ford on May 3, 1975. You can read the whole speech at www.fordlibrarymuseum .gov/library/document/0122/1252308.pdf.

Note how President Ford uses humor to entertain in this opening about journalist Helen Thomas. He continues with this lighthearted banter as he singles out other press members.

> I do appreciate that rather kind and gentle introduction because Helen Thomas has a well-earned reputation for speaking her own mind. I can remember some years ago, when I was still a congressman, Helen and I were walking down Pennsylvania Avenue when we passed one of those scales that gives you your weight and your fortune—all for a penny. Helen said, "Why don't you try it? I might get a scoop." So, I got on the scale, put in a penny, a card came out, and it said: "You are handsome, debonair, sophisticated, a born leader of men, a silver-tongued orator, and some day you will make your mark in history." Helen leaned over, looked at the card, and said, "It has your weight wrong, too!"...

Toward the end of the speech, President Ford moves into a more serious message about the press being respectfully part of his "extended family."

> ... I see the first family as being an extended family—one that draws in and includes all the men and women who make the White House a living, breathing, and functioning body. It encompasses a handful of Fords, completely and comfortably surrounded by staff and press alike. We are not just Jerry, Betty, Susan, Jack, Steve, and Mike—but Bob, Helen, Ron, Fran, Frank, and a few hundred others as well.
>
> We work together. We laugh together. We exchange ideas, facts, and speculations. We interact. We cannot function well without each other. This is the stuff that families are made of.
>
> And like all families, we have our disagreements. We take in and assimilate individual attitudes, concerns, interests, and information. Then we shine the spotlight of our unique perceptions on each problem, each new challenge. Your spotlight is not mine—mine is not yours. Sometimes we differ. But the essence and glory of the true family is this: decisions and conclusions may be questioned—but motivation and commitment are not. We speak our differences in trust. We accept that we are travelers heading toward the same destination. It is only the road that has to be determined. This is the first family I know we all want to be a part of. We have shared some of these feelings here tonight. We should never aspire to less. Thank you and good night.

Chapter 17: Review

ASSESSING YOUR KNOWLEDGE

17.1 What Are Special Occasion Speeches?

Objective 17.1: **DESCRIBE THE PURPOSE OF SPECIAL OCCASION SPEECHES**

A special occasion speech has the general purpose to celebrate, commemorate, inspire, or entertain.

- Speeches to celebrate will honor or highlight a person, group, institution, place, or event.
- Speeches to commemorate pay tribute to or remember a person, group, institution, place, or event.
- Speeches to inspire are created to motivate, stir, encourage, or arouse the audience.
- Speeches to entertain all have the general goal to amuse, delight, and engage the audience for the purpose of enjoyment, with a bit of wisdom or tribute thrown in, depending on the occasion.

→ See pages 400–401.

17.2 What Is the Creative Process for Special Occasion Speaking?

Objective 17.2: **EXPLAIN THE CREATIVE PROCESS FOR SPECIAL OCCASION SPEAKING**

Special occasion speeches are some of the most creative. The five basic activities in the process follow the same structure as for other speeches—starting, researching, creating, presenting, and listening and evaluating—but certain steps are emphasized more. For example, determining the purpose and type of a special occasion speech often relates more to the specific occasion rather than the audience, and your language choices can be more celebratory or inspirational than in other speeches.

→ See pages 402–403.

17.3 How Do You Write a Special Occasion Speech?

Objective 17.3: **SUMMARIZE HOW TO WRITE A SPECIAL OCCASION SPEECH**

You create a special occasion speech much like you would any other speech, with more focus on the occasion and your purpose.

- Determine the purpose and type of speech.
- Analyze the audience and the situation.
- Focus on a central idea.
- Research the speech.
- Outline and organize the speech.
- Practice the speech.
- Evaluate for the standard and unique qualities of the special occasion speech.

→ See pages 404–407.

17.4 What Are the Types of Special Occasion Speeches?

Objective 17.4: **DESCRIBE THE TYPES OF SPECIAL OCCASION SPEECHES**

- Toasts or roasts are speeches to celebrate. A toast is a ritual expressing honor or goodwill to a person, group, institution, or event, punctuated by taking a drink. A roast is a humorous tribute to a person.
- A speech of introduction presents to the audience an event's next or main speaker.
- A speech of award presentation is a speech given when you are the individual announcing the recipient(s) of an award, prize, or honor.
- A speech of award acceptance is the response an award recipient gives after receiving an award, prize, or honor.
- Eulogies and tributes are commemorative speeches. Eulogies are given at ceremonies such as funerals, marking the death of an individual. A tribute commemorates lives or accomplishments of people, groups, institutions, or events. A tribute can be given with the recipient present, or posthumously. Tributes are given at such events as award ceremonies, banquets, and retirement dinners.
- Speeches of inspiration strive to motivate, encourage, move, and/or arouse an audience in a positive manner. They may be given at religious events, graduations, motivational events, rallies, or conventions.
- After-dinner speeches are usually given with the general purpose to entertain but with a relevant message.

→ See pages 408–419.

TERMS TO REMEMBER

special occasion speech (400)
speeches to celebrate (401)
speeches to commemorate (401)
speeches to inspire (401)
speeches to entertain (401)
toast (408)
roast (408)
speech of introduction (410)
speech of award presentation (411)
speech of award acceptance (412)
eulogy (413)
tribute (413)
speech of inspiration (414)
after-dinner speech (418)

Practical Pointers for Tab 8

FAQs

When can I use humor in a special occasion speech?

As with any other speech, humor can be useful in a special occasion speech. Humor can even be helpful in eulogies when used appropriately. All uses of humor must be appropriate to the audience, the guest of honor, and the occasion. Here are some tips to follow:

- Test your humor on a friend, mentor, or family member who will be honest with you about its appropriateness (and whether or not it is funny).
- Use humor that focuses on your speech's general purpose and central idea. Humor should not be your general purpose or central idea.
- Remember, your speech is not about you and how funny you are. In most special occasion speeches, you shouldn't tell jokes about yourself.
- Don't laugh at your own jokes.
- Balance jokes with sincerity.
- Humor should be lighthearted, not mean-spirited.
- Don't make jokes about race, ethnicity, religion, gender, sexual orientation, height, age, or weight.
- Don't be crude or risqué, especially in wedding toasts.
- Use jokes that offer a funny insight into the person, group, event, place, or institution.
- Keep your jokes short.

I've been asked to give a wedding toast, and I am still not sure about what to say. What should I include?

Wedding or commitment ceremony toasts are the most common type of toast given. Here is a standard format:

- If you haven't been introduced, say who you are—especially if less than 50 percent of the audience knows you.
- Thank the person or persons hosting the wedding or ceremony. You can even be a bit vague if this is complicated. For example, "Thank you to everyone responsible for this happy occasion and for sharing your joy with us."
- Connect to the couple in some way. Tell a short story that focuses attention on them. For example, you could choose one of these ideas:
  - Tell about the first time you met the couple.
  - Tell about how they met.
  - Highlight how you have seen them change since they met. Focus on the positive.
  - Use a famous quotation that relates to the couple, to illustrate their love.
  - Don't include remarks about past relationships or the honeymoon.

ADDITIONAL SUPPORT

www.inspirational-quotes.info

twitter.com/motivational?lang=en

www.values.com/inspirational-quotes

www.brainyquote.com/quotes/topics.html

TAB 9
Speaking in Professional & Group Settings

9
PROFESSIONAL & GROUP SETTINGS
Chapters 18–19

18 ON-THE-JOB SPEAKING

Meeting Room

In business, communication is everything.[1]

ROBERT KENT

18.1 How Do You Effectively Communicate in an Interview?

1 Prepare to Conduct an Interview
2 Prepare to Be Interviewed

Whether you are the interviewer or the interviewee, conducting and giving a successful job interview is difficult work that is important to the future of a business and your career. Interviewing in the digital age has become even more complicated. Interviews can now be (and often are) conducted by phone, computer, or videoconferencing.

1

Prepare to Conduct an Interview

One of the best ways to learn how to conduct an interview is to observe someone else who is good at interviewing. If you know you will be in a position to interview candidates, try to observe senior employees as they interview others. You should pay attention to questions that seem to elicit a genuine response and the overall feeling of the interview.

Also, be sure to coordinate with your human resources (HR) office. Know what your company's standard procedures are. If your HR office offers sessions on how to conduct interviews, attend them.

Be conscious of the type of interviewer you need to be. Some interviewers are very aggressive and deliberately try to put the interviewee in a stressful situation to gauge how he or she will handle it. Still others will ask questions designed to elicit a behavioral response: "What would you do if…?"

You're only as good as the people you hire.[2]

RAY KROC

Here are some general guidelines.

1. Meet with your HR personnel to determine what you can and cannot ask during an interview. It is illegal to ask about age, marital status, children, childcare arrangements, religion, sexual orientation, citizenship, where a person lives and with whom, clubs or social organization membership, arrest record, or how someone was discharged from the military. Requesting personal information (such as height, weight, and/or disabilities) is prohibited as well. However, you can ask if a person is able to do a certain task or test them in some cases. You should ask your HR office if testing is acceptable.

2. Closely review the cover letter, the résumé, and any other material provided by the applicant. Research past employment and positions. Make note of how long the applicant has held previous and similar positions; if she or he was promoted and how often; and any other indications of job successes, failures, or concerns. You might ask for an explanation of any positive or negative issues.

3. Set up a time and location. Allow 45 to 60 minutes for each interview, and select a location that is comfortable and quiet (no phones). Do not let the location intimidate the candidate unless that is your intent. Tell the candidate what she or he should bring, if anything. You might ask for a list of references, a writing sample, or a résumé if that was not a part of the application materials.

4. Construct a list of questions. Using a set of standard questions asked of all candidates may be the best way to ensure a fair selection process. You may need to clear these questions with HR. Begin with general discussion to ease the candidate into the process—for example, "Tell me about yourself." Most people can and are willing to talk about themselves. Then move to complex questions such as:

Why do you feel you are a good candidate for this position?

What have you done in the past that you feel has helped you to prepare for this position?

Tell me about a time you felt you went above and beyond the call of duty at work.

5. Observe the person closely: Is the candidate dressed appropriately? Well-groomed? Does he or she look you in the eye and shake your hand firmly? Is the candidate energetic and enthusiastic?

6. When listening to the person's answers, pay attention to content and how comfortable or uncomfortable he or she was in answering. Does the response sound generic or overly prepared?

7. When specific job qualifications are important, you might set up a numeric ranking system for those qualifications and total the scores for each candidate. However, do not rely on this system alone.

8. Think about how the candidate's personality will fit in with other employees and the goal of the business.

9. Check references and/or conduct background checks if required.

10. If possible, have several members at your organization interview the candidate.

2

Prepare to Be Interviewed

Alex is graduating from college in a few months and is concerned about interviewing. He worked for his dad's landscape business throughout most of high school and college. The only time he has been interviewed was for an on-campus job, and the hiring professor already knew him and asked few questions. So Alex has not had the opportunity to create a résumé or take part in a formal interview. He is not sure how to begin the process or where to find information.

Like Alex, if you truly want a job, you have to work at it. You may be required to take several tests, participate in many interviews, and/or provide sample work—all to help you stand out from the rest as the right candidate. Trying to find the right job can be as time-consuming as a full-time job and takes dedication. Even getting an interview requires that you dedicate time and care to your application. You should always type, proofread, and update any material you send as part of your application. Tailor the material to the job and the hiring organization.

THE APPLICATION

Although filling out and creating your application package is not directly related to oral communication, it is the first step to getting the job interview. Many of the skills you have discovered in this book can also apply to the application process. You want to build strong ethos from the beginning and succinctly sell yourself as the best candidate. If your application is messy, incomplete, or too general, the reader will view you as a poor applicant. The checklist to the right can help you with the application process.

TIP: Finding Help with Interviewing

While you are still connected with a college or university, use the available resources created to help you with landing your first job.

- If your institution has a career center, ask them for help with the application process, creating a résumé, and/or setting up a mock interview session.
- Look for examples and guidance from Internet sources or at your local libraries.
- Attend any special sessions at your institution designed to help you succeed, such as workshops on how to handle yourself at a business dinner and how to recognize illegal interview questions. Such sessions can offer practical advice.
- Take classes designed to assist you. Often a major will have one class designed for mentoring you as you move out into your field, and some communication or business courses are created for this very purpose.

CHECKLIST for Your Application

❑ Did I tailor my letter, résumé, and/or application to the job, requirements, and organization?

❑ Did I type and proofread my letter, résumé, and/or application? (Have someone else also check it.)

❑ Did I update my résumé and reference list? (Always ask permission to list someone as a reference, and give him or her a copy of the job description and your current résumé.)

BEFORE THE INTERVIEW

Once you have an interview scheduled, prepare for it much like you would for a speech. An interview is like an informative and persuasive speech rolled into one. You want to tell (inform) the potential employers about you and persuade them to hire you. You need to research the audience and the topic (the hiring organization and you, respectively); create and craft what you want to cover in the interview; prepare for how you will present yourself; and evaluate the effectiveness of the interview. Much of the information from Tabs 1 through 5 of this book will assist you, and the table below gives additional strategies.

WHAT SHOULD YOU DO?	HOW CAN YOU DO IT?
Research the job.	• Search on the Internet or at the library for information related to the job. • Interview someone with insight into the specifics of such a job. If interviewing someone as research, ask him/her to suggest questions you should ask of the potential employer. • Try to find information about salaries in your area, duties of the job, opportunity for advancement, and other elements important to you.
Research the hiring organization.	• Check news articles, press releases, the organization's website, annual reports, trade journals, and other specialized publications. • Talk to someone with ties to the organization, if appropriate and possible. • Try to get a feel for the company's focus, hiring practices, growth, and employee satisfaction.
Prepare an introduction of yourself and a closing statement.	• Often, the first thing the interviewer will say to you is "Tell me a bit about yourself." Be ready to talk about some of your professional and personal traits and experiences that might interest the interviewer. • Review your résumé so that you are very familiar with the content and layout.
Research and prepare for questions you may be asked.	• Look up standard interview questions in books, in magazines, and online. • Craft and practice your answers to them.

Prepare questions to ask the interviewer(s).	• Use the information you gathered when researching the job and the hiring organization and create some questions. Search online for help. Type in "questions to ask employers during interview" or something similar.
	• Some examples:
	  What are the organization's future plans for growth?
	  Are there training or educational opportunities with this position?
	  What are the normal promotion steps for this position?

Be very familiar with your application material.	• Read over ALL your application material several times. • If any issues in the material might cause concerns for an employer, prepare a response to those possible concerns. • Think about how the material shows that you are the best candidate for the position. Prepare to cover any issues you think are especially important.

THE INTERVIEW DAY

On the day of the interview, do some last-minute research to see if anything has changed related to the organization where you will interview. You can do this by checking the organization's website, the local newspaper, or other possible local sources. If you discover something that raises a question for you about the organization, mention it or ask your interviewer about the developments during the interview, if possible and appropriate. Here are a few pointers for getting yourself ready.

Dressing for Success

Dress for the interview and the job you are applying for. Try to discover the organization's approved dress code and dress slightly more formally than the code for the organization or position.

In most interviews today, men should wear traditional business attire (dark, conservative suits; white, long-sleeved shirts; and silk ties that are not flashy). Women should wear a conservative (dark is best) suit or dress and avoid distracting jewelry or makeup. Both men and women should remove unusual body piercings or other distracting ornamentation and avoid wearing perfumes, colognes, or scented lotions. You should be well groomed and your clothes pressed. You want to be memorable as a potential asset, not stick out for the wrong reasons.

Getting to the Interview

Plan your arrival, including how to get to the location. You want to arrive early enough that you can sit somewhere quietly and look over your notes one last time. Being late to an interview is unacceptable for almost any reason. Be on time.

Before entering the building, switch off your digital watch alarm, cell phone, or anything else that could make noise. Never use one of these devices or take a call or message during an interview. It is a sure way to lose the job.

Being Interviewed

Give a good, firm handshake and make direct eye contact with the interviewer(s); first impressions begin there, and they are hard to reverse. Try to chat for a few seconds to seem personable and to calm your nerves.

When answering questions:

- Be confident.
- Show enthusiasm.
- Make eye contact.
- Articulate your words.
- Use correct grammar and language appropriate to the position.
- Watch for and respond appropriately to nonverbal cues.
- Ask questions at the appropriate times.
- Try to find just the right vocal speed. You do not want to rush or be too hesitant.
- Strive to be conversational. Construct answers that are more than one word or sentence but not too long or complex.
- Never make up information or lie. If you don't know something, say so—though also be careful not to do that too much. If you find that you frequently need to say you don't know, then you weren't prepared.

End with an enthusiastic conclusion. Ask when you might hear something, and give a firm handshake and thank-you as you leave.

Redirecting Illegal Questions

Due to federal and state laws, prospective employers are prohibited from asking certain questions that are not related to the job you are applying for. Most questions that relate to personal information are illegal. Therefore, the interviewer should not ask questions related to your marital status, race, ethnicity, gender, religion, disabilities, country of origin, sexual preferences, age, or arrest record.

Interviewers may accidentally or intentionally ask an illegal question nonetheless. If the interviewer is asking illegal questions, you will need to decide if this is a legal matter that needs to be pursued or if this is simply not the job for you. However, during the interview, you should try to steer the question back to your qualifications for the job. The table below offers some response options.

AFTER THE INTERVIEW

Send a thank-you e-mail or note the day after the interview.

Evaluate your feelings about your performance and the interview process. Assess the content of your responses, your delivery, and the effectiveness of the materials you submitted as your application. Evaluate them as you would a speech.

→ Refer to the speech evaluation guidelines in Chapter 13 if needed.

If you do not get the job and you think it is appropriate, ask the interviewer if he or she would offer you suggestions on how to improve your skills or tell you what was the deciding factor in not getting the job. Be careful not to make this a defensive question. Frame it as a growth moment for you.

Make a list of things you want to change or work on before your next interview. Practice interviewing with someone else. Try to interview as much as possible to continue improving.

ILLEGAL QUESTION	EFFECTIVE RESPONSE
Are you a U.S. citizen?	"I am authorized to work in the United States."
How will you deal with children (or your spouse) and business travel?	"I can meet the needs of my travel and work schedule." "I have nothing in my personal life that would prevent me from doing a good job or would compromise the organization." Try to follow with a positive, related question, such as: "My experiences traveling for business and training have always been beneficial and positive. What kind of travel will this position require?"

18.2 How Do You Create a Business Presentation?

1 **Starting**
2 **Researching**
3 **Creating**
4 **Presenting**
5 **Evaluating**

Most of the time, business presentations will be either reports or recommendations.

REPORTS

Oral **reports** are forms of informative speaking designed to present business-related information to others. What you report on is tied to your profession or expertise, but some general topics might be to:

- Account for resource usage such as supplies, hours, and employees.
- Update coworkers or other departments on project progress or concerns.
- Announce findings.
- Offer professional insight and expertise.
- Introduce new information, products, or purchases.

RECOMMENDATIONS

Recommendations are proposals arguing for a belief or course of action and, therefore, are a form of on-the-job persuasion. This presentation often asks the audience to:

- Approve of your proposal.
- Adopt your ideas or solutions.
- Buy your product or services.

The process for creating a public speech works for a business presentation with minor changes. For example, what you need to know about your audience becomes more focused and related to the professional setting. Remember to consider each of the five basic activities of the creative process.

1

Starting

When reporting information or making recommendations in the workplace, forgetting to consider who will be present is one of the most common mistakes. You still need to think about the personal beliefs, values, attitudes, and needs audience members might have in relationship to your topic and the workplace.

For example, you may have a negative or hostile audience if you are a director presenting information about your area within the company and several other directors—who have concerns that your area is getting too much of the company's resources—are present. Or, if the company president is attending, you should be future oriented for the betterment of the company. You should seek to answer:

- Who will attend? Will any guests or key players in the organization (such as the president, a client, or an outside vendor) attend?

- What level of knowledge and understanding will the audience have about your topic? If key players are present, is their level of knowledge or understanding different?

- Given the knowledge and understanding of your audience, what types of questions or concerns are they likely to have?

- If you are making a recommendation, is there anyone in the audience that you could enlist as an advocate to help support your viewpoint?

- Given your knowledge of the audience members, what do you want them to understand, remember, or do?

- How might the speaking situation influence your message and/or the audience? What is the occasion, time of day, and place? What is the current climate within the workplace?

Once you have an idea of the audience, the depth of the topic, and the situation, you need to create a specific purpose and central idea just as you would for an informative or persuasive speech. Some examples might be:

SPECIFIC PURPOSE	CENTRAL IDEA
To inform the board of directors about the efficiency of the Technology Help Desk	The Technology Help Desk has seen a significant increase in efficiency during the past 12 months.
SPECIFIC PURPOSE	CENTRAL IDEA
To persuade the board of directors to invest in new software to track accounting transactions	Accounting software by Account Now will decrease human error, speed up transactions, and create necessary tracking information for yearly audits.

→ See Tab 1 for help with audience or situation analysis, a specific purpose, or a central idea.

CHECKLIST for a Business Presentation Specific Purpose and Central Idea

❑ Does my specific purpose contain my general purpose, my audience reference, and my objective?

❑ Does my central idea focus on one topic?

❑ Is my central idea a complete declarative sentence?

❑ Are both clear and concise? Do they relate to the audience and situation?

2

Researching

Researching for a business report or recommendation may involve some of the same support materials and options for locating such materials as the more traditional public speech (the Internet, the library, interviews, or surveys).

However, presentations in the workplace often require that you do more in-house research, such as collecting pertinent information from peers or those who report to you, asking for statistics or facts from other departments or vendors (someone who supplies a service or product to your organization), or searching out corporate-created documentation.

These types of support materials may even need to be created for your presentation. Most organizations have in-house procedures and forms required for the generation of statistics and facts. Your manager will often know the proper protocol or who to contact. Some organizations have places on their websites dedicated to forms and directions for such requests.

When making a recommendation, you should demonstrate how your suggestion is good for the entire organization and not just your department or area. If the recommendation involves change, be prepared to help your audience see how the change is in their best interest. Change is scary for most people, so try to anticipate objections and research/prepare a rebuttal for each one. Finally, research any recent issues that could positively or negatively influence your recommendation. Recognize those issues in your presentation, and try to highlight or eliminate them as a variable in coworkers' acceptance of your recommendation.

Start your research early. You might need to rely on someone else's schedule, and you should follow the same principles and guidelines outlined for selecting, testing, and locating support materials.

→ See Tab 2 for detailed help with researching.

CHECKLIST for Researching a Business Presentation

❏ What sources outside of workplace ones can I use to support my speech? What could local libraries, Internet sources, and interviews offer me? What government agency (city, state, or federal) could be helpful?

❏ What in-house documentation could offer support for my speech?

❏ Would it be helpful to interview managers or staff directly related to my area and other areas in the company?

❏ What recent issues could positively or negatively influence my speech, both inside and outside the company?

PRACTICING ETHICS: Honest Recommendations

When making recommendations, you should hold yourself to the same ethical considerations you use when trying to persuade others.

- Do not hide or omit relevant information.
- Do not manipulate information to make it appear better than it is.
- Use ethical sources and cite them appropriately.

3

Creating

Sketch out a working outline to help you visualize the materials you will need for the presentation and to help you focus. The majority of workplace presentations are shorter than 20 minutes. Three main points work best for this time frame, but your topic or organizational strategy might suggest a different number of points. Just keep in mind your time constraint.

Once you have collected your support materials, create the preparation outline. The chronological, topical, or spatial strategies are used most often in reports.

CHRONOLOGICAL:

The lab's budget from the past three years, the current year's budget, and the projections for the next three years demonstrate effective resource allocation.

TOPICAL:

Our current expenditures for employee benefits are divided between health, disability, and retirement.

SPATIAL:

The new conveyor system is most efficient in the creation, assembly, and packaging sectors.

Causal, comparative, or problem–solution strategies are most common for recommendations.

CAUSAL:

Poor response time, ineffective equipment, and inferior materials account for low consumer satisfaction.

COMPARATIVE:

Our current inventory tracking software is better than TrackWright's.

PROBLEM–SOLUTION:

Investing more money in bonuses, benefits, and employee education will improve employee retention.

Other strategies may work as well for either your report or recommendation. For example, Monroe's motivated sequence works well in an effective sales presentation.

Remember to use links between each part of your presentation to guide your listeners. The introduction and conclusion to your report or recommendation should have the same functional parts as any speech. In an on-the-job presentation, you are likely to use startling statements, narration or anecdotes, questions, and quotations as your attention-getting devices or WOW statements.

→ See Tab 3 for more help with creating your outlines.

4

Presenting

The type of language you use should be appropriate to you, your audience, and the occasion. No matter your profession, your workplace will have a certain level of professional language, and you should strive to meet it—or to be just a little better.

For the most part, you want to use formal language when speaking on the job. When using formal language, be careful not to take shortcuts such as using contractions (*y'all*), colloquialisms (*all y'all*), slang (*dude*), acronyms, abbreviations, or jargon. Such language can appear to be sloppy, lazy, or confusing at best. Interculturally, informal language can be confusing and misunderstood.

Most often, you will present your reports and recommendations extemporaneously. Your delivery should be enthusiastic. Good eye contact, especially with key people, is important to build the credibility of your message and your ethos.

If you are planning to use a presentation aid, rehearse with it. You should:

- Have multiple backups (e.g., your PowerPoint or Prezi presentation on the computer and on a jump drive in the event the computer must be replaced).

- Have extra equipment if possible. For example, a spare bulb for the projector can save valuable time. Check the equipment early to have extra time to solve issues.

- Know the technical assistance personnel and contact numbers. Have a phone available.

- Create handouts or paper copies of your slide presentation. If something major goes wrong, you can distribute the handouts. For general use after your presentation, you could make your slides available on a website. Be sure to include the URL in your presentation.

- If a website is an important part of your presentation, figure out what you will do if the site suddenly is not available or goes out partway through your presentation. Be prepared for anything.

You might need to give your report via speakerphone, videoconferencing, or web conferencing equipment, so know how to use it and know your organization's etiquette for these procedures. You should:

- Make sure someone has tested all the connections just prior to the meeting.

- Make sure phone numbers are correct if conducting a phone conference.

- Ask everyone at the remote sites if they can adequately hear and/or see.

Pages 228–233 offer advice on conducting mediated presentations.

→ See Tab 4 for help with presenting in general.

PRACTICING ETHICS: Principled Employees

When you consider being an ethical and successful speaker on the job, you must:
- Be open to differences.
- Use reliable evidence, logic, and reasoning.
- Be sensitive to the power of language.
- Be dedicated and thorough in citing sources.
- Accept responsibility for your communication.
- Support and endorse freedom of expression.

5

Evaluating

As the speaker or an audience member, try to listen critically, not defensively. Because business presentations are connected to your profession and livelihood, you can quickly become defensive. Withhold judgment until you have heard the entire message. As a speaker, respect the knowledge, expertise, and perspective your audience members bring to the presentation and listen to their suggestions.

After each presentation, seek out someone in the audience who can mentor you as a professional speaker. Ask him or her to evaluate your effectiveness. If you are an audience member and have praise for or concerns about a fellow employee's speaking abilities or delivery methods, offer constructive evaluation.

Sometimes, businesses will ask you to complete a formal written evaluation of a report or recommendation. These evaluations tend to be general and focused on content.

→ See Chapter 12 for detailed help with listening critically.

→ See Chapter 13 for more on evaluating your and others' presentations.

CHECKLIST for Shaping a Business Presentation

❏ How might my topic influence the professional lives of my audience? How could that interfere with or support my message?
❏ What can I use to grab their attention?
❏ How might the workplace environment interfere with or support my message?
❏ What is an appropriate delivery style for this situation? How can I improve on my confidence level to help the audience listen better?
❏ During the presentation, what cues are the audience members sending me, and how can I address or use them beneficially?

CHECKLIST for Listening in the Workplace

❏ Am I giving the speaker my full attention? Did I turn off electronic devices that might distract me? Did I put away work or papers that might distract me?
❏ Am I actively listening to the content of the message?
❏ Am I critically listening to the content?
❏ If the topic is sensitive for me, am I being careful not to become defensive? Am I listening to the content rather than crafting a defensive response?
❏ Am I effectively giving feedback to the speaker?

Building Improvement Session, Thursday 12:00–2:00 pm

1. Did you find the content of this session helpful? If so, what was its most useful aspect for you?
2. What did you find less helpful about the content of the session? What would you like more information on?
3. Was the presentation effective?
4. Were the audiovisual aids and handouts effective?
5. What improvements can you offer?

18.3 How Do You Effectively Communicate in a Meeting?

1 Lead
2 Participate

In many jobs, meetings can be a significant part of your regular activities whether you are a leader or a participant. Meetings are a specific form of communicative interaction that can have different goals, such as sharing information, brainstorming ideas, making decisions, creating materials, or motivating employees. Some meetings are formal, conducted under strict rules, ethics, and customs. Usually formal meetings best fit civic organizations, clubs, and government. Informal meetings are more common in the workplace but should adhere to rules, ethics, and appropriate customs.

1

Lead

If you are leading the meeting, these guidelines will help you conduct an effective and productive meeting.

- Have a purpose and share it. Holding an unnecessary, undefined meeting wastes time and lowers morale.

- Create an agenda and send a copy to each attendee. An agenda is a written document outlining the meeting's goal and what will be covered during the meeting, item by item. Depending on your workplace norms or what works best for you as a leader, your agenda could simply list each item to be considered during the meeting or it could be very detailed. Detailed agendas often list how each item will be considered (for information, for discussion, or for action), who is presenting the item, and how much time will be spent on each item. In either case, you want your information to be specific enough that participants can prepare accordingly. Include the date, time, and location of the meeting.

- If the meeting was called suddenly, quickly type an agenda to be distributed at the beginning of the meeting or take a few minutes to outline orally what will be covered.

- If you will call on someone to speak, make sure he or she is aware of when and for how long. Give the person enough notice to prepare.

- Set beginning and ending times for the meeting, and share this information with participants in advance. Make sure you can see a clock or watch during the meeting.

- Select a room large enough to accommodate known participants and maybe a few extra, in case a participant invites someone else. Make sure all necessary equipment is present and working before the start of the meeting.

- Start your meetings on time and end when you said you would, even if you are not finished.

- Arrive a few minutes early and chat with participants. By doing so, you personalize your relationship with the group and give them time to talk "off topic" about things that might otherwise come up during the meeting.

- Turn off your cell phone, unnecessary computers, or other distracting devices. Doing so in front of the participants can be a subtle hint that they should do the same. Close the door to minimize interruptions.

- Conduct introductions if new participants or guests are present.

- Keep control of the meeting. Do not let a participant take it over or monopolize the time. Limit the amount of time someone can speak, and try to engage all participants. Be energetic and focused.

- Save enough time at the end of the meeting to summarize what transpired, divide up responsibilities or tasks, ask if there are any questions, and thank the participants for their input.

- If needed, arrange a time and date for the next meeting.

2
Participate

Participants share the responsibility of using meeting time wisely and productively. As a participant, you should:

- Respond quickly when asked to participate in a meeting. You may be important to an agenda item, and the meeting may need to be rescheduled if you cannot attend.

- Read the agenda as soon as you get it, to see what you need to prepare. Anticipate how you might respond to questions about each item, and do your research.

- Be on time. This includes mediated meetings. Late arrivals are obvious and annoying. They will interrupt the flow of the meeting and could cause unnecessary repetition of information already discussed.

- During the meeting, actively listen and pay attention, focus on the agenda items, and keep your discussion to a minimum. Allow others to participate, and try not to interrupt. Be enthusiastic.

- Ask questions when appropriate, and write down your follow-up responsibilities.

→ See Chapter 19 for additional information on leading and participating in small group situations such as meetings.

TIP: Applying Public Speaking Skills

Even though the focus of this book is oral communication, you can apply many of the skills learned here to written forms of communication. For example, formal working outlines are much like meeting agendas.

18.4 How Do You Effectively Communicate in a Review?

Reviews (or performance appraisals) are part of a process to assess and discuss employee work performance. They are usually conducted by the employee's supervisor or manager and can include human resources staff. Like the evaluation process discussed in Chapter 13, reviews seek to recognize strengths and accomplishments, identify areas needing improvement, and offer suggestions. This process usually occurs annually but can be more frequent for various reasons. A review usually includes some type of standard evaluation sheet and an oral discussion of the employee's performance. A good evaluation should describe the work behavior, judge its worth, and logically justify that view based on rational norms.

→ See Chapter 13 for more on how to evaluate.

RECEIVING REVIEWS

Even when you have had a great year at work, the review process can seem a bit nerve-racking. So meet the evaluation process head on with a commitment to do an even better job next year. Listen critically, not emotionally, to what the evaluator is suggesting. Do not let other employees influence your response to the evaluation process. Be confident that if you do a good job, it will be reflected in the evaluation. For more insights into the process, read through the next section on giving reviews.

> **TIP: Stay Positive**
>
> Remember what Chapter 13 suggests about the positive aspects of evaluation.
> - Evaluation is a "good thing."
> - Evaluation teaches critical thinking.
> - Evaluation builds your confidence.
> - Evaluation makes you better.

GIVING REVIEWS

If you are a manager, evaluating your employees is one of your most significant tasks. Your evaluation can, and often should, influence an employee's morale, retention, and the rewards he or she will receive. Here are a few suggestions:

- Locate a standard evaluation form. Your organization may have one that you must use and is consistent with all areas of the organization. If not, you can make one by researching what others use or collecting examples from the Internet and other written sources. Make sure you include a place for your signature, the employee's signature, and the date you discussed the evaluation. You might include a section where the employee can add two or three goals for the coming year.

- Employees should never be surprised by your reviews if you have given them feedback throughout the year. As a manager or supervisor, you should consistently mentor and advise those who report to you. This review process should simply be a summary of your periodic conversations with each employee.

- If the evaluation form allows for explanation, provide details. The employee will be better able to improve or maintain a good work ethic if he or she understands the issues.

- On the written form, try to start with the good and follow with suggestions for improvement. Find a location for the oral review that is not threatening (unless, in extreme cases, that is necessary). Be confident in your evaluation but not authoritarian. Using a friendly and conversational approach recognizes that this is often a difficult process for employees.

- Ask if the employee understands the evaluation or has any concerns with it. Try to come to a consensus on the value of the suggestions. Before ending the evaluation, both of you should sign and date the forms. Make a copy for the employee.

CONFIDENCE BOOSTER

The great football coach Vince Lombardi once said, "Confidence is contagious. So is the lack of confidence." So surround yourself with colleagues who are confident and positive in their jobs. Demonstrate confidence in what you do—it will uplift others and you too.

EMPLOYEE PERFORMANCE EVALUATION

Employee Name: .... Position: ....

Department: ....

Evaluation Purpose: .... Annual .... Evaluation Date: ....

New Employee .... Other ....

Position Knowledge
Consider ability to apply knowledge to daily activities:

☐ Below expectations   ☐ Marginal expectations   ☐ Meets expectations   ☐ Frequently exceeds expectations   ☐ Consistently exceeds

Comments: ....

Chapter 18: Review

ASSESSING YOUR KNOWLEDGE

18.1 How Do You Effectively Communicate in an Interview?

Objective 18.1: **DESCRIBE HOW TO EFFECTIVELY COMMUNICATE IN AN INTERVIEW**

- As an interviewer, prepare to conduct the interview: meet with human resources, review the candidate's file, set up a time and location, and construct questions. During the interview, observe and listen closely to the candidate. Think about how the candidate will fit job requirements and the office environment. Check references.
- As an interviewee, tailor your letter, résumé, and/or application to the job. Always proofread and update any document you send to the potential employer. Prepare for the interview by researching the job and the organization. Practice introducing yourself, and prepare questions to ask the interviewer. The day of the interview, dress appropriately, arrive early, and be confident. Afterward, send a thank-you note.

→ See pages 424–429.

18.2 How Do You Create a Business Presentation?

Objective 18.2: **DEMONSTRATE HOW TO CREATE A BUSINESS PRESENTATION**

Most of the time, you will give either an oral report or a recommendation. Oral reports are a form of informative speaking designed to present business-related information to others. Recommendations are proposals arguing for a belief or course of action. The process of creating a public speech works for a business presentation with minor changes.

- Start by conducting an audience analysis of who will be there and might react to you and your topic. Consider the situation and how detailed you need to be about the topic. Then, create a specific purpose and central idea, keeping in mind the information you gained from the analysis.
- Conduct the necessary research. Presentations in the workplace may involve some of the same types of research as any speech but often require more in-house research. Remember to collect pertinent information from peers or those reporting to you, and ask for information from other departments or vendors. The key to on-the-job research is to start early. You may need to wait for a response to a request.
- The majority of workplace presentations are 20 minutes or less. Sketch out your working outline early, and create your preparation outline once you have conducted your research.
- You will give most workplace presentations extemporaneously. Think about your language, how to use presentation aids, and if you will be giving a mediated presentation.
- Listen to and evaluate a business presentation objectively.

→ See pages 430–435.

18.3 How Do You Effectively Communicate in a Meeting?

Objective 18.3: **EXPLAIN HOW TO EFFECTIVELY COMMUNICATE IN A MEETING**

In many jobs, meetings will be a significant part of your regular activity whether you are a leader or a participant.

- As a leader, conduct meetings only if they are necessary and defined. Create a detailed agenda when possible. Notify those you might call on during the meeting. Set beginning and ending times and stick to them. Select a room that will work well for each meeting. Prepare yourself and the room, and conduct necessary introductions. Save time at the end to summarize and divide up tasks. If needed, arrange the next meeting.
- As a participant, share the responsibility for using meeting time wisely. Be prepared for the meeting, focus on the agenda during the meeting, and ask appropriate questions.

→ See pages 436–437.

18.4 How Do You Effectively Communicate in a Review?

Objective 18.4: **SUMMARIZE HOW TO EFFECTIVELY COMMUNICATE IN A REVIEW**

Reviews are part of a process to assess and discuss work performance. If you are receiving a review, consider the process a "good thing," listen objectively, and be confident you can do a better job. If giving a review, use the appropriate form for your organization or create one, give feedback throughout the year so an employee is not surprised at the formal review, be detailed, and give positive marks as well as concerns. Ask if the employee understands the issues and possible ways to improve.

→ See pages 438–439.

TERMS TO REMEMBER

reports (430)
recommendations (430)
reviews (438)

19

SPEAKING IN SMALL GROUPS

People who work together will win, whether it be against complex football defenses or the problems of modern society.[1]

VINCE LOMBARDI

19.1 What Is a Small Group?

Determining an exact definition of a small group is difficult because the term *small* is so ambiguous. Small could be two, 20, or more, depending on what you are comparing it to. However, some parameters can help you define what constitutes small group communication.

First, what number of people constitutes a small group? Two people communicating with each other is called a *dyad*. According to Katherine Adams and Gloria Galanes in *Communicating in Groups*, dyads function differently because they immediately cease to exist if one person leaves the dyad, and they do not have multiple communication networks or leadership hierarchies. Therefore, a **small group** must include at least three people. The upper number is more complicated. Indeed, if you asked several communication scholars for a limit, most would say it falls somewhere between seven and 20, with the majority preferring seven to 12 communicators.

What communication scholars can agree on is defining small group communication based on how the process works. **Small group communication** occurs when three or more people unite over time for a common purpose, feel a sense of belongingness, and have the ability to influence each other and the outcome. Most often, these people come together in face-to-face interaction, but today, virtual groups are possible. **Virtual small groups** function much like other small groups, only they may never, or rarely, meet face-to-face; they interact primarily through electronic media.

SMALL GROUP TYPES

Small groups can be either social or working groups. **Social groups** form when individuals come together informally for the purpose of socializing. These groups may use an activity in place of a major goal, as a means for gathering and interacting. For example, a group of friends may meet once a month as a gourmet club, fixing meals and swapping recipes. The goal is to socialize, and the gourmet theme is the means.

Working groups are more formal and are created to work on a specific task. A study group you form for a particular class is a working group.

The table below describes the different types of working groups you might encounter in your personal and professional lives.

TIP: Group Development

Identifying the stage a group is having the most trouble with will help you assist the group to move on and to be productive.

SMALL GROUP DEVELOPMENT

According to Bruce Tuckman and Mary Ann Jensen in "Stages of Small-Group Development Revisited," when small groups form, they go through five phases.

- **Forming:** The group creates its identity, seeks the leader's guidance and direction, and determines membership and roles.

- **Storming:** The group starts focusing on its goal and may become complex as power and relationship issues emerge.

- **Norming:** Occurs after the conflict of the storming phase is expressed and addressed. The members begin to outline necessary tasks and assignments to achieve their goal.

- **Performing:** The "real work" phase where the group conducts the work necessary to make a decision or solve a problem.

- **Terminating/Reforming:** The end point for the entire group. The group is done with that task and either disbands or reforms with a new goal.

TYPE OF BUSINESS OR CIVIC WORKING GROUP	WHAT IS IT?
Decision-making group	A group that draws conclusions and decides policies for action
Problem-solving group	A group united to solve a particular problem
Focus group	A group that addresses an issue and searches for the best solution
Brainstorming team	A group charged with generating ideas but not evaluating them
Project team	A group consisting of members with the necessary expertise to perform all the activities required to create and produce a product, service, etc.
Advisory group	A group of experts who offer skilled advice to an individual or group that needs to make a decision
Quality assurance group	A group that works to improve the quality of an organization's products, services, etc.

19.2 What Roles Can You Play in a Small Group?

1 Leader
2 Member

When a small group is formed, you will either play the role of leader or member. A leader is sometimes called a chairperson (or chair). As a member of the group, your role will be further defined as the group moves through the development phases.

1

Leader

During small group communication, a *leader* is a person who guides the group toward its goal. The tools for analyzing and researching a speech's audience, situation, and topic will help when leading a group. For example, leaders need to analyze a group's membership to determine strengths and weaknesses. Leaders will also analyze the situation surrounding the group's task and the broader audience that its decisions will affect. Developing a specific purpose and central idea that encapsulate the group's goal will focus group activities.

In some groups, although rarely in a working group, you may not have a leader. This absence of leadership usually evolves and works best when each member has equal influence and status or in groups such as advisory or focus groups. Recognizing the type of leader you are will help you determine how to relate to other group members.

TYPE OF LEADER	HOW IS THIS LEADER CHOSEN?
Implied leader	When other group members defer to a member because of her or his rank, expertise, or other characteristics
Designated leader	By election or appointment when the group is formed
Emergent leader	When a member evolves as leader during the early stages of the group's formation

➜ See Tab 1 for help with audience or situational analysis and focusing on a topic.

LEADERSHIP STYLES

Leadership style refers to how a leader chooses to lead or influence the group. The leader may select the style based on what he or she is comfortable with or what is necessary with the group members and situation.

The three leadership styles are:

Authoritarian leaders (also called *autocratic*) assume and maintain control over the group. Such leaders tell their groups what needs to be done, and how, and ask for minimal advice from the members. Although authoritarian leaders can be demanding and controlling, they are effective in situations where the solution to a problem is obvious and simply needs to be carried out; time is short; members are new to the workplace or situation; or there is a crisis or disaster. This style is not a license to degrade, abuse, or threaten, and it requires a wise use of power.

Democratic leaders (also called *participative*) involve group members in decision-making and/or creative processes. These leaders guide the discussion and offer insight. Here, either the group makes the final decision or the leader maintains control over the final decision. This leadership style works best when you need the knowledge and expertise of others.

Laissez-faire leaders (also called *delegative* or *free rein*) give group members complete freedom with the process necessary to reach the goal. However, the leader is still responsible for the the final decisions. This style of leadership works best when members are capable of analyzing the situation and doing something about it. However, the laissez-faire style is often misused, leaving the group confused and frustrated.

TASKS OF A LEADER

The main responsibility of a leader is to facilitate and manage the types of communication (procedural, task, and maintenance) required to reach a group's goal.

Procedural communication includes the routine interactions necessary for group functions, such as:

- Establishing the places, dates, and times the group will meet
- Setting and distributing the agenda
- Finding a room, setting up equipment, and taking care of personal needs (water, coffee, comfortable space, etc.)
- Preparing and distributing materials
- Taking notes or minutes or appointing someone else to do so
- Summarizing at the end of each meeting

Task communication includes the necessary interactions during the group meetings to keep the group on task to reach its goal. These interactions include:

- Helping the group with decision-making or problem-solving processes
- Helping research and collect information
- Pushing the group to consider all options
- Assigning tasks to each member
- Helping the group reach a consensus

Maintenance communication activities involve creating and maintaining effective interpersonal relationships within the group:

- Controlling conflict and bad behavior
- Determining if members are fulfilling their tasks
- Creating and maintaining a supportive environment

2

Member

Usually, you will assume the responsibility of group member. Although the situation will dictate the number of group members, many communication scholars suggest that the most effective groups have seven to nine members and a leader. With too few members, you might not have the necessary knowledge base; too many members will impede the decision-making process. In a classroom setting, groups of four or five seem to work well.

As a member, you will bring your expertise to the group, be given special tasks to complete, and take on certain membership roles. Members can use audience and situational analysis to examine who and what will be affected by a group's decisions and to conduct research to guide those decisions. Outlining can help organize ideas.

Positive member roles are clustered as either group task or group interaction roles. If you take on a **group task role**, your behavior will assist the group with completing tasks and the group goal. A **group interaction role** helps create and maintain a positive climate and interpersonal relationships.

Not all group member roles are positive, however. A member (or members) of the group might play a **self-centered role** by focusing on his or her own needs.

Based on Thomas E. Harris and John C. Sherblom's text *Small Group and Team Communication*, the table on page 449 outlines the various roles members may play in a group.

→ See Tab 1 for help with analysis, Tab 2 for research guidance, and Tab 3 for outlining ideas.

PRACTICING ETHICS: 5-C Principles

To be a productive and ethical member of a small group, you must act in a responsible way. Recognize and dedicate yourself to the 5-C principles of small group membership to become a productive and ethical participant.

Commitment:
Be willing to give the group your complete attention, and align your personal goals with the group's goal. Do not impair or destroy the group goal by manipulating others for a personal goal.

Confidential:
Often, sensitive issues are discussed by groups, so be respectful of privacy and personal conversation. Only share group discussions outside of the small group when appropriate.

Coalesce:
Allow the group members to come together and work *with*—rather than against—each other. Avoid interpersonal conflicts by being civil, courteous, respectful, and inclusive. Encourage all to contribute.

Contribute:
Use your talent for the betterment of the group and complete your tasks. An effective group requires *every* member to be responsible.

Concentrate:
Stay on task and focus on the group goal. Do not hijack the discussion.

GROUP TASK ROLES (Positive)	**Initiator** proposes and prods the group for new ideas, goals, plans, activities, etc.
	Elaborator asks for clarification, expands on ideas or suggestions, and develops thoughts.
	Coordinator puts ideas together, organizes, and promotes cooperation.
	Summarizer pulls work and ideas together and makes connections to previous work and discussion.
	Recorder takes good notes on the proceedings, prepares minutes, or creates reports.
	Evaluator thinks critically and offers effective analysis of ideas.
	Information giver or seeker researches for data, facts, and other materials related to the goal of the group.
	Opinion giver draws conclusions about group actions or discussion based on his or her beliefs, values, interpretations, and judgments.
	Clarifier asks for more details to make the group's discussion less ambiguous.
	Consensus taker asks how the group feels about issues, discussions, or actions.
	Agenda setter suggests a path or procedure to take or how to make a decision.
GROUP INTERACTION ROLES (Positive)	**Encourager** reinforces group cohesiveness by recognizing and openly appreciating contributions.
	Supporter tends to follow the lead of other members by supporting and agreeing with others' proposals or ideas.
	Harmonizer works to relieve tension by mediating, compromising, or offering new suggestions.
	Gatekeeper allows all members to have a say in the process.
	Observer focuses on observing and commenting on the process the group is taking.
	Standard setter helps set and enforce standards, rules, and norms.
	Tension reliever works at making members feel at ease with each other by encouraging informality, using humor, and/or developing a group spirit.
SELF-CENTERED ROLES (Negative)	**Blocker** blocks progress by *constantly* objecting, repeatedly bringing up old issues, and refusing to accept or support a group decision.
	Attacker prevents effective collaboration by harshly criticizing and threatening others.
	Avoider does not contribute, refuses to deal with conflict, hides emotions, and cannot take a stance.
	Dominator controls, interrupts, and refuses to listen to other options or opinions.
	Attention seeker is always boasting and calling attention to herself/himself or engages in games or humor for attention.
	Joker engages in games and humor that distract group work.
	Special-interest pleader pleads for his or her own subgroup or special interest at the expense of group time and resources.

19.3 How Do Groups Make Decisions or Solve Problems?

Often groups are brought together to make a decision or to solve a problem. Even a class's small group assignments frequently complete one of these tasks. Numerous decision-making methods are available, and many are variations of reflective thinking, first identified by philosopher John Dewey (1910).

Harris and Sherblom outline one of these variations, called the **DECIDE model**, for decision making and problem solving. Their unique approach makes it easy to remember the steps, and with slight modifications, DECIDE resembles the creative process for any type of public speaking. The table on the next page explains each step. You can use this model as an outline or to plan tasks for any group you are part of that needs to solve a problem. The next time you are in a student group with an assignment, think of the assignment as a problem to solve and use this model to do so.

1
STARTING

2
RESEARCHING

3
CREATING

4
PRESENTING
➔ See pages 452–453

5
LISTENING & EVALUATING

THE DECIDE MODEL

THE STEPS	WHAT NEEDS TO BE ESTABLISHED	EXAMPLES
Define the goal and problem	What are the group objectives? What is the problem? Why, when, where, how, and for whom is it a problem?	The 5,000 jobs lost last year are a concern for the city, industry, housing market, and taxpayers, as they demonstrate a loss in growth and potential.
Examine issues preventing goal success	What is causing the problem, and how severe is it? To reach your goal, what would be satisfactory, realistic, or achievable?	The closing of major industries and lost jobs in higher education and the medical field seem to be the sources of the problem. This job loss is 50 percent more than in 2008. Our goal is to reduce the number of jobs lost by 25 percent (still above 2008).
Consider alternatives	What are the criteria or standards for solving the problem? What are potential solutions?	Potential solutions are to rally for more state funding of higher education and medicine or to work at attracting new businesses.
Initiate a decision	Which solution is the best according to the group?	Because the state budget is being drastically cut, rallying for more state funds seems useless. Therefore, we should work to bring more new businesses to town.
Develop a plan	How will you implement the solution?	We will create tax cut incentives, build assistance programs, and step up public relations activities to attract growing industries.
Evaluate the results	Did the solution work? Was it too costly?	Although somewhat costly initially to the city and still high, the lost-job rate did drop 15 percent, which was better than for any other city in the state.

PRACTICING ETHICS: Avoiding Groupthink

Avoid groupthink. *Groupthink* is the willingness to conform to what the group thinks at the moment rather than to critically think about the issue and potentially come to a better conclusion. According to Adams and Galanes, thoroughly exploring the problem (vigilance), encouraging "anything goes" brainstorming, establishing norms for evaluating conclusions, preventing leaders from stating preferences too early, and inviting outside input will help prevent groupthink.

19.4 How Do Groups Present Their Findings?

1 **Determine the Format**
2 **Create the Presentation**
3 **Give the Presentation**
4 **Listen and Evaluate**

1

Determine the Format

Once a group comes to a decision, the members may need to present their findings or decisions to a larger audience. There are five group presentation formats.

Group oral report:

A speech reporting the findings, conclusions, and decisions of the group and given by the group leader or someone selected from the group to do so. A question and answer session may follow.

Forum:

An interactive session between the audience and the small group. Here, the audience can offer their comments as well as ask questions. A forum may follow a symposium or prepared speech. Forums require significant knowledge of the topic.

Symposium:

A series of short reports by each group member, presented to an audience. Each report is coordinated to prevent duplication of information. A moderator introduces and connects each speech and summarizes after all are given. There may be a question and answer session.

Colloquium:

A public discussion between the group members in front of a public audience. The members usually have divergent views, a moderator facilitates, and the audience may participate in a question and answer session.

Panel discussion:

Usually led by a moderator or chairperson, this format is designed to give information about an issue, problem, or recommendation.

2
Create the Presentation

- Determine the goal and central idea of the presentation. As with an informative or persuasive speech, this step requires analyzing your audience and the situation as well as narrowing your topic. Make sure each group member understands and supports the goal and focus of the presentation.
  → See Chapter 3 for help with focusing a central idea.
- Adhere to your presentation format.
- Assign individual tasks. If you agree to do something, do it.
- Create preparation and delivery outlines for each member. Think about electing someone to serve as moderator to help connect the individual parts. Moderators should also try to facilitate interaction between the presenters and the audience.
  → See Tab 3 for more on creating outlines.
- Use language appropriate to the audience and situation. Define any specialized terms.

CHECKLIST for Creating Group Presentations
- ❏ Has my group determined the goal?
- ❏ Does each member have an assigned task?
- ❏ Did we create preparation and delivery outlines?
- ❏ Do we have a moderator?
- ❏ Have we created necessary presentation aids? Are they consistent?
- ❏ Have we practiced enough to be effective?

3
Give the Presentation

- Create necessary presentation aids. If each member creates his or her own, try to coordinate them.
- Rehearse as a group several times. Working with each other and using the presentation aids will uncover any trouble spots. Time your presentation to ensure that you are within the limit. Panels and forums are usually extemporaneous or impromptu. Symposiums and oral reports may be delivered extemporaneously, from a manuscript, or from memory.
- Dress for the occasion.
- Use technology if appropriate and available.
  → Refer to Tab 4 for help with language, delivery, or presentation aids.

4
Listen and Evaluate

- Listen/watch for verbal and nonverbal feedback from your audience and respond.
- Be ready to take and answer questions.
- Evaluate the presentation for its effectiveness.
  → See Tab 5 for guidance on listening and evaluating.

CONFIDENCE BOOSTER
Practicing with your group will build confidence, so encourage the group to practice several times. Incorporate ways to interact with your presentation aids or other group members to lessen your apprehension.

Chapter 19: Review

ASSESSING YOUR KNOWLEDGE

19.1 What Is a Small Group?

Objective 19.1: **DESCRIBE WHAT CONSTITUTES A SMALL GROUP**

A small group must include at least three people, with an upper limit of between seven and 20 people, depending on the scholarly definition. Small group communication occurs when three or more people unite over time for a common purpose, feel a sense of belongingness to the group, and have the ability to influence others and the outcome. Such groups might meet face-to-face or as virtual small groups. Social and working groups are the two types of small groups.

Small group development goes through five phases.

- When a group creates its identity, seeks guidance and direction from the leader, and determines membership and roles, it is in the *forming* phase.
- When the group starts to focus on its goal and possibly experiences the complexity of power and relationship issues, the group is in the *storming* phase.
- When the group begins to outline necessary tasks and assignments, this is the *norming* phase.
- The *performing* phase is where the group conducts the work necessary to make a decision or solve a problem.
- The final phase is the *terminating/reforming* phase. The group is done with that task and either disbands or reforms with a new goal.

→ See pages 444–445.

19.2 What Roles Can You Play in a Small Group?

Objective 19.2: **IDENTIFY ROLES YOU CAN PLAY IN A SMALL GROUP**

In small groups, you will be either a leader or a member.

As a leader:
Implied, *designated*, and *emergent* are the three types of leaders, based on how the leader is selected for the position. There are also three leadership styles, which refer to how a leader chooses to lead or influence the group. The *authoritarian leader* assumes and maintains control over the group. The *democratic leader* involves group members in decision-making and/or creative processes. The *laissez-faire leader* gives group members complete freedom with the process necessary to reach the goal. The main responsibility of a leader is to facilitate and manage the types of communication (procedural, task, and maintenance) required to reach a group's goal.

As a member:
As a group member, you will bring your expertise to the group, be given special tasks, and take on certain membership roles. Positive membership roles are clustered as either group task or group interaction roles. Negative or potentially unproductive roles are self-centered roles.

→ See pages 446–449.

19.3 How Do Groups Make Decisions or Solve Problems?

Objective 19.3: **SUMMARIZE HOW GROUPS MAKE DECISIONS OR SOLVE PROBLEMS**

There are numerous decision-making methods available. However, the DECIDE model, by Harris and Sherblom, resembles the creative process for any type of public speaking discussed in this book. The six steps to the model are:
• Define the goal and problem.
• Examine issues preventing goal success.
• Consider alternatives.
• Initiate a decision.
• Develop a plan.
• Evaluate the results.
Decision-making methods such as this one will help you avoid groupthink. Groupthink is the willingness to conform to what the group thinks now rather than to critically think about the issue and potentially come to a better conclusion.

➜ See pages 450–451.

19.4 How Do Groups Present Their Findings?

Objective 19.4: **EXPLAIN HOW GROUPS PRESENT THEIR FINDINGS**

To present findings, the group must decide on the format (group oral report, forum, symposium, colloquium, or panel discussion), create the presentation, give the presentation, listen and watch for the audience's feedback, and evaluate the presentation.

➜ See pages 452–453.

TERMS TO REMEMBER

small group (444)
small group communication (444)
virtual small groups (444)
social groups (445)
working groups (445)
forming (445)
storming (445)
norming (445)
performing (445)
terminating/reforming (445)
implied leader (446)
designated leader (446)
emergent leader (446)
authoritarian leaders (447)
democratic leaders (447)
laissez-faire leaders (447)
procedural communication (447)
task communication (447)
maintenance communication (447)
group task role (448)
group interaction role (448)
self-centered role (448)
DECIDE model (450)
groupthink (451)

Practical Pointers for Tab 9

FAQs

I've never been a group leader before. How do I do it?

Being an effective leader takes good observation skills, time, and practice. When you are part of a group, make a conscious effort to note what other effective leaders do. Pay particular attention to how they facilitate the procedural, task, and maintenance communication of each group. Try to make notes about what works, what doesn't, and when. Put yourself in the position to lead when possible. The act of doing will help you learn what works for you and what does not. Most leaders are confident, ethical, prepared, and future oriented. They listen well to others, are resourceful, communicate clearly, and are supportive when possible.

How do I deal with members who take on unproductive behavior in a group?

You will remember from Chapter 19 that the roles of blocker, attacker, avoider, dominator, attention-seeker, joker, and special-interest pleader are all negative, self-centered membership roles. They can be very destructive if allowed to control the group. Both the leader and the other members of the group need to help prevent these behaviors from influencing the group productivity. Here are some suggestions:

- Model effective or positive behavior yourself.
- Try to pull decisions away from the person or behavior that they exhibit.

- Ignore the behavior and it might go away (however, don't rely on this technique too long).
- Praise effective behavior within the group.
- Return to the goals outlined in the agenda.
- Limit the amount of time each member has to speak when offering input or engaging in a discussion.
- If you are a member of the group, meet with the group leader for advice on how to deal with the behavior.
- If you are the leader, you might need to take this particular member aside and discuss the ineffective behavior and potential consequences.

ADDITIONAL SUPPORT

For more support for interviewing, search online for sites and articles such as these:

offices.trincoll.edu/depts_career/guides /resume.shtml

www.themuse.com/advice/the-ultimate -interview-guide-30-prep-tips-for-job -interview-success

careerservices.princeton.edu/ undergraduate-students/interviews -offers/preparing-interviews

For more information about illegal interview questions, try such sites as:

http://www.workforce.com/articles /interview-questions-legal-or-illegal

www.businessinsider.com/illegal -interview-questions-2015-4?op=1

NCA's Learning Outcomes in Communication

In 2015, the National Communication Association (NCA) revealed learning outcomes for graduates with a Communication degree. Although this course is considered general education and not representative of an entire degree curriculum, it is one of the foundational courses dedicated to a major communication skill, public speaking, which is central to the discipline and represents the discipline to those on the outside. As part of a curriculum that offers basic skills to the general student body and may feed into the communication major, it is important for this book to address all of the outcomes and many of the related abilities at an introductory level.

The following pages (458–469) provide a quick reference to key places where *DK Guide to Public Speaking* addresses NCA's learning outcomes. Note that only the relevant abilities taught in the course are listed. For the complete list of abilities and more information about NCA's Learning Outcomes in Communication project, see www.natcom.org/LOC.

CONTENTS

NCA information that appears on pages 457–469 comes from the National Communication Association, "What Should a Graduate with a Communication Degree Know, Understand, and Be Able to Do?" (NCA, 2015). Reprinted with permission of NCA, www.natcom.org.

LOC #1: Describe the Communication Discipline and Its Central Questions

ABILITIES	REFER TO ...
• Articulate the importance of communication expertise in career development and civic engagement.	**Tab 1 STARTING** **Chapter 1** 1.1 When will you use the skills offered in this book? *2–3* 1.5 How can you be an ethical public speaker? *14–17* **Tab 9 SPEAKING IN PROFESSIONAL & GROUP SETTINGS** **Chapter 18** On-the-job speaking, *423–439* **Chapter 19** Speaking in small groups, *443–453*

LOC #2: Employ Communication Theories, Perspectives, Principles, and Concepts

ABILITIES	REFER TO ...
• Explain Communication theories, perspectives, principles, and concepts. • Apply Communication theories, perspectives, principles, and concepts.	**Tab 1 STARTING** **Chapter 1** Overview of public speaking, *1–21* **Chapter 2** 2.1 Why do you need to know your audience and situation? *26–27* 2.2 What do you need to know about your audience? *28–29* 2.3 What specific traits do you need to investigate? *30–35* **Tab 2 RESEARCHING** **Chapter 5** Selecting and testing support materials, *103–123* **Tab 4 PRESENTING** **Chapter 9** Using language successfully, *191–207*

LOC #2: Employ Communication Theories, Perspectives, Principles, and Concepts (continued)

LOC #3: Engage in Communication Inquiry

ABILITIES

- Apply Communication scholarship.

REFER TO ...

Practicing Ethics boxes throughout the book

Tab 1 STARTING

Chapter 1
1.5 How can you be an ethical public speaker?
14–17

Tab 2 RESEARCHING

Chapter 5
Selecting and testing support materials, *103–123*

Tab 3 CREATING

Chapter 7
Organizing the speech body, *155–169*

Chapter 8
Introducing and concluding your speech, *173–187*

Tab 4 PRESENTING

Chapter 9
9.1 What makes language so important? *192–195*

Chapter 10
10.5 How do you prepare for a mediated
presentation? *228–233*

Tab 5 LISTENING & EVALUATING

Chapter 12
Listening, *269–281*

Chapter 13
Evaluating speeches, *285–295*

Tab 6 SPEAKING TO INFORM

Chapter 14
The informative speech, *299–331*

LOC #3: Engage in Communication Inquiry (continued)

LOC #4: Create Messages Appropriate to the Audience, Purpose, and Context

ABILITIES	REFER TO …
	All chapters in *DK Guide to Public Speaking* support this learning outcome. Some specific discussions for each ability include:

ABILITIES

- Locate and use information relevant to the goals, audiences, purposes, and contexts.

- Select creative and appropriate modalities and technologies to accomplish communicative goals.

- Adapt messages to the diverse needs of individuals, groups, and contexts.

REFER TO …

All chapters in *DK Guide to Public Speaking* support this learning outcome. Some specific discussions for each ability include:

Tab 2 RESEARCHING

Chapter 4
Locating support materials, *67–99*

Chapter 5
Selecting and testing support materials, *103–123*

Tab 4 PRESENTING

Chapter 10
10.5 How do you prepare for a mediated presentation? *228–233*

Chapter 11
Using presentation aids, *237–265*

Practicing Ethics boxes throughout the book

Tab 6 SPEAKING TO INFORM

Chapter 14
14.2 What is the creative process for informative speaking? *302–303*
14.3 How do you choose a focused informative topic? *304–311*

Tab 7 SPEAKING TO PERSUADE

Chapter 15
Tools for persuading, *335–355*

Chapter 16
16.1 What is the creative process for persuasive speaking? *360–361*
16.2 How do you choose a focused persuasive topic? *362–369*

Tab 8 SPEAKING ON SPECIAL OCCASIONS

Chapter 17
17.3 How do you write a special occasion speech? *404–407*

LOC #4: Create Messages Appropriate to the Audience, Purpose, and Context (continued)

• Present messages in multiple communication modalities and contexts.

LOC #4: Create Messages Appropriate to the Audience, Purpose, and Context (continued)

- Adjust messages while in the process of communicating.

- Critically reflect on one's own messages after the communication event.

Tab 1 STARTING

Chapter 2
2.6 How can you adapt to your audience and situation during the speech? *42–43*

Tab 4 PRESENTING

Chapter 10
Delivering your speech, *211–233*

Practicing Ethics boxes throughout the book

Tab 5 LISTENING & EVALUATING

Chapter 13
Evaluating speeches, *285–295*

Tab 6 SPEAKING TO INFORM

Chapter 14
14.7 How do you evaluate an informative speech? *330–331*

Tab 7 SPEAKING TO PERSUADE

Chapter 16
16.6 How do you evaluate a persuasive speech? *388–395*

Tab 8 SPEAKING ON SPECIAL OCCASIONS

Chapter 17
17.3.7 Evaluate the special occasion speech, *407*

Tab 9 SPEAKING IN PROFESSIONAL & GROUP SETTINGS

Chapter 18
18.2.5 Evaluating, *435*

Chapter 19
19.4.4 Listen and evaluate, *453*

LOC #5: Critically Analyze Messages

ABILITIES

- Identify meanings embedded in messages.
- Articulate characteristics of mediated and non-mediated messages.
- Recognize the influence of messages.
- Engage in active listening.
- Enact mindful responding to messages.

REFER TO ...

LOC #6: Demonstrate the Ability to Accomplish Communicative Goals (Self-Efficacy)

ABILITIES

- Identify contexts, situations, and barriers that impede communication self-efficacy.
- Perform verbal and nonverbal communication behaviors that illustrate self-efficacy.
- Articulate personal beliefs about abilities to accomplish communication goals.
- Evaluate personal communication strengths and weaknesses.

REFER TO …

Confidence Booster boxes throughout the book

Practicing Ethics boxes throughout the book

Tab 1 STARTING

Chapter 1
1.3 How can you be a successful public speaker? *6–9*
1.4 How can you overcome a fear of public speaking? *10–13*
1.5 How can you be an ethical public speaker? *14–17*

Tab 4 PRESENTING

Chapter 9
Using language successfully, *191–207*

Chapter 10
Delivering your speech, *211–233*

Tab 5 LISTENING & EVALUATING

Chapter 12
Listening, *269–281*

Chapter 13
Evaluating speeches, *285–295*

LOC #7: Apply Ethical Communication Principles and Practices

ABILITIES

- Identify ethical perspectives.
- Articulate the ethical dimensions of a communication situation.
- Choose to communicate with ethical intention.
- Propose solutions for (un)ethical communication.
- Evaluate the ethical elements of a communication situation.

REFER TO ...

Practicing Ethics boxes throughout the book

Tab 1 STARTING

Chapter 1
1.5 How can you be an ethical public speaker? *14–17*

Tab 2 RESEARCHING

Chapter 4
4.7.2 Be an ethical researcher, *97*

Tab 5 LISTENING & EVALUATING

Chapter 13
Evaluating speeches, *285–295*

Tab 7 SPEAKING TO PERSUADE

Chapter 16
16.6 How do you evaluate a persuasive speech? *388–395*

Tab 9 SPEAKING IN PROFESSIONAL & GROUP SETTINGS

Chapter 18
18.1 How do you effectively communicate in an interview? *424–429*

LOC #8: Utilize Communication to Embrace Difference

ABILITIES

- Recognize individual and cultural similarities and differences.
- Appreciate individual and cultural similarities and differences.
- Respect diverse perspectives and the ways they influence communication.
- Articulate one's own cultural standpoint and how it affects communication and world view.
- Demonstrate the ability to be culturally self-aware.
- Adapt one's communication in diverse cultural contexts.

REFER TO …

Tab 1 STARTING

Chapter 1
1.3.1 Be audience centered, *7*
1.5.2 Support and endorse freedom of expression, *15*
1.5.3 Value diversity, *15*

Chapter 2
Getting to know your audience and situation, *25–43*

Tab 4 PRESENTING

Chapter 9
Using language successfully, *191–207*

Chapter 10
Delivering your speech, *211–233*

Tab 5 LISTENING & EVALUATING

Chapter 12
12.4 What can prevent effective listening? *276–277*

Tab 6 SPEAKING TO INFORM

Chapter 14
14.3.1 Get to know the audience and situation, *304–305*
14.4 How do you research the informative speech? *312–313*

Tab 7 SPEAKING TO PERSUADE

Chapter 16
16.2.1 Get to know the audience and situation, *362–363*

Tab 8 SPEAKING ON SPECIAL OCCASIONS

Chapter 17
17.3.2 Analyze the audience and situation, *405*

LOC #9: Influence Public Discourse

ABILITIES

- Explain the importance of communication in civic life.
- Utilize communication to respond to issues at the local, national, and/or global level.
- Advocate a course of action to address local, national, and/or global issues from a Communication perspective.
- Empower individuals to promote human rights, human dignity, and human freedom.

REFER TO …

Many Practicing Ethics features

Glossary

abbreviation A shortened form of a word or phrase, used to represent the full form. (Chapter 9)

acronym A word formed from the initials or other parts of several words. (Chapter 9)

ad hominem The fallacy of attacking the person instead of challenging an argument. (Chapter 16)

ad populum The fallacy of arguing a claim is accurate because many people believe it or do it. (Chapter 16)

after-dinner speech A speech with the general purpose to entertain but also containing a relevant message. (Chapter 17)

analogy A way of explaining the unfamiliar by comparing and contrasting it to what is familiar. (Chapter 5)

appeal to tradition The fallacy of assuming something is best or correct because it is traditional. (Chapter 16)

appeals The means by which speakers prove or establish the arguments they are making. (Chapter 15)

appearance A person's physical choices of dress and grooming practices. (Chapter 10)

appreciative listening Listening for recreation or enjoyment. (Chapter 12)

arbitrary The principle that the relationship between a word and what it stands for is random, subjective, or coincidental. (Chapter 9)

argument A reason or a series of reasons given to support an assertion. (Chapter 15)

argument by analogy The conclusion that something will be accurate for one case if it is true for another similar case. (Chapter 15)

argument by authority An argument dependent on the ethos and authority of others whose testimony you use to support a claim. (Chapter 15)

argument by cause An argument that demonstrates a relationship between two events or factors by focusing on the premise that one caused the other to occur. (Chapter 15)

argument by deduction An argument constructed of a series of general statements that together prove correct the claim/conclusion. (Chapter 15)

argument by induction Predicting probability, this argument reasons from specific cases to a general statement. (Chapter 15)

articulation How completely and clearly you utter a word. (Chapter 10)

asynchronous engagements Communication events that occur when the speaker and audience interaction is not in real time. (Chapter 10)

attending The phase of hearing when a person pays attention to a given sound or equivalent stimulus. (Chapter 12)

attention-getter An opening statement, image, or action that grabs the audience's interest. (Chapter 8)

attitudes Learned, persistent psychological responses, predispositions, or inclinations to act one way or feel a particular way toward something. (Chapters 2, 15)

audience The person or persons receiving the speaker's message and contributing feedback. (Chapters 1, 2)

audience and situation analysis A systematic investigation of the characteristics that make the audience and speaking situation unique. (Chapter 2)

audience centered A way of speaking that recognizes the audience's unique characteristics and viewpoints. (Chapters 1, 2)

audio clips Recordings of sound only. (Chapter 11)

auditory learners People who learn best by listening and through effective use of sound. (Chapter 14)

authoritarian leaders Leaders who assume and maintain control over small groups by telling the groups what needs to be done, and how, and asking for minimal advice from the members. (Chapter 19)

background The speaker's and audience's identities and life experiences. (Chapter 1)

backing Additional support to prove a warrant in an argument. (Chapter 15)

bar graphs Visuals consisting of vertical or horizontal bars that represent sets of data. (Chapter 11)

behaviors The unconcealed actions or reactions people have, often in response to stimuli, related to their attitudes, beliefs, and values. (Chapter 15)

beliefs The ideas a person accepts as plausible based on interpretation and judgment. (Chapters 2, 15)

blatant plagiarism Occurs either when speakers take an entire speech or document and present it as their own or when speakers take pieces of information from other sources and link the parts together, creating an entire speech out of someone else's words, ideas, or illustrations. (Chapter 1)

blog A website or web page that contains regular postings by its author(s) and may allow visitors to post comments. (Chapter 4)

body The central portion of the speech, made up of the main points, the multiple layers of subordinate points, and links. (Chapter 6)

brainstorming The process of stimulating creative thinking through free association or clustering. (Chapter 3)

brief examples Specific instances illustrating a single general notion. (Chapter 5)

causal strategy An organizational strategy used when the audience needs to understand the cause and effect or consequences of something, by either leading up to a particular result or backtracking from the effect to the cause. (Chapter 7)

central idea The concise, single sentence summarizing and/or previewing what a speaker will say during a speech; also called a thesis statement, theme, or subject sentence. (Chapter 3)

central processing Being motivated to listen to and think critically about a message. (Chapter 15)

channel The means of getting the message across, such as a voice over the airwaves or visual messages in the form of nonverbal and visual aids. (Chapter 1)

character The measure of a speaker's intentions and concern for the audience as perceived by the audience. (Chapter 15)

charisma How a speaker's personality is perceived by the audience. (Chapter 15)

charts Visual summaries of complex or large quantities of information. (Chapter 11)

chronological strategy An organizational strategy that moves through steps in a process or develops a timeline. (Chapter 7)

citations The oral and written credits for the original sources of the support materials used for a speech. (Chapter 5)

claim An assertion made in an argument. (Chapter 15)

clichés Overused words or phrases that have lost their effect. (Chapter 9)

closed-ended questions Questions that prompt one-word or short answers (often "yes" or "no"). (Chapters 2, 4)

coercion The act of forcing a person, via threats or intimidation, to do something against his or her will. (Chapter 15)

cognitive dissonance theory A theory emphasizing the human need to be in a harmonious (consonant) state and that conflicting attitudes, values, beliefs, ideas, or behaviors can cause an inharmonious (dissonant) feeling. (Chapter 15)

common ground The overlap within the speaker's and audience's identities and life experiences. (Chapter 1)

communication apprehension Fears about engaging in a communicative interaction with one or more persons. (Chapter 1)

comparative advantage A strategy to convince an audience that one thing is better than another, by comparing the two. (Chapter 7)

comparative strategy An organizational strategy using the practice of compare and contrast. (Chapter 7)

comparison The act of pointing out similarities between two or more ideas, things, factors, or issues. (Chapter 5)

competency The audience's perception of how knowledgeable the speaker is about a topic. (Chapter 15)

conclusion The ending of the speech, which allows the speaker one last moment to reinforce the main ideas as well as "wow" the audience. (Chapters 6, 8)

connotative meaning The emotional and personal reaction a person may have to a word. (Chapter 9)

contrast The act of pointing out differences between two or more ideas, things, factors, or issues. (Chapter 5)

critical listening Listening carefully to a message to judge it as acceptable or not. (Chapter 12)

critical thinking The careful, deliberate determination of whether one should accept, reject, or suspend judgment about a claim or information and the degree of confidence with which one accepts or rejects it. (Chapter 12)

culture The system or learned patterns of beliefs, values, attitudes, norms, practices, customs, and behaviors shared by a large group of people that are taught from one generation to the next. (Chapters 2, 9)

databases Extensive collections of published works, such as magazine, newspaper, and journal articles, all in electronic form. They contain descriptions, citation information about the articles, and often the full text of the articles. (Chapter 4)

DECIDE model An approach for decision making and problem solving that has six steps: defining the goal, examining issues preventing success, considering alternatives, initiating a decision, developing a plan, and evaluating the results. (Chapter 19)

decoding The process of interpreting messages. (Chapter 1)

definitions Brief explanations designed to inform the audience about something unfamiliar. (Chapter 5)

delivery outline An outline that maintains the structure of the preparation outline while eliminating much of the detail, contains delivery hints, and is used during the speech. (Chapter 6)

demagogue A speaker who stirs up the audience's feelings by strong provocation. (Chapter 16)

democratic leaders Leaders who involve group members in the decision-making and/or creative processes. (Chapter 19)

denotative meaning The accepted meaning of a word, which can be found in the dictionary. (Chapter 9)

derived ethos The credibility the audience assigns a speaker during a speech. (Chapter 15)

description The stage of evaluation when the evaluator offers what he or she saw and heard. (Chapter 13)

descriptive statistics Numerical facts or data that describe or summarize characteristics of a population or a large quantity of data. (Chapter 5)

designated leader A leader elected or appointed by the group when it is formed. (Chapter 19)

design principles Principles relating to the arrangement and placement of various elements of visual aids for optimum effect. (Chapter 11)

dialect The way a culture or coculture pronounces and uses language. (Chapter 10)

direct eye contact The act of a speaker briefly looking into audience members' eyes. (Chapter 10)

drawings Maps, sketches, diagrams, plans, or other nonphotographic representations. (Chapter 11)

egocentrism The tendency for an audience to be interested in the topics that relate and matter to them. (Chapter 12)

either-or fallacy The fallacy of considering only two options when more are possible. (Chapter 16)

elaboration likelihood model (ELM) Suggests that people process persuasive messages based on their commitment or involvement, by either central or peripheral processing. (Chapter 15)

emblems Speech-independent or culturally learned gestures that have a direct verbal translation. (Chapter 10)

emergent leader A group member who evolves as the leader during the early stages of the group's formation. (Chapter 19)

empathic listening Listening for the purpose of giving the speaker emotional support. (Chapter 12)

encoding The process of conveying messages. (Chapter 1)

enthymeme A truncated syllogism that omits an obvious minor premise. (Chapter 15)

enunciation The ability to use distinctiveness and clarity while saying linked whole words. (Chapter 10)

environmental barriers External noise or conditions within the speech location that interrupt the listener's ability to concentrate, such as movement, heat, cold, or hard seats. (Chapters 2, 12)

ethics A set of standards that guide you to good and honorable behavior. (Chapter 1)

ethnicity Traits that stem from national and religious affiliations. (Chapter 2)

ethnocentrism The notion that one's culture is superior to other cultures. (Chapters 1, 15)

ethos Appeal of reliability or credibility. (Chapters 1, 15)

eulogy A speech presented after a person's death. (Chapter 17)

evaluation A detailed description of a speech's successes and/or the improvements needed, which is grounded in a justified judgment. (Chapter 13)

evidence The information that proves a claim to be accurate. (Chapter 15)

examples Specific instances or cases that embody or illustrate points in a speech. (Chapter 5)

expectancy-outcome values theory A theory suggesting that people will evaluate the cost, benefit, or value related to making change in an attitude, value, belief, or behavior to decide if it is worthwhile or not. (Chapter 15)

expert testimony Firsthand knowledge or opinions from someone the audience recognizes as a specialist in a field related to the speech's topic. (Chapter 5)

extemporaneous speaking Delivery method in which the speaker plans out, rehearses, and delivers the speech from an outline of key words, phrases, and delivery notes. (Chapter 10)

extended examples Detailed stories, narratives, illustrations, or anecdotes allowing the audience to linger on the vivid, concrete images the examples create. (Chapter 5)

external noise Any environmental or linguistic barrier to effective listening that originates outside of the listener's mind and body. (Chapters 2, 12)

facial expressions The use of facial features and muscles to convey a speaker's internal thoughts and feelings. (Chapter 10)

facts Verifiable bits of information about people, events, places, dates, and times. (Chapter 5)

fallacy A faulty argument or error in logic. (Chapter 16)

false analogy The fallacy of comparing two things that are not similar or are dissimilar in a radical or important way related to the claim. (Chapter 16)

faulty emotional appeal The fallacy of using only emotional appeal or unethically manipulating an audience's emotions to get them to accept a claim. (Chapter 16)

faulty syllogism A flawed argument in which the major premise, minor premise, and/or conclusion is not factual. (Chapter 15)

faulty use of authority A fallacy caused by using information or testimony from someone who is not a legitimate authority on the subject. (Chapter 16)

feedback The verbal or nonverbal messages encoded by the audience and decoded by the speaker. (Chapter 1)

figurative analogy Compares and contrasts two essentially different things. (Chapter 5)

fillers Unnecessary sounds, words, or phrases that serve no purpose and do not add to the understanding of the message, such as "um." (Chapters 9, 10)

First Amendment Amendment to the U.S. Constitution establishing freedom of speech by stating, "Congress shall make no law … abridging the freedom of speech, or the press …" (Chapter 1)

flowcharts Charts that diagram step-by-step development through a procedure, relationship, or process. (Chapter 11)

follow-up questions New questions the interviewer produces based on the interviewee's answers to questions during an interview. (Chapter 4)

forming The small group development stage in which the group creates its identity, seeks guidance and direction from the leader, and determines membership and roles. (Chapter 19)

general purpose The unrestricted aim of a speech. (Chapter 3)

gestures The use of the body or parts of it (hands, arms, eyes, or head) to convey a message or feeling during a speech. (Chapter 10)

graphs Visual representations of numerical (statistical) information that demonstrate relationships or differences between two or more variables. (Chapter 11)

group interaction role A role in which a small group member helps create and maintain a positive climate and interpersonal relationships within the group. (Chapter 19)

group task role A role in which a small group member assists the group with completing tasks and the group goal. (Chapter 19)

groupthink The willingness to conform to what the group thinks at the moment rather than to critically think about the issue and potentially come to a better conclusion. (Chapter 19)

hasty generalization A fallacy in which a general conclusion is drawn without sufficient support materials. (Chapter 16)

hearing Occurs when sound waves strike the eardrum and spark a chain reaction that ends with the brain registering the sound. (Chapter 12)

hits A list of web pages, files, and images related to the terms entered into a search engine. (Chapter 4)

hybrid engagements Communication engagements that occur when part of a speaker's audience is interacting in real time and a subset of the audience is not. (Chapter 10)

hypothetical examples Examples based on the potential outcomes of imagined scenarios. (Chapter 5)

idea bank A list of general words and phrases that could be speech topics. (Chapter 3)

identification The human need and willingness to understand as much as possible the feelings, thoughts, motives, interests, attitudes, and lives of others. (Chapter 1)

identity Made up of a person's beliefs, values, and attitudes. (Chapter 2)

identity knowledge The speaker's understanding of what makes the audience distinctive. (Chapter 2)

illustrators Gestures that are speech dependent or closely linked to what is being said, which help demonstrate the message. (Chapter 10)

implied leader A type of leader that develops when other group members defer to the member because of her or his rank, expertise, or other characteristics. (Chapter 19)

impromptu speaking Delivery method in which the speaker has little or no time for preparation or rehearsal prior to giving the speech. (Chapter 10)

inferential statistics Numerical facts or data that aim to draw conclusions about a larger population by making estimates based on a smaller sample of that population. (Chapter 5)

inflection Varying the pitch of one's voice to demonstrate enthusiasm, excitement, concern, and dedication to the topic. (Chapter 10)

informative listening Listening to gain insight or comprehension, which emphasizes concentrating on language, ideas, and details as well as remembering the knowledge gained. (Chapter 12)

informative speaking Speaking to give the audience completely new knowledge, skills, or understanding about a topic or to increase their current knowledge, skills, or understanding. (Chapter 14)

initial ethos The audience's perception of a speaker before the speech starts. (Chapter 15)

internal noise Any physiological or psychological barrier to effective listening that originates within the body or mind of the listener. (Chapters 2, 12)

internal previews Links that indicate what is next in the speech. (Chapter 6)

internal reviews Links that summarize the information just stated in the previous section of a speech. (Chapter 6)

interviews Information-gathering sessions where one person asks another person or a group a series of prepared questions. (Chapters 2, 4)

introduction The opening of a speech, used to grab the audience's attention, preview the speech, and focus in on the topic. (Chapters 6, 8)

jargon The specialized or technical vocabulary used among members of a profession. (Chapter 9)

judgment The stage of evaluation where the evaluator offers what was good or not about a speech. (Chapter 13)

justification The stage of evaluation where the evaluator explains why something was good or not about a speech. (Chapter 13)

kinesthetic learners People who learn best by experiencing or touching. (Chapter 14)

laissez-faire leaders Leaders who allow their group members complete freedom with the process necessary to reach the group goal. (Chapter 19)

lay testimony Firsthand knowledge or opinion from a peer or an ordinary person other than the speaker, who bears witness to his or her own experiences and beliefs. (Chapter 5)

line graphs Visuals containing numerical points plotted on a horizontal axis for one variable and on a vertical axis for another; the points are then connected to make a line. (Chapter 11)

linguistic barriers External noise or barriers to listening that occur when the verbal and nonverbal messages from the speaker are unfamiliar to or misunderstood by the listener. (Chapters 2, 12)

links Words, phrases, or sentences that make a logical connection between the parts of the body of the speech and/or thoughts. (Chapter 6)

listening The conscious learned act of paying attention, assigning meaning, and responding to a verbal or nonverbal message. (Chapter 12)

literal analogy Compares and contrasts two like things. (Chapter 5)

logical learners People who learn best when they have to reason or think conceptually and abstractly. (Chapter 14)

logos Appeals to the audience's ability to reason logically through statistics, facts, and testimony to reach a conclusion. (Chapters 1, 15)

main points The essential ideas or claims about a topic that comprise the body of a speech. (Chapters 3, 6)

maintenance communication Communication that involves creating and maintaining effective interpersonal relationships within a group. (Chapter 19)

manuscript speaking Delivery method in which a speaker reads word for word from a copy of the speech. (Chapter 10)

Maslow's hierarchy of needs The theory that humans have a hierarchical set of needs that must be met, starting with the lower, more basic needs and progressing to the higher, less basic needs. (Chapters 2, 15)

mean An average of a set of numbers. (Chapter 5)

median The middle value in a set of numbers arranged in increasing order. (Chapter 5)

mediated presentations Presentations that use technology as a channel outside of the speaker or audience to exchange a message. (Chapter 10)

memorized speaking Delivery method in which the speaker delivers a speech from memory exactly as written. (Chapter 10)

message The verbal and nonverbal ideas encoded by the speaker and decoded by the audience. (Chapter 1)

mindfulness The speaker is conscientiously aware of and paying attention to the distinctions of uniqueness within the audience. (Chapter 2)

mode The number that occurs the most in a set of numbers. (Chapter 5)

models Three-dimensional representations. (Chapter 11)

monotone A vocal quality that is constant in pitch, which can be distracting and boring. (Chapter 10)

Monroe's motivated sequence A five-step organizational strategy that motivates an audience to action based on their needs. (Chapters 7, 15)

movement The speaker's use of motion and space during a speech. (Chapter 10)

multimedia The combination of multiple presentation aids (still images, graphs, text, sound, and video) into one choreographed production. (Chapter 11)

mythos Appeals to the audience's sense of history in the larger culture and the need to be a member of that culture; draws on feelings such as patriotism, pride, and valor. (Chapter 15)

negotiation skill The ability to respond to audience differences through sensitivity, politeness, willing adjustment, and collaboration. (Chapter 2)

no-citation plagiarism Occurs when speakers fail to give source credit to a specific part of their speech that has been taken from another source. (Chapter 1)

noise Any unwanted pleasant or unpleasant barrier that prevents effective listening and/or interferes with the message and/or feedback. (Chapters 1, 12)

non sequitur A fallacy in which an argument's conclusion is not connected to the premises. (Chapter 16)

norming The phase of small group development that occurs after the conflict of the storming phase is expressed and addressed. The members begin to outline necessary tasks and assignments to achieve their goal. (Chapter 19)

objective The part of the specific purpose that describes the outcome or behavior the speaker wants the audience to experience or adopt. (Chapter 3)

open-ended questions Questions that allow for discussion and longer responses. (Chapters 2, 4)

oral evaluations Brief overviews, delivered in oral form, describing what the evaluator saw and felt about a speech. (Chapter 13)

organizational charts Charts illustrating the structure or chain of command in an organization. (Chapter 11)

parallelism The arrangement of words, phrases, or sentences in similar patterns. (Chapter 7)

paraphrasing Restating material in a simpler format using the speaker's own words. (Chapter 5)

passivity syndrome Mistakenly believing, as an audience member, that the speaker is entirely responsible for the effectiveness of the message. (Chapter 12)

pathos Appeals to emotions. (Chapters 1, 15)

pause Slowing down the speaking rate or stopping during a speech for effect. (Chapter 10)

performing The phase of small group development in which the group conducts the "real work" necessary to make a decision or solve a problem. (Chapter 19)

peripheral processing Not paying close attention to an argument, or superficially accepting an argument. (Chapter 15)

personal testimony The speaker's experience or point of view. (Chapter 5)

personal traits Audience demographics, or traits such as age, gender, sexual orientation, household type, education, occupation, income, and disabilities. (Chapter 2)

persuasion A deliberate attempt by the speaker to create, reinforce, or change the attitudes, beliefs, values, and/or behaviors of the listener. (Chapter 15)

persuasive speaking Speaking with the general purpose to persuade. (Chapter 15)

photographs Two-dimensional photographic representations. (Chapter 11)

physiological barriers Internal noise such as hunger, sickness, disabilities, pain, or other bodily conditions that can prevent or constrain the listening process. (Chapters 2, 12)

pictographs Bar graphs that use pictures instead of bars. (Chapter 11)

pie graphs Circular graphs with sections representing a percentage of a given quantity. (Chapter 11)

pitch How high or low a person's voice is in frequency, which is determined by how fast or slow the vocal cords vibrate. (Chapter 10)

plagiarism Intentional or accidental use without proper credit of all or a portion of the words, ideas, or illustrations created by someone else. (Chapter 1)

popular sources Publications or sources written for general readers. (Chapter 5)

population The larger group of individuals represented by a small survey group. (Chapter 4)

post hoc ergo propter hoc The fallacy of assuming that because one event comes after another, the first event caused the second. (Chapter 16)

posture A speaker's body position and stance during a speech. (Chapter 10)

preparation outline The detailed, full-sentence outline of a speech. (Chapter 6)

presentation aids Two- or three-dimensional visual items, video footage, audio recordings, and/or multimedia segments that support and enhance a speech. (Chapter 11)

prestige testimony Firsthand knowledge or opinions from a person known for his or her popularity, fame, attractiveness, high-profile activities, and/or age. (Chapter 5)

primacy model Suggests putting the strongest arguments first in the body of the speech, to persuade the audience early in the speech. (Chapter 16)

primary sources Original sources of information, such as photographs, autobiographies, and letters. (Chapter 5)

problem–solution strategy An organizational strategy that demonstrates a problem and explains or advocates a solution. (Chapter 7)

procedural communication The routine communication necessary for a group to function, such as setting the agenda. (Chapter 19)

pronunciation The standard or commonly accepted way to make a word sound. (Chapter 10)

proposition of fact An assertion made in a persuasive speech's central idea to prove something factual—that it is accurate or not. (Chapter 15)

proposition of policy An assertion made in a persuasive speech's central idea that seeks to prove a need for a new or different policy. (Chapter 15)

proposition of value An assertion made in a persuasive speech's central idea that seeks to make a value judgment on what has worth or importance. (Chapter 15)

psychological barriers Internal noise in the form of emotional conditions that may prevent the listener from focusing on and absorbing a message, such as fear, prejudice, or boredom. (Chapters 2, 12)

psychological traits The needs and motivations of the audience. (Chapter 2)

qualifiers Information in an argument that softens the effect of reservations on a claim. (Chapter 15)

quotations Words or passages originally written or said by someone other than the speaker. (Chapter 8)

race The biological differences of humankind often noticeable in physical markers such as color or texture of hair, color of skin and eyes, shape of facial features, and bodily build and proportions. (Chapter 2)

rate The speed at which a person speaks. (Chapter 10)

rationale The stage of evaluation where the evaluator offers the logic or norm behind his or her justification. (Chapter 13)

read/write learners People who learn best when information is transmitted via the effective use of words and, often, visual representations of words. (Chapter 14)

reasoning The rational thinking that humans do to reach a conclusion or to justify beliefs or acts. (Chapter 15)

receiving The physiological process of hearing. (Chapter 12)

recency model Suggests beginning the body of the speech with the weakest argument and ending with the strongest, to persuade the audience. (Chapter 16)

recommendations Business proposals arguing for a belief or course of action. (Chapter 18)

reflexivity Occurs when a speaker takes a moment to consider himself or herself in relation to the speech and vice versa. (Chapter 13)

remembering The final stage of listening, in which the listener retains information. (Chapter 12)

reports Forms of informative speaking designed to present business-related information to others. (Chapter 18)

reservation Information in an argument that notes a claim may not be true all the time. (Chapter 15)

responding The phase of listening in which feedback or a reply is given to the messages that have been processed. (Chapter 12)

reviews Performance appraisals or job-related evaluations. (Chapter 18)

rhetorical questions Questions that the speaker does not expect the audience to answer, which are used for effect rather than to gain knowledge. (Chapter 8)

roast A humorous tribute to a person. (Chapter 17)

sample The surveyed portion of a larger population. (Chapter 4)

schemes Speech devices or language techniques that finesse word order or repeat sounds, words, phrases, sentences, or grammatical patterns. (Chapter 9)

scholarly sources Sources written for readers who are specialists in their academic or professional fields. (Chapter 5)

search engines Specific tools used to locate information on the web. (Chapter 4)

secondary sources Sources that build upon other (often primary) sources by citing, reviewing, quoting, and/or paraphrasing the other materials or sources. (Chapter 5)

self-centered role A role in which a small group member focuses on his or her own needs. (Chapter 19)

signposts Words or phrases that signal to the audience where they are with regard to related thoughts or what is important to remember. (Chapter 6)

situation The location and time in which the process of communication takes place. (Chapters 1, 2)

slippery slope The fallacy of arguing that a small event sets off a chain reaction to disaster. (Chapter 16)

small group A group of at least three and up to about 20 people who unite over time for a common purpose. (Chapter 19)

small group communication Interaction in a group of three or more people who unite over time for a common purpose, feel a sense of belongingness, and have the ability to influence each other and the outcome. (Chapter 19)

social groups Informal groups that form when individuals unite for the purpose of socializing. (Chapter 19)

social traits Relate to how the audience is affected by or identifies with other groups of people. (Chapter 2)

sources Any books, magazines, journals, blogs, websites, e-mail, interviews, or other such resources that contribute information to the creation of a speech. (Chapter 4)

spatial strategy An organizational strategy recognizing space as a method of arrangement. (Chapter 7)

speaker The person who initiates and is responsible for most of the message. (Chapter 1)

speaking competence How well the speaker communicates with others. (Chapter 2)

special occasion speech A speech given to celebrate, commemorate, inspire, or entertain. (Chapter 17)

specific purpose A single statement combining the general purpose, a specific audience, and the speaker's objective. (Chapter 3)

speech anxiety Feelings of uneasiness and fearfulness about preparing or giving a speech. (Chapter 1)

speeches to celebrate Speeches that honor or highlight a person, group, institution, place, or event. (Chapter 17)

speeches to commemorate Speeches that pay tribute to or remember a person, group, institution, place, or event. (Chapter 17)

speeches to entertain Speeches with the general goal to amuse, delight, and engage the audience for the purpose of enjoyment, with a bit of wisdom or tribute thrown in. (Chapter 17)

speeches to inspire Speeches that motivate, stir, encourage, or arouse the audience. (Chapter 17)

speech of award acceptance The response a speaker gives after receiving an award, prize, or honor. (Chapter 17)

speech of award presentation A speech given to announce the recipient(s) of an award, prize, or honor. (Chapter 17)

speech of inspiration A speech that strives to motivate, encourage, move, or arouse an audience in a positive manner. (Chapter 17)

speech of introduction A speech that introduces the next or main speaker. (Chapter 17)

speech to actuate A speech with the purpose of asking an audience to take action. (Chapter 15)

speech to convince A speech with a goal to create a new or change an existing attitude belief, value, or behavior for the audience. (Chapter 15)

speech to describe A speech that describes an object, a person, an animal, a place, or an event. (Chapter 14)

speech to explain A speech that explains or clarifies a concept or issue. (Chapter 14)

speech to instruct A speech that teaches or demonstrates a process. (Chapter 14)

speech to report An oral report or briefing. (Chapters 14, 18)

speech to stimulate A speech focused on overcoming apathy in an audience or reinforcing an existing, attitude belief, value, or behavior. (Chapter 15)

standard of balance The standard that the main points in a speech should be equal or nearly equal to each other in importance and length. (Chapter 6)

statistics Numerical facts or data that are summarized, organized, and tabulated to present significant information about a given population. (Chapter 5)

stereotyping The false or oversimplified generalizing applied to individuals based on group characteristics. (Chapter 2)

storming The phase of small group development in which the group begins focusing on its goal and may become complex as power and relationship issues emerge. (Chapter 19)

storyboarding The act of sketching out the content for and arranging the sequence of visual aids. (Chapter 11)

strategy A plan designed to achieve a goal, particularly concerning the relationship and arrangement of a speech's main points. (Chapter 7)

straw person The fallacy of ignoring key components of a person's actual position and substituting a misrepresented version of his/her claim. (Chapter 16)

subpoints Subordinate points that offer information to support and relate back to the main points of a speech. (Chapter 6)

support materials Any information that explains, elaborates, or validates your speech topic. Also called evidence. (Chapter 4)

surveys Series of questions used to collect quantifiable information from a population. (Chapters 2, 4)

syllogism The classical form of deductive reasoning, featuring major and minor premises and a conclusion. (Chapter 15)

symbolic The principle that a word represents what it is referring to either by association, resemblance, or convention. (Chapter 9)

synchronous engagements Communication engagements that occur when the speaker and the audience interact in real time via some sort of mediation. (Chapter 10)

tables Visuals consisting of numbers or words arranged in rows, columns, or lists. (Chapter 11)

target audience The primary group of people the speaker wants to persuade or engage. (Chapter 16)

task communication The necessary interactions a leader must make during small group meetings to keep the group on task to reach its goal. (Chapter 19)

terminal ethos The audience's perception of the speaker after the speech is finished. (Chapter 15)

terminating/reforming The fifth phase of small group development, in which the group either disbands or reforms with a new goal. (Chapter 19)

testimony Firsthand knowledge or opinions, either your own or from others. (Chapter 5)

toast A speech expressing honor or goodwill to a person, group, institution, or event, punctuated by taking a drink. (Chapter 17)

topical strategy An organizational strategy used when a strong inherent or traditional division of subtopics exists within the main topic. (Chapter 7)

transactional process The fluid process of communication where the speaker and the listener participate equally by simultaneously sending and receiving information to and from one another. (Chapter 1)

transitions Words or phrases signaling movement from one point to another and how the points relate to each other. (Chapter 6)

tribute A speech that commemorates the lives or accomplishments of people, groups, institutions, or events, either with the recipient present or posthumously. (Chapter 17)

tropes Language techniques that transform or enhance ordinary words. (Chapter 9)

understanding The phase of the listening process in which meaning is applied to a sound or equivalent stimulus. (Chapter 12)

values The enduring principles related to worth or what a person sees as right or wrong, important or unimportant, and desirable or undesirable. (Chapters 2, 15)

variety The fluctuation, change, or adjustment of a speaker's volume, pitch, rate, and pauses. (Chapter 10)

video clips Footage from television, movies, or any other type of video. (Chapter 11)

virtual small groups Small groups that function much like other small groups but never, or rarely, meet face to-face and instead interact primarily through electronic media. (Chapter 19)

visual learners People who learn best by obtaining and processing information visually. (Chapter 14)

volume How loud or soft the speaker's voice is. (Chapter 10)

warrants Assumptions that act as links between the evidence and the claim in an argument. (Chapter 15)

websites Online sites that consist of multiple, unified pages beginning with a home page, created and maintained by an individual, group, business, or organization. (Chapter 4)

working groups Formal groups that are created to work on a specific task. (Chapter 19)

working main points The early drafts of a speaker's main points that are subject to change during the course of research. (Chapter 3)

working outline A brief, usually handwritten, outline of the body of the speech used to guide research and organize thoughts during the early stages of creating a speech. (Chapters 3, 6)

written evaluations Assessments given in written form. (Chapter 13)

Bibliography

Adams, Katherine, and Gloria J. Galanes. *Communicating in Groups: Applications and Skills.* 7th ed., McGraw-Hill, 2009, pp. 12–13, 132.

American Association of Retired Persons. "What Skills Are Employers Looking For?" *AARP Work Search*, www.aarpworksearch.org/Inside /Pages/HowEmployableAmI.aspx. Accessed 29 July 2015.

Aristotle. "De Anima." *The Basic Works of Aristotle*, translated by J. A. Smith, edited by Richard McKeon, Random House, 1941, pp. 554–81.

---. "De Caelo." *The Basic Works of Aristotle*, translated by J. L. Stocks, edited by Richard McKeon, Random House, 1941, p. 404.

---. *The Poetics of Aristotle*. Translated by Preston H. Epps, U of North Carolina P, 1942.

---. "Rhetorica." *The Basic Works of Aristotle*, translated by W. Rhys Roberts, edited by Richard McKeon, Random House, 1941, pp. 1325–451.

Burke, Kenneth. *A Rhetoric of Motives*. U of California P, 1969, p. viii.

Carson, Rachel L. *Under the Sea-Wind: A Naturalist's Picture of Ocean Life*. 1st ed., Simon & Schuster, 1941, p. xiii.

Colby, Sandra L., and Jennifer M. Ortman. *Projections of the Size and Composition of the U.S. Population: 2014 to 2060*. No. P25-1143, U.S. Census Bureau, March 2015, www.census.gov/content/dam /Census/library/publications/2015/demo/p25 -1143.pdf.

Corbett, Edward J., and Robert J. Connors. *Classical Rhetoric for the Modern Student*. 4th ed., Oxford UP, 1999, pp. 62–71.

Doyle, Arthur Conan. *The Hound of the Baskervilles*. Grosset & Dunlap Publishers, 1902, p. 36.

Duarte, Nancy. *Slide:ology: The Art and Science of Creating Great Presentations*. O'Reilly Media, 2008, pp. 13, 83, 222.

Ferrell, O. C., and Michael Hartline. *Marketing Strategy*. 3rd ed., Thomson South-Western, 2005, p. 236.

Festinger, Leon. *A Theory of Cognitive Dissonance*. Stanford UP, 1957.

Fishbein, Martin, and Icek Ajzen. *Belief, Attitude, Intention, and Behavior: An Introduction to Theory and Research*. Addison-Wesley, 1975, p. 6.

Fleming, Neil D., and Colleen Mills. "Not Another Inventory, Rather a Catalyst for Reflection." *To Improve the Academy*, vol. 11, 1992, pp. 137–55.

Frymier, Ann Bainbridge, and Marjorie Keeshan Nadler. *Persuasion: Integrating Theory, Research, and Practice*. 2nd ed., Kendall Hunt Publishing, 2010, p. 34.

Gardner, Howard. *Frames of Mind: The Theory of Multiple Intelligences*. Basic Books, 2011.

Harris, Thomas E., and John C. Sherblom. *Small Group and Team Communication*. 5th ed., Allyn & Bacon, 2011, pp. 46–47, 154.

Hofstede, Geert. *Culture's Consequences: Comparing Values, Behaviors, Institutions, and Organizations Across Nations*. 2nd ed., SAGE Publications, 2001.

International Listening Association. "What is ILA?" *ILA*, www.listen.org. Accessed 20 July 2015.

Lancaster, Lynne C., and David Stillman. *When Generations Collide*. HarperCollins Publishers, 2002, 18–32.

Littlejohn, Stephen W., and Karen A. Foss. *Theories of Human Communication*. 9th ed., Thomson Wadsworth, 2008, p. 91.

Lippmann, Walter. "The Indispensable Opposition." *Atlantic Monthly*, vol. 164, no. 2, 1939, p. 188.

Maslow, Abraham. *Motivation and Personality*. Harper & Row, Publishers, 1954, pp. 80–106.

McCroskey, James C. *An Introduction to Rhetorical Communication*. 9th ed., Routledge, 2006.

Monroe, Alan H. *Principles and Types of Speech*. Scott, Foresman, 1935.

Moore, Brooke Noel, and Richard Parker. *Critical Thinking*. 4th ed., Mayfield Publishing, 1995, p. 4.

National Association of Colleges and Employers. "Job Outlook: The Candidate Skills/Qualities Employers Want, the Influence of Attributes." *NACE*, 12 Nov. 2014, www.naceweb.org/s11122014/job-outlook-skills-qualities-employers-want.aspx.

Ogden, Charles K., and Ivor A. Richards. *The Meaning of Meaning*. 6th ed., Harcourt Brace Jovanovich, Publishers, 1944.

Pandit, Vivek. *We Are Generation Z: How Identity, Attitudes, and Perspectives Are Shaping Our Future*. Brown Books, 2015.

Pelias, Ronald J., and Tracy Stephenson Shaffer. *Performance Studies: The Interpretation of Aesthetic Texts*. 2nd ed., Kendall Hunt Publishing, 2007, pp. 181–95.

Petty, Richard E., and John T. Cacioppo. *Communication and Persuasion: Central and Peripheral Routes to Attitude Change*. Springer-Verlag, 1986.

Richter, Jean Paul Friedrich. *Levana; Or, The Doctrine of Education*. Translated by A.H., George Bell and Sons, 1891, p. 309.

Robles, Marcel M. "Executive Perceptions of the Top 10 Soft Skills Needed in Today's Workplace." *Business Communication Quarterly*, vol. 75, no. 4, 2012, pp. 453–65. *Business Source Complete*, doi: 10.1177/1080569912460400.

Sagan, Carl. *The Demon-Haunted World: Science as a Candle in the Dark*. Random House, 1996, pp. 209–17.

Shirky, Clay. *Here Comes Everybody: The Power of Organizing Without Organizations*. The Penguin Press, 2008, p. 165.

Sleep Disorders Center. "Relaxation Techniques." *University of Maryland Medical Center*, 3 Aug. 2010, www.umm.edu. Accessed 10 Aug. 2010.

Syrus, Publius. *The Moral Sayings of Publius Syrus, A Roman Slave*. Translated by Darius Lyman, Jr., L. E. Barnard, 1856, p. 43.

"Ted.com." *Alexa*, 2016, www.alexa.com/siteinfo/ted.com. Accessed 6 Apr. 2016.

Toulmin, Stephen Edelston. *The Uses of Argument*. Cambridge UP, 1958, pp. 94–145.

Toulmin, Stephen, Richard Rieke, and Allan Janik. *An Introduction to Reasoning*. 2nd ed., Macmillan Publishing, 1984, pp. 129–75.

Tuckman, Bruce W., and Mary Ann C. Jensen. "Stages of Small-Group Development Revisited." *Group and Organization Studies*, vol. 2, 1977, pp. 419–27.

United States, Census Bureau. "Current Population Survey, 2010 Annual Social and Economic Supplement." *United States Census Bureau*, Nov. 2010, www.census.gov/hhes/www/cpstables/032010/perinc/new03_001.htm. Accessed 4 Dec. 2012.

Notes

CHAPTER 1
1. Gerald Ford, *A Time to Heal* (Harper & Row, 1979), 50.
2. David G. Myers and Malcolm A. Jeeves, *Psychology through the Eyes of Faith* (Christian College Coalition, 1987), 139.

CHAPTER 2
1. Norman Katlov, *The Fabulous Fanny: The Story of Fanny Brice* (Alfred A. Knopf, 1953), 71.

CHAPTER 3
1. Charles Lamb, "The Genteel Style in Writing," *The Last Essays of Elia* (Home Book Co., [1892?]), 103. The punctuation in this quotation has been modernized.

CHAPTER 4
1. Joan Bauer, *Best Foot Forward* (Penguin Group, 2005), 141.

CHAPTER 5
1. Robert I. Fitzhenry, editor, *The Harper Book of Quotations*, 3rd ed. (Quill/HarperResource, 1993), 398.

CHAPTER 6
1. Thomas Mann, *The Magic Mountain*, vol. 1, translated by H. T. Lowe-Porter (Alfred A. Knopf, 1927), 312.

CHAPTER 7
1. C. William Pollard, *The Soul of the Firm* (ServiceMaster Co., 1996), 123.

CHAPTER 8
1. Franklin Delano Roosevelt, "Pearl Harbor Address to the Nation," Joint Session of Congress (8 Dec. 1941), Washington, address.

CHAPTER 9
1. Sonia Sotomayor, "NYU Commencement Address," *Archives of Women's Political Communication* (16 May 2012), www.womenspeecharchive .org/women/profile/speech/index .cfm?ProfileID=296&SpeechID=5473.
2. Sojourner Truth, "Ain't I a Woman?" Women's Convention (May 1851), Akron, speech.
3. Ludwig Wittgenstein, *Tractatus Logico-Philosophicus*, edited by C. K. Ogden (Harcourt, Brace, 1922), 149.

CHAPTER 10
1. Although commonly attributed to Aristotle, this quotation originates from Will Durant's summation of Aristotle's ideas in *Ethics*, book II, chapter 4, and book I, chapter 7. See Will Durant, *The Story of Philosophy: The Lives and Opinions of the World's Greatest Philosophers* (Pocket Books, 1991), 76.

CHAPTER 11
1. Nancy Duarte, *Slide:ology: The Art and Science of Creating Great Presentations* (O'Reilly Media, 2008), 222.

CHAPTER 12
1. Rachel Naomi Remen, *Kitchen Table Wisdom: Stories That Heal* (Riverhead Books, 2006), 143.

CHAPTER 13
1. Publius Syrus, *The Moral Sayings of Publius Syrus, A Roman Slave*, translated by Darius Lyman, Jr. (L. E. Barnard, 1856), 23.

CHAPTER 14
1. United Nations, " 'If Information and Knowledge Are Central to Democracy, They Are Conditions for Development,' Says Secretary-General" (United Nations, 23 June 1997), www.un.org/press /en/1997/19970623.sgsm6268.html.

CHAPTER 15
1. Ludwig Wittgenstein, *On Certainty*, translated by Denis Paul and G. E. M. Anscombe, edited by G. E. M. Anscombe and G. H. von Wright (Harper & Row, 1969).

CHAPTER 16
1. Henry David Thoreau, *Walden*, 19th ed. (Houghton, Mifflin, 1882), 331.

CHAPTER 17
1. Titus Maccius Plautus, *Asinaria*, edited by Ferruccio Bertini (R.A.D.A.R., 1968), 104.

CHAPTER 18
1. Marty Blalock, "Why Good Communication Is Good Business," *Wisconsin Business Alumni Update* (Board of Regents of the U of Wisconsin, 23 Dec. 2005), about.pdpsolutions.com/bm.doc /goodcommunication.pdf.
2. Laura Harris, *Surrender to Win* (Greenleaf Book Group Press, 2009), 147.

CHAPTER 19
1. Donald T. Phillips, *Run to Win: Vince Lombardi on Coaching and Leadership* (St. Martin's Press, 2001), 22.

Credits

CHAPTER 1

Photos: Tab 1 Fiona Crawford Watson/Moment Open/Getty Images; **1** Manuela Schewe-Behnisch/EyeEm/Getty Images; **2** Realistic Reflections/Alamy Stock Photo; **4** Skynesher/E+/Getty Images; **6** Hero Images/Getty Images; **10** IS581/Image Source/Alamy Stock Photo; **14** Skynesher/E+/Getty Images; **18** Bounce/Cultura/Getty Images; **20** Vernon Wiley/Vetta/Getty Images.

Text: 7, Excerpt from A Time to Heal: The Autobiography of Gerald R. Ford by Gerald R Ford. Published by Harper and Collins, © 1979; **7,** Quote by Michelangelo; **7,** Quote by Martin Luther King Jr; **9,** Quote by Publilius Syrus; **13,** Copyright © by University of Maryland Medical Center. Used by permission of University of Maryland Medical Center; **15,** Excerpt from First Amendment from U.S Constitution. Published by U.S Constitution, © 1979; **15,** Excerpt from On the Heavens by Aristotle. Published by Harvard University Press, © 1939; **21,** Excerpt from Psychology Through the Eyes of Faith by David G. Myers, Malcolm A. Jeeves and Nicholas Wolterstorff. Published by Christian College Coalition, © 1987.

CHAPTER 2

Photos: 24–25 Andres Rodriguez/Fotolia; **26** Hero Images/Getty Images; **28** William Perugini/123RF; **30** VM/E+/Getty Images; **36** Walter Zerla/easyFotostock/Age Fotostock; **38** Moodboard/Cultura/Getty Images; **42** HeroImages/Getty Images.

Text: 6, Excerpt from The Fabulous Fanny: The Story of Fanny Brice by Norman Katkov. Published by Alfred A. Knopf, © 1953; **31,** Based on When Generations Collide by Lynne Lancaster and David Stillman and We Are Generation Z by Vivek Pandit; **32,** Lisa A. Ford-Brown, DK Dorling Kindersley; **34,** Lisa A. Ford-Brown, DK Dorling Kindersley; **34,** From U.S Census Bureau. Published by U.S Census Bureau, © 2010; **41,** Book Shot of Statistical Abstract of the United States 2015. Published by Bernan Press, © 2015; **41,** Screenshot of U.S Census 2020, U.S Census Bureau; **41,** Screenshot of U.S Government Web Portal, USA.gov.

CHAPTER 3

Photos: 46–47 Andresr/E+/Getty Images; **48** Hero Images/Getty Images; **54** Blend Images/Age Fotostock; **56** remik44992/Age Fotostock; **62** Image Source/Getty Images.

Text: 49, Lisa Ford-Brown; **50,** Lisa Ford-Brown; **54** Excerpt from The Genteel Style in Writing in The Last Essays of Elia by Charles Lamb. Published by Home Book Co., © 1892; **58,** Lisa Ford-Brown; **60,** Lisa Ford-Brown.

CHAPTER 4

Photos: Tab 2 Steve Fleming/Moment/Getty Images; **67** Martin Barraud/OJO Images/Getty Images; **68** BillionPhotos.com/Fotolia; **70** CJG - Technology/Alamy Stock Photo; **74** White House; **76** nd3000/Fotolia; **81** Stillfx/Fotolia; **82** Africa Studio/Fotolia; **85** Blend Images/Brand X Pictures/Getty Images; **86** Shock/Fotolia; **88** Hill Street Studios/Blend Images/Getty Images; **92** Wdstock/E+/Getty images; **96** Gala_Khan/Shutterstock.

Text: 69, From Columbia College website. Copyright © by Columbia College. Used by the permission of Columbia College; **72,** From Water Efficient Maize for Africa (WEMA). Copyright © by Monsanto Company. Used by permission of Monsanto Company; **72,** From Water Efficient Maize for Africa (WEMA). Copyright © by Monsanto Company. Used by permission of Monsanto Company; **73,** From Central Missouri Honor Flight. Copyright © 2015 by Central Missouri Honor Flight. Used by the permission of Central Missouri Honor Flight; **73,** From Central Missouri Honor Flight. Copyright © 2015 by Central Missouri Honor Flight. Used by the permission of Central Missouri Honor Flight; **74,** From The Employment Situation in November by Jason Furman, Published by Executive Branch of Government; **74,** From White House website, Executive Branch of Government; **75,** From Artist Statement by Annette Kennedy. Copyright © by Annette Kennedy.Used by permission of Annette Kennedy; **75,** From Annette Kennedy website. Copyright © by Annette Kennedy. Used by the permission of Annette Kennedy; **77,** From University of Colorado library. Copyright © by University of Colorado library. Used by permission of University of Colorado library; **79,** Reprinted courtesy of JSTOR. JSTOR © 2016. All rights reserved; **80,** From The Spunky Coconut Cookbook, Published by Apidae Press/AJB Design Inc;

81, From Paris Attacks Show the Good and Bad of High-Tech Revolution by Matthew Schofield. Copyright © 2015 by Miami Herald. Used by permission of Newscom; **82,** From Mountains in the Sea by Gregory S. Stone. Published by National Geographic Society, © 2012; **83,** From Better Nutrition Every Day, by National Institutes of Health (NIH), 2015; **83,** From NIH News In Health website, National Institutes of Health (NIH); **84,** From Bookshot of Journal of Film and Video. Copyright © by The University of Illinois Press. Used by permission of The University of Illinois Press; **85,** Quote by Joan Bauer; **87,** From Pearson Education, Longman Dictionary Of American English, 4th Ed., ©2008. Reprinted and Electronically reproduced by permission of Pearson Education, Inc., New York, NY.

CHAPTER 5

Photos: 102–103 Vernon Wiley/Vetta/ Getty Images; **104** Monkey Business/ Fotolia; **110** Igor Mojzes/Fotolia; **114** Phil Boorman/Cultura/Getty Images; **118** Creativa Images/Fotolia; **120** Ralf Mohr/Alamy Stock Photo.

Text: 104, From E-Marketing,7e by Raymond Frost and Judy Strauss. Published by Pearson Education, © 2013; **105,** From New CDC estimates Underscore the Need to Increase Awareness of a Daily Pill that Can Prevent HIV Infection by Tom Frieden, Published by Centers for Disease Control and Prevention © 2015; **105,** Lisa A. Ford-Brown, DK Guide To Public Speaking, 3Ed., © 2017. Pearson Education, Inc., New York, NY; **107,** From The New England Journal of Medicine, Bisola O. Ojikutu and Valerie E. Stone, Women, Inequality, and the Burden of HIV, 352. Copyright © 2005

Massachusetts Medical Society. Reprinted with permission from Massachusetts Medical Society. **108,** Lisa A. Ford-Brown, DK Guide To Public Speaking, 3Ed., © 2017. Pearson Education, Inc., New York, NY; **108,** From "Congressional Job Approval Averages Meager 16% in 2015" by Jeffrey M. Jones in Gallup. Published by Gallup Poll Monthly, © 2015; **118,** From "A Blueprint for a Carbon Free America" by Craig Welch, Published by National Geographic Society, © 2015; **118,** Quote from Rhetoric by Aristotle; **119,** Lisa A. Ford-Brown, DK Guide To Public Speaking, 3Ed., © 2017. Pearson Education, Inc., New York, NY; **119,** Lisa A. Ford-Brown, DK Guide To Public Speaking, 3Ed., © 2017. Pearson Education, Inc., New York, NY; **119,** Lisa A. Ford-Brown, DK Guide To Public Speaking, 3Ed., © 2017. Pearson Education, Inc., New York, NY; **123,** From Child Passenger Safety, Safety Alert, published by National Transportation Safety Board, © 2012.

CHAPTER 6

Photos: Tab 3 Eduardo Jose Bernardino/E+/Getty Images; **127** Cathy Yeulet/123RF; **128** Bruno135/123RF; **130** Westend61/ Getty Images; **136** Hero Images/ Getty Images; **144** Jens Lennartsson/ Maskot/Getty Images; **146** PeopleImages.com/DigitalVision/ Getty Images; **148** Juj Wnn/Moment Open/Getty Images.

Text: 128, Excerpt from The Magic Mountain, Vol. 01 by Thomas Mann. Published byAlfred A. Knopf, Inc., © 1927; **130,** Lisa Ford-Brown; **134,** Lisa A. Ford-Brown; **135,** Lisa A. Ford-Brown and DK Dorling Kindersley; **136,** Lisa A. Ford-Brown, DK Dorling

Kindersley; **138–141,** Lisa A. Ford-Brown, DK Dorling Kindersley; **142–143,** Lisa A. Ford-Brown, DK Dorling Kindersley; **150–151,** Lisa Ford-Brown.

CHAPTER 7

Photos: 154–155 PNC/Digital Vision/Getty Images; **156** Tetra Images/Getty Images; **164** Fuse/ Getty Images.

Text: 158, Lisa Ford-Brown; **160,** Lisa Ford-Brown; **163,** Excerpt from Marketing Strategy by O. C. Ferrell and Michael D. Hartline. Published by Thomson South-Western, © 2005; **163,** Lisa Ford-Brown; **166,** Lisa Ford-Brown.

CHAPTER 8

Photos: 172–173 Fuse/Getty Images; **174** HeroImages/Getty Images; **176** ERproductions Ltd/ Blend Images/Getty Images; **180** Tek Images/Science Photo Library/Getty Images; **182** Caiaimage/Caiaimage/ Robert Daly/OJO+/Getty Images; **184** Izabela Habur/E+/Getty Images; **186** Hero Images/Getty Images.

Text: 174–175, "Student Interview, Ashley Hardy, Pearson Education"; **177,** Excerpt from Impaired Driving: Get the Facts. Published by Centers for Disease Control and Prevention, © 2015; **177,** "Student Interview, Rachel K. Wester, Pearson Education"; **177,** Excerpt from Under the Sea-wind: A Naturalist's Picture of Ocean Life by Rachel Carson. Published by Simon and Schuster, Inc., © 1941; **178,** Lisa Ford-Brown; **179,** From Remarks by The President at White House Correspondents' Association Dinner by Barack Obama. Published by The White House, © 2015; **179,** From Remarks by the President on Osama Bin Laden by Barack Obama.

Cultura/Getty Images; **256** Eduardo Rivero/Fotolia; **256** Eduardo Rivero/Fotolia; **256** Eduardo Rivero/Fotolia; **256** Kryssia Campos/Moment Open/Getty Images; **258** HeroImages/Getty Images; **264** Tom Merton/Caiaimage/Getty Images.

Text: 241, Graph/chart originally published in Dire Predictions: Understanding Global Warming, by Michael E. Mann and Lee R. Kump, © 2008 Dorling Kindersley Limited. These graphs based on original data documented in the Fourth Assessment Report of the IPCC. Used by permission of DK Publishing; **242,** Copyright © 2016 Pearson Education; **242,** Graph/chart originally published in Dire Predictions: Understanding Global Warming, by Michael E. Mann and Lee R. Kump, © 2008 Dorling Kindersley Limited. These graphs based on original data documented in the Fourth Assessment Report of the IPCC. Used by permission of DK Publishing; **243,** Graph/chart originally published in Dire Predictions: Understanding Global Warming, by Michael E. Mann and Lee R. Kump, © 2008 Dorling Kindersley Limited. These graphs based on original data documented in the Fourth Assessment Report of the IPCC. Used by permission of DK Publishing; **244,** Excerpt from Slide:ology: The Art and Science of Creating Great Presentations by Nancy Duarte. Published by O'Reilly Media, Inc., © 2008; **254,** Excerpt from Slide:ology: The Art and Science of Creating Great Presentations by Nancy Duarte. Published by O'Reilly Media, Inc., © 2008; **255,** Dorling Kindersley, kids.lovetoknow.com, and animals.sandiegozoo.org; **257,** Lisa A. Ford-Brown and DK Dorling Kindersley; **260,** PowerPoint 2016,

Windows 10, Microsoft Corporation. **262–263,** Screenshot of Prezi. Used with permission from Prezi Inc; **268,** Lisa Ford-Brown.

CHAPTER 12

Photos: Tab 5 Grady Coppell/Photographer's Choice RF/Getty Images; **268** Walter Lippmann; **270** KidStock/Blend Images/Getty Images; **272** imagebroker/Alamy Stock Photo; **274** Rawpixel/Fotolia; **276** Dave & Les Jacobs/Blend Images/Alamy Stock Photo; **278** Poba/E+/Getty Images; **280** HeroImages/Getty Images.

Text: 269, Excerpt from Kitchen Table Wisdom: Stories That Heal by Rachel Naomi Remen. Published by Penguin Group, © 2006; **271,** Quote by Walter Lippmann; **275, 282,** Excerpt from Critical Thinking by Brooke Noel Moore and Richard Parker. Published by Mayfield Publishing Company, © 1995; **275,** Quote by Carl Sagan.

CHAPTER 13

Photos: 284–285 Arturbo/E+/Getty Images; **286** Steve Debenport/E+/Getty Images; **290** Karramba Production/Fotolia; **292** Chris Ryan/Ojo Images/Age Fotostock;

Text: 285, Excerpt from The Moral Sayings of Publius Syrus, a Roman Slave by Publius Syrus. Published by L.E. Bernard & Company © 1856; **288,** Excerpt from The Hound of the Baskervilles by Arthur Conan Doyle. Published by George Newnes © 1902.

CHAPTER 14

Photos: Tab 6 Petar Chernaev/E+/Getty Images; **299** Sharplaninac/Fotolia; **300** Westend61 GmbH/Alamy Stock Photo; **302** kzenon/123RF; **304** Dreaming Andy/

Fotolia; **312** Michael Simons/123RF; **314** Hongqi Zhang/123RF; **320** Bruce P. Brown; **328** Inspirestock Inc./Alamy Stock Photo; **330** Hongqi Zhang/123RF.

Text: 313, Based on: Fleming, Neil D. and Colleen Mills. "Not Another Inventory, Rather a Catalyst for Reflection." To Improve the Academy. 11 (1992): 137-155. Print; and Gardner, Howard. Frames of Mind: The Theory of Multiple Intelligence. New York: Basic Books, 2011; **316,** Quote by Kofi Annan from If Information and Knowledge are Central to Democracy, They are Conditions for development, Says Secretary-General; **318–327,** Lisa Ford-Brown; **319,** Lisa Ford-Brown; **319,** Lisa Ford-Brown.

CHAPTER 15

Photos: Tab 7 George Doyle/Stockbyte/Getty Images; **334** Age Fotostock; **336** Hybrid Images/Cultura/Getty Images; **338** Ariel Skelley/Blend Images/Getty Images; **340** Luke Frazza/AFP/Newscom; **344** Rungroj Yongrit/european pressphoto agency b.v./Alamy Stock Photo; **348** Sam Edwards/OJO Images/Getty Images; **352** Tommi Kokkola Photography/Moment/Getty Images.

Text: 337, Excerpt from Belief, Attitude, Intention and Behavior: An Introduction to Theory and Research, by Martin Fishbein, Icek Ajzen. Published by Addison-Wesley Publishing © 1975; **340,** Excerpt from Oklahoma Bombing Memorial Prayer Service Address by President Bill Clinton; **341,** Excerpt from Statement by the President in His Address to the Nation by President George W. Bush; **342,** Lisa Ford-Brown; **343,** Lisa Ford-Brown;

347, Lisa Ford-Brown; **348,** Quote from On Certainty by Ludwig Wittgenstein translated by Denis Paul, .E.M.Anscombe Basil Blackwell. Published by HarperCollins © 1969; **349,** Based on Keep Chickens! Tending Small Flocks in Cities, Suburbs, and Other Small Spaces, Barbara Kilarski; Chickens in Your Backyard: A Beginner's Guide, Rick and Gail Luttmann.

CHAPTER 16

Photos: 358 MarkGabrenya/E+/Getty Images; **360** JGI/Jamie Grill/Blend Images/Getty Images; **362** Hero Images/Getty Images; **370** Alvarez/Vetta/Getty Images; **372** Yuri Arcurs/Alamy Stock Photo; **376** Amana images inc./Alamy Stock Photo; **386** Hill Street Studios/Blend Images/Getty Images; **388** Hero Images/Getty Images.

Text: 359, Quote by Henry David Thoreau; **364,** ©EBSCO Information Services, 2013. All rights reserved; **371,** Lisa Ford-Brown; **386,** Quote by President Barack Obama; **392,** Quote by Eldridge Cleaver.

CHAPTER 17

Photos: Tab 8 Ladi Kim/Alamy Stock Photo; **398–399** hxdbzxy/123RF; **400** C Flanigan/FilmMagic/Getty Images; **402** Mihailomilovanovic/E+/Getty Images; **404** Hero Images/Getty Images; **408** Jeff Greenberg/Age Fotostock.

Text: 401, Quote by Titus Maccius Plautus from Asinaria. Published by Editrice R.A.D.A.R, © 1968; **413,** Speech by Harry Reid, Reid Eulogy For Senator Daniel Inouye: To Everything A Season, © 2012; **414,** Copyright by John J. Yonker. Used by permission of John J. Yonker; **415,** Speech by Kimberly Albrecht-Taylor. Copyright © 2010 Kimberly Albrecht-Taylor. Used by permission of Kimberly Albrecht-Taylor; **415,** Quote by Agnes George de Mille in Wit and Wisdom of Famous American Women by Evelyn L. Beilenson and edited by Ann Tenenbaum, © 1986; **416,** Quote by Kenneth Haigh in Theater Arts, Volume 42 edited by Edith Juliet Rich Isaacs. Published by Theater Arts Magazine, © 1958; **417,** Quote by Alan Alda; **419,** Speech by Gerald Ford at White House Correspondents Dinner, © 1975.

CHAPTER 18

Photos: Tab 9 Steve Debenport/E+/Getty Images; **422–423** PeopleImages/E+/Getty Images; **424** Stephen Coburn/123RF; **430** Lamb/Alamy Stock Photo; **436** Eric Audras/PhotoAlto sas/Alamy Stock Photo; **438** Sjenner13/123RF.

Text: 423, Quote by Robert Kent in Why Good Communication Is Good Business by Marty Blalock. Published by The Board of Regents of the University of Wisconsin System, © 2005; **424,** Quote by Ray Kroc in Surrender to Win: Regain Sanity by Strategically Relinquishing Control by Laura Harris. Published by Greenleaf Book Group, © 2008; **427,** Lisa Ford-Brown.

CHAPTER 19

Photos: 442–443 Image Source/Getty Images; **444** Sam Edwards/Caiaimage/OJO+/Getty images; **446** Jeff Greenberg/age Fotostock; **450** Maskot/Getty Images; **452** Hero Images/Getty Images.

Text: 443, Excerpt from Run to Win: Vince Lombardi on Coaching and Leadership by Donald T. Phillips. Published by St. Martin's Press, © 2002; **445,** Lisa Ford-Brown; **445,** Lisa Ford-Brown; **449,** HARRIS, THOMAS E.; SHERBLOM. JOHN C.. SMALL GROUP AND TEAM COMMUNICATION, 5th Ed, ©2011, pp 46, 47, 154. Reprinted and Electronically reproduced by permission of Pearson Education, Inc. Upper Saddle River, New Jersey; **451,** HARRIS, THOMAS E.; SHERBLOM. JOHN C.. SMALL GROUP AND TEAM COMMUNICATION, 5th Ed, ©2011, pp 46, 47, 154. Reprinted and Electronically reproduced by permission of Pearson Education, Inc. Upper Saddle River, New Jersey.

ENDMATTER

Reprinted with the permission of the National Communication Association (NCA). For more information on NCA's Learning Outcomes in Communication project, see www.natcom.org/LOC.

Index

icons used in creating, 242
line graphs, 241
pictographs, 242
pie graphs, 243
time shown on, 242
Great speeches as attention-getter, 179
Group interaction role, **448**–449
Group oral report, 452
Group task role, **448**–449
Groupthink, **451**
Guided imagery, 13

H

Handouts, 250
Harmony, appeal to, 346
Harris, Thomas E. *(Small Group and Team Communication)*, 448, 450
Hartline, Michael *(Marketing Strategy)*, 163
Hasty generalization, **390**
Hearing, **272**, 273
Henry, Will, 103
Here Comes Everybody (Shirky), 195
Historical/recent events as attention-getter, 179
Hits, **70**
Hofstede, Geert
Culture's Consequences, 34
Value Dimension model, 34–35
Humor
as attention-getter, 178, 179
ethics in, 185
as "WOW" statement, 185
Hybrid engagements, **229**
Hybrid mediated presentations, 229
Hyperbole, 205
Hypothetical examples, **106**

I

Idea bank, **49**–52
brainstorming and, 50–51
general purpose and, 52
informative speeches and, 306
persuasive speeches and, 364
presentation aids and, 257
topic ideas and, searching for, 49
Identification, **7**

Identity, **29**
Identity knowledge, **27**
Illustrations
as attention-getter, 177
as support material, 106
as "WOW" statement, 184
Illustrators, **220**
Image unity in presentation aids, 255
Implied leader, **446**
Impromptu speaking, 223, **223**
Inferential statistics, **108**
Inflection, **212**
Informative listening, **275**
Informative speaking, 299–331, **300**
audience for, 304–305
body of, 314–315, 323–326
central idea in, 310
commiting to strategy for, 316–317
conclusion in, 320–321, 326–327
creative process for, 302–303
delivery of, 329
ethics in, 300
evaluating, 330–331
idea bank for, 306
informative topic in, 307
introduction in, 320–322, 320–323, 322–323
language in, 328
listening in, 330
main points of, 318
organizational strategy for, 317
outline of, 314–315
presentation aids in, 329
purpose of, 308
research in, 312–313
situation, 304–305
support materials for, 319
topic, 304–311
types of, 301, 309
working outline of, 311
Informative speech, 161
Informative topic
in informative speeches, 307
Initial ethos, **342**
Instructor, evaluation by, 294
Interlibrary loan (ILL) service, 76
Internal noise, **43**, **277**

Internal previews, **145**
Internal reviews, **145**
Internet
attention-getters on, tips for locating, 179
finding support materials on, 70–75, 86–87
library on, 76, 86 (*See also* Library)
Interview, 88, 424–429
after, strategies for, 429
application for, 426
in audience and situation analysis, 39
before, strategies for, 427
benefits of, 88
conducting, 90, 424–425
day of, strategies for, 428
dressing for, 428
ethics in, 89, 91
getting the interview, strategies for, 428
guidelines, 39
interviewees, finding, 88
media-assisted, 91
oral citation for, sample, 90
preparing to be interviewed, 89, 426–429
questions (*See* Interview questions)
recording, 89
support materials gathered in, 88–91
time and location for, 89
Interview questions, 89, 90
answering, strategies for, 428
closed-ended, 39
illegal, 429
open-ended, 39
Introduction, **129**, 174–175
attention-getters in, 174
audience relevance in, 175
credibility built in, 175
delivering, tips for, 175
in informative speeches, 320–322, 320–323, 322–323
organizing, 180–181
in persuasive speeches, 376, 377–378